A MAIMONIDES

Library of Jewish Studies

A MAIMONIDES READER

Edited, with introductions and notes, by

ISADORE TWERSKY

BEHRMAN HOUSE, INC. | PUBLISHERS |

ACKNOWLEDGMENTS

The author and publisher thank the following for permission to reprint:

American Academy for Jewish Research for Boaz Cohen, tr., *Epistle to Yemen,* in Abraham Halkin, *Iggeret Teman.* © 1952 by American Academy for Jewish Research.

Bloch Publishing Company for selections from Arthur David, tr., *The Commentary to Mishnah Aboth.* © 1968 by Arthur David.

Boys Town Publishers for selections from Moses Hyamson, tr., *Mishneh Torah,* Books I and II (1962).

Columbia University Press for selections from Joseph I. Gorfinkle, tr., *The Eight Chapters.* © 1912 by Columbia University Press.

East and West Library for selections from Franz Kobler, ed., *A Treasury of Jewish Letters.* © 1952 by Ararat Publishing Society, Ltd.

Hebrew Union College for selections adapted from Abraham Cronbach, "The Maimonidean Code of Benevolence," *Hebrew Union College Annual,* XX. © 1947 by the Hebrew Union College.

Judaism for Arnold J. Wolf, tr., "Maimonides on Immortality and the Principles of Judaism" (*Helek: Sanhedrin, Chapter Ten*). © 1966 by the American Jewish Congress.

The Macmillan Company for Ralph Lerner, tr., "Letter on Astrology," from Ralph Lerner and Muhsin Mahdi, eds., *Medieval Political Philosophy.* © 1963 by the Free Press of Glencoe, a division of the Macmillan Company.

The Soncino Press, Ltd. for selections from Charles B. Chavel, tr., *The Commandments.* © 1967 by the Soncino Press, Ltd.

The University of Chicago Press for selections from Shlomo Pines, tr., *The Guide of the Perplexed.* © 1963 by the University of Chicago.

Yale University Press for selections from *The Code of Maimonides,* Books III, V–VI, VIII–XIV. © 1949, 1950, 1951, 1954, 1956, 1957, 1961, 1962, 1965 by Yale University Press.

LIBRARY OF CONGRESS CATALOGING IN PUBLICATION DATA

Moses ben Maimon, 1135-1204.
  A Maimonides reader.

  (Library of Jewish studies)
  Bibliography: p. 483
  1. Judaism—Works to 1900. I. Twersky, Isadore,
ed. II. Title.
BM545.A45T9   1972   296.3   76-160818
ISBN 0-87441-206-4

For
Mosheh, Tzipporah, and Mayer,
with love

CONTENTS

❀

GUIDE OF THE PERPLEXED

$$\text{\textcolor{gray}{⟨◈⟩}}$$

PREFACE

R*ABBI MOSES BEN MAIMON*, known in Hebrew literature as
the Rambam and in Western culture since the Renaissance as
Maimonides, is unquestionably one of the outstanding figures of
Jewish history—a figure, moreover, whose commanding influence
has been widely recognized by non-Jews as well as Jews. As early as
the fourteenth century, a rabbinic scholar applied to Maimonides the
phrase (adapted from Mal. 1:11), "his name is great among the
nations." And the seventeenth-century English humanist Jeremy
Taylor called him, in a simple, suggestive phrase, that "famous Jew"
par excellence. As a result, even those generally unacquainted with
or uninterested in the basic phenomena and major trends of Jewish
history react to the name of this "famous Jew."

The reactions are quite varied, however, for Maimonides' impact
was as protean as it was widespread. He is known as a Talmudist,
whose magisterial reformulation of Jewish law became the object of
microscopic study by later generations of scholars; as a correspondent,
whose authoritative, compassionate, and enlightening letters were
treasured by Jewish communities throughout the world; as a rationalist, whose careful and searching exposition of Judaism became both
paradigm and challenge to all concerned with Jewish theology and
philosophy; as a philosopher, whose proofs of the existence of God or
whose allegorical interpretation of the Bible were copied and adapted
by non-Jewish scholastics; as a student of Aristotle—and of ancient
philosophy and science in general—whose own writings mark an
important stage in the history of Aristotelianism and medieval
Hellenism; and as a creative thinker who approached problems of
intellect, sensibility, and will with passion and vigor.

In the interest of precision, however, it is helpful to delineate two main aspects of this multifaceted figure—the real and the post-humous. There is, first, the rabbi and philosopher who lived in Spain and North Africa in the twelfth century, who was a court physician and a leader of his people, and who wrote many influential works—some of them epoch-making—in the major areas of medieval concern: law, theology, and medicine. This Maimonides, who helped fashion post-Talmudic Judaism and fix its contours, is the subject of scholarly investigation and scientific research, of articles and monographs probing details of his works and seeking, by means of philological and historical criticism, to determine their relationship to Jewish and general sources.

"Great men not only make history, they are also consumed by history." Hence the second, posthumous, Maimonides. This Maimonides has been continuously recreated and refashioned in successive generations. He has been singled out as an awe-inspiring ally or a formidable antagonist; his works have been animatedly studied, reinterpreted, denounced, and appropriated; his motives and announced goals have been scrutinized and reflected through the lenses of change and contemporary contingency.

Posterity speaks with many voices, and the voices abound in contradiction and paradox. Maimonides has been the hero—sometimes the villain—of conservative theologians and radical philosophers, of atavists and inconoclasts, of single-minded Talmudists and students of comparative jurisprudence, of physicians and metaphysicians. Mystics have carried on a protracted, often intense, flirtation with him. The extraordinary measure of esteem and reverence in which he has been held has alternated with hostility, intemperate condemnation, and outright contempt. Stimulant to some, irritant to others, he has scarcely ever evoked an attitude of indifference or nonchalance. Some have seen him as a multifaceted but essentially harmonious personality, others as tense and complex, riddled, whether consciously or unconsciously, with paradox and inconsistency. Indeed, the long and vivid chronicle of contradictory attitudes and motifs which constitutes the posthumous development of the Maimonidean saga is itself a major theme of Jewish history.

The purpose of this volume is to acquaint the reader with the first Maimonides by exposing him directly to the form, content, and scope of the Maimonidean legacy, its fastidiousness of thought and expression, its fusion of tradition and innovation, its cold intellectualism and warm humanity, its rationalism and piety, its emphases and ambiguities. The serious reader will quickly realize that much of Maimonidean writing is characterized, in Ben Jonson's phrase, by "a newness of sense and antiquity of voice," and must be read with care and imagination. Maimonides has never been merely of antiquarian interest. As has been the case in the past, contemporary readers will surely adapt Maimonides and transform him; they will be guided, instructed, and provoked by him, reading insights into or out of his statements. They may see him as the forerunner of critical scholarship, of cultural Zionism, of natural religion, interpret or misinterpret him in terms of nationalism or universalism, existentialism or idealism, orthodoxy or liberalism. And thus, if the volume will have succeeded in its primary purpose, that of providing a measure of objective knowledge about the real Maimonides, it will inevitably help also to extend the ongoing history of the second Maimonides, for every generation confronts him anew.

In determining the plan to follow in arranging the material to be included in this volume, I considered three options. The first was to adopt a topical-conceptual scheme and organize the selections from the various Maimonidean works under such standard rubrics as God, man, Torah, ethics, etc. Another was to follow the chronological order and arrange the selections according to their dates of composition, thus showing literary development and aspects of continuity and change. I have chosen instead to establish Maimonides' major work, the *Mishneh Torah*, as the central pillar of this volume, excerpting liberally from its fourteen books, and then relating the other selections to it, thereby allowing a certain unity to emerge out of the matrix of the *Mishneh Torah*.

I adopted this third alternative because I felt that it was imperative to convey a clear idea of the scope and structure and style of the *Mishneh Torah*, the flower of Jewish jurisprudence. Paradoxically, while the *Mishneh Torah* was intended for everyone, great and small, and the *Guide* for a small elite, the former is not generally studied, certainly not by English-reading audiences. As a matter of fact, the *Mishneh Torah* is only now being made available in a complete English translation by the Yale University Press. In giving substantive selections I hope to demonstrate that the *Mishneh*

Torah is the best possible introduction to the thought and outlook of Maimonides in all its diversity, tension, and originality.

Moreover, it is my hope that experiencing the scope of the *Mishneh Torah* will help dispel from the reader's mind the widespread misconception which equates Judaism with a narrow legalism. The *Mishneh Torah* covers physics, metaphysics, ethics, psychology, dietetics, astronomy, everything from creation to the *eschaton*; it allows one, in short, to glimpse the full sweep and dialectic of Judaism. This is all the more noteworthy for being accomplished within the confines of a work of jurisprudence, a work which purports to be a comprehensive code of law.

Related to this aim is the more general need of according *halakhah* its due. *Halakhah* has constituted the mainstream of Judaism and Jewish history, and yet most modern writers since the period of Enlightenment have shown little sympathy for or understanding of it. They have tended to view it as a barren, stultifying discipline which yields neither intellectual benefit nor spiritual satisfaction. Even writers who acknowledge its importance and centrality feel that treating it in English would be cumbersome and perhaps unintelligible. In the view that *halakhah* is the most characteristic expression of Judaism and the most typical manifestation of the Jewish way of life, this volume attempts to present large amounts of *halakhic* material—"softened," to be sure, by its relation to or integration with philosophical and ethical material. To the extent that the Maimonidean presentation of this material is characteristic of post-Talmudic Judaism as a whole, it should be of even greater interest and relevance.

In order to preserve the sequence of the *Mishneh Torah* and allow the reader to make his way independently through its many parts, it seemed best to print the excerpts from the *Mishneh Torah* material first. These are followed by the *Guide of the Perplexed*. Selections from Maimonides' commentaries and letters appear at the end. The brief introductions to the selections are for the most part descriptive, underscoring some of the themes which should be read with special care. The cross references indicated in the footnotes are intended to help the reader perceive the essential integrity of the material presented, as well as to suggest how practically all of it could be subsumed under statements and implications found in the *Mishneh Torah*.

The translations presented below are taken from a variety of sources, and no attempt has been made to revise or standardize them. A few instances of mistranslation or stylistic awkwardness have been eliminated.

I am deeply grateful to Neal Kozodoy for his valuable advice and editorial assistance. Special thanks are due Andrew Amsel of Behrman House for his courtesy and helpfulness in seeing the book through the press, and Carolyn I. Cross of Harvard's Department of Near Eastern Languages and Literatures for her patience and skill in typing successive drafts of the introductory materials.

MAIMONIDES' biography immediately suggests a profound paradox. A philosopher by temperament and ideology, a zealous devotee of the contemplative life who eloquently portrayed and yearned for the serenity of solitude and the spiritual exuberance of meditation, he nevertheless led a relentlessly active life that regularly brought him to the brink of exhaustion. A harassed physician and conscientious leader of his community, he combined an arduous professional routine with unabated scholarship, vigorous creativity, and literary productivity. Maimonides' life was a mosaic of anxiety, tribulation, and, at best, incredibly strenuous work and intellectual exertion. This is perhaps the first matter worthy of attention for the modern reader, accustomed for the most part to comfort, leisure, and even affluence.

Maimonides was born in 1135 in Cordova, at one time the greatest center of Jewish learning and general Islamic culture; his father was a prominent judge and respected scholar. His entry into adolescence—just as he was becoming a bar mitzvah (1148)—was filled with gloom and despair because of the invasion of Spain by the Almohades, fanatical, puritanical Muslims who presented all non-Muslims with the radical choice of conversion or death. Some Spanish Jews chose martyrdom, others fled, while many reluctantly took

1

upon themselves a life of duplicity and ambivalence, creating a searing gap between their public Muslim-like behavior and their private adherence to Judaism. The colorful history of the Jews in Islamic Spain, which reached unusual heights in its material and intellectual development, was coming to an abrupt, inglorious end. The Maimonidean family, uprooting itself from its ancestral home, where eight generations of scholars had served as rabbis and judges, entered into a turbulent decade of flight and nomadism,* wandering through southern Spain and northern Africa (ca. 1148–1158) and finally settling for several years in the city of Fez (c. 1159–1165) where the Almohades also ruled with Spartan rigor and inquisitorial zeal. Life continued to be filled with apprehension, pretense, and defamation, theological indictment and physical harassment.

In 1165, heeding the advice which he had given to his perplexed, despairing fellow Jews—and which he would repeat to the distraught Jews of Yemen some years later—to flee the land of persecution at all costs, "without considering separation from family or loss of wealth," Maimonides undertook a hazardous sea voyage from Morocco to the land of Israel, which was then the scene of the crusades. During this particular period, the Latin Kingdom of Jerusalem, momentarily triumphant, was enjoying politico-military ascendancy over the Muslims; since its religious fanaticism equaled its political power, Maimonides found no haven in the Holy Land. His wanderings continued. It may even be that he regarded his trip primarily as a pilgrimage. His journey from Morocco to Palestine, as described in a statement quoted by a sixteenth-century writer (R. Eleazar Azikri), ended in prayer at the Western Wall:

> On Sunday evening, the fourth of the month of Iyar, I went to sea; on Sabbath, the tenth of Iyar, in the year 4925, a heavy gale arose,

---

*The rather common experience of wandering and homelessness was described by Moses ibn Ezra (d. 1135) in one of his poems:

> I am weary of roaming about the world, measuring its expanse; and am not yet done.
> I walk with the beasts of the forest and I hover like a bird of prey over the peaks of the mountains.
> My feet run about like lightning to the far ends of the earth, and I move from sea to sea.
> Journey follows journey, but I find no resting place, no calm repose.

Quoted in Yitzhak Baer, A History of the Jews in Christian Spain (Philadelphia, 1961), I, pp. 61–62.

the sea was turbulent and we were in danger of drowning. I vowed to observe these two days as strict fast days for myself, my family and all my household, and to order my descendants to keep these fasts also in future generations and to give charity in accordance with their means. I further vowed to observe the tenth of Iyar in complete seclusion and to devote the day to prayer and study. On that day, God alone was with me on the sea; so upon the anniversary of this day, I wish to be alone with God and not in the company of man, unless I am compelled to.

On Sunday evening, the third of Sivan, I landed safely in Acre and thus escaped persecution. The day on which we set foot in the land of Israel I vowed to observe as a day of festivity and joy accompanied by the distribution of gifts to the poor, I as well as my offspring in future generations.

Tuesday, the fourth of Marheshvan, in the year 4926, we arrived in Jerusalem from Acre after a dangerous journey. I entered the site of the great and holy Temple and prayed there on Thursday, the sixth of Marheshvan.

In any event, this experience of terrified flight from the lands of Islam and implacable hostility on the part of the powers of Christianity is in some respects reminiscent of the general fate of the Jews caught between the fierce rivalries of Christian and Muslim.*

His extraordinary difficulties in pursuing his studies during these years of instability and exile and the profound sense of uprootedness and precariousness which permeated his thought are poignantly portrayed in several of Maimonides' writings from this period. In the epilogue to his *Commentary on the Mishnah* (c. 1168), he writes:

In concluding this work according to my plans, I pray to God that He save me from errors. Whoever finds occasion to criticize me, or knows of a better interpretation of any of the laws, should call my attention to it and graciously forgive me. Every righteous and intelligent person will realize that the task I undertook was not simple or easy of fulfillment. In addition, I was agitated by the distress of our time, the exile which God had decreed upon us, the fact that we are being driven from one end of the world to the other. Perhaps we have received reward for this, inasmuch as exile atones for sin. God knows, there are some laws which I explained while on the road; some matters I collected while on board ship. Besides, I also devoted myself to the study of other sciences. The reason that led me to

*Judah ha-Levi (d. 1140) wrote: "The son of the servant-maid [Ishmael, i.e. Islam] pursues us with his hate; we turn pleading to Esau [i.e. Christianity] and he tears us like a wild beast." See Yitzhak Baer, *Galut* (New York, 1947), p. 33.

describe my situation in detail was my desire to justify my critics; they should not be blamed for criticizing me. May God reward them, and I will regard them as friends, for they do godly work. The description of the conditions under which I wrote this commentary will explain why its completion required such a long time.

The prologue to his *Epistle to Yemen* (1172) echoes a similar refrain:

Verily, I am one of the humblest of scholars from Spain whose prestige was lowered in exile. Although I always study the ordinances of the Lord, I did not attain to the learning of my forebears, for evil days and hard times overtook us; we did not abide in tranquility. We labored and had no rest. How could we study the law when we were being exiled from city to city, and from country to country? I pursued the reapers in their paths and gathered ears of grain, both the rank and the full ones, as well as the withered and the thin ones. Only recently have I found a home. Were it not for the help of God, I would not have culled the store I did and from which I continually draw.

After making his way southward from Acre through Jerusalem to Hebron, Maimonides settled in Cairo, an important, strategically located center of the Arab world, with a large, heterogeneous Jewish community. The first years in Egypt were punctuated by the death of his father, his own prolonged illness, intermittent strife—personal and communal—instigated by both Jews and Muslims, and, in 1173, the crushing blow: the death of his younger brother David, a well-to-do, enterprising merchant who had been supporting the entire family, and who was drowned in the Indian Ocean while on a business trip. Maimonides could not be consoled in his mourning. A letter written several years later (c. 1184) evokes the mood of agony and anguish and notes the residue of grief:

In Egypt I met with great and severe misfortunes. Illness and material losses came upon me. In addition, various informers plotted against my life. But the most terrible blow which befell me, a blow which caused me more grief than anything I have experienced in my life, was the death of the most perfect and righteous man, who was drowned while traveling in the Indian Ocean.

For nearly a year after I received the sad news, I lay ill on my bed struggling with fever and despair. Eight years have since passed, and I still mourn, for there is no consolation. What can console me? He grew up on my knees; he was my brother, my pupil. He was engaged in business and earned money that I might stay at home and continue my studies. He was learned in the Talmud and in the Bible and an accomplished grammarian. My one joy was to see him. Now my joy has been changed into darkness; he has gone to his eternal home, and has left me prostrated in a strange land. Whenever I come across his handwriting or one of his books, my heart grows faint within me, and my grief reawakens. In short: "I will go down into the grave unto my son mourning." Were not the study of the Torah my delight, and did not the study of wisdom divert me from my grief, "I should have succumbed in my affliction."

Soon after, he began to practice medicine and, thanks to his erudition, skill, and conscientiousness, became the house physician of Saladin's vizier and one of the most respected court physicians. Simultaneously, he emerged as the untitled leader of the Jewish community, combining the duties of rabbi, local judge, appellate judge, administrative chief responsible for appointing and supervising community officials, and overseer of the philanthropic foundations—to which he was especially dedicated.* His professional and communal commitments—resulting in working hours which present-day scholars and professionals would find appalling—were not unrelated, for Maimonides was absolutely determined to guarantee his independence and self-sufficiency. He received no financial aid or official remuneration from the Jewish community; as a matter of fact, he violently opposed and condemned those scholars or religious functionaries who relied on communal support. Some of his most passionate and animated prose was elicited by his distaste for this practice, which he tried—unsuccessfully—to eliminate. His own painful consistency in this regard lends all the more pathos and determination to his writing.

Maimonides apparently married twice. His first wife, about whom we know very little, died in Egypt, and he later remarried. His only son Abraham, who was to become the official head (nagid) of the Jewish community in Egypt and the zealous defender and interpreter of the total—halakhic and theological—Maimonidean legacy, was born in 1187. Maimonides lavished fond attention on his son,

*Maimonides' career thus reflects still another aspect of the intellectual and political experience of the Jews in Spain, and under Islam generally. The influential courtier who then becomes leader of the Jewish community and is usually a versatile scholar and benevolent patron of learning is typical of Jewish history in Spain. The tradition begins with Hasdai ibn Shaprut (d. 976) who was court physician, diplomatic troubleshooter, scientific translator, and father of Jewish culture in Cordova and, indeed, in all of Spain; it reaches a high point in Samuel ha-Nagid (d. 1053) who was an authoritative rabbinic scholar, a notable poet, a skillful polemicist, as well as vizier of the king, commander-in-chief of the armed forces, and head of the Jewish community.

whom he described as possessing modesty and integrity as well as a fine intellect. Although only seventeen at the time of his father's death (1204), Abraham was able still to absorb an impressive amount of his father's teaching and in his own works he cites many interpretations and opinions transmitted to him orally by his illustrious father. The son's commentary on the Bible, his voluminous *Complete Guide for the Pious* (*Kifayat al-'Abidin*), the *Treatise on Aggadot*, and numerous letters and responsa are thus important sources of Maimonidean doctrine. All his duties and commitments notwithstanding, Maimonides must have found time to "teach his son Torah." Indeed, we have here a good example of a sustained aristocracy of the intellect and spirit, and it is interesting to follow the literary history of this family, starting with R. Maimon's Letter of Consolation, over many generations.

Aspects of Maimonides' medical practice and intellectual preoccupations are described in a candid letter (1191) to Joseph b. Judah, the favorite and trusted disciple for whom he composed the *Guide of the Perplexed*:

> I inform you that I have acquired in medicine a very great reputation among the great, such as the Chief Qadi, the princes, . . . and other grandees from whom I do not ordinarily receive any fee. As for the ordinary people, I am placed too high for them to reach me. This obliges me continually to waste my day in Cairo visiting the [noble] sick. When I return to Fostat, the most I am able to do, for the rest of the day and night, is to study medical books, which are so necessary for me. For you know how long and difficult this art is for a conscientious and exact man who does not want to state anything which he cannot support by argument and without knowing where it has been said and how it can be demonstrated. This has further resulted in the fact that I find no time to study Torah; the only time I am able to read the Bible is on Saturday. As for other sciences, I have no time to study them at all and this distresses me very much. Recently I received all of Averroes' commentaries on Aristotle . . . and my impression is that he explicates the author's views properly, but I have not yet found the time to read all his books.

The most revealing piece of personal testimony about Maimonides' professional and communal schedule is to be found in his letter of 1199 to Samuel ibn Tibbon, the Hebrew translator of the *Guide of the Perplexed*:

Now God knows that in order to write this to you I have escaped to a secluded spot, where people would not think to find me, sometimes leaning for support against the wall, sometimes lying down on account of my excessive weakness, for I have grown old and feeble. With regard to your wish to come here to me, I cannot but say how greatly your visit would delight me, for I truly long to commune with you, and would anticipate our meeting with even greater joy than you. Yet I must advise you not to expose yourself to the perils of the voyage, for beyond seeing me, and my doing all I could to honor you, you would not derive any advantage from your visit. Do not expect to be able to confer with me on any scientific subject, for even one hour either by day or by night, for the following is my daily occupation. I dwell at Misr [Fostat] and the Sultan resides at Kahira [Cairo]; these two places are two Sabbath days' journey [about one mile and a half] distant from each other. My duties to the Sultan are very heavy. I am obliged to visit him every day, early in the morning; and when he or any of his children, or any of the inmates of his harem, are indisposed, I dare not quit Kahira, but must stay during the greater part of the day in the palace. It also frequently happens that one or two of the royal officers fall sick, and I must attend to their healing. Hence, as a rule, I repair to Kahira very early in the day, and if nothing unusual happens, I do not return to Misr until the afternoon. Then I am almost dying with hunger. I find the antechamber filled with people, both Jews and Gentiles, nobles and common people, judges and bailiffs, friends and foes—a mixed multitude, who await the time of my return.

I dismount from my animal, wash my hands, go forth to my patients, and entreat them to bear with me while I partake of some slight refreshment, the only meal I take in the twenty-four hours. Then I attend to my patients, write prescriptions for their various ailments. Patients go in and out until nightfall, and sometimes even, I solemnly assure you, until two hours and more in the night. I converse and prescribe for them while lying down from sheer fatigue, and when night falls, I am so exhausted that I can scarcely speak.

In consequence of this, no Israelite can have any private interview with me except on the Sabbath. On this day the whole congregation, or at least the majority of the members, come to me after the morning service, when I instruct them as to their proceedings during the whole week; we study together a little until noon, when they depart. Some of them return, and read with me after the afternoon service until evening prayers. In this manner I spend that day. I have here related to you only a part of what you would see if you were to visit me. Now, when you have completed for our brethren the translation you have commenced, I beg that you will come to me but not with the hope of deriving any advantage from your visit as regards your studies; for my time is, as I have shown you, excessively occupied.

His physical infirmity and all these apparently stultifying conditions notwithstanding, Maimonides was constantly studying, teaching, and writing. He may have chafed under the tensions and pressures, but he never fell to brooding and self-pity; he sometimes described his difficulties in elegiac prose but did not allow them to paralyze his work. He began writing early—with zeal, almost with a sense of mission—and continued writing prodigiously to the end of his life. His writing, in essence, was a work of art and a labor of love. Even if he had enjoyed optimal conditions of comfort and security, unlimited research and secretarial assistance, it would still be hard to understand how he could have produced what he did.

His youthful works, composed for the most part during his wanderings in southern Spain, include the *Millot ha-Higgayon* and the *Ma'amar ha-Ibbur*, both written in Arabic.* The first is a treatise on logic which "offers a clear and concise exposition of the most important logical terms and also of some physical, metaphysical, and ethical terms used in the discussion of logical theory. It is therefore not only a handbook on logic but also an introduction to philosophy, as the terms 'logic' and 'philosophy' were then understood" (I. Efros, *Maimonides' Treatise on Logic*, p. 3). The second describes, as simply as possible, with a minimum of technical jargon and scientific window-dressing, the rationale, mechanics, and astronomical principles of the Jewish calendar—an area in which *halakhah* and natural science were intermingled. The complexity of his writing and its skillful integration of diverse disciplines are foreshadowed in this treatise. The so-called "Renaissance man," the scholar who aspires to universal knowledge and successfully cultivates a variety of interests, who achieves diversity without sacrificing profundity or succumbing to dilettantism, reveals himself here.† Certainly the scope of his learned

*The exact date of composition of these works is not clear; I rely on the conventional bibliographic view in listing these works as youthful.

†Yedaya Bedersi, writing in 1305, in southern France, praises Maimonides as having the understanding of Aristotle in philosophy, of Euclid in geometry, of Ptolemy in astronomy, and of Galen and Hippocrates in medicine.

achievements—like that of many of the Jews of the "Golden Age" in Spain—is another general point worthy of attention for the modern reader, living in an age of ever-increasing specialization and atomization. It is noteworthy also that these early works were composed in response to specific requests. In other words, Maimonides' multifaceted erudition and constructive expository skills were already known and appreciated during his adolescence. His reputation as teacher and guide was already growing.

In 1158, at the age of 23, he began writing his pioneering commentary on the Mishnah, a task which was to engage his attention for the next ten years. During the same period he also completed two other works which, for a variety of reasons, remained marginal in the later history of Talmudic literature and interpretation: a brief commentary on those three sections of the Babylonian Talmud which were regularly studied in the Spanish schools, and a compendium of laws found in the Palestinian Talmud. The first represented a conventional preoccupation of rabbinic scholars, while the purpose of the second was more original: to cull all those sections of the rather neglected Palestinian Talmud which would shed light on the normative Babylonian Talmud, explain obscurities, fill in halakhic details, and by such use automatically enhance the importance of the Palestinian Talmud. In common with other scholars of North Africa (primarily in Kairwan) and Spain, Maimonides was devoted to the study of the Palestinian Talmud and eager to extend its popularity and influence.

Throughout his life, Maimonides was to write hundreds of responsa, decisions concerning the interpretation or application of the law, letters of advice, comfort, or arbitration to all parts of the world: Yemen, Baghdad, Aleppo, Damascus, Jerusalem, Alexandria, Marseilles, and Lunel. Some were curt answers providing the authoritative opinion required; others were balanced expositions of moot points; still others were small monographs which Maimonides himself considered as treatises which would henceforth be available for all to consult. In other words, the writing and despatching of a comprehensive responsum was equivalent to publication of a book, for important responsa were customarily copied, collected, and widely circulated. Maimonides' responsa are significant not only for presenting an X-ray picture of a creative mind at work but also for illuminating through frequent cross references the method, motivation, or meaning of his major legal and philosophical works. The most notable of the early letters and occasional pieces are the *Epistle on Conversion* (*Iggeret ha-Shemad*) and the *Epistle to Yemen* (*Iggeret Teman*).

Iggeret ha-Shemad (c. 1161–2) is a broadside, a real polemical treatise. It was not written in answer to a specific inquiry or request for guidance, but was rather Maimonides' passionate reaction to the *halakhic* decision rendered by a certain scholar who, totally insensitive to the plight of those tormented Jews under Almohade rule who succumbed to inexorable pressures and feigned acceptance of Islam, had unqualifiedly read them out of the Jewish community and, by his insensitivity and practically clinical detachment, had greatly increased their anguish and despondency. Maimonides, following in the footsteps of his father who had previously written a highly emotional Letter of Consolation* for the same audience, sought to bolster the sagging spirits of his brethren and to save the Jewish community from total demoralization and disintegration. The letter is unique in that Maimonides reacted viscerally as well as intellectually; he did not limit his response to rigorous *halakhic* reasoning and interpretation but went out of his way to marshal every possible argument, legal, theological, and rhetorical, and cited a profusion of *aggadic* passages in order both to discountenance his opponent and to discredit the views which he had propounded.

The *Epistle to Yemen* was written in response to a specific inquiry from the Jews of Yemen concerning the religious persecutions in that country (begun about 1165) which were compounded by the seductive, conversionary preaching of a recent apostate and the unsettling pronouncements of a self-proclaimed messiah. In this responsum Maimonides reviews among other things the entire history of persecutions of the Jews, the special animosity which Christianity and Islam, the derivative monotheistic systems, feel toward Judaism, and the inviolable unity of the Bible and rabbinic tradition.

*"And it is necessary that we should rely upon God, and believe in Him, and not doubt His promises, just as we do not doubt His existence, nor should we fear that He will cast us off when He has promised to draw us near unto Him, nor should the great prosperity of the nations terrify us, or what they assert, or what they hope for, because we confide in God, and put faith in His promises. And in spite of their victory over us, and their anger against us, and our subjection to them, and the renewal of our calamities with the renewal of day and night . . . we must still reflect upon that which He has promised us, and upon that which we hope, and then the weary souls will have rest, and their fears be allayed, for there must needs be repose and healing after this unhappiness, there must needs be enlargement after this straitness." See "Maimon ben Joseph's Letter of Consolation" in Franz Kobler, *A Treasury of Jewish Letters* (Philadelphia, 1954), v. I, p. 168.

He tries especially to cope with the "problem of history," to confront the recurrent facts of catastrophe and decimation, to explain the ubiquitousness of suffering: "people witnessed our feebleness and noted the triumph of our adversaries and their dominion over us." As a result, "the hearts of some people have turned away, uncertainty befalls them and their beliefs are weakened." Maimonides writes in order to mitigate this distress and supply comfort and counsel stemming from a long-range, philosophical view of history. Punishment does not mean repudiation by God. Faith in God's promises to Israel must be as firm as faith in His existence. "As it is impossible for God to cease to exist, so is Israel's destruction and disappearance from the world unthinkable." The letter—eloquent and philosophical on the one hand, sensitive and empathetic on the other—won for Maimonides a special place in the hearts of Yemenite Jews who, as a token of gratitude and reverence, included the name of Maimonides in the recitation of the kaddish. The Yemenites remained ardent students, copyists, and commentators of Maimonidean writings through the ages.

Maimonides' major works—major by dint of their unfailing originality, impressive size, and abiding influence—are: the *Commentary on the Mishnah* (*Perush ha-Mishnah*), *Book of Commandments* (*Sefer ha-Mitzvot*), *Mishneh Torah* (also known as *Yad ha-Hazakah*), *Guide of the Perplexed* (*Moreh Nevukhim*).

The *Commentary on the Mishnah* should be seen in light of the fact that although the Mishnah was prior to the Talmud in point of time, it gradually became subservient to and assimilated in the Talmud as a unit of study. Consequently, while several, practically complete commentaries on the Talmud were in existence by the end of the eleventh century, commentaries on the Mishnah were rare and fragmentary. In an effort to rehabilitate the Mishnah as a legitimate, self-sufficient unit of study, Maimonides intended his commentary to serve both as an *introduction* to the Talmud—this follows from the nature of the Mishnah—and as a *review* of the Talmud—this follows from the nature of his commentary which summarizes different interpretations and indicates the normative conclusions. He here combines minute textual study, even lexicographical annotation, with conceptual analysis, both of which are necessary for a comprehensive commentary. He often digresses in his commentary in order to elab-

orate a theological principle or elucidate a philosophic issue, for, as he confesses, "expounding a single principle of religion is dearer to me than anything else that I might teach."
Similarly, he is already preoccupied here with a problem that was to engage him intermittently for the rest of his life and was also becoming a staple, central theme of Jewish intellectual history: the metaphorical interpretation of the aggadic, or non-legal sections of the Talmud. Apparently implausible passages of aggadic literature had to be made reasonable and meaningful. As a matter of fact, most medieval scholars were convinced that aggadah—in common with certain Biblical passages—could not and should not be taken literally, for it was initially intended to convey metaphysical insights and basic truths, which could be uncovered and identified only by judicious interpretation. Non-literal interpretations were indispensable companions to literal understanding; aggadic texts had an intrinsic multiplicity of meanings, and a simple literalism would not do them justice.
We should note, of course, that the process of interpreting or deriving insight from texts and the habit of reading apriori, firmly grasped doctrines into the texts have to be carefully and honestly balanced. In the history of textual interpretation, one is not always sure whether something is being cleverly inferred from a text or whether it is being subtly read into the text. Both, to be sure, keep the text vibrant and relevant and provide continuity where discontinuity might have appeared. In any event, to borrow a phrase from Lovejoy, we might say that the problem of aggadic exegesis for Maimonides was "to disengage its serious philosophic content from the poetic imagery." Maimonides informs us in the Commentary on the Mishnah that he was planning a special commentary which would classify, explain, and rationalize the aggadah. He later abandoned the idea of composing such a commentary and, he tells us, the Guide of the Perplexed which was devoted in great part to matters of exegesis and allegory was intended as partial replacement for this work. This statement raises the history of aggadah to a higher level than is usually accorded to it and also puts the Guide in a different perspective, suggesting that the Guide is part of the aggadic as well as of the philosophic tradition.
Embedded in this pioneering commentary on the Mishnah are a number of independent monographs which have their own focus and integrity and can be—indeed have been—studied independently. First

is the general introduction which may properly be described as the first comprehensive, sophisticated inquiry into the theoretical, historical, and doctrinal foundations of the Oral Law—the act of revelation and, particularly, the process of transmission and on-going interpretation. Maimonides emphasizes that the Oral Law is a completely rational enterprise, subject to its own canons of interpretation, and brooking no suprarational interference. It follows that even prophecy is of little relevance to the juridical process. Only the prophecy of Moses was legislative—and, therefore, unique; all subsequent prophecy was exhortatory, based on moral persuasion, and could not create new laws (see also *Guide*, II, ch. 39). A thousand prophets would not, therefore, outweigh a thousand and one jurists, for the juridical principle of majority rule, absolutely indifferent to claims of special inspiration or heavenly instruction, would prevail. The Torah "is not in heaven" (Deut. 30:12).

Maimonides here addresses himself, for systematic as well as, apparently, for polemical reasons, to a question which is at the very core of any authoritative system, be it law or philosophy: how is one to reconcile diversity of opinion with authority and certitude? How can divergent views—in which the Talmud abounds—crop up in a legal system which claims to derive from revelation and uninterrupted tradition? Maimonides' answer introduces a sharp distinction between two components of the Oral Law: tradition, which is complete, absolute, and never subject to dispute; and the laws arrived at by accepted canons of interpretation.

The first group contains laws which have no foundation whatsoever in the Biblical text but are based solely on tradition—for example, the requirement that the *tefillin*, phylacteries, should be square and black. It also includes laws which are ascertainable by independent reasoning and which can be related to a Biblical text by careful exegesis but whose validity and authority are based on tradition, on direct, continuous practice—for example, the interpretation of "beautiful fruit" in Leviticus 23:40 as referring to the *etrog*, the citron, or the interpretation of "an eye for an eye" in Exodus 21:24 as meaning monetary compensation. Such laws have always been unequivocal and apodictic.

The second group, which accounts for the bulk of the Oral Law, is based on interpretation, inference, and analogy, on judicial review, and becomes part of authoritative tradition only after its conclusions have been agreed upon, after the norms have been established by majority decision or other principles of the juridical process. Only this area, which is in the hands of man, is subject to dispute and open to divergence; consensus of interpretation could not always be expected and was not necessary. The core of tradition thus remains free of controversy.*

The section of the Mishnah commentary concerned with the methodology of text interpretation and the explanation of the term "world to come" also stands as an independent monograph. The chapter (*Perek Helek*) in the Talmudic tractate Sanhedrin beginning "All Israelites have a share in the world to come . . ." provides Maimonides with the pretext for a lengthy excursus on Jewish belief. After debunking crude, materialistic conceptions of the world to come and identifying the religious concept of the world to come with the philosophical notion of the immortality of the soul, Maimonides defines the term "Israelites" by formulating the famous thirteen principles or articles of faith which every Israelite is expected to endorse. The thirteen principles may conveniently be reduced to three basic categories: (1) God—His existence, unity, incorporeality, and eternity, and the prohibition of idolatry; (2) the Law—prophecy, uniqueness of Mosaic prophecy, divine origin of the Written and Oral Law, and the eternity and immutability of the Law; (3) beliefs relating to reward and punishment—God's omniscience, divine compensation for good and evil, coming of the Messiah, and resurrection.

It seems most probable that this dogmatic structuring of Judaism was not undertaken in order to formulate a creed or catechism but was part of a philosophical-theological program which reflected Maimonides' intellectualism. It said, in effect, that there is a minimum of theoretical insight and true conceptual knowledge which even an unsophisticated, philosophically-innocent believer must possess. The difference, consequently, between such a person and the

---

*The following accusation, found in the writing of a twelfth-century apostate from Judaism to Islam, shows how urgent was the need to deal with this problem:

> Then it follows that in every single problem about which two of your legists disagreed, each will sustain his belief in the matter with a tradition going back to God. Thus, vileness pervades them to such a degree that they ascribe to God contradictory commands on any given problem.

See Samau'al Al-Maghribi, *Silencing the Jews*, ed. M. Perlmann (New York, 1964), p. 39. One of the ways by which Judah ha-Levi sought to weaken the authority of philosophy and tarnish its glory was by underscoring the dissension which characterizes its development, its conceptual infirmity and lack of certitude; see, *e.g.*, *Kuzari*, V, 14.

philosopher would be in the mode of acquiring true beliefs: blind conformity and unquestioning acceptance versus intellectual perception and rational demonstration. Both, however, would have a common set of beliefs. This discussion, in turn, becomes the point of departure for all subsequent investigation of Jewish dogma (e.g., by Crescas, Albo, and Abarbanel), and indeed for the very question of whether Judaism has dogma, whether it has a distinct creed or consists solely of deeds—a question which has been at the center of modern theologies and critiques of Judaism from Spinoza and Moses Mendelssohn on the one hand to Kant and Hegel on the other.

A third, self-contained unit of this commentary is the introduction to *Pirke Avot* (Ethics of the Fathers), usually entitled *Eight Chapters*. This may be described as a psychological-ethical treatise; its basis is psychology while its goal is ethics. It contains the fullest presentation of Maimonides' theory of the golden mean, which defines virtues as psychological dispositions between extremes of excess and deficiency. The "good deed is equibalanced, maintaining the mean between two bad extremes." For example, generosity is seen as the median point between stinginess and extravagance; courage is the mean between recklessness and cowardice. The last chapter contains an unequivocal affirmation of human freedom and, concomitantly, the rejection of all views (e.g. astrology or divine predestination) which would undermine free will. Without freedom to choose and act there would be no ethics. As Maimonides says in the *Mishneh Torah*, freedom is the "pillar of the Law and the commandments" and "every human being may become righteous like Moses our Teacher, or wicked like Jeroboam, wise or foolish, merciful or cruel, niggardly or generous." Man has the power and freedom to chart his own course.

Maimonides' *Book of Commandments* belongs to a conventional genre of rabbinic literature, inaugurated in the eighth century, which was based on the Talmudic reference to 613 divine commandments. While there has been general agreement on the number of 613, there has been no agreement on which commandments deserve to be included in the enumeration. Dismissing his predecessors with a few lines of devastating critique, Maimonides suggests fourteen guiding principles which should help bring about a consensus. These principles contain provocative assumptions as well as profound insights. For example, Maimonides contended that laws derived from Scripture by use of the traditional means of exegesis are not to be included in the enumeration, for they are considered rabbinic rather than Biblical in origin. The ninth principle introduces an interesting classification of laws: (1) beliefs and opinions—e.g., to acknowledge the unity of God; (2) actions—e.g., to offer sacrifices; (3) virtues and traits of character—e.g., to love one's neighbor; (4) speech—e.g., to pray. What is especially significant about this four-fold classification is its all-inclusiveness and its repudiation—intentional or incidental but clear and convincing—of a narrow "legalism" in the pejorative sense that is often attached to the term as a description of Judaism. This ambitious attempt to add rigor and objectivity to the enumeration by classifying Jewish law, defining the differences between Biblical and rabbinic commandments, differentiating between general exhortations and specific commands, is the novel and original part of the book. The enumeration itself was preparatory to his code and was designed to insure its comprehensiveness. He needed an exact, exhaustive list of commandments in order to guard against forgetfulness and omissions in his *Mishneh Torah*.

The *Mishneh Torah*, to which a large section of this volume is devoted, was completed about 1178 after a decade of painstaking work. Its novelty and importance may best be understood by noting five features,* to which Maimonides himself called attention in various places and which he considered as the distinctive characteristics of this work.†

(1) Language. Maimonides chose the Hebrew of the Mishnah rather than the Hebrew of the Bible or the Aramaic of the Talmud. Biblical Hebrew was inadequate and Talmudic Aramaic was too difficult, and he wanted his work to be easily intelligible to as large an audience as possible. This meant, incidentally, that we find here substantial portions of the Talmud translated into a fluent, rather

---

*The following is based upon a full analysis of the respective themes in my forthcoming book, *The Mishneh Torah of Maimonides* (Yale University Press).

†Needless to say, Maimonides did not appear out of a whirlwind or in a vacuum. He is part of a sturdy succession of Talmudists (e.g., R. Isaac Alfasi, R. Joseph ibn Migas) who influenced him significantly, and yet much about his writing is new and we should be prepared to confront and recognize this novelty. The search for "influence" should not eclipse the possibility of originality.

felicitous Hebrew. Maimonides took great pains with his style; his use of Hebrew and his development of a rich, flexible style that enabled him to write with precision, brevity, and elegance were exacting, novel undertakings, for we know from the plaintive testimony of such writers as Judah ha-Levi and Moses ibn Ezra that contemporary Hebrew was in a sad state.

(2) Arrangement and classification. Maimonides abandoned the sequence of the Mishnah and created a new topical-pedagogical arrangement—one that would not do violence to the subject matter and that would also be educationally sound. Classification is, of course, a prerequisite for codification and necessitates interpretation, sustained conceptualization, a large measure of abstraction, and a synoptic view of the entire body of material. Classification deals not only with clear, given data but with latent assumptions and relations that must be rationally perceived; for in order to group a and b together, their common denominator, which is not always explicit, must be established. Legal classification concerns itself not only with the sum total of individual laws but with the concept of law per se. John Gray quotes the saying "that he who could perfectly classify the law would have a perfect knowledge of the law." There is neither antecedent nor sequel in rabbinic literature for such an ambitious attempt at classification. If, as Aristotle said, "it is the business of the wise man to order," Maimonides displayed great wisdom in his ordering and structuring of halakhah.

(3) Codificatory form. Maimonides chose to present the massive material in crisp, concise form, moving at a quick tempo, eliminating indeterminate debate and conflicting interpretations, and formulating as a rule unilateral, undocumented decisions. He emphasized that he wanted to write a code, not a commentary. The fact remains, however, that the Mishneh Torah is not a monolithic, cut and dried code in the conventional sense, but is in many respects a commentary cast in codificatory form, abounding in interpretations, bits of exegesis (Biblical, halakhic, and aggadic), historical surveys, explanations of tricky phrases and subtle concepts. It occasionally cites sources, mentions names of authorities, and describes personal views and practices. It not only summarizes normative patterns of behavior but expounds in capsule form the entire Law. It is a manual of study as well as a guide to practice.

(4) Scope. One of the truly revolutionary aspects of the Mishneh Torah is its all-inclusive scope, obliterating accidental distinc-

tions between the practical and the theoretical. Maimonides opposed
the pervasive tendency, reflected in his own youthful commentaries,
to study only those parts of the Talmud which were of practical
value and immediate relevance. He insisted that the abstruse, "antiquated" sections of the Talmud—Zeraim and Kodashim—were not
inferior to Moed and Nashim and should receive equal time and consideration. Maimonides knew that many of these treatises were "bristling with fundamental difficulties and even the greatest masters find
it hard to comprehend them," but this was no justification for continued neglect. Laws momentarily impracticable because of historical
or geographical circumstances—e.g., laws concerning sacrifices or the
Land of Israel—and laws relating to the messianic period should be
studied and known, and were accordingly codified as precisely and
minutely as laws of prayer, holiday observance, and marital relations.
Maimonides aimed at comprehensiveness, at producing an all-
embracing corpus of Jewish law so that "discerning students ... will
have no need to roam and ramble about in other books in search of
information." His intention was to codify everything concerning
"that which is forbidden or permitted, clean or unclean, and the
other rules of the Torah," but he also included statements "that have
only an academic value"—such as rules governing the visibility of the
new moon—"in order to make the Torah great and glorious" (Is.
42:21).

(5) Fusion of halakhah and philosophy. As part of the overall
unity of learning, Maimonides tried to bring about the unity of practice and concept, external observance and inner meaning, visible
action and invisible experience, law and philosophy. This unification
of the practical, theoretical, and theological components is actually
underscored by Maimonides in a letter to a student in which he
describes the twofold objective of the Mishneh Torah: to provide an
authoritative compilation of laws and also of "true beliefs." This aim
is not confined to Book I, which briefly summarizes the metaphysical
and ethical postulates of Judaism, talks about improvement of the
moral qualities, and encourages learning and teaching, for "if knowledge is not achieved, no right action and no correct opinion can be
achieved." There are also pointed philosophic comments, rationalistic directives, ethical insights and theological principles incorporated
into other parts of the Mishneh Torah. Maimonides' systematization
of the halakhah includes a good measure of ethicization, spiritualiza-
tion, and rationalization. Ethical assumptions are spelled out and

made explicit. Ideals concretized in a particular law are articulated. While not too many laws are actually rationalized, the mandate to engage in rationalization, to penetrate to their essence and their real motive powers, "to meditate upon the laws of the Holy Torah and to comprehend their full meaning" is clearly issued in the *Mishneh Torah*. It takes within its purview, in other words, not only the laws but the theological stimuli and ethical underpinnings which suffuse the legal details with significance and spirituality. A law code which instructs as well as commands, it is an instrument of education and edification, for law itself is an educative force leading to ethical and intellectual perfection. Law must, therefore, be understood and appreciated as well as obeyed and implemented.

The *Guide of the Perplexed*, Maimonides' philosophic testament par excellence, was composed (sometime between 1185 and 1190) for a special kind of reader, described by him as follows:

It is not the purpose of this treatise to make its totality understandable to the vulgar or to beginners in speculation, nor to teach those who have not engaged in any study other than the science of the Law—I mean the legalistic study of the Law. For the purpose of this treatise and of all those like it is the science of Law in its true sense. Or rather its purpose is to give indications to a religious man for whom the validity of our Law has become established in his soul and has become actual in his belief—such a man being perfect in his religion and character, and having studied the sciences of the philosophers and come to know what they signify. The human intellect having drawn him on and led him to dwell within its province, he must have felt distressed by the externals of the Law and by the meanings of the above-mentioned equivocal, derivative, or amphibolous terms, as he continued to understand them by himself or was made to understand them by others. Hence he would remain in a state of perplexity and confusion as to whether he should follow his intellect, renounce what he knew concerning the terms in question, and consequently consider that he has renounced the foundations of the Law. Or he should hold fast to his understanding of these terms and not let himself be drawn on together with his intellect, rather turning his back on it and moving away from it, while at the same time perceiving that he had brought loss to himself and harm to his religion. He would be left with those imaginary beliefs to which he owes his fear and difficulty and would not cease to suffer from heartache and great perplexity.

Maimonides also indicates a second function:

> ... namely, the explanation of very obscure parables occurring in the books of the prophets, but not explicitly identified there as such. Hence an ignorant or heedless individual might think that they possess only an external sense, but no internal one. However, even when one who truly possesses knowledge considers these parables and interprets them according to their external meaning, he too is overtaken by great perplexity. But if we explain these parables to him or if we draw his attention to their being parables, he will take the right road and be delivered from his perplexity. That is why I have called this treatise the *Guide of the Perplexed.*

The concern of the *Guide* is thus, on the face of it, hermeneutical, methodological, and interpretive; its raw material consists of knotty, often disconcerting passages from Biblical and rabbinic literature, aligned with concepts and images drawn from philosophic and scientific literature. In essence, however, the *Guide* covers a wide spectrum of staple philosophic problems such as the claims of reason versus revelation; the existence, unity, and incorporeality of God (i.e., the theory of attributes, the problem of anthropomorphism, cosmological and ontological proofs for the existence of God); the freedom of God's action; creation of the world; problems of physics; miracles and natural law; prophecy; evil; providence; the reasons for the commandments of the Torah and the insistence that divine commandments are not arbitrary. Maimonides' views on basic problems of religious philosophy are not very different from those of his predecessors (e.g., Saadyah Gaon or Bahya ibn Pakuda, Abraham ibn Ezra or Abraham ibn Daud) whom he sometimes criticizes or else simply ignores. All medieval religious philosophers shared basic principles, had common characteristics, and agreed on fundamental conceptions of metaphysics, physics, and ethics—in other words, God, the universe, and man. The main difference lies in his form of argumentation and methods of demonstration, in a more rigorously scientific approach based on what were considered to be unimpeachable Aristotelian doctrines. For he was convinced that "the works of Aristotle are the roots and foundations of all works on the sciences" and that "Aristotle's intellect represents the extreme of human intellect."* He

---

*Nevertheless, we should not forget that he was also a critic of Aristotle and revised many aspects of traditional Aristotelianism; see, for example, *Guide*, II, on creation. Medieval religious philosophy would be unintelligible without this flexibility and intellectual agility, the fusion of dependence and independence.

would not, therefore, settle for a shoddy defense of, or rickety apology for, religion—and that explains why Maimonides, in common with Muslim philosophers such as Al-farabi (whose philosophical acumen Maimonides admired), mercilessly exposed the inadequacies and inconstancies of the Kalam, the system on which Muslim theology was erected. The Mutakallimun, practitioners of this unsound and unsatisfying philosophy, are repeatedly upbraided by Maimonides. He sought a candid confrontation with philosophy and an honest demonstration of the importance and supremacy of religious tradition. He addressed himself to the implicit antagonism between religion with its insistence upon the necessity and value of action, and philosophy with its insistence upon the excellence and superiority of contemplation—the "ultimate perfection" which consists only of rational opinions without "actions or moral qualities" (Guide, III, ch. 27). He was concerned with but not stymied by the difficulties involved in transferring philosophic concepts to religion or identifying religious notions with philosophic postulates. It is in this sense—and notwithstanding Maimonides' recognition of the fallibility of reason as a guide to truth, of the necessary limitations of philosophy as a body of knowledge and the resultant need to criticize or revise certain philosophic conceptions in light of religious belief—that the Guide marks the peak of medieval Jewish rationalism.

Actually, Maimonides was caught on the horns of a painful dilemma. He was fully aware of the dangers, and indeed of the limitations, of philosophy, of the need for prudence and discretion in the dissemination of rationalistic views, of the fact that the philosopher would always be part of an intellectual elite far removed from—and often suspect by—the mass of simple believers. This accounts for the dialectic of the Guide, which aims to enlighten some people without disconcerting others. Maimonides warns the reader that the Guide contains premeditated, carefully wrought contradictions. In common with the Biblical allegories and aggadic parables, the Guide must manage to communicate with different people on different levels. But despite these difficulties,* he remained unswervingly committed to the supremacy of speculative theology, convinced that all people

*This dialectic and these difficulties continue to befuddle and divide students of the Guide concerning Maimonides' true intention and actual religious stance. There is little agreement among scholars in this area. Professor Leo Strauss has repeatedly focused attention on the esoteric, allusive, heterodox, and contradictory in the writings of Maimonides. See my review of his position in Speculum, XLI (1966), pp. 555-58.

should pursue it "to the extent of their ability" and "according to the measure of their apprehension." Any esotericist, convinced of the validity and usefulness of his doctrine, eventually has to evangelize his cause and face the dangers of popularization. Maimonides emphasized his attitude with the following homiletical flourish:

> One of the parables generally known in our community is that comparing knowledge to water. Now the sages, peace be on them, explained several notions by means of this parable; one of them being that he who knows how to swim brings up pearls from the bottom of the sea, whereas he who does not know, drowns. For this reason, no one should expose himself to the risks of swimming unless he has been trained in learning to swim (Guide, I, ch. 34).

Like swimming in deep water, the pursuit of philosophic knowledge demands multiple skills, patient preparation, and extraordinary tenacity. The training is long and hard but indispensable if one is to achieve the goal and enter the palace (see Guide, III, ch. 51).

Maimonides' philosophic posture may thus be seen as reflecting his innate conviction that "it is through wisdom, in an unrestricted sense, that the rational matter that we receive from the Law through tradition, is demonstrated" (Guide, III, ch. 54), and this real wisdom is the goal toward which every person must strive. "The opinions [of the Torah] should first be known as being received through tradition, then they should be demonstrated." Belief is not just assent to a body of truth, but "belief is the affirmation that what has been represented is outside the mind just as it has been represented in the mind" (Guide, I, ch. 50).

It is important that his intellectual position, however, which may be presented as typically rationalist, should be seen also from the historical perspective. It arose from a specific milieu and was an answer to the perplexity of the times. Maimonides must be seen against the background of Muslim philosophers (from Al-farabi and Avicenna to Averroes) who either provided his immediate sources or determined the general climate of philosophic opinion and its characteristic tendencies. Philosophy was widespread, and rationalism was a common modality of thought, almost a way of life. Left alone, unharnessed and untrammeled, it could destroy positive religion and produce skepticism, agnosticism, and relativism. Heresy and antinomism became real dangers. Muslim theologians were agonizing over this problem and Christian scholastics would soon have their prolonged confrontation with it.

The beliefs of Judaism had to be expounded systematically and with sophistication while the practices of Judaism had to be endowed with rationality and significance. R. Bahya ibn Pakuda, anticipating Maimonides' very phraseology, submitted that his *Hovot ha-Levavot* (Duties of the Heart) was designed "to show the way to the perplexed." R. Saadyah Gaon's description of the circumstances that motivated the composition of his *Emunot ve-Deot* (Beliefs and Opinions), although written in Baghdad, is also pertinent: "I saw men sunk, as it were, in a sea of doubt and overwhelmed by the waves of confusion and there was no diver to bring them up from the depths and no swimmer to come to their rescue." Maimonides' summation and evaluation of R. Saadyah Gaon's activities (in the *Epistle to Yemen*) is noteworthy: "For the Jews of his time were perplexed and misguided. The divine religion might well nigh have disappeared had he not encouraged the pusillanimous and diffused, disseminated, and propagated by word of mouth and pen a knowledge of its underlying principles. He believed, in all earnestness ... that he would inspire the masses with hope for the truth." One is tempted to discern autobiographical allusions in this panegyric; the paragraph might well have been written with regard to Maimonides' own activities.

We should add that this projection of Maimonides against the backdrop of twelfth-century science and rationalism is not merely a result of our modern historical sense. Maimonides was sensitive to the challenges and complexities of his time, was aware of the essential universality of philosophy, and stressed the need to present Judaism within such a general framework. There is, in other words, a conscious sense of "outer-directedness" in his philosophizing, an awareness of the profile of the Jews "in the eyes of the nations" and a need to project continuously the image of a "wise and understanding people" (Deut. 4:7). Literalism and unphilosophical thinking will only result in the other peoples saying that "this little people is foolish and ignoble."

Although religious rationalism did not begin with Maimonides, it came to be totally identified with him. Protagonists and antagonists would draw the lines of their positions in relation to Maimonides. To a great extent, subsequent Jewish intellectual history may be seen as a debate concerning the wisdom and effectiveness of the Maimonidean position. Adherents of philosophy unequivocally asserted the primacy of the intellectual experience and cognitive attainment in Judaism and, consequently, the indispensability of philosophy. Philosophic knowledge as a duty was the nuclear notion of their program. Man is duty bound to realize his intellectual potential, for "his ultimate perfection is to become rational in actu, I mean to have an intellect in actu; this would consist in his knowing every- thing concerning all the beings that it is within the capacity of man to know in accordance with his ultimate perfection" (Guide, III, ch. 27).

There is, furthermore, a religious dimension to intellectual attainment. There is a religious obligation to apply one's intellect to the study of the world. "It is known and certain that the love of God does not become closely knit in a man's heart till he is continuously and thoroughly possessed by it and gives up everything else in the world for it; as God commanded us, 'with all your heart and with all your soul' (Deut. 6:5). One only loves God with the knowledge with which one knows Him; according to the knowledge will be the love. If the former be little or much, so will the latter be little or much. A person ought therefore to devote himself to the understand- ing and comprehension of those sciences and studies which will inform him concerning his Master, as far as it lies in human faculties to understand and comprehend" (Mishneh Torah, Book I, Laws of Repentance, ch. X). The protagonists of philosophy did not conceal the fact that they found perfunctory piety or unexamined traditional- ism uncongenial and that routine Talmudism divorced from spiritual animation was not at the top of their scale of values. A prominent component of the philosophic apologia is also the desire to show the world (i.e., fellow intellectuals) that Judaism has not forfeited its claim to, or skill in, philosophy and science. In common with their first-century coreligionists of Alexandria, they were deeply conscious, in H. A. Wolfson's words, of "the social significance of the philo- sophical interpretation of Scripture either as a means of satisfying the inquiring minds among the Jews or as a means of defending Judaism against the attacks" of antagonistic non-Jews. In their view, it was one of the lasting achievements of Maimonides that he helped restore lustre and dignity to Judaism by commanding the respectful attention of Christians and Moslems.

Opponents of philosophy vigorously condemn the development of rationalism and its detrimental consequences, are hostile to studies tainted by foreign origin and philosophical associations, and view the indiscriminate spread of allegorism as potentially disruptive of the Jewish tradition. The rationalization of the commandments and the reduction of the law, in some cases, to pragmatic-utilitarian categories were considered to be the prelude to antinomism, and contempt for traditional Jewish practices. They feared the victory of the "God of Aristotle" (as defined by Judah ha-Levi) who is removed from and unconcerned with human affairs, who is not accessible in prayer, who would not and could not intervene miraculously in the natural course of events. In short, the reasons for opposition to philosophy and religious rationalization as articulated in the introduction to the *Emunot ve-Deot* remained valid: "there are people who disapprove of such an occupation, being of the opinion that speculation leads to unbelief and is conductive to heresy." Maimonides also reproduces the view of those who contended that philosophic inquiry "undermines the foundations of law" (*Guide*, I, ch. 33). Some—Hasdai Crescas in the fourteenth century is a good example—simply wanted to disentangle religion from philosophy, to extricate faith from the clutch of reason, and establish the complete independence of religion, even when philosophy purported to be in agreement with it. Religion should not be dependent on or subservient to anything.

The whole debate revolved around Maimonides—and, in many ways, still does. For Maimonides represents a type of mentality and suggests a direction of thought concerning which neutrality is impossible. In the final analysis, two conflicting ideal types were juxtaposed: a traditional puritanism which is distrustful of secular culture and insists on the absolute opposition between divine wisdom and human wisdom; and religious rationalism which is convinced of the interrelatedness and complementarity—indeed the essential identity—of divine and human wisdom, of religion and culture, and strives doggedly for their integration.*

Maimonides' literary career was concluded with the composition of some ten medical treatises. These have been summarily characterized by Dr. M. Meyerhof as varied and useful monographs on individual diseases and drugs, based to a large extent on Arabic medical literature. While hardly pioneering in the field, his medical texts illustrate his vast erudition and the high ethical standards he brought in his approach to medicine.

*See, for example, H. A. Wolfson, *Philo* (Cambridge, 1962), p. 21 ff., 64. *The Philosophy of the Church Fathers* (Cambridge, 1964), p. 7 ff; also C. Dawson, *Religion and Culture* (New York, 1958), p. 175.

A synoptic view of Maimonides' work attests to its remarkable unity and systematic progression. In spite of changes, evolution of thought, allusive presentation of certain ideas, and outright contradictions, his work adds up to a judicious interpretation and systematic presentation of Jewish belief and practice. As it moves from one literary form to another, from textual explication to independent exposition, and from one level of exposition to another, one would think he had had a master plan from the very beginning to achieve his overarching objective: to bring law and philosophy—two apparently incongruous attitudes of mind, two jealous rivals—into fruitful harmony. We see him consistently espousing a sensitized view of religion and morality, demanding a full and uncompromising but inspired and sensitive observance of the law, openly disdaining the perfunctory, vulgar view of the masses, searching for the ultimate religious significance of every human action, and urging a commitment to and quest for wisdom and perfection. He wanted to unify mood and medium, to integrate the thought of eternity with the life of temporality, to combine religious tradition with philosophical doctrine. He knew that this could not be done easily or indiscriminately but he was convinced that the very attempt, though fraught with danger, was indispensable for true religious perfection. It may be said that Maimonides allowed religious rationalization, which had led a sort of subliminal existence in earlier rabbinic writing, to claim and obtain legitimacy and dignity.

Such an integrative view of Maimonides has significant repercussions for the study of his writings and warns against the widespread, misleading tendency on the part of students to fragmentize Maimonides' works. Throughout the ages, scholars have often set up a dichotomy between Maimonidean law and Maimonidean philosophy, or have even isolated different components of his legal legacy (i.e., have studied the code without the commentary or responsa). This failure to see and study Maimonides in his totality has often obscured the historical vision, blurred the real forms of his intellectual achievement, and erased his individuality.

There are, moreover, certain pre-eminent traits which are common to all of Maimonides' writings and these should be boldly underscored. Maimonides never tired of emphasizing that he wrote with great care and precision, that his ideas were rigorously reasoned, his balanced sentences were meticulously formulated, and the sections of his various writings were thoughtfully organized. He disclaimed anything haphazard or incidental, writing only "after reflection and deliberation and careful examination of true opinions as well as untrue ones." Concerning the *Guide* he said: "The diction of this treatise has not been chosen at haphazard, but with great exactness and exceeding precision, and with care to avoid failing to explain any obscure point." His rigorous attitude in general was described in the *Epistle on Conversion*: "It is not proper to speak publicly unless one has rehearsed what he wants to say many times and studied it well. This is how the rabbis interpreted the verse in Job 28:27–28. 'Then did He see it and declare it; He established it and searched it out.' And only after this punctilious preparation did He speak: 'and He said to man.'"

The compliment which the French encyclopedist Diderot paid to the German philosopher Leibniz is applicable to Maimonides: "He combined two great qualities which are almost incompatible with one another—the spirit of discovery and that of method." His writings are marked not only by ordered intelligibility and terse summation but also by creativity and originality. Sometimes he himself called attention to the "spirit of discovery" which permeated his work, as when he declared the *Mishneh Torah* to be a work of unprecedented scope and arrangement, for not since R. Judah the Prince redacted the Mishnah had anyone undertaken to rework and reformulate the entire *halakhah*. In the introduction to the *Guide* he claims to write about topics "which have not been treated by any of our scholars . . . since the times of our captivity." He did not engage in popularization in any conventional sense; he was a molder and architect of ideas.

Another outstanding feature of Maimonides was his intellectual honesty and courage, unintimidated by pressure, dissatisfaction, or potential censure. In his *Commentary on the Mishnah* he addressed himself to a certain problem even though he knew that his views would be uncongenial to most—or even all—of the great scholars; he proceeded "oblivious of predecessors or contemporaries." Elsewhere in that work he repudiates the method of R. Saadyah Gaon who used obviously fallacious arguments, which he himself did not accept, just for the purpose of vanquishing his opponents. In the *Eight Chapters* he asserts: "Let what others have said be compared with our opinion, and the truth will surely prevail." He was sensitive to the fact that his innovating code of law would give rise to abundant and vehement criticism—he even listed the kinds of critics that would rise against him—but this awareness did not deflect him from his course. Concerning the *Guide*, Maimonides says:

> I am the man who when the concern pressed him and his way was straitened and he could find no other device by which to teach a demonstrated truth other than by giving satisfaction to a single virtuous man while displeasing ten thousand ignoramuses—I am he who prefers to address that single man by himself, and I do not heed the blame of those many creatures.

Maimonides also felt the need to resist the tyranny of the published word. Most readers tend to dismiss something as obviously erroneous if it contradicts an earlier book; even scholars do not always examine a work critically in an effort to establish its intrinsic worth and plausibility but merely compare it with older books. Maimonides opposed the pervasive mood of intellectual conservatism which accepts anything published as authoritative, anything old and familiar as correct, and anything novel as suspect. Independent judgment and honest criticism must play an important role. In the Letter on Astrology, Maimonides exclaims:

> The great sickness and the grievous evil consist in this: that all the things that man finds written in books, he presumes to think of as true—and all the more so if the books are old.

A special aspect of this radical honesty and courage is his determination to "accept the truth from whatever source it proceeds." In other words, non-Jewish sources are equally relevant and valid. This inflexible determination is formulated early in the *Eight Chapters*:

> I have gleaned [the ideas] from the words of the wise occurring in the Midrashim, in the Talmud, and in other of their works as well as from the words of the philosophers, ancient and recent, and also from the works of various authors, as one should accept the truth from whatever source it proceeds.

It is repeated emphatically in the *Mishneh Torah*, where Maimonides extols the wise men of Greece and insists upon the indispensability of their scientific writings:

> ... all this is part of the science of astronomy and mathematics, about which many books have been composed by Greek sages— books that are still available to the scholars of our time. But the books which had been composed by the sages of Israel, of the tribe of Issachar, who lived in the time of the Prophets, have not come

down to us. But since all these rules have been established by sound and clear proofs, free from any flaw and irrefutable, we need not be concerned about the identity of their authors, whether they were Hebrew prophets or Gentile sages. For when we have to do with rules and propositions which have been demonstrated by good reasons and have been verified to be true by sound and flawless proofs, we rely upon the author who has discovered them or has transmitted them, only because of his demonstrated proofs and verified reasoning.

The importance of this principle for his philosophical and medical works is quite transparent.

While much of his writing has—or has been invested with—the quality of timelessness, Maimonides did not write in an historical vacuum, and it would be wrong to uproot him from his moorings in time and place. Explicitly and implicitly he addressed himself to the socio-political realities, spiritual problems, and intellectual challenges of his generation. To be sure, he left his imprint on his age and on future ages, but his age left its imprint on him as well. We may, in other words, learn a great deal from his writings about the intellectual and religious confrontations of his period: about the decline and fall of the Gaonate, the nature and seriousness of the Karaite attack on rabbinic tradition, the divisiveness within the Jewish community, the demands and problems of contemporary rationalism, the posture of Judaism vis-à-vis Christianity and Islam, the history—accomplishments and lacunae—of rabbinic and philosophic literature, the prevalent forms and methods of Biblical and Talmudic study, the varieties of Jewish and non-Jewish intellectual and religious experience.

A strong pedagogic sense, finally, motivates his writing. Starting with his youthful works on logic and astronomy, he shows himself eager to teach, to transmit knowledge, and to guide his readers. Failure to share one's knowledge with others would be tantamount to "robbing one who deserves the truth of the truth, or begrudging an heir his inheritance" (Guide, III, introduction). His own words in the Guide of the Perplexed (II, ch. 37) best express this: "A man endowed with knowledge does not set anything down for himself in order to teach himself what he already knows. But the nature of that intellect is such that it always overflows and is transmitted from one who receives that overflow to another one who receives it after him. . . ."

MISHNEH TORAH

*T*HE Mishneh Torah, the first serious attempt, since the redaction of the Mishnah by R. Judah the Prince, at a comprehensive survey, classification, and codification of Jewish law, changed the entire landscape of rabbinic literature. Although it did not attain its goal—it was not adopted as the universal Jewish code nor were its really novel features (scope and arrangement) imitated by later codifiers—the Mishneh Torah did become the pièce de résistance of all Talmudic study through the ages. Any advanced student of the Talmud would invariably consult the Mishneh Torah, attempt to reconstruct the latent processes of Maimonides' reasoning, and compare his formulations with alternative constructions. The Mishneh Torah was like a prism through which practically all Talmudic study had to pass.

Although confident about the need, value, and ultimate acceptance of his code, Maimonides anticipated criticism and opposition on the grounds of his (a) having omitted source references and presented unilateral, unsubstantiated decisions and (b) having included a heady dose of philosophic exposition and comment. He also felt that jealous people "would defame its praiseworthy features and pretend" that such a summary was totally superfluous for them. Such criticism was indeed forthcoming and it markedly influenced the spread and study of the Mishneh Torah.

Maimonides' introduction to the code contains a brief history of

33

the Oral Law and its transmission, and explains the reasons for the eventual emergence of a literary corpus (Mishnah and Talmud) embodying the oral tradition. A suggestive parallel is drawn between the socio-political conditions which necessitated the compilation of the Mishnah and those of Maimonides' own time. Maimonides was convinced that there is a significant correlation between political decline and intellectual atrophy. His survey includes a dispassionate, mildly pejorative, evaluation of the literary achievements of the Geonim and calls attention to the role of regionalism and local custom in Jewish law. Only Talmudic law represents a consensus and is universally binding for the entire Jewish people; post-Talmudic developments in halakhah—e.g., Geonic ordinances or communal enactments—are restricted in their application.

The following selections from the Mishneh Torah illustrate for the most part Maimonides' original interpretations, new emphases, striking formulations, or interpolations of ethical and philosophical motifs into Talmudic material. I have included a few sections which show Maimonides' organization and rephrasing of standard halakhic material in his own clear, vigorous prose, and through which Maimonides emerges as an effective mouthpiece for historical Judaism. There are also sections where well-known Talmudic material is interpreted and presented in such a way that a new pattern of meanings seems to emerge.

ALL the precepts which Moses received on Sinai, were given together with their interpretation, as it is said, "And I will give to you the tables of stone, and the law, and the commandment" (Ex. 24:12). "The law" refers to the Written Law; "the commandment," to its interpretation. God bade us fulfill the Law in accordance with "the commandment." This commandment refers to that which is called the Oral Law. The whole of the Law was written by Moses our Teacher before his death, in his own hand. He presented a scroll to each tribe and deposited one in the Ark for a testimony, as it is said, "Take this book of the law and put it by the side of the Ark of the Covenant of the Lord your God, that it may be there for a witness against you" (Deut. 31:26). "The commandment," which is the interpretation of the Law, he did not write down but gave a charge concerning it to the Elders, to Joshua, and to the rest of Israel, as it is said, "All this which I command you, that shall you do; you shall not add to, nor diminish from it" (ibid. 4:2). Hence, it is styled the Oral Law.

See *Book of Commandments*, introduction; Letter to Joseph ibn Gabir; *Guide of the Perplexed*, introduction and I, ch. 71.

Although the Oral Law was not committed to writing, Moses taught the whole of it, in his court, to the seventy elders as well as to Eleazar, Phineas, and Joshua—all three of whom received it from Moses. To Joshua, his disciple, our teacher Moses delivered the Oral Law and charged him concerning it. So too, Joshua, throughout his life, taught orally. Many elders received the Oral Law from Joshua. Eli received it from the elders and from Phineas. Samuel, from Eli and his court. David, from Samuel and his court. . . .

R. Judah, our teacher, the saint, compiled the Mishnah. From the time of Moses to that of our teacher, the saint, no work had been composed from which the Oral Law was publicly taught. But in each generation, the head of the then existing court or the prophet of that time wrote down for his private use a memorandum of the traditions which he had heard from his teachers, and which he taught orally in public. So too, every student wrote down, according to his ability, the exposition of the Torah and of its laws, as he heard them, as well as the new matter evolved in each generation, which had not been received by tradition but had been deduced by application of the thirteen hermeneutical rules and had been adopted by the Supreme Court. This was the method in vogue till the time of our teacher, the saint.

He gathered together all the traditions, enactments, interpretations, and expositions of every portion of the Torah, that had either come down from Moses our Teacher or had been deduced by the courts in successive generations. All this material he redacted in the Mishnah, which was diligently taught in public, and thus became universally known among the Jewish people. Copies of it were made and widely disseminated, so that the Oral Law might not be forgotten in Israel.

Why did our teacher, the saint, act so and not leave things as they were? Because he observed that the number of disciples was diminishing, fresh calamities were continually happening, the wicked government was extending its domain and increasing in power, and Israelites were wandering and emigrating to distant countries. He therefore composed a work to serve as a handbook for all, the contents of which could be rapidly studied and not be forgotten. Throughout his life, he and his colleagues were engaged in giving public instruction in the Mishnah. . . .

All these sages . . . were the great men of the successive generations; some of them were presidents of colleges, some Exilarchs, and some were members of the great Sanhedrin; besides them were thousands and myriads of disciples and fellow-students. Ravina and Rav Ashi closed the list of the sages of the Talmud. It was Rav Ashi who compiled the Babylonian Talmud in the land of Shinar (Babylon), about a century after Rabbi Johanan had compiled the Palestinian Talmud. These two Talmuds contain an exposition of the text of the Mishnah and an elucidation of its abstruse points and of the new subject matter that had been added by the various courts from the days of our teacher, the saint, till the compilation of the Talmud. The two Talmuds, the Tosefta, the Sifra and the Sifre, and the Toseftot are the sources, from all of which is elucidated what is forbidden and what is permitted, what is unclean and what is clean, what is a penal violation and what involves no penalty, what is fit to be used and what is unfit for use, all in accordance with the traditions received by the sages from their predecessors in unbroken succession up to the teachings of Moses as he received them on Sinai. From these sources too, are ascertained the decrees, instituted by the sages and prophets, in each generation, to serve as a protecting fence about the Law, in accordance with Moses' express injunction, "You shall keep My charge" (Lev. 18:30), that is, "Ordain a charge to preserve My charge." From these sources a clear conception is also obtained of the customs and ordinances, either formally introduced in various generations by their respective authorities or that came into use with their sanction; from these it is forbidden to depart, as it is said, "You shall not turn aside from the sentence which they shall declare to you, to the right hand, nor to the left" (Deut. 17:11). So too these works contain the clearly established judgments and rules not received from Moses, but which the Supreme Court of each generation deduced by applying the hermeneutical principles for the interpretation of the Law, and which were decided by those venerable authorities to be the law—all of which, accumulated from the days of Moses to his own time, Rav Ashi put together in the Gemara.*

After the Court of Rav Ashi, who compiled the Gemara which was finally completed in the days of his son, an extraordinarily great dispersion of Israel throughout the world took place. The people emigrated to remote parts and distant isles. The prevalence of wars and the march of armies made travel insecure. The study of the

*See Book XIV, Rebels, ch. I; also Book III, Sanctification of the New Moon, V, 3.

Torah declined. The Jewish people did not flock to the colleges in their thousands and tens of thousands as heretofore; but in each city and country, individuals who felt the divine call gathered together and occupied themselves with the Torah; studied all the works of the sages; and from these learned the method of legal interpretation.

If a court established in any country after the time of the Talmud made decrees and ordinances or introduced customs for those residing in its particular country or for residents of other countries, its enactments did not obtain the acceptance of all Israel because of the remoteness of the Jewish settlements and the difficulties of travel. And as the court of any particular country consisted of individuals (whose authority was not universally recognized), while the Supreme Court of seventy-one members had, several years before the compilation of the Talmud, ceased to exist, no compulsion is exercised on those living in one country to observe the customs of another country; nor is any court directed to issue a decree that had been issued by another court in the same country. So too, if one of the Geonim taught that a certain way of judgment was correct, and it became clear to a court at a later date that this was not in accordance with the view of the Gemara, the earlier authority is not necessarily followed but that view is adopted which seems more reasonable, whether it be that of an earlier or later authority.

The foregoing observations refer to rules, decrees, ordinances, and customs that originated after the Talmud had been compiled. But whatever is already mentioned in the Babylonian Talmud is binding on all Israel. And every city and country is bound to observe all the customs observed by the sages of the Gemara, promulgate their decrees, and uphold their institutions, on the ground that all the customs, decrees, and institutions mentioned in the Talmud received the assent of all Israel, and those sages who instituted the ordinances, issued the decrees, introduced the customs, gave the decisions, and taught that a certain ruling was correct, constituted the total body or the majority of Israel's wise men. They were the leaders who received from each other the traditions concerning the fundamentals of Judaism in unbroken succession back to Moses our Teacher, upon whom be peace.

The sages, however, who arose after the compilation of the Talmud, studied it deeply and became famous for their wisdom, are called Geonim. All these Geonim who flourished in the land of Israel, Babylon, Spain, and France, taught the method of the

Talmud, elucidated its obscurities, and expounded the various topics with which it deals. For its method is exceedingly profound. Furthermore, the work is composed in Aramaic mixed with other languages—this having been the vernacular of the Babylonian Jews at the time when it was compiled. In other countries, however, as also in Babylon in the days of the Geonim, no one, unless specially taught, understood that dialect. Many applications were made to the Gaon of the day by residents of different cities, asking for explanations of difficulties in the Talmud. These, the Geonim answered, according to their ability. Those who had put the questions collected the responses which they made into books for study. The Geonim also, at different periods, composed commentaries on the Talmud. Some of them explained specific laws; others, particular chapters that presented difficulties to their contemporaries; others again expounded complete treatises and entire orders of the Talmud. They also made compilations of settled rules as to things permitted or forbidden, as to infractions which were penal or were not liable to a penalty. All these dealt with matters in regard to which compendia were needed, that could be studied by one not capable of penetrating to the depths of the Talmud. This is the godly work in which all the Geonim of Israel engaged, from the completion of the Talmud to the present date which is the eighth year of the eleventh century after the destruction of the Second Temple.*

In our days, severe vicissitudes prevail, and all feel the pressure of hard times. The wisdom of our wise men has disappeared; the understanding of our prudent men is hidden. Hence, the commentaries of the Geonim and their compilations of laws and responses, which they took care to make clear, have in our times become hard to understand so that only a few individuals properly comprehend them. Needless to add that such is the case in regard to the Talmud itself—the Babylonian as well as the Palestinian—the *Sifra*, the *Sifre* and the *Tosefta*, all of which works require, for their comprehension, a broad mind, a wise soul, and considerable study, and then one can learn from them the correct practice as to what is forbidden or permitted, and the other rules of the Torah.

On these grounds, I, Moses the son of Maimon the Sefardi, bestirred myself, and, relying on the help of God, blessed be He, intently studied all these works, with the view of putting together

*Cf. to this date (1177), Book III, Sanctification of the New Moon, XI, 16; Book VII, Laws of the Sabbatical Year, X, 4.

the results obtained from them in regard to what is forbidden or permitted, clean or unclean, and the other rules of the Torah—all in plain language and terse style, so that thus the entire Oral Law might become systematically known to all, without citing difficulties and solutions or differences of view, one person saying so, and another something else—but consisting of statements, clear and convincing, and in accordance with the conclusions drawn from all these compilations and commentaries that have appeared from the time of Moses to the present, so that all the rules shall be accessible to young and old, whether these appertain to the (Pentateuchal) precepts or to the institutions established by the sages and prophets, so that no other work should be needed for ascertaining any of the laws of Israel, but that this work might serve as a compendium of the entire Oral Law, including the ordinances, customs, and decrees instituted from the days of our teacher Moses till the compilation of the Talmud, as expounded for us by the Geonim in all the works composed by them since the completion of the Talmud. Hence, I have entitled this work *Mishneh Torah* (Repetition of the Law), for the reason that a person who first reads the Written Law and then this compilation, will know from it the whole of the Oral Law, without having occasion to consult any other book between them.

I have seen fit to arrange this compendium in large divisions of the laws according to their various topics. These divisions are distributed in chapters grouped according to subject matter. Each chapter is subdivided into smaller paragraphs so that they may be systematically memorized. Among the laws in the various topics, some consist of rules in reference to a single Biblical precept. This would be the case when such a precept is rich in traditional matter and forms a single topic. Other sections include rules referring to several precepts when these all belong to one topic. For the work follows the order of topics and is not planned according to the number of precepts, as will be explained to the reader.

The total number of precepts that are obligatory for all generations is 613. Of these, 248 are affirmative; their mnemonic is the number of bones in the human body. 365 precepts are negative and their mnemonic is the number of days in the solar year.

Blessed be the all-merciful who has aided us.

These are the 613 precepts which were orally imparted to Moses on Sinai, together with their general principles, detailed applications, and minute particulars. All these principles, details, particulars, and the exposition of every precept constitute the Oral Law, which each court received from its predecessor. There are other precepts which originated after the Sinaitic Revelation, were instituted by prophets and sages, and were universally accepted by all Israel. Such are the reading of the Scroll of Esther (on Purim), the kindling of the Hanukkah lights, fasting on the Ninth of Av. . . . Each of these precepts has its special interpretations and details, all of which will be expounded in this work.

All these newly established precepts, we are duty bound to accept and observe, as it is said, "You shall not turn aside from the sentence which they shall declare to you, to the right hand, nor to the left" (Deut. 17:11). They are not an addition to the precepts of the Torah. In regard to what, then, did the Torah warn us, "You shall not add thereto, nor diminish from it" (ibid. 13:1)? The purpose of this text is to teach us that a prophet is not permitted to make an innovation and declare that the Holy One, blessed be He, had commanded him to add it to the precepts of the Torah or had bidden him to abrogate one of these 613 precepts. But if the Court, together with the prophet living at the time, institute an additional precept as an ordinance, judicial decision, or decree, this is not an addition (to the precepts of the Torah). For they did not assert that the Holy One, blessed be He . . . ordered the reading of the Scroll of Esther at the appointed time. Had they said this, they would have been adding to the Torah. We hold, however, that the prophets, in conjunction with the Court, enacted these ordinances, and commanded that the Scroll of Esther be read at the appointed time so as to proclaim the praises of the Holy One, blessed be He, recount the salvations that He wrought for us, and that He was ever near when we cried to Him, and that we should therefore bless and laud Him and inform future generations how true is the reassurance of the Torah in the text, "For what great nation is there that has God so near to them, as the Lord our God is [to us], whensoever we call upon Him" (ibid. 4:7). In this way every precept, affirmative or negative, instituted by the Scribes, is to be understood.*

I have seen fit to divide this work into fourteen books.

---

*This refutes the Karaite contention that Talmudic law is an illegitimate accretion to Biblical law. See also the anti-Karaite polemic in Book VIII, Daily Offerings, VII, 11; and Book III, Sabbath, ch. II; Commentary on the Mishnah, Avot 1:3.

MAIMONIDES explains that he could not compose a comprehensive work on the details of practical precepts while ignoring the fundamentals of essential beliefs; he felt compelled to prefix a philosophical-theological prolegomenon to his code, thereby underscoring the unity of the philosophical and the legal components of Judaism. Book I contains Maimonides' summary of the essential beliefs and guiding concepts which provide the ideological and experiential substructure of Judaism.

The reader should be especially attentive to the following points:

(1) The identification of physics and metaphysics with classical rabbinic teachings (Basic Principles, II, 12; IV, 10–13) and the inclusion of these sciences in the Oral Law (Study, I, 11–12). Generally the chapters on Study—especially chapter III—throb with vitality. Maimonides' usual reticence and restrained formulation are slackened; the statements about the universality of the obligation of study and its absolute precedence are emphatic and vigorous.

(2) One sanctifies God's name not only by martyrdom but by leading a dedicated life of integrity and honesty (Basic Principles, V, 11; Moral Dispositions, ch. VI). Even in normal circumstances,

religion does not demand extremism or self-mortification; indeed, the doctrine of the golden mean is a most poignant, barbed repudiation of all forms of monasticism and asceticism, including Islamic Sufism whose spiritual claims apparently fascinated many Jews (Moral Dispositions, chs. I–III; see Eight Chapters, ch. IV).

(3) Maimonides' conception of the history of religion, affirming—contrary to the modern evolutionary view—that monotheism was the original state of belief and idolatry a corruption of it (Idolatry, ch. I). Abraham is depicted as a vigorous iconoclast, crusading against the rampant polytheism of his day, engaging people in ideological debate and argumentation. His life is a paradigm of ethical activism. (Cf. Guide, II, ch. 39; III, chs. 29 and 51.) In rejecting astrology and other superstitious practices or beliefs, Maimonides insists that this rejection be motivated by rational conviction; routine conformity without absolute conviction is inadequate (Idolatry, ch. XI).

(4) The description of a disinterested love of God, with no desire for any kind of reward, as the highest and purest form of religious commitment (Repentance, ch. X). In this context, Maimonides introduces the stunning interpretation of the Song of Songs as an allegory of the soul's relation to or communion with God.

BASIC PRINCIPLES OF THE TORAH

Chapter 1

❲ 1 The basic principle of all basic principles and the pillar of all sciences is to realize that there is a First Being who brought every existing thing into being. All existing things, whether celestial, terrestrial, or belonging to an intermediate class, exist only through His true existence.

❲ 2 If it could be supposed that He did not exist, it would follow that nothing else could possibly exist.

❲ 3 If, however, it were supposed that all other beings were nonexistent, He alone would still exist. Their non-existence would not involve His non-existence. For all beings are in need of Him; but He, blessed be He, is not in need of them nor of any one of them. Hence, His real essence is unlike that of any of them.*

❡ 4   This is what the prophet means when he says, "But the Eternal is the true God" (Jer. 10:10); that is, He alone is real, and nothing else has reality like His reality. The same thought the Torah expresses in the text: "There is none else besides Him" (Deut. 4:35); that is: there is no being besides Him, that is really like Him.

❡ 6   To acknowledge this truth is an affirmative precept, as it is said, "I am the Lord your God" (Ex. 20:2; Deut. 5:6). And whoever permits the thought to enter his mind that there is another deity besides this God, violates a prohibition; as it is said, "You shall have no other gods before Me" (Ex. 20:3; Deut. 5:7), and denies the essence of religion—this doctrine being the great principle on which everything depends.

❡ 8   That the Holy One, blessed be He, is not a physical body, is explicitly set forth in the Pentateuch and in the Prophets, as it is said "(Know therefore) that the Lord, He is God in Heaven above, and upon the Earth beneath" (Deut. 4:39); and a physical body is not in two places at one time. Furthermore, it is said, "For you saw no manner of similitude" (ibid. 4:15); and again it is said, "To whom then will you liken Me, or shall I equal?" (Is. 40:25). If He were a body, He would be like other bodies.

❡ 9   Since this is so, what is the meaning of the following expressions found in the Torah: "Beneath His Feet" (Ex. 24:10); "Written with the finger of God (ibid. 31:18); "The hand of God" (ibid. 9:3); "The eyes of God" (Gen. 38:7); "The ears of God" (Num. 11:1); and similar phrases? All these expressions are adapted to the mental capacity of the majority of mankind who have a clear perception of physical bodies only. The Torah speaks in the language of men. All these phrases are metaphorical, like the sentence "If I whet my glittering sword" (Deut. 32:41). Has God then a sword and does He slay with a sword? The term is used allegorically and all these phrases are to be understood in a similar sense. That this view is correct is proved by the fact that one prophet says that he had a vision of the Holy One, blessed be He, "Whose garment was white as snow" (Dan. 7:9), while another says that he saw Him "with dyed

*See Guide, I, ch. 69.

garments from Bozrah" (Is. 63:1). Moses our Teacher himself saw Him at the Red Sea as a mighty man waging war (Ex. 15:3) and on Sinai, as a congregational reader wrapped (in his *tallit*)—all indicating that in reality He has no form or figure. These only appeared in a prophetic vision. But God's essence as it really is, the human mind does not understand and is incapable of grasping or investigating. And this is expressed in the scriptural text "Can you, by searching, find out God? Can you find out the Almighty to perfection?" (Job 11:7).*

¶ 12   This being so, the expressions in the Pentateuch and books of the Prophets already mentioned, and others similar to these, are all of them metaphorical and rhetorical, as for example, "He that sits in the heavens shall laugh" (Ps. 2:4), "They have provoked Me to anger with their vanities" (Deut. 32:21), "As the Lord rejoiced" (*ibid.* 28:63), etc. To all these phrases, applies the saying "The Torah speaks in the language of men." So too, it is said "Do they provoke Me to anger?" (Jer. 7:19); and yet it is said "I am the Lord, I change not" (Mal. 3:6). If God were sometimes angry and sometimes rejoiced, He would be changing. All these states exist in physical beings that are of obscure and mean condition, dwelling in houses of clay, whose foundation is in the dust. Infinitely blessed and exalted above all this, is God, blessed be He.

Chapter 2

¶ 1   This God, honored and revered, it is our duty to love and fear; as it is said "You shall love the Lord your God" (Deut. 6:5), and it is further said "You shall fear the Lord your God" (*ibid.* 6:13).

¶ 2   And what is the way that will lead to the love of Him and the fear of Him? When a person contemplates His great and wondrous works and creatures and from them obtains a glimpse of His wisdom which is incomparable and infinite, he will straightway love Him, praise Him, glorify Him, and long with an exceeding longing to know His great Name; even as David said, "My soul thirsts for God, for the living God" (Ps. 42:3). And when he ponders these matters, he will recoil frightened, and realize that he is a small creature, lowly and obscure, endowed with slight and slender intelligence, standing in the presence of Him who is perfect in knowledge. And so David said "When I consider Your heavens, the work of Your fingers—what

*See *Guide*, I, chs. 26, 33, and 46.

is man that You are mindful of him?" (Ps. 8:4–5). In harmony with these sentiments, I shall explain some large, general aspects of the works of the Sovereign of the Universe, that they may serve the intelligent individual as a door to the love of God, even as our sages have remarked in connection with the theme of the love of God, "Observe the Universe and hence, you will realize Him who spoke and the world was."*

¶ 9 All beings, except the Creator, from the highest angelic form to the tiniest insect that is in the interior of the earth, exist by the power of God's essential existence. And as He has self-knowledge, and realizes His greatness, glory, and truth, He knows all, and nothing is hidden from Him.

¶ 10 The Holy One, blessed be He, realizes His true being, and knows it as it is, not with a knowledge external to Himself, as is our knowledge. For our knowledge and ourselves are separate. But as for the Creator, blessed be He, His knowledge and His life are One, in all aspects, from every point of view, and however we conceive Unity. If the Creator lived as other living creatures live, and His knowledge were external to Himself, there would be a plurality of deities, namely: He himself, His life, and His knowledge. This however, is not so. He is One in every aspect, from every angle, and in all ways in which Unity is conceived. Hence the conclusion that God is the One who knows, is known, and is the knowledge (of Himself)—all these being One. This is beyond the power of speech to express, beyond the capacity of the ear to hear, and of the human mind to apprehend clearly. Scripture, accordingly says "By the life of Pharaoh" and "By the life of your soul" but not "By the life of the Eternal." The phrase employed is "As God lives"; because the Creator and His life are not dual, as is the case with the life of living bodies or of angels. Hence too, God does not apprehend creatures and know them because of them, as we know them, but He knows them because of Himself. Knowing Himself, He knows everything, for everything is attached to Him, in His Being.†

¶ 11 What has been said on this topic in these two chapters is but a drop in the ocean, compared with what has to be elucidated on this subject. The exposition of all the principles alluded to in these two

*See Guide, III, ch. 28.
†See Guide, I, ch. 68.

chapters forms the so-called *Maaseh Merkavah*—"Account of the Divine Chariot" (Ezek. 1).

❡ 12   The ancient sages enjoined us to discuss these subjects privately, with only one individual, and then only if he be wise and capable of independent reasoning. In this case, the chapter headings are communicated to him, and he is instructed in a minute portion of the subject. It is left to him to develop the conclusions for himself and to penetrate to the depths of the subject. These topics are exceedingly profound; and not every intellect is able to grasp them. Solomon, in his wisdom, said, in regard to them, by way of parable: "The lambs will be for your clothing" (Prov. 27:26). Thus have the sages said, in the exposition of this parable, "matters that deal with the mystery of the universe shall be for your garment, that is, for you alone; do not expound them in public." So too, Solomon said concerning these topics "Let them be for you alone and not for strangers with you" (*ibid.* 5:17).

And he further said concerning these subjects, "Honey and milk are under your tongue" (Song of Songs 4:11). This text the ancient sages have thus explained, "The things that are like milk and honey shall be under your tongue." *

Chapter 4

❡ 10   The matters just discussed are like a drop in a bucket, and are very deep, but are not as deep as those treated in the First and Second Chapters. The exposition of the topics dealt with in the Third and Fourth Chapters, is termed *Maaseh Bereshit* (cosmogony). Our ancient sages enjoined us that these matters are not to be expounded in public, but should be communicated and taught to an individual privately.

❡ 11   What distinction is there between the *Maaseh Merkavah* (Ezek. 1) and the *Maaseh Bereshit?* The subject matter of *Maaseh Merkavah* is not expounded even to an individual unless he is wise and able to draw conclusions independently; and then, only the chapter headings are communicated to him. But the topics of the *Maaseh Bereshit* are taught to an individual; and even if he is unable to form independent conclusions we nevertheless teach him as much as he is capable of learning on these matters. Why is the subject not

*See *Guide*, introduction.

taught in public? Because not every one possesses the breadth of intellect requisite for obtaining an accurate grasp of the meaning and interpretation of all its contents.*

❴ 12   When a man reflects on these things, studies all these created beings, from the angels and spheres down to human beings and so on, and realizes the Divine Wisdom manifested in them all, his love for God will increase, his soul will thirst, his very flesh will yearn to love God. He will be filled with fear and trembling, as he becomes conscious of his own lowly condition, poverty, and insignificance, and compares himself with any of the great and holy bodies; still more when he compares himself with any one of the pure forms that are incorporeal and have never had association with corporeal substance. He will then realize that he is a vessel full of shame, dishonor, and reproach, empty and deficient.

❴ 13   The topics connected with these five precepts, treated in the above four chapters, are what our wise men called Pardes (Paradise), as in the passage, "Four went into Pardes" (Hagigah 14). And although those four were great men of Israel and great sages, they did not all possess the capacity to know and grasp these subjects clearly. Therefore, I say that it is not proper to dally in Pardes till one has first filled oneself with bread and meat; by which I mean knowledge of what is permitted and what forbidden, and similar distinctions in other classes of precepts. Although these last subjects were called by the sages "a small thing" (when they say "A great thing, Maaseh Merkavah; a small thing, the discussion of Abbayye and Rava"), still they should have the precedence. For the knowledge of these things gives primarily composure to the mind. They are the precious boon bestowed by God, to promote social well-being on earth, and enable men to obtain bliss, in the life hereafter. Moreover, the knowledge of them is within the reach of all, young and old, men and women; those gifted with great intellectual capacity as well as those whose intelligence is limited.†

Chapter 5

❴ 1   All the members of the house of Israel are commanded to sanctify the great name of God, as it is said, "But I will be hallowed

*Guide, introduction; I, chs. 33 and 71; II, ch. 29; III, introduction.

†See Guide, III, ch. 51; also, I, chs. 31–34 (on prerequisites for the study of metaphysics); Commentary on the Mishnah, Avot 3:9.

among the children of Israel" (Lev. 22:32). They are furthermore cautioned not to profane it, as it is said, "Neither shall you profane My holy name" (Lev. 22:32). How are these precepts to be applied? Should an idolater arise and coerce an Israelite to violate any one of the commandments mentioned in the Torah under the threat that otherwise he would put him to death, the Israelite is to commit the transgression rather than suffer death; for concerning the commandments it is said, "which, if a man do them, he shall live by them" (Lev. 18:5): "Live by them, and not die by them." And if he suffered death rather than commit a transgression, he himself is to blame for his death.

¶ 2 This rule applies to all the commandments, except the prohibitions of idolatry, inchastity and murder. With regard to these: if an Israelite should be told: "Transgress one of them or else you will be put to death," he should suffer death rather than transgress. The above distinction only holds good if the idolater's motive is personal advantage; for example, if he forces an Israelite to build him a house or cook for him on the Sabbath, or forces a Jewess to cohabit with him, and so on; but if his purpose is to compel the Israelite to violate the ordinances of his religion, then if this took place privately and ten fellow-Israelites were not present, he should commit the transgression rather than suffer death. But if the attempt to coerce the Israelite to transgress was made in the presence of ten Israelites, he should suffer death and not transgress, even if it was only one of the remaining commandments that the idolater wished him to violate.

¶ 3 All the foregoing applies to a time free from religious persecution. But at a period when there is such persecution, such as when a wicked king arises, like Nebuchadnezzar and his confederates, and issues decrees against Israel, with the purpose of abolishing their religion or one of the precepts, then it is the Israelite's duty to suffer death and not violate any one, even of the remaining commandments, whether the coercion takes place in the presence of ten Israelites or in the presence of idolaters.

¶ 4 When one is enjoined to transgress rather than be slain, and suffers death rather than transgress he is to blame for his death. Where one is enjoined to die rather than transgress, and suffers death so as not to transgress, he sanctifies the name of God. If he does so in the presence of ten Israelites, he sanctifies the name of God publicly, like Daniel, Hananyah, Mishael, and Azaryah, Rabbi Akiva and his colleagues. These are the martyrs, whom none ranks higher. Concerning them it is said, "But for Your sake are we killed all the day long; we are accounted as sheep for the slaughter" (Ps. 44:23). And to them also, the text refers, "Gather my saints together to Me, those that have made a covenant with Me by sacrifice" (Ps. 50:5). Where one is enjoined to suffer death rather than transgress, and commits a transgression and so escapes death, he has profaned the name of God. If the transgression was committed in the presence of ten Israelites, he has profaned the name of God in public, failed to observe an affirmative precept—to sanctify the name of God—and violated a negative precept—not to profane His Name. Still, as the transgression was committed under duress, he is not punished with flogging, and, needless to add, he is not sentenced by a court to be put to death, even if, under duress, he committed murder. For the penalty of death or flogging is only inflicted on one who transgresses of his own free will, in the presence of witnesses and after due warning.

❬ 11　There are other things that are a profanation of the Name of God. When a man, great in the knowledge of the Torah and reputed for his piety does things which cause people to talk about him, even if the acts are not express violations, he profanes the Name of God. As, for example, if such a person makes a purchase and does not pay promptly, provided that he has means and the creditors ask for payment and he puts them off; or if he indulges immoderately in jesting, eating, or drinking, when he is staying with ignorant people or living among them; or if his mode of addressing people is not gentle, or he does not receive people affably, but is quarrelsome and irascible. The greater a man is the more scrupulous should he be in all such things, and do more than the strict letter of the law requires. And if a man has been scrupulous in his conduct, gentle in his conversation, pleasant toward his fellow-creatures, affable in manner when receiving them, not retorting, even when affronted, but showing courtesy to all, even to those who treat him with disdain, conducting his commercial affairs with integrity, not readily accepting the hospitality of the ignorant nor frequenting their company, not seen at all times, but devoting himself to the study of the Torah, wrapped in *tallit*, and crowned with phylacteries, and doing more than his duty in all things, avoiding, however, extremes and exaggerations—such a man has sanctified God, and concerning him, Scripture says, "And He said to me, 'You are My servant, O Israel, in whom I will be glorified'" (Is. 49:3).

LAWS RELATING TO MORAL DISPOSITIONS
AND ETHICAL CONDUCT

Chapter 1*

❡ 1 Every human being is characterized by numerous moral dispositions which differ from each other and are exceedingly divergent. One man is choleric, always irascible; another sedate, never angry; or, if he should become angry, is only slightly and very rarely so. One man is haughty to excess; another humble in the extreme. One is a sensualist whose lusts are never sufficiently gratified; another is so pure in soul that he does not even long for the few things that our physical nature needs. One is so greedy that all the money in the world would not satisfy him, as it is said, "He who loves silver shall not be satisfied with silver" (Eccles. 5:9). Another so curbs his desires that he is contented with very little, even with that which is insufficient, and does not bestir himself to obtain that which he really needs. One will suffer extreme hunger for the sake of saving and does not spend the smallest coin without a pang, while another deliberately and wantonly squanders all his property. In the same way, men differ in other traits. There are, for example, the hilarious and the melancholy, the stingy and the generous, the cruel and the merciful, the timid and the stout-hearted, and so forth.

❡ 2 Between any moral disposition and its extreme opposite, there are intermediate dispositions more or less removed from each other. Of all the various dispositions, some belong to a man from the beginning of his existence and correspond to his physical constitution. Others are such that a particular individual's nature is favorably predisposed to them and prone to acquire them more rapidly than other traits. Others again are not innate, but have been either learned from others, or are self-originated, as the result of an idea that has entered the mind or because, having heard that a disposition is good for him, and should be cultivated by him, one trained himself in it till it became part of his nature.

*See *Eight Chapters*.

❨ 3 To cultivate either extreme in any class of dispositions is not the right course nor is it proper for any person to follow or learn it. If a man finds that his nature tends or is disposed to one of these extremes, or if one has acquired and become habituated to it, he should turn back and improve, so as to walk in the way of good people, which is the right way.

❨ 4 The right way is the mean in each group of dispositions common to humanity; namely, that disposition which is equally distant from the two extremes in its class, not being nearer to the one than to the other. Hence, our ancient sages exhorted us that a person should always evaluate his dispositions and so adjust them that they shall be at the mean between the extremes, and this will secure his physical health. Thus a man should not be choleric, easily moved to anger, nor be like the dead without feeling; but should aim at the happy medium; be angry only for a grave cause that rightly calls for indignation, so that the like shall not be done again. He will only desire that which the body absolutely needs and cannot do without, as it is said, "The righteous eats, to satisfy himself" (Prov. 13:25). He will only labor at his occupation to obtain what is necessary for his sustenance, as it is said, "A little that a righteous man has is better [than the riches of many wicked]" (Ps. 37:16). He will not be tight-fisted nor yet a spendthrift, but will bestow charity according to his means and give a suitable loan to whoever needs it. He will be neither frivolous and given to jesting, nor mournful and melancholy, but will rejoice all his days tranquilly and cheerfully. And so will he comport himself with regard to all his other dispositions. This is the way of the wise. Whoever observes in his dispositions the mean is termed wise.

❨ 5 Whoever is particularly scrupulous and deviates somewhat from the exact mean in disposition, in one direction or the other, is called a saint (hasid).* For example, if one avoids haughtiness to the utmost extent and is exceedingly humble, he is termed a saint, and this is the standard of saintliness. If one only departs from haughtiness as far as the mean, and is humble, he is called wise, and this is the standard of wisdom. And so with all other dispositions. The ancient saints trained their dispositions away from the exact mean toward the extremes; in regard to one disposition in one direction; in regard to another in the opposite direction. This was supererogation.

*See Guide, III, ch. 53.

We are bidden to walk in the middle paths which are the right and proper ways, as it is said, "and you shall walk in His ·ways" (Deut. 28:9).

❡ 6 In explanation of the text just quoted, the sages taught, "Even as God is called gracious, so be you gracious; even as He is called merciful, so be you merciful; even as He is called holy, so be you holy." Thus too the prophets described the Almighty by all the various attributes "long-suffering and abounding in kindness, righteous and upright, perfect, mighty and powerful," and so forth, to teach us that these qualities are good and right and that a human being should cultivate them, and thus imitate God, as far as he can.*

❡ 7 How shall a man train himself in these dispositions, so that they become ingrained? Let him practice again and again the actions prompted by those dispositions which are the mean between the extremes, and repeat them continually till they become easy and are no longer irksome to him, and so the corresponding dispositions will become a fixed part of his character. And as the Creator is called by these attributes, which constitute the middle path in which we are to walk, this path is called the Way of God and this is what the patriarch Abraham taught his children, as it is said "For I love him, because he will charge his children and his household after him, that they may keep the way of the Lord" (Gen. 18:19). Whoever walks in this way secures for himself happiness and blessing, as the text continues, "In order that the Lord might bring upon Abraham that which He spoke concerning him" (ibid. 18:19).†

Chapter 2

❡ 1 To those who are sick in body, the bitter tastes as if it were sweet, and the sweet as if it were bitter. Among sick folk, some long and yearn for things unfit for food, such as earth and charcoal, and have an aversion to wholesome foods like bread and meat, the perversity depending on the severity of the illness. Similarly, human beings whose souls are sick and love evil dispositions, hate the way that is good and are too indolent to walk therein finding it exceedingly irksome because of their sickness. And so Isaiah says of such people, "O, they that say of evil that it is good, and of good that it is

*See Guide, I, ch. 54.
†See Book VII, Gifts to the Poor, ch. X; Book III, Reading of the Megillah, II, 17.

evil, that turn darkness into light and light into darkness, who take bitter for sweet and sweet for bitter" (Is. 5:20). And of such it is also said, "Who forsake the paths of integrity to walk in the ways of darkness" (Prov. 2:13). What is the corrective for those who are sick in soul? They should go to the wise who are physicians of the soul and they will heal their maladies by instructing them in the dispositions which they should acquire till they are restored to the right path. Of those who realize that their dispositions are bad and nevertheless do not resort to the wise to be cured, Solomon says, "Wisdom and discipline, fools despise" (Prov. 1:7).

¶ 2 What is the method of effecting their cure? If one is irascible, he is directed so to govern himself that even if he is assaulted or reviled, he should not feel affronted. And in this course he is to persevere for a long time till the choleric temperament has been eradicated. If one is arrogant, he should accustom himself to endure much contumely, sit below everyone, and wear old and ragged garments that bring the wearer into contempt, and so forth, till arrogance is eradicated from his heart and he has regained the middle path, which is the right way. And when he has returned to this path, he should walk in it the rest of his days. On similar lines, he should treat all his dispositions. If, in any of them, he is at one extreme, he should move to the opposite extreme, and keep to it for a long time till he has regained the right path which is the normal mean in every class of dispositions.*

¶ 3 There are some dispositions in regard to which it is forbidden merely to keep to the middle path. They must be shunned to the extreme. Such a disposition is pride. The right way in this regard is not to be merely meek, but to be humble-minded and lowly of spirit to the utmost. And therefore was it said of Moses that he was "exceedingly meek," (Num. 12:3), not merely that he was "meek." Hence, our sages exhorted us, "Be exceedingly, exceedingly lowly of spirit" (Ethics of the Fathers 4:4). They also said that anyone who permits his heart to swell with haughtiness has denied the essential principle of our religion, as it is said, "And your heart will be proud, and you will forget the Lord your God" (Deut. 8:14). Again have they said, "Under a ban be he who is proud, even in the smallest degree." Anger, too, is an exceedingly bad passion, and one should avoid it to the last extreme. One should train oneself not to be angry

*See Book VI, Vows, XIII, 23.

even for something that would justify anger. If one wishes to arouse fear in his children and household, or in the members of a community of which he is the head, and desires to exhibit anger, so that they may amend their ways, he should make a show of anger before them, so as to correct them, but in reality, his mind should be composed like that of a man who simulates anger and does not really feel it. The ancient sages said, "He who is angry—it is the same as if he worshiped idols." They also said, "One who yields to anger—if he is a sage, his wisdom departs from him; if he is a prophet, his prophetic gift departs from him."* Those of an irate disposition—their life is not worth living. The sages therefore, charged us that anger should be avoided to such a degree that one should train oneself to be unmoved even by things that naturally would provoke anger; and this is the good way. The practice of the righteous is to suffer contumely and not inflict it; to hear themselves reproached, not retort; to be impelled in what they do by love, and to rejoice in suffering. Of them Scripture says, "And they that love Him are like the going forth of the sun in his strength" (Judges 5:31).

❬ 4 One should always cultivate the habit of silence and only converse on topics of wisdom or on matters of moment to one's existence. Of Rav, disciple of our sainted teacher (R. Judah the Prince) it was said that throughout his life he never indulged in idle conversation, of which most people's talk consists. And even of our material needs, we should not speak much. In this connection, our wise men charged, "He who multiplies words causes sin" (Ethics of the Fathers 1:17). They further said, "I have found nothing of better service to the body than silence" (ibid.). So too, in discussing Torah and wisdom, a man's words should be few but full of meaning. This, the sages express in their recommendation: "A man should always teach his disciples tersely." But where words are many and their meaning is small—that is folly, of which it is said, "For the dream comes with much discussion, and a fool's voice with an abundance of words" (Eccles. 5:2).

❬ 5 "A fence to wisdom is silence" (Ethics of the Fathers 3:17). Hence, a man should not be hasty in reply, nor talk much. He should teach his pupils gently and calmly, not shouting, and avoiding prolixity. Solomon said, "The words of the wise, spoken quietly, are heard" (Eccles. 9:17).

*See Eight Chapters, ch. VIII; Commentary on the Mishnah, Avot 2:10, 4:4.

❡ 6   It is forbidden to accustom oneself to smooth speech and flatteries. One must not say one thing and mean another. Inward and outward self should correspond; only what we have in mind, should we utter with the mouth. We must deceive no one, not even an idolater. A man, for example, must not sell to an idolater flesh from a beast that has died naturally, as if it were meat of an animal ritually slaughtered. Nor should one sell a shoe, the leather of which came from the hide of a beast that met with a natural death, allowing it to be believed that the leather had come from the hide of a ritually slaughtered animal. One must not urge another to join one at a meal, when one is aware that the invitation will not be accepted. Nor should one press upon another any marks of friendship which one knows will be declined. So too, casks of wine, which must be opened for sale, should not be broached in such a way as to deceive a guest and make him believe that they had been opened in his honor, and so forth. Even a single word of flattery or deception is forbidden. A person should always cherish truthful speech, an upright spirit, and a pure heart free from all forwardness and perversity.

❡ 7   One should not indulge in jesting and mockery nor be melancholy and mournful, but one should be cheerful. So our sages said, "Jesting and levity lead a man on to lewdness" (Ethics of the Fathers 3:17). They further charged that a man should not give way to immoderate laughter nor yet be sad and mournful, but should receive everyone with a cheerful countenance. One should also not cherish large desires—hurrying to get rich—nor be melancholy and idle, but should be contented, engage a little in secular occupation and devote oneself to the study of the Torah, and rejoice in the little one has as his portion. One should not be quarrelsome, jealous, or sensual; nor run after honor. Thus our wise men said, "Envy, lust, and ambition take a man from the world" (ibid. 4:2). In fine, in every class of dispositions, a man should choose the mean so that all one's dispositions shall occupy the exact middle between the extremes. This is what Solomon expressed in the text, "Balance the course of your steps, so that all your ways may be right" (Prov. 4:26).

Chapter 3

❡ 1   Possibly a person may say: "Since envy, cupidity, and ambition are evil qualities to cultivate and lead to a man's ruin, I will avoid them to the uttermost, and seek their contraries." A person following this principle, will not eat meat, or drink wine, or marry, or dwell in a decent home, or wear comely apparel, but will clothe himself in sackcloth and coarse wool like the idolaters' priests. This too, is the wrong way, not to be followed. Whoever persists in such a course is termed a sinner. Of the Nazirite, it is said, "He (the priest) shall make atonement for him, for the sin that he committed against the soul" (Num. 6:11). On this text, the sages comment, "If the Nazarite who only abstained from wine stands in need of an atonement, how much more so one who deprives himself of all legitimate enjoyments." The sages accordingly enjoined us that we should only refrain from that which the Torah has expressly withdrawn from our use. And no one should, by vows and oaths, inhibit to himself the use of things permitted. "Do not the prohibitions of the Torah," say our sages, "suffice you, that you add others for yourself?" In this condemnation, those are included, who make a practice of fasting; they too are not walking in the right way; our wise men prohibited self-mortification by fasting. And concerning this and similar excesses Solomon exhorts us, "Be not overrighteous, nor excessively wise. Wherefore should you be desolate?" (Eccles. 7:16).*

❲ 3   He who regulates his life in accordance with the laws of hygiene, with the sole motive of maintaining a sound and vigorous physique and begetting children to do his work and labor for his benefit, is not following the right course. A man should aim to maintain physical health and vigor, in order that his soul may be upright, in a condition to know God. For it is impossible for one to understand sciences and meditate upon them when he is hungry or sick, or when any of his limbs is aching. And in cohabitation, one should set one's heart on having a son who may become a sage and a great man in Israel. Whoever throughout his life follows this course will be continually serving God, even while engaged in business and even during cohabitation, because his purpose in all that he does will be to satisfy his needs so as to have a sound body with which to serve God. Even when he sleeps and seeks repose, to calm his mind and rest his body, so as not to fall sick and be incapacitated from serving God, his sleep is service of the Almighty. In this sense, our wise men charged us, "Let all your deeds be for the sake of God" (Ethics of the Fathers 2:17). And Solomon, in his wisdom, said, "In all your ways know Him, and He will make your paths straight" (Prov. 3:6).

*See *Eight Chapters*, ch. IV; *Commentary on the Mishnah*, Avot 2:12.

Chapter 4

❡ 1 Since by keeping the body in health and vigor one walks in the ways of God—it being impossible during sickness to have any understanding or knowledge of the Creator—it is a man's duty to avoid whatever is injurious to the body, and cultivate habits conducive to health and vigor.

❡ 20 Whoever lives in accordance with the directions I have set forth has my assurance that he will never be sick until he grows old and dies; he will not be in need of a physician, and will enjoy normal health as long as he lives. . . .

❡ 23 No scholar may live in a city that does not have the following ten officials and institutions: a physician, a surgeon, a bathhouse, a lavatory, a source of water supply such as a stream or spring, a synagogue, a schoolteacher, a scribe, a treasurer of charity funds for the poor, a court that has authority to punish with flogging and imprisonment.

Chapter 5

❡ 1 Even as a sage is recognized by his wisdom and moral principles which distinguish him from the rest of the people, so ought he to be recognized in all his activities, in his food and drink, in the fulfillment of his marital obligations, in attention to excretory functions, in his talk, walk, dress, management of his affairs and business transactions. All these activities should bear the mark of exceeding refinement and orderliness. For example, a scholar will not be a glutton but will eat food conducive to health; and of such food he will not eat to excess. He will not be eager to fill his stomach, like those who gorge themselves with food and drink till the body swells. Concerning such people, Scripture says, "I will spread dung on your faces" (Mal. 2:3). This text, our wise men say, refers to those who eat and drink and spend all their days as if they were holidays. They are the people who exclaim, "Eat and drink for tomorrow we die" (Is. 22:13). This is how the wicked eat. They are reprobated in the verse, "For all tables are full of filthy vomit, and no place is clean" (Is. 28:8). The wise man, on the contrary, will only partake of one or two courses, of which he will consume as much as he needs to sustain him. Thus Solomon said, "The righteous eats to satisfy himself" (Prov. 13:25).

❡ 12 A person is forbidden to declare all his property derelict or devote it to the sanctuary and thus become a public charge. . . .

❡ 13 The scholar conducts his business affairs honestly and in good faith. His nay is nay; his yea, yea. In his accounts, he is strict (in meeting his obligations). At the same time, when buying, he is liberal and does not drive a hard bargain. He pays promptly for his purchases. He declines to act as a surety or trustee; nor will he accept a power of attorney. In commercial matters, he acknowledges liability even where the law would not hold him liable; his principle being to keep his word and not change it. If others have been adjudged liable to him, he is considerate, and even forgives them the amount due. He grants benevolent (interest-free) loans and does favors. He will not encroach on another man's business, and throughout his life will not vex a human being. In short, he belongs to the class of those who are persecuted but do not persecute, who are reviled but do not revile. A man who acts thus is commended in the Scriptural text, "And He said to me, you are My servant, Israel, in whom I glory" (Is. 49:3).

Chapter 6

❡ 1 It is natural to be influenced, in sentiments and conduct, by one's neighbors and associates, and observe the customs of one's fellow citizens. Hence, a person ought constantly to associate with the righteous and frequent the company of the wise, so as to learn from their practices, and shun the wicked who are benighted, so as not to be corrupted by their example. So Solomon said, "He that walks with the wise, shall be wise; but the companion of fools shall smart for it" (Prov. 13:20). And it is also said, "Happy is the man who has not walked in the counsel of the wicked" (Ps. 1:1). So too, if one lives in a country where the customs are pernicious and the inhabitants do not go in the right way, he should leave for a place where the people are righteous and follow the ways of the good. If all the countries of which he has personal knowledge, or concerning which he hears reports, follow a course that is not right—as is the case in our times—or if military campaigns or sickness debar him from leaving for a country with good customs, he should live by himself in seclusion, as it is said, "Let him sit alone and keep silence" (Lam. 3:28). And if the inhabitants are wicked reprobates who will not let him stay in the country unless he mixes with them and adopts their evil practices, let him withdraw to caves, thickets, or deserts, and not habituate himself to the ways of sinners, as it is said "O that I were in the wilderness, in a lodging place of wayfaring men" (Jer. 9:1).*

❨ 2 It is an affirmative precept to attach oneself to sages and their disciples, so as to learn from their example; as it is said, "And unto Him shall you cleave" (Deut. 10:20). But can a human being cleave to the *Shekhinah?* Our wise men explained this text thus: "Attach yourself to sages and their disciples." A man should, accordingly, strive to win a scholar's daughter for a wife, and should give his daughter in marriage to a scholar. He should eat and drink in the company of scholars, give them opportunities to do business, and cultivate their society in every relation, as it is said, "And to cleave unto Him" (*ibid.* 11:22). So too, our sages exhorted us, "Sit in the dust of their feet, and drink their words thirstily" (Ethics of the Fathers 1:4).

❨ 3 It is incumbent on every one to love each individual Israelite as himself, as it is said "You shall love your neighbor, as yourself" (Lev. 19:18). Hence, a person ought to speak in praise of his neighbor and be careful of his neighbor's property as he is careful of his own property and solicitous about his own honor. Whoever glorifies himself by humiliating another person, will have no portion in the world to come.

❨ 4 To love the proselyte who comes to take refuge beneath the wings of the *Shekhinah* is the fulfillment of two affirmative precepts. First, because he is included among neighbors (whom we are commanded to love). And secondly, because he is a stranger, and the Torah said, "Love you therefore the stranger" (Deut. 10:19). God charged (us) concerning the love of the stranger, even as He charged us concerning love of Himself, as it is said, "You shall love the Lord your God" (*ibid.* 6:5). The Holy One, blessed be He, loves strangers, as it is said, "And He loves the stranger" (*ibid.* 10:18).†

❨ 5 Whoever entertains in his heart hatred of any Israelite, transgresses a prohibition, as it is said, "You shall not hate your brother in your heart" (Lev. 19:17). The violation of this precept is, however,

---

*See *Eight Chapters*, ch. IV; *Epistle to Yemen; Commentary,* Avot 2:4.

†See Letter to an Inquirer; also, Book XII, Sales, XIV, 15–16; Slaves, VIII, 11.

not punished with flogging, as no overt act is involved. The Torah, in this text, only warned against hatred in the heart. But any one who smites or reviles his neighbor, although he is not permitted to do so, is not infringing the precept, "You shall not hate your brother."

¶ 6 When a man sins against another, the injured party should not hate the offender and keep silent, as it is said concerning the wicked, "And Absalom spoke to Amnon neither good nor evil, for Absalom hated Amnon" (II Sam. 13:22). But it is his duty to inform the offender and say to him "Why did you do this to me? Why did you sin against me in this matter?" And thus it is said, "You shall surely rebuke your neighbor" (Lev. 19:17). If the offender repents and pleads for forgiveness, he should be forgiven. The forgiver should not be obdurate, as it is said, "And Abraham prayed unto God (for Abimelech)" (Gen. 20:17).

¶ 7 If one observes that a person committed a sin or walks in a way that is not good, it is a duty to bring the erring man back to the right path and point out to him that he is wronging himself by his evil courses, as it is said, "You shall surely rebuke your neighbor" (Lev. 19:17). He who rebukes another, whether for offenses against the rebuker himself or for sins against God, should administer the rebuke in private, speak to the offender gently and tenderly, and point out that he is only speaking for the wrongdoer's own good, to secure for him life in the world to come. If the latter accepts the rebuke, well and good. If not, he should be rebuked a second, and a third time. And so one is bound to continue the admonitions, till the sinner assaults the admonisher and says to him "I refuse to listen." Whoever is in a position to prevent wrongdoing and does not do so is responsible for the iniquity of all the wrongdoers whom he might have restrained.

¶ 8 He who rebukes another must not at first speak to the offender harshly so as to put him to shame, as it is said, "And you shall not suffer sin because of him" (Lev. 19:17). Our rabbis explained this text as follows: "Since it might have been supposed that you are to rebuke the sinner till he changes color, therefore it is said 'And you shall not bear sin because of him.'" Hence, the inference that it is forbidden to put an Israelite to shame, especially in public. Although one who puts another to shame is not punished with flogging, still it is a grave offense. And thus the sages said, "He who shames another in public has no portion in the world to come." One ought, therefore, to beware of publicly shaming anyone, whether he be young or old. One should not call a person by a name of which he feels ashamed, nor relate anything in his presence which humiliates him. This applies to matters between man and man. But in regard to duties to God, if an individual, after having been privately rebuked, does not repent, he should be shamed in public; his sin should be openly declared; he is to be reviled, affronted, and cursed till he returns to the right course. This was the method followed by all the prophets of Israel.

❡ 9 If one who has been wronged by another does not wish to rebuke or speak to the offender because the latter is a very common person or mentally defective, and if he has sincerely forgiven him, and neither bears him ill-will nor rebukes him—he acts according to the standard of saints. All that the Torah objects to is harboring ill-will.

❡ 10 A man ought to be especially heedful of his behavior toward widows and orphans, for their souls are exceedingly depressed and their spirits low. Even if they are wealthy, even if they are the widow and orphans of a king, we are specifically enjoined concerning them, as it is said, "You shall not afflict any widow or fatherless child" (Ex. 22:21). How are we to conduct ourselves toward them? One must not speak to them otherwise than tenderly. One must show them unvarying courtesy; not hurt them physically with hard toil, or wound their feelings with harsh speech. One must take greater care of their property than of one's own. Whoever irritates them, provokes them to anger, pains them, tyrannizes over them, or causes them loss of money, is guilty of a transgression, and still more so if one beats them or curses them. Though no flogging is inflicted for this transgression, its punishment is explicitly set forth in the Torah (in the following terms): "My wrath shall wax hot, and I will slay you with the sword" (ibid. 22:23). He who created the world by His word made a covenant with widows and orphans that when they will cry out because of violence, they will be answered, as it is said, "If you afflict them in any wise—for if they cry at all unto Me, I will surely hear their cry" (ibid. 22:22). This only applies to cases where a person afflicts them for his own ends. But if a teacher punishes orphan children in order to teach them Torah or a trade or lead them in the right way—this is permissible. And yet he should not treat them like others, but make a distinction in their favor. He should guide them gently, with the utmost tenderness and courtesy, whether they are bereft of a father or mother, as it is said, "For the Lord will plead their cause" (Prov. 22:23). To what age are they to be regarded in these respects as orphans? Till they reach the age when they no longer need an adult on whom they depend to train them and care for them, and when each of them can provide for all his wants, like other grown-up persons.

Chapter 7

❲ 1   Whoever tells tales about another person violates a prohibition, as it is said, "You shall not go up and down as a tale-bearer among your people" (Lev. 19:16). And although no flogging is inflicted, it is a grave offense, and leads to the death of many souls in Israel. Hence, this precept is followed immediately by the sentence, "Neither shall you stand idly by the blood of your neighbor" (ibid. 19:16). For an example of the tragic consequence of this transgression, read what happened after Doeg's report concerning the priests of Nob (I Sam. 22:6–19).

❲ 5   If one indulges in evil speech about a person, whether in his presence or in his absence, or makes statements which, if repeated, would tend to hurt him physically or injure him financially, distress or alarm him—all this is evil speech. If a statement of this character has been made in the presence of three persons, the subject matter is regarded as public and generally known, and if one of the three repeats it, he is not guilty of evil speech, provided he had no intention to give the story wider currency.

❲ 6   All such persons are scandal-mongers in whose neighborhood it is forbidden to reside; and still more is it forbidden to cultivate their society and listen to them. The sentence passed upon our forefathers in the wilderness was confirmed only because they were guilty of the sin of the evil tongue.

❲ 7   He who takes revenge violates a prohibition, as it is said, "You shall not take vengeance" (Lev. 19:18). And although he is not punished with flogging, still such conduct indicates an exceedingly bad disposition. One should rather practice forebearance in all secular matters. For the intelligent realize that these are vain things and not worth taking vengeance for. What is "taking vengeance"? The following is a case. A neighbor says to one, "Lend me your axe." He replies, "I will not lend it to you." The next day, the latter needs a similar favor from the neighbor and says to him, "Lend me your axe," and receives the reply, "I will not lend it to you, for you did not lend me your axe when I asked it of you." Any one who acts in this way is "taking vengeance." But when he comes to borrow aught, one should give what is asked cheerfully, and not repay discourtesy with discourtesy. And so in similar cases. Thus David, expressing his excellent sentiments, said "If I have requited him that did evil to me, or despoiled mine adversary . . ." (Ps. 7:5).*

❡ 8 So too, one who bears a grudge against a fellow Israelite violates a prohibition, as it is said, "Nor bear a grudge against the children of your people" (Lev. 19:18). What is "bearing a grudge?" A said to B, "Rent this house to me, or let me borrow this ox." B refuses. After a time, B comes to A to borrow or hire something. A replies, "Here it is. I lend it to you. I am not like you. I will not treat you as you treated me." One who acts thus, transgresses the commandment "You shall not bear a grudge." One should blot the thing out of his mind and not bear a grudge. For as long as one nurses a grievance and keeps it in mind, one may come to take vengeance. The Torah, accordingly, emphatically warns us not to bear a grudge, so that the impression of the wrong shall be quite obliterated and be no longer remembered. This is the right principle. It alone makes civilized life and social intercourse possible.†

LAWS CONCERNING THE STUDY OF THE TORAH

Chapter 1

❡ 8 Every Israelite is under an obligation to study Torah, whether he is poor or rich, in sound health or ailing, in the vigor of youth or very old and feeble. Even a man so poor that he is maintained by charity or goes begging from door to door, as also a man with a wife

---

*Cf. Letter to Hasdai.

†See *Guide*, III, chs. 27 and 35; also, Book I, Basic Principles of the Torah, IV, 13.

and children to support, is under the obligation to set aside a
definite period during the day and at night for the study of the
Torah, as it is said, "But you shall meditate therein day and night"
(Josh. 1:8).

¶ 9 Among the great sages of Israel, some were hewers of wood,
some drawers of water, while others were blind. Nevertheless, they
devoted themselves by day and by night to the study of the Torah.
They are included among the transmitters of the tradition in the
direct line from Moses.

¶ 10 Until what period in life ought one to study Torah? Until the
day of one's death, as it is said, "And lest they [the precepts] depart
from your heart all the days of your life" (Deut. 4:9). Whenever one
ceases to study, one forgets.

¶ 11 The time allotted to study should be divided into three parts.
A third should be devoted to the Written Law; a third to the Oral
Law; and the last third should be spent in reflection, deducing conclusions from premises, developing implications of statements, com-
paring dicta, studying the hermeneutical principles by which the
Torah is interpreted, till one knows the essence of these principles,
and how to deduce what is permitted and what is forbidden from
what one has learned traditionally. This is termed Talmud.

¶ 12 For example, if one is an artisan who works at his trade three
hours daily and devotes nine hours to the study of the Torah, he
should spend three of these nine hours in the study of the Written
Law, three in the study of the Oral Law, and the remaining three in
reflecting on how to deduce one rule from another. The words of the
Prophets are comprised in the Written Law, while their exposition
falls within the category of the Oral Law. The subjects styled Pardes
(Esoteric Studies) are included in Talmud.* This plan applies to the
period when one begins learning. But after one has become pro-
ficient and no longer needs to learn the Written Law or continually
be occupied with the Oral Law, he should, at fixed times, read the
Written Law and the traditional dicta, so as not to forget any of the
rules of the Torah, and should devote all his days exclusively to the
study of Talmud according to his breadth of mind and maturity of
intellect.†

*See Book I, Basic Principles of the Torah, IV, 13.
†See Maimonides' Introduction to Mishneh Torah.

Chapter 3

¶ 1 With three crowns was Israel crowned—with the crown of the Torah, with the crown of the priesthood, and with the crown of sovereignty. The crown of the priesthood was bestowed upon Aaron, as it is said, "And it shall be to him and to his seed after him, the covenant of an everlasting priesthood" (Num. 25:13). The crown of sovereignty was conferred upon David, as it is said, "His seed shall endure forever, and his throne as the sun before Me" (Ps. 89:37). The crown of the Torah, however, is for all Israel, as it is said, "Moses commanded us a law, an inheritance of the congregation of Jacob" (Deut. 33:4). Whoever desires it can win it. Do not suppose that the other two crowns are greater than the crown of the Torah, for it is said, "By me, kings reign and princes decree justice. By me, princes rule" (Prov. 8:15–16). Hence the inference, that the crown of the Torah is greater than the other two crowns.

¶ 2 The sages said, "A bastard who is a scholar takes precedence over an ignorant High Priest; for it is said, "More precious it is than rubies" (Prov. 3:15), that is (more to be honored is the scholar) than the High Priest who enters the innermost Sanctuary.*

¶ 3 Of all precepts, none is equal in importance to the study of the Torah. Nay, study of the Torah is equal to them all, for study leads to practice. Hence, study always takes precedence of practice.†

¶ 4 If the opportunity of fulfilling a specific precept would interrupt the study of the Torah and the precept can be performed by others, one should not interrupt study. Otherwise, the precept should be performed and then the study be resumed.

¶ 5 At the Judgment hereafter, a man will first be called to account in regard to his fulfillment of the duty of study, and afterwards concerning his other activities. Hence, the sages said, "A person should always occupy himself with the Torah, whether for its own sake or for other reasons. For study of the Torah, even when pursued from interested motives, will lead to study for its own sake" (see Pesahim 50b).

¶ 6 He whose heart prompts him to fulfill this duty properly, and to be crowned with the crown of the Torah, must not allow his mind to

---

*A play upon the word *peninim* (rubies), taken as *lifne velifnim* (High Priest who entered the Holy of Holies on the Day of Atonement).

†See *Guide*, III, ch. 36.

be diverted to other objects. He must not aim at acquiring Torah as well as riches and honor at the same time. "This is the way for the study of the Torah. A morsel of bread with salt you must eat, and water by measure you must drink; you must sleep upon the ground and live a life of hardship, the while you toil in the Torah" (Ethics of the Fathers 6:4). "It is not incumbent upon you to complete the task; but neither are you free to neglect it" (ibid. 2:21). "And if you have studied much Torah, you have earned much reward. The recompense will be proportionate to the pains" (ibid. 5:26).

⟨ 7 Possibly you may say: When I shall have accumulated money, I shall resume my studies; when I shall have provided for my needs and have leisure from my affairs, I shall resume my studies. Should such a thought enter your mind, you will never win the crown of the Torah. "Rather make the study of the Torah your fixed occupation" (Ethics of the Fathers 1:15) and let your secular affairs engage you casually, and do not say: "When I shall have leisure, I shall study; perhaps you may never have leisure" (ibid. 2:5).

⟨ 8 In the Torah it is written, "It is not in heaven . . . neither is it beyond the sea" (Deut. 30:12–13). "It is not in heaven," this means that the Torah is not to be found with the arrogant; "nor beyond the sea," that is, it is not found among those who cross the ocean. Hence, our sages said, "Nor can one who is engaged overmuch in business grow wise" (Ethics of the Fathers 2:6). They have also exhorted us, "Engage little in business and occupy yourself with the Torah" (ibid. 4:12).

⟨ 9 The words of the Torah have been compared to water, as it is said, "O everyone that thirsts, come for water" (Is. 55:1); this teaches us that just as water does not accumulate on a slope but flows away, while in a depression it stays, so the words of the Torah are not to be found in the arrogant or haughty but only in him who is contrite and lowly in spirit, who sits in the dust at the feet of the wise and banishes from his heart lusts and temporal delights, works a little daily, just enough to provide for his needs, if he would otherwise have nothing to eat, and devotes the rest of the day and night to the study of the Torah.

⟨ 10 One, however, who makes up his mind to study Torah and not to work but to live on charity, profanes the name of God, brings the Torah into contempt, extinguishes the light of religion, brings evil upon himself, and deprives himself of life hereafter, for it is forbidden to derive any temporal advantage from the words of the Torah. The sages said, "Whoever derives a profit for himself from the words of the Torah is helping on his own destruction" (Ethics of the Fathers 4:17). They have further charged us, "Make not of them a crown wherewith to aggrandize yourself, nor a spade wherewith to dig" (ibid. 4:7). They likewise exhorted us, "Love work, hate lordship" (ibid. 1:10). "All study of the Torah, not conjoined with work, must, in the end, be futile, and become a cause of sin" (ibid. 2:2). The end of such a person will be that he will rob his fellow creatures.*

❮ 11   It indicates a high degree of excellence in a man to maintain himself by the labor of his hands. And this was the normal practice of the early saints. Thus, one secures all honor and happiness here and hereafter, as it is said, "When you eat of the labor of your hands, happy shall you be, and it shall be well with you" (Ps. 128:2). Happy shall you be in this world, and it shall be well with you in the world to come, which is altogether good.

❮ 12   The words of the Torah do not abide with one who studies listlessly, nor with those who learn amid luxury and high living, but only with one who mortifies himself for the sake of the Torah, constantly enduring physical discomfort and not permitting sleep to his eyes nor slumber to his eyelids. "This is the law, when a man dies in a tent" (Num. 19:14). The sages explain the text metaphorically thus: "The Torah only abides with him who mortifies himself in the tents of the wise." And so Solomon, in his wisdom, said, "If you faint in the day of adversity, your strength is small indeed" (Prov. 24:10). He also said, "Also my wisdom stood unto me" (Eccles. 2:9). This is explained by our wise men thus, "The wisdom that I learned in wrath,† this has remained with me." The sages said "There is a solemn covenant that anyone who toils at his studies in the synagogue will not quickly forget." He who toils privately in learning, will become wise, as it is said, "With the lowly (literally, the reserved) is wisdom" (Prov. 11:2). If one recites aloud while studying, what he learns will remain with him. But he who reads silently soon forgets.

❮ 13   While it is a duty to study by day and by night, most of one's knowledge is acquired at night. Accordingly, when one aspires to win

*See Commentary, Avot 4:5.

†Play upon the word aph, meaning also and wrath. See Commentary, Avot 5:23.

the crown of the Torah, he should be especially heedful of all his nights and not waste a single one of them in sleep, eating, drinking, idle talk, and so forth, but devote all of them to study of the Torah and words of wisdom. The sages said, "That sound of the Torah has worth which is heard by night, as it is said 'Arise, cry out in the night' (Lam. 2:19). And whoever occupies himself with the study of the Torah by night—a mark of spiritual grace distinguishes him by day, as it is said, 'By day the Lord will command His lovingkindness, and in the night His song shall be with me, even a prayer unto the God of my life' (Ps. 42:9). A house wherein the words of the Torah are not heard at night will be consumed by fire, as it is said, 'All darkness is laid up for his treasures; a fire not blown by man shall consume him' (Job 20:26). 'Because he has despised the word of the Lord' (Num. 15:31)—this refers to one who has utterly neglected [the study of] the words of the Torah." And, so too, one who is able to occupy himself with the Torah and does not do so, or who had read Scripture and learned Mishnah and gave them up for worldly inanities, and abandoned and completely renounced this study, is included in the condemnation, "Because he has despised the word of the Lord." The sages said, "Whoever neglects the Torah because of wealth will, at last, be forced to neglect it owing to poverty. And whoever fulfills the Torah in poverty, will ultimately fulfill it amid wealth" (Ethics of the Fathers 4:11, with order of sentences reversed). And this is explicitly set forth in the Torah, as it is said, "Because you did not serve the Lord your God with joyfulness and with gladness of heart, by reason of the abundance of all things, therefore shall you serve your enemy" (Deut. 28:47–48). It is also said "That He might afflict you ... to do you good at your latter end ..." (ibid. 8:16).*

Chapter 5

⟨ 1   Just as a person is commanded to honor and revere his father, so is he under an obligation to honor and revere his teacher, even to a greater extent than his father; for his father gave him life in this world, while his teacher who instructs him in wisdom, secures for him life in the world to come.

⟨ 4   A disciple who is not thus qualified and nevertheless gives decisions is "wicked, foolish, and of an arrogant spirit" (Ethics of the Fathers 4:9). And of him it is said, "For she has cast down many

*See Book III, Repose on the Festivals, VI, 20.

wounded" (Prov. 7:26). On the other hand, a sage who is qualified and refrains from rendering decisions withholds knowledge of the Torah and puts stumbling blocks before the blind. Of him it is said "Even the mighty are all her slain" (Prov. 7:26). The students of small minds who have acquired an insufficient knowledge of the Torah, and yet seek to aggrandize themselves before the ignorant and among their townsmen by impertinently putting themselves forward and presuming to judge and render decisions in Israel—these are the ones who multiply strife, devastate the world, quench the light of the Torah, and spoil the vineyard of the Lord of hosts. Of such, Solomon, in his wisdom, said, "Seize for us the foxes, the little foxes that spoil the vineyard" (Song of Songs 2:15).*

⟦ 12   As pupils are bound to honor their teacher, so a teacher ought to show courtesy and friendliness to his pupils. The sages said, "Let the honor of your disciples be as dear to you as your own" (Ethics of the Fathers 4:15). A man should take an interest in his pupils and love them, for they are his spiritual children who will bring him happiness in this world and in the world hereafter.

⟦ 13   Disciples increase the teacher's wisdom and broaden his mind. The sages said, "Much wisdom I learned from my teachers, more from my colleagues; from my pupils, most of all." Even as a small piece of wood kindles a large log, so a pupil of small attainments sharpens the mind of his teacher, so that by his questions, he elicits glorious wisdom.

Chapter 6

⟦ 1   It is a duty to honor every scholar, even if he is not one's teacher, as it is said, "You shall rise up before the hoary head, and honor the face of the old man" (Lev. 19:32). "Old man" refers to one who has acquired wisdom.

⟦ 3   It is improper for a sage to put the people to inconvenience by deliberately passing before them, so that they should have to stand up before him. He should use a short route and endeavor to avoid notice so that they should not be troubled to stand up. The sages were wont to use circuitous and exterior paths, where they were not likely to meet those who might recognize them, so as not to trouble them.

*See Book XIV, Sanhedrin, XX, 8; Guide, III, introduction.

([11 It is exceedingly iniquitous to contemn sages or hate them. Jerusalem was destroyed only when its scholars were treated with contumely, as it is said, "But they mocked the messengers of God and despised His words, and scoffed at His prophets" (II Chron. 36: 16); this means that they "despised those who taught His words." So too, the text, "And if you shall abhor My statutes" (Lev. 26:15) means "if you abhor the teachers of My statutes." Whoever contemns the sages will have no portion in the world to come, and is included in the censure, "For the word of the Lord has he despised" (Num. 15:31).*

LAWS CONCERNING IDOLATRY AND THE
ORDINANCES OF THE HEATHENS

Chapter 1†

([1 In the days of Enosh, the people fell into gross error, and the counsel of the wise men of the generation became foolish. Enosh himself was among those who erred. Their error was as follows: "Since God," they said, "created these stars and spheres to guide the world, set them on high and allotted to them honor, and since they are ministers who minister before Him, they deserve to be praised and glorified, and honor should be rendered them; and it is the will of God, blessed be He, that men should aggrandize and honor those whom He aggrandized and honored just as a king desires that respect should be shown to the officers who stand before him, and thus honor is shown to the king." When this idea arose in their minds, they began to erect temples to the stars, offered up sacrifices to them, praised and glorified them in speech, and prostrated themselves before them—their purpose, according to their perverse notions, being to obtain the Creator's favor. This was the root of idolatry and this was what the idolaters who knew its fundamentals said. They did not, however, maintain that there was no God except

*See Book X, Uncleanness of Leprosy, X, 16.

† See *Guide*, I, ch. 36; II, chs. 13 and 39; III, chs. 29, 37, and 51; Letter on Astrology; *Epistle to Yemen*; Letter to Obadiah; also, Book I, Repentance, X, 2.

the particular star (which was the object of their worship). Thus
Jeremiah said, "Who would not fear You, O King of nations? For it
befits You; for as much as among all the wise men of the nations and
in all their kingdom, there is none like You. But in one thing they
are brutish and foolish. The vanities by which they are instructed are
but a stock" (Jer. 10:7–8). This means that all know that You alone
are God; their error and folly consists in imagining that this vain
worship is Your desire.

❡ 2 In course of time, there arose among men false prophets who
asserted that God had commanded and expressly told them, "Worship that particular star, or worship all the stars. Offer up to it such
and such sacrifices. Pour out to it such and such libations. Erect a
temple to it. Make a figure of it, to which all the people—the
women, children, and the rest of the folk—shall bow down." The
false prophet pointed out to them the figure which he had invented
out of his own mind and asserted that it was the figure of that particular star which had been shown him in his prophetic vision. And then
they began to make figures in temples, under the trees, on the moun-
tain-tops, and the hills. There they would assemble, bow down to the
figures, and tell all the people that this particular figure conferred
benefits and inflicted injuries and that it was proper to worship and
fear it. Their priests would say to them, "Through this worship, shall
you increase and prosper. Do this and do not do that." Other impos-
ters then sprang up who declared that the star, celestial sphere, or
angel, had communed with them, and said to them, "Worship me in
such and such fashion," had taught them a definite ritual, and said
to them, "Do this, and do not do that." So gradually the custom
spread throughout the world of worshiping figures with various
modes of worship, such as offering up sacrifices to them, and bowing
down to them.

As time gradually passed, the honored and revered Name of
God was forgotten by mankind, vanished from their lips and hearts,
and was no longer known to them. All the common people and the
women and children knew only the figure of wood and stone and the
temple edifice in which they had, from their childhood, been trained
to prostrate themselves to the figure, worship it, and swear by its
name. Even their wise men, such as priests and men of similar standing, also fancied that there was no other god but the stars and
spheres, for whose sake and in whose similitude these figures had
been made. But the Creator of the universe was known to none, and

recognized by none save a few solitary individuals, such as Enosh, Methuselah, Noah, Shem, and Eber. The world moved on in this fashion until that pillar of the world, the patriarch Abraham, was born.

After Abraham was weaned, while still an infant, his mind began to reflect. By day and by night he was thinking and wondering: "How is it possible that this [celestial] sphere should continuously be guiding the world and have no one to guide it and cause it to turn round; for it cannot be that it turns round of itself." He had no teacher, no one to instruct him in aught. He was submerged in Ur of the Chaldees, among silly idolaters. His father and mother and the entire population worshiped idols, and he worshiped with them. But his mind was busily working and reflecting until he had attained the way of truth, apprehended the correct line of thought, and knew that there is one God, that He guides the celestial sphere and created everything, and that among all that exist, there is no god besides Him. He realized that men everywhere were in error, and that what had occasioned their error was that they worshiped the stars and the images, so that the truth perished from their minds. Abraham was forty years old when he recognized his Creator. Having attained this knowledge, he began to refute the inhabitants of Ur of the Chaldees, arguing with them and saying to them, "The course you are following is not the way of truth." He broke the images and commenced to instruct the people that it was not right to serve any one but the God of the universe, to whom alone it was proper to bow down, offer up sacrifices and make libations, so that all human creatures might, in the future, know Him; and that it was proper to destroy and shatter all the images, so that the people might not err like these who thought that there was no god but these images. When he had prevailed over them with his arguments, the king (of the country) sought to slay him. He was miraculously saved and emigrated to Haran. He then began to proclaim to the whole world with great power and to instruct the people that the entire universe had but one Creator and that Him it was right to worship. He went from city to city and from kingdom to kingdom, calling and gathering together the inhabitants till he arrived in the land of Canaan. There, too, he proclaimed his message, as it is said, "And he called there on the name of the Lord, God of the universe" (Gen. 21:33). When the people flocked to him and questioned him regarding his assertions, he would instruct each one according to his capacity till he had brought him to the way of truth, and thus thousands and tens of thousands joined him. These were the persons referred to in the phrase, "men of the house of Abraham."

Abraham implanted in their hearts this great doctrine, composed books on it, and taught it to Isaac, his son. Isaac settled down, instructing and exhorting. He imparted the doctrine to Jacob and ordained him to teach it. He, too, settled down, taught and morally strengthened all who joined him. The patriarch Jacob instructed all his sons, set apart Levi, appointed him head (teacher) and placed him in a college to teach the way of God and keep the charge of Abraham. He charged his sons to appoint, from the tribe of Levi, one instructor after another, in uninterrupted succession, so that the doctrine might never be forgotten. And so it went on with ever increasing vigor among Jacob's children and their adherents till they became a people that knew God. When the Israelites had stayed a long while in Egypt, they relapsed, learned the practices of their neighbors, and, like them, worshiped idols, with the exception of the tribe of Levi, that steadfastly kept the charge of the patriarch. This tribe of Levi never practiced idolatry. The doctrine implanted by Abraham would, in a very short time, have been uprooted, and Jacob's descendants would have lapsed into the error and perversities universally prevalent.

But because of God's love for us and because He kept the oath made to our ancestor Abraham, He appointed Moses to be our teacher and the teacher of all the prophets and charged him with his mission. After Moses had begun to exercise his prophetic functions and Israel had been chosen by the Almighty as His heritage, He crowned them with precepts, and showed them the way to worship Him and how to deal with idolatry and with those who go astray after it.*

Chapter 11

(1 We should not follow the customs of the Gentiles, nor imitate them in dress or in their way of trimming the hair, as it is said, "And you shall not walk in the customs of the nation which I have cast out before you" (Lev. 20:23); "Neither shall you walk in their statutes" (ibid. 18:3); "Take heed to yourself that you be not ensnared to follow them" (Deut. 12:30). These texts all refer to one theme and warn against imitating them. The Israelite shall, on the contrary, be

*See *Guide*, II, ch. 39.

distinguished from them and be recognizable by the way he dresses and in his other activities, just as he is distinguished from them by his knowledge and his principles. And thus it is said, "And I have set you apart from the peoples" (Lev. 20:26). He shall not put on a garment like that specially worn by them nor let the lock of his hair grow in the way they do. Thus, he shall not cut the hair of the head at the sides, leaving the hair in the center untouched as they do—this is called "growing the forelock." Nor shall he cut the hair in front from ear to ear, leaving the hair at the back to grow, as they do. He shall not rear edifices resembling idolatrous temples for the gathering of multitudes, as they do. Whoever does any of these or similar things is punished with stripes.

❪ 12   One who whispers a spell over a wound, at the same time reciting a verse from the Torah, one who recites a verse over a child to save it from terrors, and one who places a scroll or phylacteries on an infant to induce it to sleep, are not in the category of sorcerers and soothsayers, but they are included among those who repudiate the Torah; for they use its words to cure the body whereas these are only medicine for the soul, as it is said, "They shall be life to your soul" (Prov. 3:22).* On the other hand, anyone in the enjoyment of good health is permitted to recite verses from the Scriptures or a psalm, so that he may be shielded by the merit of the recital and saved from trouble and hurt.

❪ 16   These practices are all false and deceptive and were means employed by the ancient idolaters to deceive the peoples of various countries and induce them to become their followers. It is not proper for Israelites who are highly intelligent to suffer themselves to be deluded by such inanities or imagine that there is anything in them, as it is said, "For there is no enchantment with Jacob, neither is there any divination with Israel" (Num. 23:23); and further, "For these nations that you are to dispossess hearken to soothsayers and diviners; but as for you, the Lord your God, has not suffered you so to do" (Deut. 18:14). Whoever believes in these and similar things and, in his heart, holds them to be true and scientific and only forbidden by the Torah, is nothing but a fool, deficient in understanding, who belongs to the same class with women and children whose intellects are immature. Sensible people, however, who possess sound mental faculties, know by clear proofs that all these practices which

*See Book II, Laws of the Mezuzah, V, 4; Guide, I, ch. 42.

the Torah prohibited have no scientific basis but are chimerical and inane; and that only those deficient in knowledge are attracted by these follies and, for their sake, leave the ways of truth. The Torah, therefore, in forbidding all these follies, exhorts us, "You shall be wholehearted with the Lord your God" (ibid. 18:13).*

LAWS CONCERNING REPENTANCE

Chapter 3

❨ 4 Although the sounding of the shofar on the New Year is a decree of the Written Law, still it has a deep meaning, as if saying, "Awake, awake, O sleeper, from your sleep; O slumberers, arouse yourselves from your slumbers; examine your deeds, return in repentance, and remember your Creator. Those of you who forget the truth in the follies of the times and go astray the whole year in vanity and emptiness which neither profit nor save, look to your souls; improve your ways and works. Abandon, every one of you, his evil course and the thought that is not good."

It is necessary, therefore, that each person should regard himself throughout the year as if he were half innocent and half guilty and should regard the whole of mankind as half innocent and half guilty. If then he commits one more sin, he presses down the scale of guilt against himself and the whole world and causes his destruction. If he fulfills one commandment, he turns the scale of merit in his favor and in favor of the whole world, and brings salvation and deliverance to all his fellow creatures and to himself, as it is said, "The righteous man is the foundation of the world" (Prov. 10:25); that is to say, he who acts justly presses down the scale of merit in favor of all the world and saves it.

Because of these considerations, all Jews are accustomed to increase their charities and other good deeds from the New Year to the Day of Atonement and engage in meritorious actions during this

*See Epistle to Yemen; Letter on Astrology; Guide, III, ch. 37.

period to a greater degree than during the rest of the year. All are accustomed to arise while it is still night and to pray in the synagogues until dawn, with fervent entreaties and supplications.*

Chapter 5†

❨ 1 Free will is bestowed on every human being. If one desires to turn toward the good way and be righteous, he has the power to do so. If one wishes to turn toward the evil way and be wicked, he is at liberty to do so. And thus it is written in the Torah, "Behold, the man is become as one of us, to know good and evil" (Gen. 3:22)—which means that the human species had become unique in the world—there being no other species like it in the following respect, namely, that man, of himself and by the exercise of his own intelligence and reason, knows what is good and what is evil, and there is none who can prevent him from doing that which is good or that which is evil. And since this is so there is reason to fear "lest he put forth his hand . . ." (ibid.).

❨ 2 Let not the notion, expressed by foolish Gentiles and most of the senseless folk among Israelites, pass through your mind that at the beginning of a person's existence the Almighty decrees that he is to be either righteous or wicked. This is not so. Every human being may become righteous like Moses our Teacher, or wicked like Jeroboam; wise or foolish, merciful or cruel, niggardly or generous, and so with all other qualities. There is no one that coerces him or decrees what he is to do, or draws him to either of the two ways; but every person turns to the way which he desires, spontaneously and of his own volition. Thus Jeremiah said, "Out of the mouth of the Most High proceeds not evil and good?" (Lam. 3:38); that is to say, the Creator does not decree either that a man shall be good or that he shall be wicked. Accordingly it follows that it is the sinner who has inflicted injury on himself; and he should, therefore, weep for and bewail what he has done to his soul—how he has mistreated it. This is expressed in the next verse, "Wherefore does a living man complain, a strong man, because of his sins" (ibid. 3:39). The prophet continues: since liberty of action is in our hands and we have, of our free will, committed all these evils, it behooves us to return in a spirit

*See Guide, III, ch. 43.

†See Eight Chapters, ch. VIII; Letter on Astrology; Guide, III, ch. 36; Commentary on the Mishnah, Avot 3:15.

of repentance, and forsake our wickedness, for we have the power to do so. This thought is expressed in the next verse, "Let us search and try our ways, and return to the Lord" (*ibid.* 3:40).

❡ 3 This doctrine is an important principle, the pillar of the Law and the commandment, as it is said, "See, I set before you this day life and good, and death and evil" (Deut. 30:15); and again it is written, "Behold, I set before you this day a blessing and a curse" (*ibid.* 11:26). This means that the power is in your hands, and whatever a man desires to do among the things that human beings do, he can do, whether they are good or evil; and, because of this faculty, it is said, "O that they had such a heart as this always" (*ibid.* 5:26), which implies that the Creator neither puts compulsion on the children of men nor decrees that they should do either good or evil, but it is all left to their discretion.*

❡ 4 If God had decreed that a person should be either righteous or wicked, or if there were some force inherent in his nature which irresistibly drew him to a particular course, or to a special branch of knowledge, to special views or activities, as the foolish astrologers out of their own fancy pretend, how could the Almighty have charged us through the prophets: "Do this and do not do that, improve your ways, do not follow your wicked impulses," when, from the beginning of his existence his destiny had already been decreed, or his innate constitution irresistibly drew him to that from which he could not set himself free? What room would there be for the whole of the Torah? By what right or justice could God punish the wicked or reward the righteous? "Shall not the Judge of all the earth act justly?" (Gen. 18:25).

Chapter 7

❡ 1 Since every human being, as we have explained, has free will, a man should strive to repent (make verbal confession of his sins) and renounce them, so that he may die penitent and thus be worthy of life in the world to come.

❡ 2 A man should always regard himself as if his death were imminent and think that he may die this very hour, while still in a state of sin. He should therefore repent of his sins immediately and not say, "When I grow old I shall repent," for he may die before he becomes

*See *Guide*, III, ch. 32.

old. So Solomon, in his wisdom, said, "Let your garments be always white, and oil on your head not be lacking" (Eccles. 9:8).

❨ 3 Do not say that one need only repent of sinful deeds such as fornication, robbery, and theft. Just as a man needs to repent of these sins involving acts, so he needs to investigate and repent of any evil dispositions that he may have, such as hot temper, hatred, jealousy, scoffing, eager pursuit of wealth or honors, greediness in eating, and so on. Of all these faults one should repent. They are graver than sinful acts; for when one is addicted to them it is difficult to give them up. And thus it is said, "Let the wicked forsake his way and the man of iniquity his thoughts" (Is. 55:7).

❨ 4 Let not the penitent suppose that he is kept far away from the degree attained by the righteous because of the iniquities and sins that he has committed. This is not so. He is beloved by the Creator, desired by Him, as if he had never sinned. Moreover, his reward is great; since, though having tasted sin, he renounced it and overcame his evil passions. The sages say, "Where penitents stand, the completely righteous cannot stand." This means that the degree attained by penitents is higher than that of those who had never sinned, the reason being that the former have had to put forth a greater effort to subdue their passions than the latter.

❨ 5 All the prophets charged the people concerning repentance. Only through repentance will Israel be redeemed, and the Torah already offered the assurance that Israel will, in the closing period of exile, finally repent, and thereupon be immediately redeemed, as it is said, "And it shall come to pass, when all these things are come upon you, the blessing and the curse which I have set before you, and you shall take it to heart among all the nations, wherever the Lord your God has driven you, and shall return to the Lord your God, and hearken to His voice according to all that I command you this day, you and your children, with all your heart, and with all your soul, that the Lord your God will turn your captivity, and have mercy upon you, and will return and gather you from all the nations, wherever the Lord your God has scattered you" (Deut. 30:1–3).

❨ 6 Great is repentance, for it brings men near to the Divine Presence, as it is said, "Return, O Israel, to the Lord your God" (Hos. 14:2). Again, it is said, "And you have not returned to Me, says the Lord" (Amos 4:6). Further, "If you return, O Israel, to Me shall you return" (Jer. 4:1), which means "If you return in repentance, you will cleave to Me." Repentance brings near those who are far away. But yesterday this person was odious before God, abhorred, estranged, an abomination. Today he is beloved, desirable, near [to God], a friend. So you find that the same expression with which God thrusts sinners away from Him, He employs to bring the penitent near to Him, whether they are individuals or communities, as it is said, "And instead of that which was said unto them: 'You are not My people,' it shall be said unto them: 'You are children of the living God'" (Hos. 2:1). Of Jeconiah, while he was wicked, it was said, "Write you this man childless, a man that shall not prosper in his days" (Jer. 22:30); "Though Coniah, the son of Jehoiakim, king of Judah, were a signet upon my right hand, yet would I pluck you therefrom" (ibid. 22:24). But after he had in his exile repented, it is said of his son, Zerubbabel, "In that day, says the Lord of Hosts, will I take you, O Zerubbabel son of Shealtiel, my servant, and will make you as a signet, says the Lord of hosts" (Haggai 2:23).

❬7 How exalted is the degree of repentance? Just last night a certain individual was separated from the Lord, God of Israel, as it is said, "Your iniquities were making a separation between you and your God" (Is. 59:2). He cries aloud and is not answered, as it is said, "Yea, when you make many prayers, I will not hear" (ibid. 1:15). He fulfills religious precepts and they are flung back in his face, as it is said, "Who has required this at your hand to tread my courts?" (ibid. 1:12); "Oh, that there were even one among you that would shut the doors, that you might not kindle fire on my altar in vain; I have no pleasure in you, says the Lord of hosts, neither will I accept an offering at your hand" (Mal. 1:10); "Add your burnt offerings to your sacrifice and eat flesh" (Jer. 7:21). Today, the same individual (having repented) is closely attached to the Divine Presence, as it is said, "And you that cleave to the Lord your God, are alive, every one of you this day" (Deut. 4:4). He cries and is immediately answered, as it is said, "And it shall come to pass that before they call I will answer" (Is. 65:24). He fulfills religious precepts and they are accepted with pleasure and with joy, as it is said, "For God has already accepted your works" (Eccles. 9:7). Yet more, they are eagerly desired, as it is said, "Then shall the offering of Judah and Jerusalem be pleasant to the Lord as in the days of old and as in ancient years" (Mal. 3:4).

Chapter 9*

❪ 1 ❫ It is known that the reward for the fulfillment of the commandments and the good to which we will attain if we have kept the way
of the Lord, as prescribed in the Law, is life in the world to come, as
it is said, "That it may be well with you, and that you may prolong
your days" (Deut. 22:7), while the retribution exacted from the
wicked who have abandoned the ways of righteousness prescribed in
the Torah is excision, as it is said, "that soul shall be utterly cut off;
his iniquity shall be upon him" (Num. 15:31). What then is the
meaning of the statement found everywhere in the Torah that if you
obey, it will happen to you thus; if you do not obey, it will be otherwise; and all these happenings will take place in this world, such as
war and peace; sovereignty and subjection; residence in the Promised
Land and exile; prosperity in one's activities and failure and all the
other things predicted in the words of the Covenant (Lev. 26, Deut.
28)? All those promises were once truly fulfilled and will again be so.
When we fulfill all the commandments of the Torah, all the good
things of this world will come to us. When, however, we transgress
the precepts, the evils that are written in the Torah will befall us.
But, nevertheless, those good things are not the final reward for the
fulfillment of the commandments, nor are those evils the last penalty
exacted from one who transgresses all the commandments. These
matters are to be understood as follows: The Holy One, blessed be
He, gave us this Law—a tree of life. Whoever fulfills what is written
therein and knows it with a complete and correct knowledge will
attain thereby life in the world to come. According to the greatness
of his deeds and abundance of his knowledge will be the measure in
which he will attain that life.

The Holy One, blessed be He, has further promised us in the
Torah that if we observe its behests joyously and cheerfully, and continually meditate on its wisdom, He will remove from us the obstacles that hinder us in its observance, such as sickness, war, famine,
and other calamities; and will bestow upon us all the material benefits which will strengthen our ability to fulfill the Law, such as
plenty, peace, abundance of silver and gold. Thus we will not be
engaged all our days in providing for our bodily needs, but will have
leisure to study wisdom and fulfill the commandment and thus
attain life in the world to come. Hence, after the assurance of mate-

*See *Commentary on Helek*, end; also Book V, Forbidden Intercourse, XIV, 3.

rial benefits, it is said in the Torah, "And it shall be righteousness to us, if we observe to do all this commandment before the Lord our God as He has commanded us" (ibid. 6:25). So too, He taught us in the Torah that if we deliberately forsake it and occupy ourselves with temporal follies, as the text says, "But Jeshurun waxed fat and wicked" (ibid. 32:15), the true Judge will deprive the forsakers of all those material benefits which only served to encourage them to be recalcitrant, and will send upon them all the calamities that will prevent their attaining the life hereafter, so that they will perish in their wickedness. This is expressed by the Torah in the text: "Because you did not serve the Lord your God with joyfulness and with gladness of heart, by reason of the abundance of all things, therefore shall you serve your enemy whom the Lord shall send against you" (ibid. 28:47–48).

Hence, all those benedictions and maledictions promised in the Torah are to be explained as follows: If you have served God with joy and observed His way, He will bestow upon you those blessings and avert from you those curses, so that you will have leisure to become wise in the Torah and occupy yourselves therewith, and thus attain life hereafter, and then it will be well with you in the world which is entirely blissful and you will enjoy length of days in an existence which is everlasting. So you will enjoy both worlds, a happy life on earth leading to the life in the world to come. For if wisdom is not acquired and good deeds are not performed here, there will be nothing meriting a recompense hereafter, as it is said, "For there is no work, no device, no knowledge, no wisdom in the grave" (Eccles. 9:10). But if you have forsaken the Lord and have erred in eating, drinking, fornication, and similar things, He will bring upon you all those curses and withhold from you all those blessings till your days will end in confusion and terror, and you will have neither the free mind nor the healthy body requisite for the fulfillment of the commandments so that you will suffer perdition in the life hereafter and will thus have lost both worlds—for when one is troubled here on earth with diseases, war or famine, he does not occupy himself with the acquisition of wisdom or the performance of religious precepts by which life hereafter is gained.

¶ 2 Hence, all Israelites, their prophets and sages, longed for the advent of Messianic times, that they might have relief from the wicked tyranny that does not permit them properly to occupy themselves with the study of the Torah and the observance of the commandments; that they might have ease, devote themselves to getting wisdom, and thus attain to life in the world to come. For in those days, knowledge, wisdom, and truth will increase, as it is said, "For the earth will be full of the knowledge of the Lord" (Is. 11:9), and it is said, "They will no more teach everyone his brother and everyone his neighbor" (Jer. 31:34), and further, "I will remove the heart of stone from your flesh" (Ezek. 36:26). Because the king who will arise from the seed of David will possess more wisdom than Solomon and will be a great prophet, approaching Moses our Teacher, he will teach the whole of the Jewish people and instruct them in the way of God; and all nations will come to hear him, as it is said, "And at the end of days it shall come to pass that the mount of the Lord's house shall be established as the top of the mountains" (Micah 4:1, Is. 2:2). The ultimate and perfect reward, the final bliss which will suffer neither interruption nor diminution, is the life in the world to come. The Messianic era, on the other hand, will be realized in this world; which will continue in its normal course except that independent sovereignty will be restored to Israel. The ancient sages already said, "The only difference between the present and the Messianic era is that political oppression will then cease."*

Chapter 10

⟨ 1 Let not a man say, "I will observe the precepts of the Torah and occupy myself with its wisdom in order that I may obtain all the blessings written in the Torah, or to attain life in the world to come; I will abstain from transgressions against which the Torah warns, so that I may be saved from the curses written in the Torah, or that I may not be cut off from life in the world to come." It is not right to serve God after this fashion for whoever does so, serves Him out of fear. This is not the standard set by the prophets and sages. Those who may serve God in this way are illiterate, women, or children whom one trains to serve out of fear, till their knowledge shall have increased when they will serve out of love.

⟨ 2 Whoever serves God out of love, occupies himself with the study of the Law and the fulfillment of commandments and walks in the paths of wisdom, impelled by no external motive whatsoever, moved neither by fear of calamity nor by the desire to obtain material benefits—such a man does what is truly right because it is truly right, and

*See Book XIV, Kings and Wars, ch. XII.

ultimately, happiness comes to him as a result of his conduct. This standard is indeed a very high one; not every sage attained it. It was the standard of the patriarch Abraham whom God called His lover, because he served only out of love. It is the standard which God, through Moses, bids us achieve, as it is said, "And you shall love the Lord your God" (Deut. 6:5). When one loves God with the right love, he will straightway observe all the commandments out of love.*

¶ 3 What is the love of God that is befitting? It is to love the Eternal with a great and exceeding love, so strong that one's soul shall be knit up with the love of God, and one should be continually enraptured by it, like a love-sick individual, whose mind is at no time free from his passion for a particular woman, the thought of her filling his heart at all times, when sitting down or rising up, when he is eating or drinking. Even intenser should be the love of God in the hearts of those who love Him. And this love should continually possess them, even as He commanded us in the phrase, "with all your heart and with all your soul" (Deut. 6:5). This, Solomon expressed allegorically in the sentence, "for I am sick with love" (Song of Songs 2:5). The entire Song of Songs is indeed an allegory descriptive of this love.†

¶ 4 The ancient sages said, "Peradventure, you will say, 'I will study Torah, in order that I may become rich, that I may be called rabbi, that I may receive a reward in the world to come.' It is therefore said, 'To love the Lord.' Whatever you do, do it out of love only." The text: "[Happy is the man who fears the Lord,] who delights greatly in His commandments" (Ps. 112:1) has been thus explained by the sages—"In His commandments—not in the reward for His commandments." So too, the greatest sages were wont specifically to exhort those among their disciples who were understanding and intelligent, "Be not like servants who minister to their master upon the condition of receiving a reward" (Ethics of the Fathers 1:3). But it is proper to be like servants who serve their master not for the sake of receiving anything; but only because he is the master, it is right to serve him; that is, serve him out of love.

¶ 5 Whoever engages in the study of the Torah in order that he may receive a reward or avoid calamities is not studying the Torah

*See *Guide*, III, ch. 52; *Commentary on the Mishnah*, Avot 1:3.
†See *Guide*, III, ch. 51.

for its own sake. Whoever occupies himself with the Torah, neither out of fear nor for the sake of recompense, but solely out of love for the Lord of the whole earth who enjoined us to do so, is occupied with the Torah for its own sake. The sages, however, said, "One should always engage in the study of the Torah, even if not for its own sake; for he who begins thus will end by studying it for its own sake." Hence, when instructing the young, women, or the illiterate generally, we teach them to serve God out of fear or for the sake of reward, till their knowledge increases and they have attained a large measure of wisdom. Then we reveal to them this secret truth, little by little, and train them by easy stages till they have grasped and comprehended it, and serve God out of love.

¶ 6 It is known and certain that the love of God does not become closely knit in a man's heart till he is continuously and thoroughly possessed by it and gives up everything else in the world for it; as God commanded us, "with all your heart and with all your soul" (Deut. 6:5). One only loves God with the knowledge with which one knows Him. According to the knowledge will be the love. If the former be little or much, so will the latter be little or much. A person ought therefore to devote himself to the understanding and comprehension of those sciences and studies which will inform him concerning his Master, as far as it lies in human faculties to understand and comprehend—as indeed we have explained in the Laws of the Basic Principles of the Torah.

*T*HE daily recitation of the Shema, prayers, and assorted benedictions, the wearing of phylacteries, and the other religious practices included in this book are described by Maimonides as "precepts which are to be constantly observed and which we have been commanded to keep in order that we may always love God and be ever mindful of Him." The emphasis is, in other words, on the regularity, frequency, or continuity of performance.

The historical survey concerning the genesis of statutory prayer is of great interest (Prayer, ch. I). The emphasis on concentration, attention, and devout meditation in prayer (ch. IV) illustrates the attempt of halakhah to fuse spontaneity and inwardness with standardization and uniformity (cf. Guide, III, ch. 51). Noteworthy is Maimonides' sharply critical attitude toward practices which he considered superstitious and unworthy (Mezuzah, V, 4), an attitude that complements the intellectualistic-spiritualistic emphasis found in other sections (Shema, I, 4; Mezuzah, VI, 13; Phylacteries, IV, 25). Maimonides explains his classification of law and justifies the inclusion of the section on circumcision here "because this is a sign in our flesh, serving as a constant reminder," even when other commandments are not being observed. The reader should be attentive to Maimonides' principles of classification; he should especially note those instances where Maimonides explicates his method or reasoning processes.

෴

RECITATION OF THE SHEMA

Chapter 1

❨ 1 The Shema is read twice every day—in the evening and in the morning, as it is said, "and when you lie down and when you rise up" (Deut. 6:7), the phrases in this text meaning at the time when men are lying down, that is, at night, and at the time when they have risen, that is, by day.

❨ 2 What does one read? Three sections as follows: the section beginning, "Hear, O Israel" (Deut. 6:4–9); that commencing, "And it shall come to pass" (ibid. 11:13–21); and that commencing, "And the Lord spoke" (Num. 15:37–41). The section beginning, "Hear, O Israel" is recited first, because it sets forth the duties of acknowledging the Unity of God, loving Him, and studying His words. This is the great and essential matter on which all depends.* Then, the passage beginning, "And it shall come to pass" is read, this containing a charge to fulfill all the other commandments. Finally the section concerning fringes is read, as it also contains a charge to remember all the commandments.

❨ 3 Although the precept to wear fringes is not incumbent at night, still the section concerning this precept is recited at night, because it mentions the departure from Egypt, which it is a duty to recall by day and at night, as it is said, "that you may remember the day of your going forth from the land of Egypt all the days of your life" (Deut. 16:3). The reading of these three sections in this order is termed, "The reading of the Shema."

❨ 4 When reciting the Shema, after concluding the first verse, one repeats in a low tone the sentence, "Blessed be the name of His glorious sovereignty for ever and ever" and then resumes the reading of

*See Book I, Basic Principles of the Torah, I, 6.

the first section in the regular order from the verse, "And you shall love the Lord your God . . ." to the end of the section. Why is the above-mentioned sentence interpolated? We have a tradition that when the patriarch Jacob, residing in Egypt, gathered his sons about him in his dying hour, he earnestly charged them concerning the Unity of God and the way of the Lord in which Abraham and his father Isaac had walked. He questioned them, saying to them, "Possibly, my sons, there is some one among you who is unworthy, and is not at one with me on the doctrine of the Unity of the Creator of the world, in the same way as our teacher Moses charged the people in the words, 'Lest there be among you a man or a woman . . . whose heart turns away this day' " (Deut. 29:17). They all answered, "Hear, O Israel, the Lord our God, the Lord is one." This means, "Our father, Israel, hear this, our [confession of faith]: 'the Lord our God is one Lord.' " The aged patriarch then ejaculated, "Blessed be the name of His glorious Sovereignty for ever and ever." Hence, all Israelites keep the custom of reciting, after the first verse of the Shema, the thanksgiving uttered by the patriarch Israel.

LAWS OF PRAYER*

Chapter 1

❨ 1 To pray daily is an affirmative duty, as it is said, "And you shall serve the Lord your God" (Ex. 23:25). The service here referred to, according to the teaching of tradition, is prayer, as it is said, "And to serve Him with all your heart" (Deut. 11:13), on which the sages commented, "What may be described as service of the heart? Prayer." The number of prayers is not prescribed in the Torah. No form of prayer is prescribed in the Torah. Nor does the Torah prescribe a fixed time for prayer. Hence, women and slaves are under an obligation to pray, this being a duty, the fulfillment of which is independent of set periods.

❨ 2 The obligation in this precept is that every person should daily, according to his ability, offer up supplication and prayer; first uttering praises of God, then with humble supplication and petition asking

*See Guide, I, ch. 59; III, ch. 32 and 52.

for all that he needs, and finally offering praise and thanksgiving to the Eternal for the benefits already bestowed upon him in rich measure.

❡ 3 One who was fluent would offer up many prayers and supplications. If one was slow of speech, he would pray as he could and whenever he pleased. Thus also, the number of separate services depended on an individual's ability. One would pray once daily; others, several times in the day. All, however, turned during prayer to the Sanctuary, in whichever direction that might be. This was the uniform practice from the times of Moses to those of Ezra.

❡ 4 When the people of Israel went into exile in the days of the wicked Nebuchadnezzar, they mingled with the Persians, Greeks, and other nations. In those foreign countries, children were born to them, whose language was confused. Everyone's speech was a mixture of many tongues. No one was able, when he spoke, to express his thoughts adequately in any one language, otherwise than incoherently, as it is said, "And their children spoke half in the speech of Ashdod and they could not speak in the Jews' language, but according to the language of each people" (Neh. 13:24).

❡ 5 Consequently, when anyone of them prayed in Hebrew, he was unable adequately to express his needs or recount the praises of God, without mixing Hebrew with other languages. When Ezra and his council realized this condition, they ordained the Eighteen Benedictions in their present order.

❡ 6 The first three blessings consist of praises of God and the last three of thanksgiving to Him. The intermediate benedictions are petitions for the things which may stand as prototypes of all the desires of the individual and the needs of the community. The object aimed at was that these prayers should be in an orderly form in everyone's mouth, that all should learn them, and thus the prayer of those who were not expert in speech would be as perfect as that of those who had command of a chaste style. For the same reason, they arranged (in a fixed form) all the blessings and prayers for all Jews so that the substance of every blessing should be familiar and current in the mouth of one who is not expert in speech.

Chapter 2

❡ 1 In Rabban Gamliel's days, the number of heretics in Israel increased. They were wont to vex the Israelites and induce them to turn away from God. When Rabban Gamliel realized that the most urgent need was to remove this evil, he composed a benediction which contains a petition to God to destroy the heretics, and incorporated it in the Eighteen Blessings so that it should be in a fixed form for all. Hence the total number of blessings in the daily service is nineteen.

❪ 2 In each of the three daily services, a person recites these nineteen blessings in their appointed order—but only if he finds that his mind is in a fit state for prayer and he is fluent in speech. But if one is distracted and harassed, or is not fluent in speech, he should recite the first three blessings, a blessing embodying the gist of all the intermediate blessings, and the last three blessings, and then he has fulfilled his duty.

❪ 3 The blessing that they ordained as a summary of the intermediate blessings is as follows: Give us understanding, O Lord, our God, to know Your ways, and circumcise our hearts to fear You. Be forgiving of us, so that we may be redeemed. Keep us far from sorrow. Make us prosperous. Cause us to dwell in the pastures of Your land. Gather the scattered from the four [corners of the earth]. Let them that go astray in the knowledge of You be judged; and over the wicked wave Your hand. Let the righteous rejoice in the rebuilding of Your city and in the re-establishment of Your temple, and in the flourishing of the horn of David, Your servant, and in the rekindling of the light of Jesse's son, Your anointed. Before we call, do You answer; before we speak, do You hearken; as it is said, "And it shall come to pass, before they call, I will answer; while they are still speaking, I will hear" (Is. 65:24); for You are He who answers in all times of trouble, who delivers and rescues from all distress, Blessed are You, O Lord, who hearkens to prayer.

Chapter 4

❪ 1 There are five requisites, the absence of which hinder the (proper) recital of a service, even when its due time has arrived: cleansing the hands, covering the body, assurance as to the cleanliness of the place where the prayers are recited, removal of distractions, and concentration of the mind.

❪ 15 Concentration of the mind—how is this condition (to be fulfilled)? Any prayer uttered without mental concentration is not prayer. If a service has been recited without such concentration, it must be recited again devoutly. A person finds that his thoughts are confused and his mind is distracted, he may not pray till he has recovered his mental composure. Hence, on returning from a journey or if one is weary or distressed, it is forbidden to pray till his mind is composed. The sages said that he should wait three days till he is rested and his mind is calm, and then he recites the prayers.

⟨ 16 What is to be understood by concentration of the mind? The mind should be freed from all extraneous thoughts and the one who prays should realize that he is standing before the Divine Presence. He should therefore sit awhile before beginning his prayers, so as to concentrate his mind, and then pray in gentle tones, beseechingly, and not regard the service as a burden which he is carrying and which he will cast off before proceeding on his way. He should, accordingly, sit awhile, after concluding the prayers, and then leave. The ancient saints were wont to pause and meditate one hour before the service, one hour after the service, and take one hour in its recital.*

⟨ 17 An intoxicated person must not pray because he cannot concentrate. If he prays, his prayer is an abomination. He must therefore recite the prayers again after he has recovered from his intoxication. A person under the influence of drink should not pray while in that condition. But if he has recited the service, it is regarded as prayer. A drunkard is one who is unable to speak in the royal presence. A person under the influence of drink is one who can speak in the presence of a king without committing error. Yet having drunk, if only a quarter of a log of wine,† one is not to pray till he is rid of the effect of the wine he has taken.

⟨ 18 So too, persons should not stand up to pray after indulging in jest, laughter, frivolity, idle talk, quarreling, or outbursts of anger, but only after the study of Torah, not however of legal discussions by which the mind is distracted, but only after the study of such themes as require no profound reflection, as for instance established rules.

⟨ 19 Prayers which are read only at periodic intervals, such as the additional service for the beginning of the month and the services for the festivals, should be first rehearsed before one stands up to recite them so that he shall not break down during their recital.

*See Guide, III, chs. 32 and 51.
†Equal in volume to one and one-half eggs.

Chapter 9

❲ 7 Whoever says in his supplications, "He that dealt mercifully with a nest of birds, forbidding the taking of the mother-bird together with the nestlings (Deut. 22:6–7) and the slaughtering of a beast and its young in one day (Lev. 22:28)—may He have mercy upon us," or offers petitions of a similar character, is silenced; for these precepts are divine decrees set forth in Scripture and have not been ordained in a spirit of compassion.* Were this the motive, the slaughtering of all animals would have been prohibited. It is also forbidden to multiply epithets and say: "O God, great, mighty, awe-inspiring, powerful, puissant," since it is beyond human power to exhaust the praises of God. One should therefore limit himself to the attributes used by Moses our Teacher, peace be upon him.†

Chapter 11

❲ 1 Wherever there are ten Israelites resident, an edifice must be fitted up, where they can assemble for worship at each period of prayer. Such a building is termed a synagogue. The residents exercise compulsory powers on each other for the purpose of erecting a synagogue and purchasing a scroll of the Law (Pentateuch), the prophetical books, and the Hagiography.

❲ 4 Synagogues and houses of study must be treated with respect. They are swept and sprinkled to lay the dust. In Spain and the West (Morocco), in Babylon and in the Holy Land, it is customary to kindle lamps in the synagogues and to spread mats on the floor on which the worshipers sit. In the lands of Edom (Christian countries) they sit in synagogues on chairs (or benches).

Chapter 12

❲ 1 Moses our Teacher established the rule for Israel that they should read the Law publicly on Sabbaths and also on the second and fifth days of the week, during the morning service, so that three days shall not elapse without hearing the Law. Ezra established the rule that the Torah should be read at the afternoon service every Sabbath, for the benefit of those who would otherwise spend the day vacuously. He also ordained that on the second and fifth days of the

*See *Guide*, III, ch. 48.
†See *Guide*, I, ch. 59.

week, three persons should be called to the reading of the Torah and that they should read not fewer than three verses each.

Chapter 13

⟨ 1 The custom prevailing through Israel is (that the reading of the Pentateuch is completed in one year). It is begun on the Sabbath after the Feast of Tabernacles, when the portion commencing *Bereshit*, "In the beginning" (Gen. 1:1), is read. On the second Sabbath, that beginning, "These are the generations of Noah" (Gen. 6:9), is read; on the third, that beginning, "And the Lord said to Abraham" (*ibid.* 12:1), and so on in regular order till the last portion is read on the Feast of Tabernacles. Some complete the reading of the Pentateuch in three years, but this is not a prevalent custom.

⟨ 11 On the Day of Atonement, in the morning service, the section read is that beginning, "After the death of the two sons of Aaron" (Lev. 16:1–34); and the lesson from the Prophets is that beginning, "For thus says the High and Lofty One" (Is. 57:15–58:14). In the afternoon service, the section read is that concerning incest, in the portion beginning, "After the death of the two sons of Aaron" (Lev. 18). The purpose aimed at is that anyone who has been guilty of any of these offenses should remember and be abashed. The third person called up reads in the Torah and recites, as the lesson from the Prophets, the Book of Jonah.

LAWS OF PHYLACTERIES

Chapter 1

⟨ 1 The four Pentateuchal sections, beginning respectively, "Sanctify to Me" (Ex. 13:1–10), "And it shall be when the Lord shall bring you" (*ibid.* 11–16)—these two being in the Book of Exodus— "Hear, O Israel" (Deut. 6:4–9) "And it shall come to pass if you shall hearken diligently" (*ibid.* 11:13–21), are written and covered with a skin. These are called *tefillin*, and are placed upon the head and bound on the arm. The omission of the point of a single letter in any one of these sections bars, according to Scriptural enactment, the use of all of them. They must all be written perfectly and in accordance with rule.

❡ 2 This is the case also with the two sections of the *mezuzah*, beginning respectively, "Hear, O Israel" (Deut. 6:4–9) and, "And it shall come to pass if you shall hearken diligently" (*ibid.* 11:13–21). If the point of a letter is missing in these two sections, the *mezuzah* may not, according to Scriptural enactment, be used. The two sections must be written perfectly. So too, a scroll of the Law, in which a single letter is missing, is unfit for use.

Chapter 4

❡ 25 The sanctity of phylacteries is a high degree of sanctity. As long as phylacteries are on a man's head and arm, he is humble and God-fearing, is not drawn into frivolity and idle talk, does not dwell on evil thoughts but occupies his mind with thoughts of truth and righteousness. A man should therefore endeavor to wear phylacteries the whole day, this being the right way of fulfilling the precept. It is said of Rav, the disciple of our sainted teacher (R. Judah the Prince), that throughout his life no one saw him without Torah, *tzitzit* (fringes on his garments), or phylacteries.

❡ 26 Although the proper mode of fulfilling the precept is to wear phylacteries the whole day, it is especially a duty to do so during the recital of prayers. The sages say, "Whoever reads the *Shema* without wearing phylacteries is regarded as testifying falsely in his own person." "Whoever does not wear phylacteries at all violates eight affirmative precepts," since in each of the four sections, the command is set forth to lay phylacteries on the head and on the arm. "Whoever wears phylacteries regularly will be blessed with longevity, as it is said, 'The Lord is upon them; they shall live' " (Is. 38:16).

፨

LAWS OF THE MEZUZAH

Chapter 5

❡ 4 It is a universal custom to write the word *Shad-dai* (Almighty) on the other side of the *mezuzah*, opposite the blank space between the two sections. As this word is written on the outside, the practice is unobjectionable. They, however, who write names of angels, holy names, a Biblical text, or inscriptions usual on seals within the *mezuzah*, are among those who have no portion in the world to come. For these fools not only fail to fulfill the commandment but they treat an important precept that expresses the Unity of God, the love of Him, and His worship, as if it were an amulet to promote their own personal interests; for, according to their foolish minds, the *mezuzah* is something that will secure for them advantage in the vanities of the world.

Chapter 6

❪ 13 A person should pay heed to the precept of the *mezuzah*; for it is an obligation perpetually binding upon all. Whenever one enters or leaves a home with the *mezuzah* on the doorpost, he will be confronted with the declaration of God's unity, blessed be His holy name; and will remember the love due to God, and will be aroused from his slumbers and his foolish absorption in temporal vanities. He will realize that nothing endures to all eternity save knowledge of the Ruler of the universe. This thought will immediately restore him to his right senses and he will walk in the paths of righteousness. Our ancient teachers said: He who has phylacteries on his head and arm, fringes on his garment, and a *mezuzah* on his door may be presumed not to sin, for he has many monitors—angels that save him from sinning, as it is said, (Ps. 34:8) "The angel of the Lord encamps round about them that fear Him and delivers them."

LAWS OF SEFER TORAH

Chapter 7

❪ 1 It is an affirmative precept binding upon every individual Israelite to write a scroll of the Law for his own use, as it is said, "Now therefore write you this song for you" (Deut. 31:19). As the Torah is not written in separate sections, this text means, "Write for yourselves the Torah in which this song is contained." Even if a person's ancestors have bequeathed a scroll to him, it is a religious duty to write a scroll at his own expense. If he writes it with his own hand, it is accounted to him as if he had received it from Sinai. If one does not know how to write a scroll, he should get others to write it for him. He who corrects a scroll, even a single letter of it, is regarded as if he had written it completely.

Chapter 8

❡ 4 As in all the scrolls I have seen, I noticed serious incorrectness in these regards; while authorities on the Massorah, who write treatises and compilations with the aim of pointing out the sections that are closed and those that are open, differ according to the variations in the scrolls on which they rely, I deemed it fit to write here a list of the sections which are closed and those which are open, as also the forms in which the songs of the Pentateuch are written·so that all the scrolls may be corrected from, and compared with, them. The copy on which I relied is the well-known Egyptian codex which contains the twenty-four books of the Scriptures and which had been in Jerusalem for several years—used as the standard text for the examination of scrolls. Everyone relied upon it because it had been examined by Ben Asher who closely studied it for many years and examined it again whenever it was being copied. This codex was the text on which I relied in the scroll of the Law that I wrote according to the rules.

Chapter 10

❡ 10 It is a duty to assign a fixed place for a scroll of the Law, and to show it extreme honor and courtesy. The words in the tables of the covenant are in every scroll of the Law. One may not expectorate before a scroll of the Law, nor indecently expose oneself before it, nor stretch out one's feet before it; nor place it upon the head in the way in which a burden is carried; nor turn one's back to it unless it is at an elevation of ten handbreadths above the person.

❡ 11 If one is traveling from place to place and had a scroll of the Law with him, he is not to put the scroll in a sack, place it on the donkey's back, and ride thereupon. If, however, he is afraid of thieves, he may do so. When there is no such apprehension, he places it in his bosom close to his heart, and continues his journey, riding. Any one, sitting before a scroll of the Law, should be inspired with a sense of earnestness, awe, and reverence, for it is a faithful witness concerning all who come into the world, as it is said, "It shall be therefore a witness against you" (Deut. 31:26).* All possible honor should be shown it. The ancient sage said, "Whoever treats the Torah with contumely will be treated with contumely by his fellow creatures. Whoever honors the Torah, will receive honor from his fellow creatures" (Ethics of the Fathers 4:8).

LAWS CONCERNING BLESSINGS

Chapter 1

(1 It is an affirmative precept of the Torah to say grace after a meal, as it is said, "And you shall eat and be satisfied and shall bless the Lord your God" (Deut. 8:10). The Torah only imposes the obligation on a person when he is satisfied; for it is said, "When you have eaten and are satisfied, you shall bless etc." According to the ordinances of the sages, however, even if one has eaten only as much food as the size of an olive, he recites grace after the meal.

(2 It is also an ordinance of the sages that before one partakes of any food, a blessing is first recited and then one eats. And however little one intends to eat or drink, the blessing is first recited and then the refreshment is taken. So too, one who wishes to smell a fragrant odor first recites the blessing and then enjoys the fragrance. Whoever partakes of any enjoyment without reciting a blessing commits a trespass. It is also an ordinance of the sages that a blessing is to be recited after eating or drinking, provided that the quantity drunk is at least a quarter of a log (equal to the volume of an egg and a half), and the food eaten is at least as much as an olive in size. A cook who is tasting food does not need to recite a blessing before or after doing so, provided that the quantity tasted is less than a quarter of a log.

(3 And just as blessings are recited when partaking of material

*Maimonides means that the scroll is a perennial reminder of the divine-human encounter. Note the different application of this verse in the introduction to the *Mishneh Torah*. See also Book IX, Festal Offerings, III, 6; *Commentary on the Mishnah*, Avot 4:6.

enjoyments, so when one is about to fulfill any precept, a blessing is said, and then the precept is performed. The sages have, moreover, instituted several blessings of praise and thanksgiving and petition, in order that when not partaking of material enjoyments or engaged in the fulfillment of religious duties we should constantly have God in mind. All blessings, accordingly, fall into three kinds: blessings recited when partaking of material enjoyments, blessings recited when fulfilling religious duties, and blessings of thanksgiving, which have the character of praise, thanksgiving, and supplication, and the purpose of which is that we should always have the Creator in mind and revere Him.

❡ 4 The forms of all the blessings were established by Ezra and his court. It is not proper to vary them, or add to or take anything away from any one of them. Whoever deviates from the form which the sages have given to the blessings is in error. Any blessing in which the name of God and His sovereignty are not mentioned is not regarded as a blessing, unless it follows immediately another blessing.

❡ 5 All blessings may be recited in any language, provided that the form instituted by the sages is followed. And even if the form has been changed, the duty of reciting the blessing is fulfilled if the name of God and His sovereignty as well as the subject matter of the blessing are mentioned, even though in a foreign tongue.

Chapter 11

❡ 2 There are some affirmative precepts in regard to which there is an obligation sedulously to strive to fulfill them; as, for example, to put on phylacteries, dwell in a booth on the Feast of Tabernacles, take in the hand a palm branch together with the other plants on that feast, hear the sound of the ram's horn on the New Year. These are termed obligatory because there is an unconditional obligation to fulfill them. Again, there are religious duties which are not obligatory but are in a sense permissive: for example, to affix a mezuzah to the doors of a house or build a parapet on the roof; since there is no obligation to live in a dwelling that requires a mezuzah to be affixed to it. One may, if one chooses, live all one's lifetime in a tent or on a ship. Similarly there is no obligation to build a house in order to erect a parapet round the roof. Every duty to God, whether permissive or obligatory, requires a blessing to be said before its fulfillment.

❡ 3 So too, all religious duties ordained by the scribes, whether these are according to their dicta, obligatory; (for example, to read the Scroll of Esther on the Feast of Purim, to kindle lights on the Eve of the Sabbath and during the Feast of Hanukkah); or whether these duties are optional,—for example, to make an *Eruv** or to wash the hands†—all require, before they are performed, the recital of a blessing, containing the formula "Who has sanctified us with Your commandments and commanded us (to perform that particular duty)." Where in the Torah did God so command us? In the text (Deut. 17:11), ". . . and according to the judgment which they tell you, you shall do." Hence, the meaning and purport of the benedictory formula is as follows, "Who has sanctified us with Your commandments among which You have commanded us to give heed to those spiritual leaders who ordained that we should kindle the Hanukkah light or read the Scroll of Esther." This applies to all the other duties ordained by the scribes.

LAWS OF CIRCUMCISION

Chapter 3

❡ 7 The foreskin is regarded as an abomination, for which the Gentiles are condemned in Scripture, as it is said, "For all the nations are uncircumcised" (Jer. 9:25). An important institution is circumcision. For the patriarch Abraham was not called perfect till he had circumcised himself, as it is said, "Walk before Me; and be perfect. And I will make My covenant between Me and you" (Gen. 17:1–2). Whoever neglects the covenant of our ancestor Abraham, and retains the foreskin or artificially obliterates the marks of circumcision, even if he has acquired much knowledge of the Torah and practices good deeds, will have no portion in the world to come.

---

*Setting aside food on the eve of a festival, to permit the cooking of food on the festival for the Sabbath, or on the eve of a Sabbath to permit carrying on the Sabbath in a court or a town.

†For prayers or meals.

❡ 8 Mark how strictly the observance of circumcision is to be regarded. Moses, although he was on a journey, did not receive indulgence a single hour for neglecting this duty. In connection with all the precepts of the Torah, three covenants were made with Israel; as it is said, "These are the words of the covenant which the Lord commanded ... besides the covenant which He made with them in Horeb" (Deut. 28:69). And in the next section it is said, "You are standing this day all of you before the Lord your God ... that you should enter into the covenant of the Lord your God" (Deut. 29:9–11). Three covenants are here mentioned. But in connection with circumcision, thirteen covenants were made with our ancestor Abraham. "And I will make My covenant between Me and you" (Gen. 17:2); "As for Me, behold, My covenant is with you" (ibid. 17:4); "And I will establish My covenant between Me and you" (ibid. 17:7); "for an everlasting covenant" (ibid. 17:7); "And as for you, you shall keep My covenant" (ibid. 17:9); "This is My covenant which you shall keep" (ibid. 17:10); "And it shall be a token of a covenant" (ibid. 17:11); "And My covenant shall be in your flesh" (ibid. 17:13); "for an everlasting covenant" (ibid. 17:13); "he has broken My covenant" (ibid. 17:14); "And I will establish My covenant with him" (ibid. 17:19); "for an everlasting covenant" (ibid. 17:19); "But My covenant I will establish with Isaac" (ibid. 17:21).

*U*NLIKE the precepts of Book II, which are to be observed constantly, the precepts treated in Book III are "fulfilled at fixed periods" only. This book therefore deals with all special days of the Jewish calendar—whether of feasting or fasting, celebration of historical success or commemoration of national calamity. Indirectly these laws illustrate the abiding contemporaneity of historical experience and the acute historical consciousness of Judaism.

Note the following: (1) the eloquent statement concerning the supremacy and nobility of human life (Sabbath, II, 1–3); (2) the description—following the exhaustive catalogue of forbidden activities—of how the Sabbath is to be observed meaningfully, infused with spirituality, and transformed into an enriching experience (Sabbath, chs. XXIV and XXX); (3) the recurrent emphasis upon the ethical and spiritual motifs of ritual performance, especially the need for compassion and generosity (Repose, ch. VI; Palm Branch, ch. VIII; Megillah, ch. II; Fast Days, ch. I); (4) the unity of all learning and, consequently, the uncontested relevance of non-Jewish sources of wisdom (Sanctification, XVII, 25); and (5) the interpretation of fasting and praying in times of crisis and adversity as a means of underscoring the providential design in all events and reminding man of his absolute dependence on God (Fast Days, chs. I and V).

SABBATH

Chapter 2

❨ 1   The commandment of the Sabbath, like all other commandments, may be set aside if human life is in danger. Accordingly, if a
person is dangerously ill, whatever a skilled local physician considers
necessary may be done for him on the Sabbath.

If it is uncertain whether the Sabbath needs to be violated or
not, or if one physician says that violation is necessary and another
says that it is not, the Sabbath should be violated, for the mere possibility of danger to human life overrides the Sabbath.

❨ 2   If it is estimated on the Sabbath that a certain treatment is
necessary and will have to be continued for eight days, one should
not say, "Let us wait until evening, so as not to violate two Sabbaths"; rather one should begin the treatment from that very Sabbath day, and as long as treatment is necessary and danger—or possibility of danger—persists, even a hundred Sabbaths may be violated.
One may light a lamp, extinguish a lamp that is disturbing the
patient, slaughter an animal, bake, cook, or heat water for the patient
to drink or to wash with. In general, insofar as the needs of a person
who is dangerously ill are concerned, the Sabbath is the same as a
weekday.

❨ 3   When such things have to be done, they should not be left to
heathens, minors, slaves, or women, lest these should come to regard
Sabbath observance as a trivial matter. They should rather be done
by adult and scholarly Israelites. Furthermore, it is forbidden to
delay such violation of the Sabbath for the sake of a person who is
dangerously ill, for Scripture says, "Which if a man do, he shall live
by them" (Lev. 18:5), that is to say, he shall not die by them. Hence
you learn that the ordinances of the Law were meant to bring upon
the world not vengeance, but mercy, lovingkindness, and peace. It is
of heretics—who assert that this is nevertheless a violation of the
Sabbath and therefore prohibited—that Scripture says, "Wherefore I

gave them also statutes that were not good, and ordinances whereby they should not live" (Ezek. 20:25).

Chapter 21

❨ 1 When Scripture says, "But on the seventh day you shall rest" (Ex. 23:12), it implies that one must refrain also from doing things which are not actual work. Such activities, prohibited by the sages on the ground that they conflict with the spirit of Sabbath rest, are many, some being forbidden because of their resemblance to prohibited kinds of work, others being forbidden as a preventive measure, lest they should lead to the doing of work that is prohibited under penalty of stoning. These activities are enumerated in the following sections.

Chapter 24

❨ 1 Some acts are forbidden on the Sabbath even though they neither resemble nor lead to prohibited work. Why then were they forbidden? Because Scripture says, "If you turn away your foot because of the Sabbath, from pursuing your business on My holy day. . . . And you shall honor it, not doing your wonted ways, nor pursuing your business, nor speaking thereof" (Is. 58:13). Accordingly, one is forbidden to go anywhere on the Sabbath in connection with his business, or even to talk about it. Thus one may not discuss with his partner what to sell on the next day, or what to buy, or how to construct a certain house, or what merchandise to take to such-and-such a place. All this and its like are forbidden, because Scripture says "nor speaking thereof"; speech is thus forbidden, but thinking of business is permitted.

❨ 2 One may not go to visit his vegetable gardens or his fields on the Sabbath in order to ascertain what they need or to observe the state of the crops, because this constitutes a walk in pursuit of his business. Similarly, one may not walk on the Sabbath to the end of the Sabbath limit and then stay there until nightfall, in order to be nearer to the place where he has business to attend to after the termination of the Sabbath, because this, too, would constitute a walk on the Sabbath in pursuit of his business.

❨ 4 . . . Prolonged idle conversation is forbidden on the Sabbath, for when Scripture says, "nor speaking thereof," it indicates that one's conversation on the Sabbath should not be the same as on weekdays.

❡ 5 It is permissible to run on the Sabbath in order to perform a religious duty, for example, to run to the synagogue or to the schoolhouse. One may also make any calculation or take any measurement that is required for a religious purpose. For example, one may measure a ritual bath to discover whether it contains the prescribed minimum quantity of water, or a piece of cloth to see whether it is large enough to be susceptible of ritual uncleanness. One may also allot charity to the poor or walk to the synagogue or to the schoolhouse—or even to a Gentile theater or hall—to attend to affairs of public concern on the Sabbath. One may discuss the betrothal of a young girl, arrange for a boy to be taught book-learning or a trade, visit the sick, or comfort people in mourning. If one visits a sick person on the Sabbath he should say, "It is Sabbath, and so I may not utter a supplication for your suffering; but your cure will come very soon!"

One may wait for nightfall at the end of the Sabbath limit in order to attend to the needs of a bride or to provide for the burial of the dead—that is, to bring a coffin or a shroud for him. In such circumstances one may say to another person, "Go to such-and-such a place first, and if you cannot get what is needed there, get it at this other place," or "If you cannot procure it for one hundred zuz, pay two hundred"; so long as no exact price is mentioned. All such acts and similar ones are permissible because they involve religious duties, and when Scripture says, "from pursuing business" (Is. 58:13), it implies that one's own business is forbidden, but God's business is permitted.

❡ 12 The sages have forbidden the moving of certain articles on the Sabbath in the way they are moved on weekdays. Why did they enact such a prohibition? The sages reasoned thus: inasmuch as the prophets have admonished us and commanded us not to walk on the Sabbath in the way we walk on weekdays, nor to converse on the Sabbath in the way we converse on weekdays—for Scripture says "nor speaking thereof" (Is. 58:13)—how much more should one refrain from moving articles on the Sabbath in the way they are moved on weekdays, in order that he should not regard the Sabbath as if it were a weekday, and so be led to lift and rearrange articles from one corner to another or from one room to another, or to put stones out of the way, or do similar things. For since one is at leisure and at home, he would look about for some occupation, and the result would be that he would not rest at all, and would disregard the Scriptural reason for the Sabbath, namely, "that your manservant and your maidservant may rest as well as you" (Deut. 5:14).

(13 Moreover, if he were to examine and move utensils used for prohibited work he might absent-mindedly handle them a little and thus be led to do prohibited work. Another reason is that there are people who have no trade or craft, but spend their whole life in idleness, such as loafers and loungers at street corners who refrain from doing work all their lives. If it were permissible to walk and talk and handle articles on the Sabbath in the ordinary weekday manner, such people would not be recognizably resting on the Sabbath at all. Accordingly, abstention from the aforementioned acts is the one form of rest which is applicable to all persons alike. It is for all these reasons that the sages have enacted a prohibition against moving articles about and, as will be explained in subsequent chapters, forbade one to move on the Sabbath any article not actually required.

Chapter 30

(1 Four duties have been formulated with reference to the Sabbath, two on Scriptural authority, and two on the authority of the scribes, being explicitly mentioned in the prophets. Scripture says "Remember" (Ex. 20:8) and "Observe" (Deut. 5:12), while the prophets explicitly mention "Honor and Delight" in the verse, "And call the Sabbath a delight, and the holy of the Lord clothed with honor" (Is. 58:13).

(2 What is meant by "honor"? This is explained by the statement of the sages that in order to honor the Sabbath one should, as a matter of religious duty, wash his face, hands, and feet with hot water on Friday, wrap himself in a fringed garment, and sit in a dignified manner waiting to receive the Sabbath, just as if one were going forth to meet the king. Indeed, the sages of old used to assemble their disciples on Friday night, put on their best clothes, and say, "Come, let us go forth to meet Sabbath, the king."

(3 Honoring the Sabbath involves also putting on clean clothes, so as not to wear the same clothes on both weekdays and Sabbaths. If one has no other change of clothes, he should let down his cloak, so that it would not look the same as it does on weekdays. Moreover, Ezra has enacted the rule that in honor of the Sabbath people should wash their clothes on Thursdays.

❲4 In order that the Sabbath should be suitably honored, it is forbidden to set a banquet or a drinking party for Friday afternoon. Furthermore, while eating and drinking are permissible until nightfall, one should, in honor of the Sabbath, refrain from having a regular meal from the time of the afternoon prayer onward, in order to enter into the Sabbath with an appetite for food.

❲5 One should set his table properly for Friday night, even if he feels no need for more than an olive's bulk of food. Similarly, one should set his table properly at the end of the Sabbath, even if he requires no more than an olive's bulk of food—in order to honor the Sabbath at both its commencement and its termination. One should also, in honor of the Sabbath, get his room ready while it is still day on Friday, by having a lamp lit, a table laid, and a couch properly spread. For all these are marks of reverence for the Sabbath.

❲6 Even if one is a person of very high rank and does not as a rule attend to the marketing or the other household chores, he should nevertheless himself perform one of these tasks in preparation for the Sabbath, for that is his way of honoring it. There were some among the sages of old who split firewood for the cooking; others cooked or salted meat, plaited wicks, lit lamps, or went to market to buy food or drink for the Sabbath, although none of these sages customarily performed such tasks on weekdays. Indeed, the more one does in the way of such preparation, the more praiseworthy he is.

❲7 What is Sabbath's delight? This is explained by the statement of the sages that one should prepare for the Sabbath the richest victuals and the choicest beverages that one can afford. The more one spends for the Sabbath and for the preparation of numerous and tasty dishes, the more praiseworthy he is. If, however, one cannot afford this, it is sufficient to make the Sabbath a delight to prepare even a plain vegetable stew, or the like. For one is not obligated to humiliate himself by begging from others in order to provide a large quantity of food for the Sabbath, and indeed the sages of old have said: "Make your Sabbath as a weekday, just so you depend not upon the charity of others."

❲8 If a person has been reared in luxury and wealth, so that all of his days are like a Sabbath, he should make his Sabbath food differ in some way from his weekday food. If no change is possible, he should at least vary the times of his meals, by eating late if he usually eats early, or early if he usually eats late.

¶ 9 It is one's duty to eat three meals on the Sabbath, one in the evening, one in the morning, and one in the afternoon; he should be particularly careful to have no less than these three meals. Even an indigent person living on charity should eat three meals on the Sabbath. If, however, an abundance of food makes one ill, or if one fasts regularly, he is exempt from the duty of eating three meals.

At each of the three meals one should have wine to drink and two whole loaves for the benediction over the breaking of the bread. The same rule applies to festival meals.

¶ 10 If one can afford it, eating meals and drinking wine on the Sabbath constitutes Sabbath's delight. It is, however, forbidden to have one's meal with wine on a Sabbath or festival during the time of the lecture in the schoolhouse, and so the custom of the righteous men of old was as follows: On Sabbath morning one would go to the synagogue for the morning service and the additional Sabbath service, then return home to eat the second meal, then go to the schoolhouse and read Scripture and Mishnah until the afternoon, then recite the afternoon service, and finally return home and sit down to the third Sabbath meal—which would include wine—eating and drinking until the termination of the Sabbath.

¶ 15 Observance of the Sabbath and abstention from idolatry are each equivalent to the sum total of all other commandments of the Law. Furthermore, the Sabbath is an eternal sign between the Holy One, blessed be He, and ourselves. Accordingly, if one transgresses any of the other commandments he is merely a wicked Israelite, but if he publicly desecrates the Sabbath he is the same as an idol worshiper, although both of these are regarded as heathens in every respect. Hence the prophet says in praise of the Sabbath observer, "Happy is the man that does this, and the son of man that holds fast by it: that keeps the Sabbath from profaning it," etc. (Is. 56:2). Furthermore, with regard to him who observes the Sabbath in full accordance with the rules thereof, and honors it and delights in it to the utmost of his ability, the prophet describes explicitly his reward in this world, over and above the reward laid up for him in the world to come, in the following verse: "Then shall you delight yourself in the Lord, and I will make you to ride upon the high places of the earth, and I will feed you with the heritage of Jacob your father; for the mouth of the Lord has spoken it" (Is. 58:14).*

*See *Guide*, III, chs. 29, 32, and 35.

REPOSE ON THE FESTIVALS

Chapter 6

⟦ 16 The commandment to honor the Sabbath and make it a delight applies equally to all the festivals. For Scripture says, "And call . . . the holy of the Lord clothed with honor" (Is. 58:13), and to each of the festivals it applies the term, "a holy convocation" (Lev. 23:2 passim; Num. 28:18 passim). We have explained the meaning of "honor" and "delight" in the Laws Concerning the Sabbath. It is likewise proper for one to refrain from having a full meal during the afternoon of the eve of a festival, just as one should refrain from it on the eve of the Sabbath, for this is one of the ways of showing honor. Furthermore, he who treats the festivals with contempt is like one who attaches himself to idol worship.

⟦ 17 The seven days of Passover, the eight days of the Feast of Tabernacles, and the other festival days, are all days on which funeral eulogies and fasting are forbidden. It is one's duty to rejoice and be of cheerful heart on these days, together with his children, his wife, his grandchildren, and all the other members of his household, for Scripture says, "And you shall rejoice in your feast, you and your son and your daughter," etc. (Deut. 16:14). Although rejoicing in this context refers to the peace offering to be brought on festivals, as we shall explain in the Laws Concerning the Festal Offering, it includes also the duty incumbent upon each man, his children, and his household, to rejoice in the appropriate manner.

⟦ 18 Thus children should be given parched ears, nuts, and other dainties; women should have clothes and pretty trinkets bought for them, according to one's means; and men should eat meat and drink wine, for there can be no real rejoicing without meat to eat and wine to drink. And while one eats and drinks himself, it is his duty to feed the stranger, the orphan, the widow, and other poor and unfortunate people, for he who locks the doors to his courtyard and eats and drinks with his wife and family, without giving anything to eat and drink to the poor and the bitter in soul—his meal is not a rejoicing in a divine commandment, but a rejoicing in his own stomach. It is of such persons that Scripture says, "Their sacrifices shall be to them as the bread of mourners, all that eat thereof shall be polluted; for their bread is for their own appetite" (Hos. 9:4). Rejoicing of this kind is a disgrace to those who indulge in it, as Scripture says, "And I will spread dung upon your faces, even the dung of your sacrifices" (Mal. 2:3).*

❡ 19 Although eating and drinking on festivals are included in the positive commandment to rejoice on those days, one should not eat and drink all day long, the proper procedure being as follows: In the morning, people should go early to the synagogue or the schoolhouse, recite the prayers and read the lesson in the Law appropriate to the day, and then return home and eat. Then they should return to the schoolhouse and study Scripture or Mishnah until noon. After noon they should recite the afternoon prayer, and then return home and eat and drink for the rest of the day until nightfall.

❡ 20 When one eats and drinks and rejoices on a festival day, he should not overindulge in wine, merriment, and frivolity, in the belief that the more he does of this the more he is fulfilling the commandment to rejoice. For drunkenness, excessive merrymaking, and frivolity are not rejoicing but madness and folly, and we were commanded to indulge not in madness and folly but in the kind of rejoicing which partakes of the worship of the Creator of all things. For Scripture says, "Because you did not serve the Lord your God with joyfulness, and with gladness of heart, by reason of the abundance of all things" (Deut. 28:47), showing that one should serve God with joyfulness, whereas it is impossible to serve God in the mood created by merriment, frivolity, or drunkenness.

THE PALM BRANCH

Chapter 8

❡ 12 Although a commandment prescribes rejoicing on all festivals, there was a day of special rejoicing in the Temple during the Feast of Tabernacles, in accordance with the verse, "And you shall rejoice before the Lord your God seven days" (Lev. 23:40). What was the procedure? On the eve of the first day of the festival, a raised section for women and a lower section for men were set up in the Tem-

*See Book I, Moral Dispositions, V, 1.

ple—to ensure that the sexes did not mix. Rejoicing began at the termination of the first day of the festival; on each of the intermediate days it began after the regular afternoon sacrifice had been offered, and went on for the rest of the day and the whole of the following night.

❨ 13 What form did this rejoicing take? Fifes sounded, and harps, lyres, and cymbals were played. Whoever could play a musical instrument did so, and whoever could sing, sang. Others stamped their feet, slapped their thighs, clapped their hands, leaped, or danced, each one to the best of his ability, while songs and hymns of praise were being recited. However, this rejoicing did not take place on the Sabbath or on the first day of the festival.

❨ 14 It was a religious duty to make this rejoicing as great as possible, but participation in it was not open to non-scholars or anyone else who wished to take part. Only the great scholars in Israel, heads of academies, members of the Sanhedrin, elders, and men distinguished for their piety and good deeds—these only danced and clapped, made music, and rejoiced in the Temple during the Feast of Tabernacles. Everyone else, men and women, came to watch and listen.

❨ 15 Rejoicing in the fulfillment of the commandment and in love for God who had prescribed the commandment is a supreme act of divine worship. One who refrains from participation in such rejoicing deserves to be punished, as it is said, "Because you did not serve the Lord your God with joyfulness, and with gladness of heart" (Deut. 28:47). If one is arrogant and stands on his own dignity, and thinks only of self-aggrandizement on such occasions, he is both a sinner and a fool. It was this that Solomon had in mind when he uttered the warning, "Glorify not yourself in the presence of the King" (Prov. 25:6). Contrariwise, one who humbles and makes light of himself on such occasions achieves greatness and honor, for he serves the Lord out of sheer love. This is the sentiment expressed by David, king of Israel, when he said, "And I will be yet more vile than this, and will be base in mine own sight" (II Sam. 6:22). True greatness and honor are achieved only by rejoicing before the Lord, as it is said, "King David leaping and dancing before the Lord," etc. (ibid. 6:16).

SANCTIFICATION OF THE NEW MOON

Chapter 11

❡ 1 From what has been stated in the preceding paragraphs (I, 6; II, 4; VI, 1), that the court used to engage in accurate calculations in order to ascertain whether or not the new crescent could be visible (on the eve of the 30th day of the month), we realize that any person with an alert spirit and curiosity for these delicate and hidden matters of scientific knowledge should be eager to learn about the methods of calculation which enable one to ascertain whether the new crescent might or might not be visible on that night.

❡ 2 As to these methods of calculation, many and great are the dissensions among the sages of the ancient peoples who used to engage in the study of astronomy and mathematics. Some great scholars blundered and overlooked certain things, and they were therefore beset by doubts. Other scholars conducted much research, yet missed the right way of performing the calculations pertaining to the visibility of the new moon: "they dived into mighty waters and came back with a potsherd in their hands."

❡ 3 In the long run, however, and after a great deal of observation and research, some scholars did find the correct methods for these calculations. Moreover, we have traditions, handed down by the sages, concerning these propositions and proofs that are not found recorded in books that are commonly accessible. Therefore I have deemed it fit to expound here the methods of these calculations in order to make them available to "every one whose heart stirred him up to come to the work to do it" (Ex. 36:2).

❡ 4 You should not, however, make light of these methods because of the fact that at the present age we no longer depend on them; for these methods are indeed remote and deep, and they constitute the Secret of the Calendar, which was known only to the great sages and which they were not permitted to reveal to anyone except to ordained and sagacious (disciples). On the other hand, the calculations which we use (for the fixed calendar) today, when there is no court qualified to proclaim the new month according to observation, are such that even schoolchildren can learn and fully grasp them in three or four days.

❡ 5 Some (readers of this book) who have studied Greek science, be they Gentile scholars or Jewish scholars, will perhaps notice that some of the methods used by me for the calculation of the visibility of the new moon operate by more or less close approximation, and they would suspect that this is due to inadvertence or ignorance on our part. Let them not give room to such a suspicion; for if we have not striven for complete exactitude (in our computations), it was only because we knew by positive mathematical proofs that such a procedure need not alarm us, since it will by no means affect the correct determination of the time of the visibility of the new moon, and this is why we have not aimed at minute exactness.

❡ 6 Similarly, should a reader observe that one or another of the methods leads to some minor shortage in the computation applicable to that method, let him realize that we have allowed that shortage intentionally; as against this, another result, obtained by another method, yields a surplus (that will balance the shortage), so that the final result will contain the correct figure, notwithstanding that it has been obtained by approximate values. In this way we were able to avoid long and complicated calculations which are of no practical value for the determination of the visibility of the new moon, and may only lead to the confusion and bewilderment of the layman, who is not trained in such matters.

Chapter 17

❡ 25 As regards the logic for all these calculations—why we have to add a particular figure or deduct it, how all these rules originated, and how they were discovered and proved—all this is part of the science of astronomy and mathematics, about which many books have been composed by Greek sages—books that are still available to the scholars of our time. But the books which had been composed by the sages of Israel, of the tribe of Issachar, who lived in the time of the prophets, have not come down to us. But since all these rules have been established by sound and clear proofs, free from any flaw and irrefutable, we need not be concerned about the identity of their authors, whether they were Hebrew prophets or Gentile sages. For when we have to do with rules and propositions which have been demonstrated by good reasons and have been verified to be true by sound and flawless proofs, we rely upon the author who has discovered them or has transmitted them only because of his demonstrated proofs and verified reasoning.*

Chapter 18

(14 . . . But the foregoing statements . . . have only an academic value; for our purpose was merely to enumerate all the rules governing the visibility of the new moon, in order to "make the law great and glorious" (Is. 42:41).

Chapter 19

(13 We have now expounded all the methods of calculation required for the determination of the visibility of the new moon and for the examination of witnesses, so that discerning students might be able to learn everything about it. Thus they shall not miss this particular branch of the many branches of the Law and will have no need to roam and ramble about in other books in search of information on matters set forth in this treatise.

"Seek out of the book of the Lord and read;
None of these [truths] shall be missing" (Is. 34:16).†

FAST DAYS

Chapter 1

(1 A positive Scriptural commandment prescribes prayer and the sounding of an alarm with trumpets whenever trouble befalls the community. For when Scripture says, "Against the adversary that oppresses you, then you shall sound an alarm with the trumpets"

*See *Eight Chapters*, foreword.
†See *Mishneh Torah*, introduction.

(Num. 10:9), the meaning is: Cry out in prayer and sound an alarm against whatsoever is oppressing you, be it famine, pestilence, locusts, or the like.

❨ 2 This procedure is one of the roads to repentance, for as the community cries out in prayer and sounds an alarm when overtaken by trouble, everyone is bound to realize that evil has come upon him as a consequence of his own evil deeds, as it is written, "Your iniquities have turned away these things, and your sins have withheld good from you" (Jer. 5:25), and that his repentance will cause the trouble to be removed.

❨ 3 If, on the other hand, the people do not cry out in prayer and do not sound an alarm, but merely say that it is the way of the world for such a thing to happen to them, and that their trouble is a matter of pure chance, they have chosen a cruel path which will cause them to persevere in their evil deeds and thus bring additional troubles upon them. For when Scripture says, "But walk contrary to Me; then I will walk contrary to you in fury" (Lev. 26:27–28), the meaning is: If, when I bring trouble upon you in order to cause you to repent, you say that the trouble is purely accidental, then I will add to your trouble the fury appropriate to such an "accident."*

❨ 17 On each fast day undertaken by a community beset by troubles, the court and the elders should remain in session at the synagogue from the end of the morning service until midday, to examine into the conduct of the citizens and to remove the obstacles to righteous living provided by transgressions. They should carefully search and inquire after those guilty of extortion and similar crimes, in order to set them apart, and those who act high-handedly, in order to humble them, and after other such matters. From midday until evening should be spent as follows: For the third quarter of the day, the Scriptural blessings and imprecations should be read, in accordance with the verse, "My son, despise not the chastening of the Lord, neither spurn His correction" (Prov. 3:11), with the lesson from the prophets consisting of admonitions having reference to the particular trouble involved. During the last quarter of the day, the afternoon service should be held and everyone, to the best of his ability, should recite supplications, cry out in prayer, and confess his sins.

*See *Epistle to Yemen*; Letter on Astrology; *Guide*, III, ch. 36.

Chapter 4

❡ 1 On each of the last seven fast days imposed on the whole community on account of deficiency of rain, the order of prayer used to be as follows: The Ark was taken out to the town's market place, and the whole population assembled attired in sackcloth. Ashes were placed upon the Ark and upon the scroll of the Law, in order to intensify the weeping and humble the people's hearts. One of the people then took some of the ashes and placed them upon the head of the patriarch and upon the head of the chief member of the court, at the spot where the phylacteries are worn, to make them feel ashamed and cause them to repent. Then everyone else took some ashes and put them on his own head.

❡ 2 Thereupon, while everybody was seated, an elder scholar stood up among them—if there was no elder scholar present, a younger scholar stood up in his place; if there was neither an elder nor a younger scholar present, someone of imposing appearance stood up instead. Addressing words of exhortation to the gathering, he spoke as follows: "My brethren, neither sackcloth nor fasting is of any avail, only repentance and good deeds, as we find in the case of Nineveh, for Scripture does not say of the men of Nineveh, 'God saw their sackcloth and their fasting,' but 'God saw their works' (Jonah 3:10), and the prophet says further, 'Rend your hearts and not your garments' (Joel 2:13)." The speaker then added further exhortations along these lines, to the best of his ability, until he reduced his listeners' hearts to submission and caused them to repent completely.

❡ 3 After the speaker finished his words of exhortation, they proceeded to recite the service, appointing as reader someone eligible to recite the prayers on such fast days. If the speaker who had addressed them with words of exhortation was eligible, he was deputized to act also as reader; otherwise another person was appointed.

❡ 4 Who was regarded as eligible to recite the prayers on such fast days? A person who was accustomed to reciting prayers and reading from the Torah, the Prophets, and the Writings; one who had small children, yet was without means and was dependent upon his labor in the field; one whose household was free from transgression—i.e., none of whose sons, household members, relatives, or other dependents was a transgressor—and who had a blameless reputation in his youth; a person of humble disposition, and held in favor by the people, and one who understood melody and had a sweet voice. If an elder could be found with all these qualifications, he was given preference; otherwise one who was not an elder was appointed to lead the congregation in prayer, so long as he answered all these requirements.

Chapter 5

❲ 1   There are days which are observed by all Israel as fasts because tragic events happened on them, the object being to stir hearts and open the way to repentance, and to remind us of our own evil deeds, and of our fathers' deeds which were like ours, as a consequence of which these tragic afflictions came upon them and upon us. For as we remember these things we ought to repent and do good, in accordance with the Scriptural verse, "And they shall confess their iniquity and the iniquity of their fathers," etc. (Lev. 26:40).

❲ 2   These fast days are the following:

Tishri 3rd, because Gedaliah the son of Ahikam was slain on that day, thus extinguishing the last remaining ember of Israel's independence and making her exile complete.

Tevet 10th, because wicked Nebuchadnezzar, king of Babylon, invested Jerusalem on that day, placing it under siege and in sore straits.

Tammuz 17th, on which five things happened: the tables of the Law were broken, the daily burnt offering ceased just before the destruction of the First Temple, the walls of Jerusalem were breached just before the destruction of the Second Temple, wicked Apostomos burned the Law and set up an idol in the Temple.

❲ 3   Av 9th, on which five things happened: the decree was issued in the wilderness that the Israelites were not to enter the Holy Land, the Temple was destroyed both the first time and the second time, a great city named Bettar was captured—it contained thousands and myriads of Israelites and had a great king whom all Israel, including the greatest scholars, thought to be the King Messiah, but he fell into the hands of the Romans who slew them all, a calamity as great as that of the destruction of the Temple—and finally, on that day predestined to misfortune, the wicked Turnus Rufus plowed up the Temple site and its surroundings, in fulfillment of the Scriptural verse, "Zion shall be plowed as a field" (Micah 3:12; Jer. 26:18).

❲ 9   . . . The practice of the pious men of old, however, was as fol-

lows: On the eve of the ninth of Av, each man in his solitude would
be served with dry bread and salt, and he would dip this in water and
eat it while seated between the oven and the stove. He would wash it
down with a pitcher of water, drunk in sadness, desolation, and tears,
like a person seated before his dead kinsman. This procedure, or one
very much like it, is the one appropriate to scholars. In all my life, I
have never eaten cooked food—even cooked lentils—on the eve of
the ninth of Av, unless this day was a Sabbath.

❨ 16 A person who beholds the ruined cities of Judea should say,
"Your holy cities have become a wilderness" (Is. 64:9), and should
rend his garment. If he beholds the ruins of Jerusalem, he should say,
"Jerusalem, a desolation" (ibid.) and likewise rend his garment. If he
beholds the ruins of the Temple, he should say, "Our holy and our
beautiful house, where our fathers praised You, is burned with fire"
(ibid. 64:10), and again rend his garment.

At what point on the approach to Jerusalem is one obliged to
rend his garment? When he is past Mount Scopus. Then, when he
reaches the Temple, he must rend his garment again. If, however,
one comes upon the Temple first, by approaching from the direction
of the wilderness, he should rend his garment first for the Temple,
and then enlarge the rent for Jerusalem.

❨ 19 All the fast days mentioned above are destined to be abolished
in the time of the Messiah; indeed, they are destined to be turned
into festive days, days of rejoicing and gladness, in accordance with
the verse, "Thus says the Lord of hosts: The fast of the fourth
month, and the fast of the fifth, and the fast of the seventh, and the
fast of the tenth, shall be to the house of Judah joy and gladness,
and cheerful seasons; therefore love you truth and peace" (Zech.
8:19).

READING OF THE MEGILLAH AND HANUKKAH

Chapter 2

❨ 16 It is also one's duty to distribute charity to the poor on Purim
day, "the poor" meaning not fewer than two persons; each should be
given a separate gift—money, a cooked dish, or some other comesti-

ble. For when Scripture says, "and gifts to the poor" (Esther 9:22), it implies at least two gifts to two poor persons. No investigation should be made of applicants for such Purim money, rather it should be given to anyone who stretches out his hand. Nor may Purim money be diverted to any other charitable purpose.

¶ 17 It is preferable to spend more on gifts to the poor than on the Purim meal or on presents to friends. For no joy is greater or more glorious than the joy of gladdening the hearts of the poor, the orphans, the widows, and the strangers. Indeed, he who causes the hearts of these unfortunates to rejoice, emulates the Divine Presence, of whom Scripture says, "to revive the spirit of the humble, and to revive the heart of the contrite ones" (Is. 57:15).

Chapter 3

¶ 1 In the time of the Second Temple, when the Greeks ruled over Israel, they issued evil decrees against them, proscribing their religion and forbidding them to study the Law and to fulfill the command-ments. They laid hands on their property and on their daughters, and they entered the Temple and made breaches in it, and defiled that which was ritually pure. And Israel was in sore straits in conse-quence thereof, and suffered great persecution, until the God of our fathers took pity on them, and saved and delivered them from the hands of the Greeks. For the Hasmonean family of high priests won a victory in which they slew the Greeks, and saved Israel from their hands. They set up a king from among the priests, and restored Israel's kingdom for a period of more than two hundred years—until the destruction of the Second Temple.

¶ 2 The day on which the Israelites were victorious over their ene-mies and destroyed them was the twenty-fifth day of Kislev. When they re-entered the Temple, they found within its precincts only one cruse of ritually pure oil, enough to burn for but a single day. Yet they kept alight with it the required number of lamps for eight days, until they could press some olives and produce new ritually pure oil.

¶ 3 Consequently, the sages of that generation ruled that the eight days beginning with the twenty-fifth of Kislev should be days of rejoicing on which the Hallel is to be recited, and that on each one of the eight nights lamps should be lit at eventide over the doors of the houses, to serve as manifestation and revelation of the miracle.

These days are known as Hanukkah. Funeral eulogies and fasting are forbidden on them, just as they are on Purim, and the lighting of lamps on them is a commandment based on the authority of the scribes, analogous to the commandment to read the Megillah.

Chapter 4

❨ 12   The commandment to light the Hanukkah lamp is an exceedingly precious one, and one should be particularly careful to fulfill it, in order to make known the miracle, and to offer additional praise and thanksgiving to God for the wonders which He has wrought for us. Even if one has no food to eat except what he receives from charity, he should beg—or sell his garment to buy—oil and lamps, and light them.

❨ 13   If one has no more than a single penny and needs wine for the sanctification benediction of the Sabbath and oil to light the Hanukkah lamp, he should give preference to the purchase of oil for the Hanukkah lamp over the purchase of wine for the sanctification benediction. Since both commandments are based on the authority of the scribes, it is best to give preference to the Hanukkah lamp, since it serves as a memorial of the miracle of Hanukkah.

❨ 14   If such a poor man needs oil for both a Sabbath lamp and a Hanukkah lamp, or oil for a Sabbath lamp and wine for the sanctification benediction, the Sabbath lamp should have priority, for the sake of peace in the household, seeing that even a Divine Name might be erased to make peace between husband and wife. Great indeed is peace, forasmuch as the purpose for which the whole of the Law was given is to bring peace upon the world, as it is said, "Her ways are ways of pleasantness, and all her paths are peace" (Prov. 3:17).

BOOK FIVE: HOLINESS

*T*HE Book of Holiness, which concerns itself with the apparently disparate themes of forbidden foods and forbidden sexual unions, is actually unified thematically because "in these two regards God sanctified us and separated us from the nations." With regard to both classes of precepts it is said, "And I have set you apart from the peoples" (Lev. 20:26 and 20:24). The book's motto, significantly, is the verse from Psalms 119:133: "Order my footsteps by Your word, and let not any iniquity have dominion over me." Its laws provide training and discipline in the art of sublime, purposive living, showing how man should strive for purity of heart and action in all spheres of life. Nothing should be perfunctory, behavioral, purely biological.

Maimonides' elaborate description of the procedure of conversion—included here, by association, because of the laws in chapter XII which forbid marriage with Gentiles—reflects his uniform insistence upon the indispensability of knowledge of the theological premises of Judaism. Note the special application and interpretation of Hosea 11:4. The concluding passage of the Laws of Slaughtering illustrates Maimonides' unflagging attempt to rationalize and spiritualize the commandments.

FORBIDDEN INTERCOURSE*

Chapter 14

❲ 1 In what manner are righteous proselytes to be received? When a heathen comes forth for the purpose of becoming a proselyte, and upon investigation no ulterior motive is found, the court should say to him, "Why do you come forth to become a proselyte? Do you not know that Israel is at present sorely afflicted, oppressed, despised, confounded, and beset by suffering?" If he answers, "I know, and I am indeed unworthy," he should be accepted immediately.

❲ 2 He should then be made acquainted with the principles of the faith, which are the oneness of God and the prohibition of idolatry. These matters should be discussed in great detail; he should then be told, though not at great length, about some of the less weighty and some of the more weighty commandments. Thereupon he should be informed of the transgressions involved in the laws of gleanings, forgotten sheaves, the corner of the field, and the poor man's tithe. Then he should be told of the punishment for violation of the commandments. How so? The court should say to him, "Be it known to you that before entering into this faith, if you ate forbidden fat, you did not incur the penalty of extinction; if you desecrated the Sabbath, you did not incur the penalty of death by stoning. But now, having become a proselyte, should you eat forbidden fat you will incur the penalty of extinction, and if you should profane the Sabbath, you will incur the penalty of death by stoning." This, however, should not be carried to excess nor to too great detail, lest it should make him weary and cause him to stray from the good way to the evil way. A person should be attracted at first only with pleasing and gentle words, as it is said first, "I will draw them with cords of a man," and only then "with bonds of love" (Hos. 11:4).

❲ 3 Just as the court should inform him of the punishment for transgression, so should they tell him of the reward for the observ-

*See Letter to Obadiah.

ance of the commandments. He should be assured that by performing these commandments he will be vouchsafed the life of the world
to come, and that there is no perfectly righteous man but the learned
man who performs these commandments properly and understands
them.

❰ 4   They should say to him further, "Be it known to you that the
world to come is treasured up solely for the righteous, who are Israel.
As for what you see that Israel is in distress in this world, it is in reality a boon which is laid up for them, because it is not granted them
to receive the abundance of good things in this world like other peoples, lest their hearts should wax haughty and they should go astray
and squander the reward of the world to come, as it is said, 'But
Jeshurun waxed fat and kicked' (Deut. 32:15)."

❰ 5   "Nevertheless, the Holy One, blessed be He, does not bring
upon them too many calamities, lest they should altogether perish.
Rather, all the heathen shall cease to exist, while they shall endure."
The court should expatiate on this point, by token of their affection
for him. If he then changes his mind and does not wish to accept, he
should be left to go on his way. But should he again accept, there
should be no further delay, and he should be at once circumcised. If
he is already circumcised, a drop of blood of the covenant should be
drawn from him, and the court should wait until he is completely
healed, after which he should be immersed.

Chapter 19

❰ 17   All families are presumed to be of valid descent, and it is permitted to intermarry with them in the first instance. Nevertheless,
should you see two families continually striving with one another, or
a family which is constantly engaged in quarrels and altercations, or
an individual who is exceedingly contentious with everyone, or is
excessively impudent, apprehension should be felt concerning them,
and it is advisable to keep one's distance from them, for these traits
are indicative of invalid descent. Similarly, if a man always casts
aspersions upon other people's descent—for instance, if he alleges
that certain families and individuals are of blemished descent and
refers to them as being bastards—suspicion is justified that he himself may be a bastard. And if he says that they are slaves, one may
suspect that he himself is a slave, since whosoever blemishes others
projects upon them his own blemish. Similarly, if a person exhibits

impudence, cruelty, or misanthropy, and never performs an act of kindness, one should strongly suspect that he is of Gibeonite descent, since the distinctive traits of Israel, the holy nation, are modesty, mercy, and lovingkindness, while of the Gibeonites it is said, "Now the Gibeonites were not of the children of Israel" (II Sam. 21:2), because they hardened their faces and refused to relent, showing no mercy to the sons of Saul, nor would they do a kindness to the children of Israel by forgiving the sons of their king, notwithstanding that Israel showed them grace at the beginning and spared their lives.*

Chapter 22

❪ 18 There is no prohibition in the whole of Scripture which the generality of the people experience greater difficulty in observing than the interdict of forbidden unions and illicit intercourse. The sages have declared that when Israel was given the commandments concerning forbidden unions, they wept and accepted this injunction with grumbling and wailing, as it is said, "weeping in their families" (Num. 11:10), i.e., weeping on account of the matter of family relations.†

❪ 19 The sages have declared further that the soul of man lusts after larceny and forbidden unions and covets them. At no time can one find a community which does not contain libertines indulging in forbidden unions and illicit intercourse. And the sages have declared also, "The majority of men are guilty of larceny, the minority of forbidden unions, and all of them together of the tendency to evil tongue."

❪ 20 Consequently, it behooves a man to subdue his inclination toward these vices and to inure himself to unbounded sanctity, pure thought, and disciplined moral disposition, so as to be saved from such transgressions. Above all, he should be on guard against improper seclusion, since this is the chief contributory factor to unchastity. The greatest of our sages used to say to their disciples, "Warn me to beware of my daughter, warn me to beware of my daughter-in-law," in order to teach their disciples not to feel embarrassed in such matters and to keep away from improper seclusion.

*See Book VII, Gifts to the Poor, X, 2.

†See Book II, Laws of Prayer, XIII, 11.

❨ 21   In like manner, man should keep away from levity, drunkenness, and lewd discourse, since these are great contributory factors
and degrees leading to forbidden unions. Nor should a man live without a wife, since married estate is conducive to great purity. But
above all this, as the sages have declared, a man should direct his
mind and thoughts to the words of Torah and enlarge his understanding with wisdom, for unchaste thoughts prevail only in the
heart devoid of wisdom, and of wisdom it is said, "a hind of love and
a doe of grace, let her breasts satisfy you at all times, with her love be
you ravished always" (Prov. 5:19).

SLAUGHTERING

Chapter 1

❨ 1   It is a positive commandment that whosoever wishes to eat of
the flesh of a domestic animal, wild beast, or bird, must first perform
shehitah upon it, and only thereafter may he eat of it, as it is said,
"and you shall kill of your herd and of your flock" (Deut. 12:21).
Scripture also says with regard to a blemished firstling, "even as the
roebuck and the hart is eaten, so shall you eat them" (ibid. 12:22).
Thus you learn that a wild beast is in the same category as a domestic animal in respect to shehitah. In regard to birds Scripture says,
"And whichsoever man . . . takes in hunting any beast or bird
that may be eaten, he shall pour out the blood thereof" (Lev.
17:13), which teaches that the slaughtering of a bird is to be performed in the same manner as the slaughtering of a beast. There is
thus but one law of shehitah applying to all of them.

❨ 4   This method of slaughtering, which is mentioned in the Torah
without definition, must needs be explained, in order to know upon
what organ of the animal shehitah is to be performed, what is the
extent of shehitah, with what instrument and when, where, and how
it is to be performed, what things invalidate it, and who may perform it. All these matters are contained in the general commandment of the Torah, "then shall you kill of your herd and your flock

as I have commanded you, and you shall eat within your gates" (Deut. 12:21), which means that Moses was commanded concerning all these matters orally, as in the case of the rest of the Oral Law, which is referred to as "commandment," as we have explained in the introduction to this work.*

Chapter 14

❡ 16 When one performs the commandment of covering up the blood, he should do it not with his foot, but with his hand, or with a knife or utensil, so as not to conduct the performance of the commandment in a contemptuous manner, thus treating God's commandments with scorn. For reverence is due not to the commandments themselves, but to Him who has issued them, blessed be He, and who delivered us from groping in the darkness by making the commandments a lamp to straighten out the crooked places and a light to teach us the paths of uprightness. And so indeed Scripture says, "Your word is a lamp to my feet, and a light to my path" (Ps. 119:105).

*See above, Maimonides' Introduction. This is the only cross reference to the introduction in the entire code.

BOOK SIX: ASSEVERATIONS

*T*HE common denominator of the four sections of this book is their concern with legal obligations and responsibilities engendered not by a person's actions but by his spoken words. The "utterance of one's lips" is sacred and, therefore, binding. Taking an oath in God's name is even a means of honoring and sanctifying Him (Oaths, ch. XI).

The following selections illustrate some significant intellectual and ethical principles emphasized by Maimonides. The passage from Oaths, ch. V, is noteworthy—perhaps unique—in indicating how the differences between the learned and unlearned have halakhic repercussions. Maimonides' defense of the use of vows when carefully regulated and properly motivated and his balanced exposition of Naziriteship are basically congruent with the philosophic stance of the Guide. Indeed, in the Guide (III, ch. 35) Maimonides states that Book VI of the Mishneh Torah is conceptually associated with Book V because the "purpose of all this is ... to put an end to the lusts and licentiousness manifested in seeking what is most pleasurable and to taking the desire for food and drink as an end." The concluding paragraph poignantly reminds us that moderation is warranted even in completely spiritual acts. There is no exaltation or idealization of poverty.

OATHS

Chapter 1

❲ 1   There are four classes of oaths: the rashly uttered oath, the vain oath, the oath arising from a bailment, and the oath arising from testimony. . . .

❲ 4   Vain oaths are likewise divisible into four types. The first is an oath stating that a known fact is not a fact. For example, if one swears that a man is a woman, or that a woman is a man, or that a pillar of marble is made of gold, or anything similar to this.

❲ 5   The second is an oath stating that a known fact which no man doubts is indeed a fact. For example, if one swears that heaven is heaven, or that a particular stone is a stone, or that two are two, or anything similar to this. For no normal person is in any doubt about such a thing, that he should need to substantiate it by an oath.

❲ 7   . . . Whosoever swears a vain oath of one of these . . . types transgresses a negative commandment. For Scripture says, "You shall not take the name of the Lord your God in vain" (Ex. 20:7). . . .

Chapter 5

❲ 22   It is well known to wise men endowed with understanding and knowledge that the sun is 170 times larger than the earth. If an ordinary person swears that the sun is larger than the earth, he is not liable to a flogging because of a false oath. For although the fact is as stated, this is not commonly known to any but the most eminent scholars, and no person is liable unless he swears about a thing well known to at least three ordinary persons, e.g., that a man is a man, or a stone a stone. Similarly, if he swears that the sun is smaller than the earth, even though this is not so, he is not liable to a flogging. For this subject is not familiar to all men, and it is therefore not like swearing that a man is a woman, as he is merely swearing about the way the sun appears to him, and he does indeed see it small. This holds good in all similar cases connected with calculations dealing with astronomical cycles, constellations, and geometrical measurements, and other scientific matters which are known only to some men.

Chapter 11

❨ 1 Just as it is a negative commandment not to swear vainly or falsely, so is it a positive commandment that whosoever becomes subject to an oath in court should swear by the Divine Name. For the Scriptural statement "And by His name shall you swear" (Deut. 6:13) is a positive commandment, and swearing by His great and holy name is one of the ways of serving God, whereby He is greatly honored and sanctified.*

❨ 2 It is forbidden to swear by any other thing jointly with His name. Whosoever associates any other thing in an oath with the name of the Holy One, blessed be He, is bound to be extirpated from the world. For none save the One, blessed be He, is fit to be accorded the honor of having men swear by His name.

❨ 3 A person is permitted—although already adjured in this respect by the oath at Mount Sinai—to swear to fulfill a commandment, in order to encourage himself; for Scripture says "I have sworn, and have confirmed it, to observe Your righteous ordinances" (Ps. 119:106).

❨ 14 Judges who administer the oath to the swearer in any language that he understands are acting properly; such was also the opinion of the Geonim. My teachers, however, taught that the oath should be administered only in the holy tongue; but this view need not be relied upon, and even though all courts customarily administer the oath in the holy tongue, the meaning of the oath should be explained to the swearer until he understands it. For the judicial oath is essentially an oath arising from a bailment. It is the general custom to administer the informal oath also in the holy tongue.

❨ 16 How is the swearer to be overawed? Those who administer the oath should say to him, "Be it known to you that the whole world was seized with trembling when the Holy One, blessed be He, said to Moses, 'You shall not take the name of the Lord your God in vain' (Ex. 20:7). Of all transgressions in Scripture it is written, 'And hold-

*See *Guide*, III, ch. 36.

ing guiltless' (Ex. 34:7), but here it is written, 'He will not hold guiltless' (Ex. 20:7). For all transgressions in Scripture the transgressor alone is punished, but here both he and his family who protect him are punished; indeed, he causes all Israel to be punished, since all Israel are sureties for one another, as it is written, 'Swearing, and lying, and killing,' etc., and after it, 'Therefore does the land mourn, and everyone that dwells therein does languish' (Hos. 4:2-3). The punishment for all transgressions in Scripture may remain suspended for two or three generations, if the transgressor possesses any merit, but here it is exacted immediately, as it is written, 'I cause it to go forth, says the Lord of hosts, and it shall enter into the house of the thief, and into the house of him that swear falsely by My name' (Zech. 5:4): 'I cause it to go forth,' *i.e.*, immediately; 'And it shall enter into the house of the thief,' i.e., one who deceives people, demanding money from his companion when he has no claim to it, and making him swear; 'Into the house of him that swears falsely by My name' is to be understood literally; 'And it shall consume it with the timber thereof and the stones thereof' (*ibid.*), *i.e.*, even things like stones which neither fire nor water can destroy are destroyed by a false oath."

(17 The full substance of this awesome admonition should be explained to the swearers in a language which they understand, so that they may comprehend the words, and so that the sinner may mend his way. If he then says, "I will not swear," he is to be held exempt and must surrender that which his companion claims. Similarly, if the plaintiff says, "I will not adjure him," and thus releases him from the claim, they may depart.

(18 If he says, "I am ready to swear," and his companion continues to press his claim, the bystanders should say one to another, "Depart, I pray you, from the tents of these wicked men" (Num. 16:26). Thereupon those who administer the oath should say to him, "We hereby administer the oath to you, not with the meaning you may give to it, but with the meaning we and the court give to it."

Chapter 12

(1 Although whosoever swears in vain or falsely is liable to a flogging, and whosoever swears an oath arising from testimony or from a bailment must bring an offering, the iniquity of the oath is not wholly expiated thereby. For Scripture says, "The Lord will not hold guiltless" (Ex. 20:7), *i.e.*, this transgressor will not be free from heavenly judgment until payment has been exacted from him also for his profanation of the great Name, of which it is written, "So that you profane the name of your God: I am the Lord" (Lev. 19:12). Hence a person should be more careful about this than about any other transgression.

❨ 2   This is one of the most grievous of sins, as we have explained in the Laws Concerning Repentance. For although it does not carry the penalty of excision or the death penalty imposed by the court, it involves desecration of the sacred Name, and this surpasses all sins.

❨ 3   If anyone swears by the heavens, the earth, the sun, or something similar, notwithstanding that he means no one but their Creator, this is no oath. Similarly, if anyone swears by one of the prophets or by one of the holy writings, although he means no one but Him who sent this prophet or commanded this writing, this is no oath. Nevertheless, while these are not oaths, the common people should be awesomely admonished concerning them and taught not to treat them frivolously, and should be given the impression that these are indeed oaths. Hence grounds for repeal should be suggested to them, and they should then be absolved from such oaths.

❨ 7   Minors who take an oath with full understanding of its significance, while under no obligation to fulfill it, should be compelled to do so, in order to train them and to deter them from taking oaths lightly. If, however, what they have sworn to do cannot be fulfilled by a child without injury to himself—for example, if he swears to fast or to eat no meat for a long time—his father or his teacher should spank him and rebuke him, and give him the impression that he is being absolved from his oath, in order to prevent him from becoming accustomed to take oaths lightly.

❨ 8   It is necessary to be exceptionally careful with children, so as to teach them to speak the truth without swearing, in order that they should not become accustomed to continual use of oaths, in the manner of the heathens. This procedure amounts to a duty incumbent upon their parents and upon the teachers of the young.*

❨ 11   It is forbidden not only to swear in vain, but to mention even without swearing one of the characteristic Names to no purpose. For Scripture has commanded "That you may fear this glorious and awesome Name, the Lord God" (Deut. 28:58), and the avoid-

*See Book XI, Theft, I, 10.

ance of mentioning Him to no purpose is included in the fear of Him. Consequently, if a person's tongue happens to slip and utters the Divine Name to no purpose, he should forthwith hasten to praise, glorify, and honor it, so that it would not have been mentioned to no purpose. For example, if he should inadvertently say "the Lord," he should immediately add "blessed be He for ever and ever," or "is great and greatly to be praised," or something like it, to prevent the Divine Name from having been uttered in vain.

❪ 12 Although it is permissible and not reprehensible to seek absolution from an oath, as we have explained—anyone whose mind is perturbed at this procedure is liable to suspicion of heresy*— nevertheless, it is proper to exercise caution in this matter, and such absolution should be granted only for the sake of a religious duty or because of dire necessity. It is best by far for a person not to swear at all, or if he breaks this rule and does swear, to suffer distress and fulfill his oath, for Scripture says, "He that swears to his own hurt and changes not," and later on, "He that does these things shall never be moved" (Ps. 15:4, 5).

ॐ

VOWS

Chapter 13

❪ 23 Whosoever makes vows in order to discipline his moral disposition and to improve his conduct displays commendable zeal and is worthy of praise. For instance, one who is a glutton and forbids to himself meat for a year or two; or one who is addicted to wine and forbids it to himself for a long time, or at least binds himself never to become inebriated; or one who runs after bribes in his eagerness to amass wealth and binds himself to accept no presents or to derive no benefit from the people of his country; or one who is proud of his good looks and vows to become a Nazirite; or anyone else who makes vows of this kind. All such vows are ways of serving God, and of them and their like the sages have said, "Vows are a fence around self-restraint."

*Karaites rejected this procedure. See also above, end of Maimonides' Introduction.

❲ 24 Yet in spite of the fact that vows are ways of serving God, one should not multiply prohibitory vows nor employ them regularly, but should rather abstain from such things as should properly be abstained from, without making vows to do so.

❲ 25 Indeed, the sages have said, "Whosoever makes a vow is as though he had built an unlawful altar." If he nevertheless transgresses and vows, it is his duty to seek absolution from the vow so that it might not become a snare before him. This, however, applies only to vows of prohibition. In the case of vows on consecration, it is one's duty to fulfill them and to seek absolution from them only under constraint, for Scripture says, "I will pay my vows to the Lord" (Ps. 116:18).

NAZIRITESHIP

Chapter 10

❲ 14 Whosoever says, "I intend to become a Nazirite if I do," or "do not do a certain thing," or something similar, is a wicked person, and this type of Naziriteship is accounted the Naziriteship of the wicked. On the other hand, whosoever vows to God in the way of holiness, does well and is praiseworthy. Of such a one Scripture says, "His consecration to God is upon his head . . . he is holy to the Lord" (Num. 6:7–8). Indeed Scripture considers him the equal of a prophet, for it says, "And I raised up of your sons for prophets, and of your young men for Nazirites" (Amos 2:11).*

VALUATIONS AND THINGS VOTIVE

Chapter 8

❲ 12 Although vows of consecration, devotion, and valuation are matters of religious duty, and it is fitting for a person to conduct

*See *Eight Chapters*, ch. IV.

himself in these things in such a manner as to subdue his inclination and avoid avarice, thus fulfilling the command of the prophets, "Honor the Lord with your substance" (Prov. 3:9), nevertheless, if he never makes any such vows, it does not matter at all, and Scripture itself bears witness to this when it says, "But if you shall forbear to vow, it shall be no sin in you" (Deut. 23:23).

⟨ 13 A person should never consecrate or devote all of his possessions. He who does the reverse acts contrary to the intention of Scripture, for it says, "of all that he has" (Lev. 27:28), not "all that he has," as was made clear by the sages. Such an act is not piety but folly, since he forfeits all his valuables and makes himself dependent upon other people who may show no pity toward him. Of such, and those like him, the sages have said, "The pious fool is one of those who cause the world to perish." Rather, whosoever wishes to expend his money in good deeds, should disburse no more than one fifth, in order that he might be, as the prophets have advised it, "one that orders his affairs rightfully" (Ps. 112:5), be it in matters of Torah or in the business of the world. Even in respect to the sacrifices which a person is obligated to offer, Scripture is sparing of his money, for it says that he may bring an offering in accordance with his means. All the more so in respect to those things for which he is not liable except in consequence of his own vow, should he vow only what is within his means, for Scripture says, "Every man shall give as he is able, according to the blessing of the Lord your God, which He has given you" (Deut. 16:17).*

*See Book I, Moral Dispositions, ch. I, V, 12; Book VII, Gifts to the Poor, ch. X; Guide, III, ch. 35.

MAIMONIDES' original classification of the "eight degrees of benevolence" is one of the gems of rabbinic literature, illustrating the need for sensitivity, tact, and graciousness in the act of charity. The formal, objective act of giving charity is deficient and defective if it is not characterized by kindness and sympathy. A benevolent act is easily vitiated by rudeness or impatience—hence the need, for example, to supplement hospitality with escorting one's guests. This is the meaning of the dictum that "the reward of charity depends entirely upon the measure of the kindness in it" (Sukkah 49b).

According to Maimonides, the purpose of most of the laws in the Book of Seeds is "instilling pity for the weak and the wretched, giving strength in various ways to the poor, and inciting us ... not to afflict the hearts of the individuals who are in a weak position." In other words, while the laws of this book are formally concerned with agriculture, tithing, first-fruits, and other gifts to the priests, the Sabbatical and Jubilee year, and related matters, they are substantively concerned with philanthropy, gifts to the needy, and the nurturing of a deep-seated altruism.

GIFTS TO THE POOR

Chapter 10

❡ 1 We are obligated to be more scrupulous in fulfilling the commandment of charity* than any other positive commandment because charity is the sign of the righteous man, the seed of Abraham our Father, as it is said, "For I know him, that he will command his children ... to do righteousness" (Gen. 18:19). The throne of Israel is established and the religion of truth is upheld only through charity, as it is said, "In righteousness shall you be established" (Is. 54:14). Israel is redeemed only through charity, as it is written, "Zion shall be redeemed with judgment and they that return of her with righteousness" (ibid. 1:27).

❡ 2 No man has ever become impoverished by giving charity and no evil or damage has ever resulted from charity, as it is said, "and the work of righteousness is peace" (Is. 32:17).

Whosoever displays mercy to others will be granted mercy himself, as it is said, "And He will grant you mercy, and have compassion upon you, and multiply you" (Deut. 13:18).

If someone is cruel and does not show mercy, there are sufficient grounds to suspect his lineage, since cruelty is found only among the other nations, as it is said, "They are cruel and will not show mercy" (Jer. 50:42).

All Jews and those attached to them are like brothers, as it is said, "You are sons to the Lord your God" (Deut. 14:1), and if a brother will not show mercy to his brother, then who will have mercy on him? And to whom can the poor of Israel look for help—to those other nations who hate and persecute them? They can look for help only to their brethren.

❡ 3 Whosoever refuses to give charity is called Belial, the same term which is applied to idol-worshipers. With regard to idol-worshipers it is said, "Certain base fellows [literally, children of

*The Hebrew word tzedakah is translated throughout as both righteousness and charity. See Guide, III, ch. 53; also ch. 39.

Belial*] have gone out" (Deut. 13:14), and with regard to those who refuse to give charity it is said, "Beware that there be not a base [Belial] thought in your heart." (ibid. 15:9); and he is called a wicked man, as it is said, "The tender mercies of the wicked are cruel" (Prov. 12:10); and he is called a sinner, as it is said. "And he cries to the Lord against you, and it be sin in you" (Deut. 15:9).

The Holy One, blessed be He, is close to the cries of the poor, as it is said, "You hear the cries of the poor" (paraphrase of Job 34:28). Therefore, one should heed their cries, for a covenant has been made with them, as it is said, "And when he will cry to Me I shall listen because I am merciful" (Ex. 22:26).

❡ 4 Whosoever gives charity to a poor man ill-manneredly and with downcast looks has lost all the merit of his action even though he should give him a thousand gold pieces. He should give with good grace and with joy and should sympathize with him in his plight, as it is said, "Did I not weep for him that was in trouble? Was not my soul grieved for the poor?" (Job 30:25). He should speak to him words of consolation and sympathy, as it is said, "And I gladdened the heart of the widow" (ibid. 29:13).

❡ 5 If a poor man requests money from you and you have nothing to give him, speak to him consolingly. It is forbidden to upbraid a poor person or to shout at him because his heart is broken and contrite, as it is said, "A broken and contrite heart, O God, You will not despise" (Ps. 51:19), and it is written, "To revive the spirit of the humble, and to revive the heart of the contrite" (Is. 57:10). Woe to him who shames a poor man. Rather one should be as a father to the poor man, in both compassion and speech, as it is said, "I am a father to the poor" (Job 29:15).

❡ 6 He who persuades and constrains others to give shall have a reward greater than that of the giver himself, as it is said, "And the work of righteousness shall be peace" (Is. 32:17). Concerning such that solicit charity (for others) and their like, it is said, "And they that turn the many to righteousness [shall shine] as the stars" (Dan. 12:3).

❡ 7 There are eight degrees of charity, one higher than the other. The highest degree, exceeded by none, is that of the person who assists a poor Jew by providing him with a gift or a loan or by accepting him into a business partnership or by helping him find employ-

*In Hebrew bene beliyaal.

ment—in a word, by putting him where he can dispense with other people's aid. With reference to such aid, it is said, "You shall strengthen him, be he a stranger or a settler, he shall live with you" (Lev. 25:35), which means strengthen him in such manner that his falling into want is prevented.

❡ 8 A step below this stands the one who gives alms to the needy in such manner that the giver knows not to whom he gives and the recipient knows not from whom it is that he takes. Such exemplifies performing the meritorious act for its own sake. An illustration would be the Hall of Secrecy in the ancient sanctuary where the righteous would place their gift clandestinely and where poor people of high lineage would come and secretly help themselves to succor.

The rank next to this is of him who drops money in the charity box. One should not drop money in the charity box unless one is sure that the person in charge is trustworthy, wise, and competent to handle the funds properly, as was Rabbi Hananya ben Teradyon.

❡ 9 One step lower is that in which the giver knows to whom he gives but the poor person knows not from whom he receives. Examples of this were the great sages who would go forth and throw coins covertly into poor people's doorways. This method becomes fitting and exalted, should it happen that those in charge of the charity fund do not conduct its affairs properly.

❡ 10 A step lower is that in which the poor person knows from whom he is taking but the giver knows not to whom he is giving. Examples of this were the great sages who would tie their coins in their scarves which they would fling over their shoulders so that the poor might help themselves without suffering shame.

❡ 11 The next degree lower is that of him who, with his own hand, bestows a gift before the poor person asks.

❡ 12 The next degree lower is that of him who gives only after the poor person asks.

❡ 13 The next degree lower is that of him who gives less than is fitting but gives with a gracious mien.

❡ 14 The next degree lower is that of him who gives morosely.

❡ 15 There have been great sages who, before praying, would give a coin to the needy, because it is said, "I will behold your face in righteousness" (Ps. 17:15).

¶ 16 A species of charity is the maintenance of one's minor sons and daughters who have passed the age at which the father is obligated to support them, provided the purpose of such maintenance be that of educating the sons in sacred lore and of keeping the daughter in the right path, removed from shame. Similarly to be classed as charity is the maintenance of one's father and mother.

In giving charity, precedence should be accorded to one's own relatives.

He who lets poor people and orphans partake of food and drink at his table shall call upon the Lord and find, to his delight, that the Lord will answer, as it is said, "Then shall you call and the Lord will answer" (Is. 58:9).

¶ 17 The sages have enjoined that one's domestics should consist not of bondmen but of poor folk and orphans. Better to employ the latter and let the descendants of Abraham, Isaac, and Jacob benefit from one's possessions than to have that advantage go to the seed of Ham. Day by day, one who adds to the number of his bondmen augments the world's sin and iniquity. But hour by hour, one who takes the poor as members of his household increases virtue and merit.

¶ 18 A man should always exert himself and should sooner endure hardship than throw himself, as a dependent, upon the community. The sages admonished, "Make your Sabbath a weekday, sooner than become dependent." Even one who is learned and honored should, if impoverished, work at various trades, yes, despicable trades, in order to avoid dependency. Better to strip the hides of beasts that have sickened and died than to tell people, "I am a great sage, my class is that of a priest, support me." Thus spoke the sages.

Outstanding scholars worked as hewers of wood, as carriers of beams, as drawers of garden water, as iron workers, as blacksmiths, rather than ask anything of the community and rather than accept any proffered gratuity.*

¶ 19 He who, having no need of alms, obtains alms by deception will, ere he die of old age, fall into a dependency that is real. Such a person comes under the characterization: "Cursed is the man that trusts in man" (Jer. 17:5).

One, however, who does stand in need, and who, like an aged or sick or afflicted person, cannot live without help but who, in his pride, declines to accept help is a shedder of blood, guilty of

*Cf. above, Book I, Study, ch. III; Book III, Sabbath, XXX, 7.

attempts on his own life. Out of his misery, he gets naught but tres-
passes and sins.

But one, impoverished otherwise, who endures privation and
exerts himself and lives a life of hardships rather than burden the
community will, ere he die of old age, possess the means out of
which he will succor others. Concerning such a person, it is written,
"Blessed is the man that trusts in the Lord" (Jer. 17:7).

SABBATICAL YEAR AND THE JUBILEE

Chapter 13

⟨ 12 Why did the tribe of Levi not acquire a share in the Land of
Israel and in its spoils together with their brothers? Because this tribe
was set apart to serve God and to minister to Him, to teach His
straight ways and righteous ordinances to the multitudes, as is written:
"They shall teach Jacob Your ordinances and Israel Your law"
(Deut. 33:10). Therefore, they were set apart from the ways of the
world; they do not wage war like the rest of Israel, nor do they inherit
land or acquire anything for themselves by their physical prowess.
They are rather the army of God, as is written: "Bless, Lord, his substance" (ibid. 33:11).* He, blessed be He, acquires (goods) for them,
as is written: "I am your portion and your inheritance" (Num. 18:20).

⟨ 13 Not only the tribe of Levi but every single individual from
among the world's inhabitants whose spirit moved him and whose
intelligence gave him the understanding to withdraw from the world
in order to stand before God to serve and minister to Him, to know
God, and he walked upright in the manner in which God made him,
shaking off from his neck the yoke of the manifold contrivances which
men seek—behold, this person has been totally consecrated and God
will be his portion and inheritance forever and ever. God will acquire
for him sufficient goods in this world just as he did for the priests and
Levites. Behold, David, may he rest in peace, says: "Lord, the portion
of my inheritance and of my cup, You maintain my lot" (Ps. 16:5).

*The word "hayil," translated as substance, also means "army."

BOOK EIGHT: SERVICE

BOOK NINE: SACRIFICES

*T*HE historical period during which part of the law was in abeyance
was, in Maimonides' opinion, an anomaly, a fleeting moment in the
pattern of eternity. The real historical dimensions were those in
which the Torah and its precepts were fully realized, that is, the time
after the restoration of the Davidic dynasty when "all the ancient
laws will be reinstituted ... sacrifices will again be offered, the Sabbatical and Jubilee years will again be observed . . ." (Book XIV,
Kings, ch. XI). Consequently, the Mishneh Torah attends to such
"antiquated" subjects as laws pertaining to the Temple and sacrifices.
One is impressed with the meticulousness and the exhaustiveness
which characterize Maimonides' treatment of the Temple, its sanctity, its architecture, its vessels, the duties of the priests and Levites
attending to it, the detailed regulations concerning communal and
individual offerings. In terms of the study of the law, there should be
no differences between the theoretical and the practical.

The following points deserve special attention:

(1) When speaking of "things which are for the sake of God,"
Maimonides mentions, all in the same breath, consecrating objects,
constructing synagogues, and feeding the hungry (Things Prohibited,

VII, 11). *All require true nobility of soul and generosity of spirit and are antagonistic to greediness and pettiness. All are divinely oriented. Compare the passage in Book XII (Sales, ch. XXII) where Maimonides rules that obligating oneself for charitable contributions conforms to the same procedure as consecrating objects to God.*

(2) The selection from Daily Offerings is a good example of anti-Karaite polemics, insisting upon the inseparability and inviolability of the oral and written traditions. The Karaite repudiation of the rabbinic-Talmudic tradition was a serious challenge and irritant to rabbinic scholars, who regularly responded to this challenge. (See Book III, Sabbath, II, 3; Book VI, Oaths, XII, 12.)

(3) Trespass, VIII, 8 is the classic formulation of the Maimonidean directive "to seek out the reasons for all commandments," to try to penetrate to the essence and real motive powers of the laws of the Torah, coupled with the warning to obey all laws even when we fail to understand or rationalize them.

(4) The above program is briefly repeated in the last selection from Book IX (Substitute Offerings, IV, 13) where Maimonides notes, in addition, that the purpose of the laws is to discipline man's evil tendencies and train him to overcome the innate inclination to greed and miserliness. Maimonides also alludes here to his basic theory (see Guide, III, ch. 27) that the Law in its entirety seeks to "improve the soul" by inculcating true beliefs and to "improve the body" by developing practical and moral virtues.

(5) The description and interpretation of the special assembly prescribed in Deut. 31:10—the reading of the Torah, with its emphasis on the experiential rather than intellectual aspects (Festal Offerings, ch. III)—should be read with care.

(6) The arrangement of material in these two books presents a problem for the reader interested in the classification of law (see introduction to Book III); Maimonides' statement that Book VIII deals with "regular public sacrifices" while Book IX covers "sacrifices brought by private individuals" is not entirely borne out by the facts.

◈

THE TEMPLE

Chapter 2

❨ 1 The site of the altar was defined very specifically and was never to be changed. For it is said: "This is the altar of burnt-offering for Israel" (I Chron. 22:1). It was on the site of the Temple that the patriarch Isaac was bound. For it is said: "And get you into the land of Moriah" (Gen. 22:2); and in the Book of Chronicles it is said: "Then Solomon began to build the house of the Lord at Jerusalem in Mount Moriah, where the Lord appeared to David his father; for which provision had been made in the Place of David, in the threshing-floor of Ornan the Jebusite" (II Chron. 3:1).

❨ 2 Now there was a tradition known to all that the place where David and Solomon built the altar in the threshing floor of Araunah was the same place where Abraham built the altar upon which he bound Isaac. This, too, was the place where Noah built an altar when he came out of the Ark. It was also the place of the altar upon which Cain and Abel offered sacrifice. There it was that Adam offered a sacrifice after he was created. Indeed Adam was created from that very ground; as the sages have taught: Adam was created from the place where he made atonement.*

Chapter 6

❨ 16 Now why is it my contention that as far as the Sanctuary and Jerusalem were concerned the first sanctification hallowed them for all time to come, whereas the sanctification of the rest of the Land of Israel, which involved the laws of the Sabbatical year and tithes and like matters, did not hallow the land for all time to come? Because the sanctity of the Sanctuary and of Jerusalem derives from the Divine Presence, which could not be banished. Does it not say "and I will bring your sanctuaries to desolation" (Lev. 26:31), wherefrom the sages have averred: even though they are desolate, the sanctuaries retain their pristine holiness.

*See Guide, III, ch. 45.

By contrast, the obligations arising out of the land as far as the Sabbatical year and the tithes are concerned had derived from the conquest of the land by the people (of Israel), and as soon as the land was wrested from them the conquest was nullified. Consequently, the land was exempted by the Law from tithes and from (the restrictions of) the Sabbatical year, for it was no longer deemed the land of Israel.

When Ezra, however, came up and hallowed (the land), he hallowed it not by conquest but merely by the act of taking possession. Therefore, every place that was possessed by those who had come up from Babylonia and hallowed by the second sanctification of Ezra is holy today, even though the land was later wrested from them; and the laws of the Sabbatical year and the tithes appertain thereto in the manner we have described in Laws Concerning Heave Offering.

THINGS PROHIBITED

Chapter 7

❨ 11   If all kinds (of oil) were valid for meal offerings, why did the sages rank their quality? So that one would know which was the very best, which were equal in value, and which was the least valuable; so that he who wished to earn merit for himself might bend his greedy inclination and make broad his generosity and bring an offering from the finest, from the very best of the species that he was bringing. Behold it is said in the Torah: "And Abel, he also brought of the firstlings of his flock and of the fat thereof. And the Lord had respect unto Abel and to his offering" (Gen. 4:4).

The same principle applies to everything which is done for the sake of the good God; namely, that it be of the finest and the best. If one builds a house of prayer, it should be finer than his private dwelling. If he feeds the hungry, he should give him of the best and the sweetest of his table. If he clothes the naked, he should give him of the finest of his garments. Hence if he consecrated something to God, he ought to give of the best of his possessions. Thus Scripture says: "all the fat is the Lord's" (Lev. 3:16).

DAILY OFFERINGS

Chapter 7

⟪ 11   This sheaf of waving would come from barley—a ruling transmitted from Moses our Teacher.

How was it brought? On the eve of the festival day messengers of the court would go out and tie the grain in bundles while still attached to the ground, so that it would be easy to reap. (People from) all the towns close by would gather, so that it would be reaped with much ado. Three se'ah of barley would be reaped by three men, in three baskets, with three sickles. As soon as it grew dark each reaper would say to all who were standing by, "Has the sun set?" They would answer him, "Yes!" "Has the sun set?" "Yes!" "Has the sun set?" "Yes!" "Is this a sickle?" They would answer him, "Yes!" "Is this a sickle?" "Yes!" "Is this a sickle?" "Yes!" "Is this a basket?" They would answer him, "Yes!" "Is this a basket?" "Yes!" "Is this a basket?" "Yes!" If it was on a Sabbath, he would ask them, "Is today the Sabbath?" and they would answer, "Yes!" "Is today the Sabbath?" "Yes!" "Is today the Sabbath?" "Yes!" After that he would say to them, "Shall I reap?" and they would answer him, "Reap!" "Shall I reap?" "Reap!" "Shall I reap?" "Reap!" Everything was repeated three times.

Why was all this necessary? Because of the erring people who deviated from the community of Israel in the days of the Second Temple, maintaining that when Scripture says (concerning the sheaf of waving) "on the morrow, after the Sabbath" (Lev. 23:11), it refers to the Sabbath of Genesis. The sages, however, have learned from oral tradition that this verse refers not to the Sabbath but to the festival day of Passover. This was the opinion at all times of the prophets and the Sanhedrin of every generation, namely, that the sheaf was being waved on the 16th of Nisan, whether it was a weekday or a Sabbath.

Behold it is said in the Torah: "And you shall eat neither bread, nor parched corn, nor fresh ears, until this selfsame day" (Lev. 23:14); and it is said: "And they did eat of the produce of the land on the morrow after the Passover, unleavened cakes and parched corn" (Josh. 5:11). Should you contend that the Passover happened to fall on a Sabbath—as the fools claim*—the question would arise: How could Scripture have made the permission to eat of the new grain depend upon a circumstance which was not the essential and determining factor but merely incidental? Rather, it is clear that since Scripture did make the matter depend upon "the morrow after the Passover," it was this morrow of the Passover that was the determining cause by which the new grain became permissible, without regard to the day of the week on which "the morrow" happened to fall.

TRESPASS

Chapter 8†

¶ 8 It is fitting for man to meditate upon the laws of the holy Torah and to comprehend their full meaning to the extent of his ability. Nevertheless, a law for which he finds no reason and understands no cause should not be trivial in his eyes. Let him not "break through to rise up against the Lord lest the Lord break forth upon him" (Ex. 19:24); nor should his thoughts concerning these things be like his thoughts concerning profane matters. Come and consider how strict the Torah was in the law of trespass! Now if sticks and stones and earth and ashes became hallowed by words alone as soon as the name of the Master of the Universe was invoked upon them, and anyone who comported with them as with a profane thing committed trespass and required atonement even if he acted unwittingly, how much more should man be on guard not to rebel against a commandment decreed for us by the Holy One, blessed be He, only because he does not understand its reason; or to heap words that are not right against the Lord; or to regard the commandments in the manner he regards ordinary affairs.

*The Karaites.
†See *Guide*, III, chs. 27, 31, and 35; also *Eight Chapters*, ch. IV.

Behold it is said in Scripture: "You shall therefore keep all My statutes, and all Mine ordinances, and do them" (Lev. 20:22); whereupon our sages have commented that "keeping" and "doing" refer to the "statutes" as well as to the "ordinances." "Doing" is well known; namely, to perform the statutes. And "keeping" means that one should be careful concerning them and not imagine that they are less important than the ordinances. Now the "ordinances" are commandments whose reason is obvious, and the benefit derived in this world from doing them is well known; for example, the prohibition against robbery and murder, or the commandment of honoring one's father and mother. The "statutes," on the other hand, are commandments whose reason is not known. Our sages have said: My statutes are the decrees that I have decreed for you, and you are not permitted to question them. A man's impulse pricks him concerning them and the Gentiles reprove us about them, such as the statutes concerning the prohibition against the flesh of the pig and that against meat seethed with milk, the law of the heifer whose neck is broken, the red heifer, or the scapegoat.

How much was King David distressed by heretics and pagans who disputed the statutes! Yet the more they pursued him with false questions, which they plied according to the narrowness of man's minds, the more he increased his cleaving to the Torah; as it is said: "The proud have forged a lie against me; but I with my whole heart will keep Your precepts" (Ps. 119:69). It is also said there concerning this: "All Your commandments are faithful; they persecute me falsely, help You me" (ibid. 119:86).

All the (laws concerning the) offerings are in the category of statutes. The sages have said that the world stands because of the service of the offerings; for through the performance of the statutes and the ordinances the righteous merit life in the world to come. Indeed, the Torah puts the commandment concerning the statutes first; as it is said: "You shall therefore keep My statutes, and Mine ordinances which if a man do, he shall live by them" (Lev. 18:5).

The following two treatises, Festal Offerings and Substitute Offerings, are from Book IX, Sacrifices.

FESTAL OFFERINGS

Chapter 2

¶ 14 ... When a man sacrifices a festal peace offering or a peace offering of rejoicing he should not eat of it with his children and his wife alone and think that he thus fulfills his entire duty; but it is incumbent upon him to give joy to the poor and the unfortunate, for it is said: "And the Levite, and the stranger, and the fatherless, and the widow" (Deut. 16:14). In proportion to his riches he should suffer them all to eat and to drink.

And if a man ate his sacrifices and did not suffer these also to rejoice with him, of him it is said: "Their sacrifices shall be to them as the bread of mourners, all that eat thereof shall become unclean, for their bread shall be for their appetite" (Hos. 9:4).

The duty toward the Levite surpasses all, since he has neither portion nor possession, nor has he any dues from the flesh of the offerings. Therefore a man should invite Levites to his table to give them cause to rejoice. Or he should give them gifts of flesh, together with their tithes, that they may find therein enough for their needs. But he who forsakes the Levite and gives him no cause to rejoice or is dilatory in paying him his tithes at the feast transgresses a negative commandment, for it is said: "Take heed to yourself that you forsake not the Levite" (Deut. 12:19).*

Chapter 3

¶ 1 It is a positive commandment to assemble all Israelites, men, women, and children, after the close of every year of release when they go up to make the pilgrimage, and in their hearing to read chapters from the Law which shall keep them diligent in the commandments and strengthen them in the true religion, for it is said: "At the end of every seven years, in the set time of the year of release, in the Feast of Tabernacles, when all Israel is come to appear ... assemble the people, the men and the women and the little ones, and your stranger that is within your gates ..." (Deut. 31:10 ff.).

¶ 2 Whosoever is exempt from the law to "appear before the Lord" is exempt from the law "assemble the people," except women and children and the uncircumcised. But he who is unclean is exempt

*See Book III, Repose on the Festivals, ch. VI.

from the law "assemble the people," for it is said: "when all Israel is
come to appear," and such a one is unfit to "come to appear." And it
is obvious that it is incumbent upon those of doubtful or double sex,
since it is incumbent upon women.

❡ 3 When do they read? At the close of the first festival day of the
Feast of Tabernacles, which is the beginning of the mid-festival days
of the feast in the eighth year.

It is the king who reads in their hearing; and the reading used to
be in the Court of the Women. He may read sitting, but if he reads
standing this is deemed praiseworthy.

Where does he read? From the beginning of the Book of Deuteronomy, "These are the words . . ." to the end of the section "Hear,
O Israel . . ." (Deut. 6:4); and he resumes at "And it shall come to
pass if you shall hearken . . ." (ibid. 11:13), and thence begins again
at "You shall surely tithe . . ." (ibid. 14:22 ff.), reading from "And
You shall surely tithe" in due order until the end of the blessings
and the cursings (ibid. 27:15–28:69) as far as "besides the covenant
which He made with them in Horeb." And there he breaks off.

❡ 4 How does he read? Trumpets are blown throughout all Jerusalem to assemble the people and a high pulpit which was made of
wood is brought and set up in the midst of the Court of the
Women. The king goes up and sits thereon so that they may hear his
reading and all Israel who go up to keep the feast gather round him.
The minister of the synagogue takes a scroll of the Torah and gives it
to the chief of the synagogue, and the chief of the synagogue gives it
to the prefect, and the prefect to the High Priest and the High Priest
to the king, to do him honor through the service of many men. The
king receives it standing, but if he pleases he may sit. He opens it
and looks in it and recites a benediction in the way which all do who
read the Torah in the synagogue. He reads the chapters which we
have cited until he comes to the end, when he rolls up the scroll and
recites a benediction after it in the way it is recited in synagogues.

He adds seven benedictions, and these are they:
"Look favorably, O Lord our God, upon Your people Israel . . .";
"We give thanks to You . . ."; "You have chosen us from among all
nations . . ." as far as "who sanctifies Israel and the appointed seasons"; and he recites them in the way the benedictions are recited in
the tefillah. These three benedictions are in accordance with their
established form.

In the fourth he prays for the Temple that it may endure concluding it with "Blessed are You, O Lord, who dwells in Zion."

In the fifth he prays for Israel that its kingdom may endure, concluding it with "Blessed are You, O Lord, who has made choice of Israel."

In the sixth he prays for the priests, that God may accept their ministration, concluding it with "Blessed are You, O Lord, who sanctifies the priests."

In the seventh he offers supplication and prayer, according as he is able, concluding it with "O Lord, save Your people Israel, for Your people are in need of salvation; blessed are You, O Lord, who hears prayer."

❡ 5   The reading of the Torah and the benedictions must be in the holy language, as it is said: "You shall read this Law" (Deut. 31:11)—in its very language, even though foreign tongues are spoken there.

❡ 6   As for proselytes who do not know the Law, they must make ready their heart and give ear attentively to listen in awe and reverence and trembling joy, as on the day when the Law was given on Sinai. Even great scholars who know the entire Law must listen with utmost attention. Even if there is any who cannot hear, he should keep his heart intent on this reading, for Scripture has ordained it solely for the strengthening of true religion; and a man should so regard himself as though the Law was now laid upon him for the first time and as though he now heard it from the mouth of the Lord, for the king is an ambassador to proclaim the words of God.

SUBSTITUTE OFFERINGS

Chapter 4

❡ 13   ... Although the statutes in the Law are all of them divine edicts, as we have explained at the close of Laws Concerning Sacrilege, yet it is proper to ponder over them and to give a reason for them, so far as we are able to give them a reason. The sages of former times said that King Solomon understood most of the reasons for all the statutes of the Law. It seems to me that in so far as Scripture has said: "Both it and that for which it is changed shall be holy" (Lev. 27:10)—as also in that matter whereof it has said: "And if he that sanctified it will redeem his house then he shall add the fifth part of the money of your valuation" (*ibid.* 17:15)—the Law has plumbed the depths of man's mind and the extremity of his evil impulse. For it is man's nature to increase his possessions and to be sparing of his wealth. Even though a man had made a vow and dedicated something, it may be that later he drew back and repented and would now redeem it with something less than its value. But the Law has said, "If he redeems it for himself he shall add the fifth." So, too, if a man dedicated a beast to a sanctity of its body, perchance he would draw back, and since he cannot redeem it, would change it for something of less worth. And if the right was given to him to change the bad for the good he would change the good for the bad and say, "It is good." Therefore Scripture has stopped the way against him so that he should not change it, and has penalized him if he should change it and has said: "Both it and that for which it was changed shall be holy." And both these laws serve to suppress man's natural tendency and correct his moral qualities. And the greater part of the rules in the Law are but "counsels from of old" (Is. 25:1), from Him who is "great in counsel" (Jer. 32:19), to correct our moral qualities and to keep straight all our doings. And so He says: "Have not I written you excellent things of counsels and knowledge, that I might make you know the certainty of the words of truth, that you might bring back words of truth to them that sent you" (Prov. 22:20).

*M*AIMONIDES' detailed treatment of the laws of cleanness and uncleanness, together with his exhaustive presentation of the laws pertaining to the Temple and its sacrifices (Books VIII and IX), reflects his determination to break down all barriers between the theoretical and the practical and to codify Jewish law in its encyclopedic totality. The subject matter is unusually complex, "bristling with fundamental difficulties which even the greatest masters find hard to comprehend." This book should, therefore, be seen as a highpoint in Maimonides' interpretation and systematization of the Talmud.

The following passages illustrate Maimonides' attempt to rationalize some of the most difficult precepts of Judaism. Apparently irrational, arbitrary laws of purity and impurity are endowed with symbolic value and purposiveness. Even though human understanding may not succeed in fathoming the reasons of such ceremonial laws, the attempt should be made. The description of the inexorable growth and escalation of evil, steadily spreading its influence, is written with verve and poignancy (Leprosy).

The reader should be attentive to Maimonides' original interpretation and creative application of Biblical verses.

UNCLEANNESS OF LEPROSY*

Chapter 16

〖 10   "Leprosy" is a comprehensive term covering sundry incompatible matters. Thus, whiteness in a man's skin is called leprosy; the falling off of some of his hair on the head or the chin is called leprosy; and a change of color in garments or in houses is called leprosy.

Now this change in garments and in houses which Scripture includes under the general term leprosy was no normal happening, but was a portent and a wonder among the Israelites to warn them against slanderous speaking. For if a man uttered slander the walls of his house would suffer a change; if he repented the house would again become clean. But if he continued in his wickedness until the house was torn down, leather objects in his house on which he sat or lay would suffer a change: if he repented they would again become clean. But if he continued in his wickedness until they were burned, the garments which he wore would suffer a change: if he repented they would again become clean. But if he continued in his wickedness until they were burned, his skin would suffer a change and he would become leprous and be set apart and exposed all alone until he should no more engage in the conversation of the wicked, which is raillery and slander.

Now on this matter there is a warning in Scripture which says, "Take heed in the plague of leprosy ... remember what the Lord your God did to Miriam by the way" (Deut. 24:9). That is to say, consider what befell Miriam the prophetess, who spoke against her brother, even though she was older than he and had nurtured him on her knees and had put herself in jeopardy to save him from the sea. Now she did not speak despitefully of him but erred only in that she put him on a level with other prophets; nor was he resentful about all these things, for it is said, "Now the man Moses was very meek" (Num. 12:3). Nevertheless, she was forthwith punished with leprosy. How much more then does this apply to wicked and foolish people who are profuse in speaking great and boastful things!

*See Book I, Moral Dispositions, II, 3 and ch. VII; Guide, I, ch. 59; III, ch. 47.

Therefore it is proper that he who would direct his way aright should keep himself far from their company and speak not with them, that he be not caught in the net of the wicked and in their foolishness.

Now the way of the company of the scornful and wicked is this: In the beginning they are profuse in vain words, as in the matter whereof it is said, "A fool's voice comes through a multitude of words" (Eccles. 5:2). Then they go on to speak to the discredit of the righteous, as in the matter whereof it is said, "Let the lying lips be dumb which speak arrogantly against the righteous" (Ps. 31:19). Then they become accustomed to speak against the prophets and to discredit their words, as in the matter whereof it is said, "But they mocked the messengers of God and despised his words and scoffed at his prophets" (II Chron. 36:16). Then they go on to speak against God and to deny the very root of religion, as in the matter whereof it is said, "And the children of Israel did impute things that were not right to the Lord their God" (II Kings 17:9); moreover it is said, "They have set their mouth against heaven and their tongue walks through the earth" (Ps. 73:9). What brought it to pass that they set their mouth against heaven? Their tongue, which first walked through the earth.

Such is the conversation of the wicked, occasioned by their idling at street corners, in the gatherings of the ignorant, and in the feastings of drunkards. But the conversation of the worthy ones in Israel is none other than words of Torah and wisdom; therefore the Holy One, blessed be He, aids them and bestows wisdom upon them, as it is said, "And they that feared the Lord spoke together every man to his neighbor, and the Lord listened and heard. And a book of remembrance was written before Him for them that feared the Lord and that thought upon His name" (Mal. 3:17).

UNCLEANNESS OF FOODSTUFFS

Chapter 16

(12 Although it is permissible to eat unclean foodstuffs and to drink unclean liquids, the pious of former times used to eat their common food in conditions of cleanness, and all their days they were wary of every uncleanness. And it is they who were called Pharisees, "separated ones," and this is a higher holiness. It is the way of piety that a man keep himself separate and go apart from the rest of the people and neither touch them nor eat and drink with them. For separation leads to the cleansing of the body from evil deeds, and the cleansing of the body leads to the hallowing of the soul from evil thoughts, and the hallowing of the soul leads to striving for likeness with the *Shekhinah*; for it is said, "Sanctify yourselves therefore and be holy" (Lev. 11:44), "for I the Lord who sanctify you am holy" (*ibid.* 21:8).*

IMMERSION POOLS

Chapter 11

❨ 12   It is plain and manifest that the laws about uncleanness and cleanness are decrees laid down by Scripture and not matters about which human understanding is capable of forming a judgment; for behold, they are included among the divine statutes. So, too, immersion as a means of freeing oneself from uncleanness is included among the divine statutes. Now "uncleanness" is not mud or filth which water can remove, but is a matter of Scriptural decree and dependent on the intention of the heart. Therefore the sages have said, if a man immerses himself, but without special intention, it is as though he has not immersed himself at all.

Nevertheless we may find some indication (for the moral basis) of this: just as one who sets his heart on becoming clean becomes clean as soon as he has immersed himself, although nothing new has befallen his body, so, too, one who sets his heart on cleansing himself from the uncleanness that beset men's souls—namely, wrongful thoughts and false convictions—becomes clean as soon as he consents in his heart to shun those counsels and brings his soul into the waters of pure reason. Behold, Scripture says, "And I will sprinkle clean water upon you and you shall be clean; from all your uncleanness and from all your idols will I cleanse you" (Ezek. 36:25).

May God, in His great mercy, cleanse us from every sin, iniquity, and guilt. Amen.

*See introduction to Book V; *Guide*, III, ch. 47.

*M*AIMONIDES describes Book XI as containing precepts "concerning civil relations which . . . cause damage to property or injury to the person." The reader is thus plunged directly into the core of Jewish civil and criminal law that guided the Jewish community in all its vicissitudes and transmutations. Unlike the laws of sacrifices, these remained alive and relevant at all times.

The selections show, among other things, how the aspiration to morality and equity—what is often described as the "duties of virtue"—informs all parts of the positive law. Unimpeachable integrity in human relations is of overriding importance; actions which jeopardize the civility and stability of society are most objectionable (e.g., Theft, VII, 12; Murder, IV, 9). Respect for human dignity is of pervasive and paramount concern (Wounding, ch. III; V, 10). Sensitivity is encouraged in every conceivable way (Murder, XIII, 14). There is always room—in all spheres—for ethical, supra-legal deeds; the individual is invited—not commanded—to move beyond the letter of the law (Robbery, XI, 17; Murder, XIII, 4).

Items of special historical and socio-political interest are:
(1) the detailed statements concerning taxation and the distinc-

tion between legitimate versus tyrannical rights of government
(Robbery, ch. V);

(2) the permissibility of condemning informers to death because
of the especially heinous nature of their crime (Wounding, ch.
VIII).

THEFT

Chapter 1

¶ 1   Whoever steals property worth a *perutah* (penny) or more
transgresses the prohibition: "You shall not steal" (Lev. 19:11).
Breach of this prohibition is not punished by flogging, since theft
must be repaid, Scripture having condemned the thief to make restitution. It makes no difference whether one steals the property of an
Israelite or the property of a heathen, or whether one steals from an
adult or from a minor.

¶ 2   On the authority of Scripture, it is prohibited to steal an object
of however small a value. It is also forbidden to steal in jest, or to
steal an object with the intention of returning it, or with the intention of paying for it. All these acts are forbidden, lest one become
accustomed to practicing them.

¶ 10   It is proper for the court to impose corporal punishment upon
minors for theft, the punishment being made in proportion to their
strength, in order that they should not become accustomed to stealing. The same procedure should be followed if they do other damage.
Similarly, if slaves steal or do damage, they should be severely beaten
in order that they should not become accustomed to doing damage.

Chapter 5

¶ 1   It is prohibited to buy from a thief any property he has stolen,
such buying being a great sin, since it encourages criminals and
causes the thief to steal other property. For if a thief finds no buyer,

he will not steal. Of this Scripture says, "Who is partner with a thief hates his own soul" (Prov. 29:24).

Chapter 7

❲ 1 If one weighs with weights that are deficient by the standards agreed upon in his locality, or measures with a measuring vessel deficient by the agreed standards, he violates a negative commandment, for Scripture states, "You shall do no unrighteousness in judgment, in length, in weight, or in measure" (Lev. 19:35).

❲ 2 Although one who measures or weighs falsely steals thereby, he need not pay double but need only pay for the deficiency in measure or weight. Nor is flogging inflicted for breach of this prohibition, since there is a liability to pay.

❲ 3 If one keeps in his house or in his shop a false measure or weight, he transgresses a negative commandment, for Scripture states, "You shall not have in your bag diverse weights" (Deut. 25:13). It is even forbidden to use a false measure as a urinal, for although one does not buy or sell with it himself, someone who does not know that it is deficient might come and use it for measuring. There is no flogging for breach of this prohibition because it does not involve action.

❲ 8 If one measures or weighs incorrectly in dealing with an Israelite or a heathen, he transgresses a negative commandment and must repay. It is similarly forbidden to deceive a heathen about an account, and one must be scrupulous with him. For since Scripture, even in a case where a heathen is subject to our rule, says, "And he shall reckon with his purchaser" (Lev. 25:50), how much more does this apply to a heathen not subject to our rule. This offense is included in the statement, "For an abomination to the Lord your God are all that do such things, even all that do unrighteously" (Deut. 25:16)—that is, in any manner.

❲ 12 The punishment for unjust measures is more severe than the punishment for immorality, for the latter is a sin against God only, the former against one's fellowman. If one denies the binding character of the commandment relating to measures, he denies in effect the Exodus from Egypt, which was the basis of the commandments;

but if one acknowledges the commandment relating to measures, he thereby acknowledges the Exodus from Egypt, which rendered all the commandments possible.

Chapter 8

❬ 1 There is a positive commandment to adjust balances, weights, and measures accurately and to calibrate them very carefully at the time of their manufacture, for Scripture says, "Just balances, just weights, a just *ephah*, and a just *hin*, shall you have" (Lev. 19:36). Similarly, in measuring land great care must be taken to calculate the area of land according to the principles laid down in works on geometry, for even a finger's breadth of land should be regarded as if it were filled with saffron.

❬ 3 A land surveyor should not measure one person's share in the summer and another person's share in the winter because the rope shrinks during the summer. Therefore, if one uses a rod or an iron chain or a similar instrument in measuring, the time of year is immaterial.

❬ 4 Weights may not be made of tin or lead or other similar metals because these rust and wear away, but they should be made of polished stone or glass or onyx or the like.

❬ 20 It is the duty of the court to appoint inspectors in every province and in every district to visit the shops, adjust balances and measures, and fix prices. If they find anyone with an inaccurate weight or measure or a faulty balance, they have the right to flog him according to his power of endurance, and to fine him whatever sum the court thinks fit, in order to ensure conformity. If anyone forces up the price and sells at a high price, they may flog him and compel him to sell at the market price.

ROBBERY AND LOST PROPERTY

Chapter 1

❬ 1 If one robs another of property worth as much as a *perutah* he transgresses a negative commandment, for it is said, "You shall not

... rob him" (Lev. 19:13). No flogging is incurred for breach of this prohibition, since Scripture has transformed it into a positive commandment, for if one commits robbery, he is obliged to make restitution, as it is said, "He shall restore that which he took by robbery" (ibid. 5:23), which is a positive commandment. Even if he burns the robbed property, he does not incur flogging, since he is obliged to repay its value, and any prohibition the transgression of which may be repaired by restitution does not entail flogging.

❡ 2 On the authority of Scripture, it is forbidden to take by robbery anything whatever (even if its worth is less than a perutah). Even a heathen must not be robbed nor may money due him be withheld. And if one does rob him or withhold money due him, he must make restitution.

❡ 3 Who is deemed a robber? One who takes another's property by force. Thus if one snatches an object from another's hand, or enters another's premises without his permission and takes articles, or if one seizes another's slave or his animal and makes use of them, or if one enters another's field and eats its produce, or commits any similar act, he is deemed a robber, as we find it exemplified in the Scripture verse: "And he plucked the spear out of the Egyptian's hand" (II Sam. 23:21).

❡ 4 Who is deemed guilty of unlawful withholding? One who, having come into possession of another person's money with the latter's consent, withholds it forcibly and does not return it upon the other's demand. Such is the case if one who has a loan or wages due him from another claims his due but cannot get it from his debtor because he is an overbearing and hardhearted person. It is of this that Scripture says, "You shall not oppress your neighbor" (Lev. 19:13).

❡ 9 If one covets the male slave or the female slave or the house or goods of another, or anything that it is possible for him to acquire from the other, and he subjects the other to vexation and pesters him until he is allowed to buy it from him, then he transgresses the negative commandment, "You shall not covet" (Ex. 20:14), even if he pays him a high price for it. No flogging is incurred for breach of this prohibition, since it does not involve action. Nor does one transgress this prohibition until he buys the object that he covets, as is exemplified by Scripture when it says, "You shall not covet the silver and gold that is on them nor take it to you" (Deut. 7:25)—thus implying that the transgression of coveting is effected only when accompanied by action.

❨ 10 If one desires another's house or his wife or his goods or any similar thing that he might buy from him, he transgresses a negative commandment as soon as he thinks in his heart how he is to acquire the desired object and allows his mind to be seduced by it. For Scripture says, "You shall not desire" (Deut. 5:18), and desire is a matter of the heart only.

❨ 11 Desire leads to coveting, and coveting to robbery, for if the owner does not wish to sell, even when he is offered a high price and is greatly importuned, it will lead the coveter to rob him, as it is said, "And they covet houses and seize them" (Micah 2:2). Moreover, if the owner should stand up to him to protect his property and prevent the robbery, this may lead to bloodshed. You can learn this from the story of Ahab and Naboth (cf. I Kings 21).

❨ 12 You thus learn that one who covets transgresses one prohibition, and if he acquires the desired object by bringing pressure upon the owner, or by requesting it of the owner, he transgresses two prohibitions, for this is why Scripture says, "You shall not covet" (Ex. 20:14), and "You shall not desire" (Deut. 5:18). If he then goes on to commit robbery, he transgresses three prohibitions.

❨ 13 If one robs another of property worth a perutah, it is regarded as if he took his life, for Scripture says, "So are the ways of everyone that is greedy of gain, he takes away the life of the owners thereof" (Prov. 1:19). Nevertheless, if property taken by robbery no longer exists, and the robber wishes to repent and comes of his own accord to return the value of the robbed property, the sages have ruled that this should not be accepted from him. Instead, he should be helped and forgiven, so as to encourage penitents in the right path. And if one accepts the value of robbed property, he does not act in the spirit of the sages.

Chapter 5

❨ 1 It is forbidden to buy from a robber property obtained by robbery, and it is also forbidden to assist him in making alterations to enable him to acquire title to it. For if one does this or anything similar to it, he encourages transgressors and himself transgresses the commandment, "You shall not put a stumbling block in front of the blind" (Lev. 19:14).

❡ 9 When persons are presumably robbers and all their property is presumably obtained by robbery, because they are robbers by occupation, such as tax collectors and bandits, it is forbidden to benefit from them since the presumption is that their occupation involves robbery. Nor may small coins be changed into denar from their till, since everything there is presumed to have been obtained by robbery.

❡ 10 If tax collectors take away one's coat and give him another instead, or if they take away his ass and give him another instead, he may keep the one given him because this is regarded as a transaction of sale and the presumption is that the owner has already abandoned hope of recovery. Nor does the recipient know for certain that it is property obtained by robbery. But if he is a conscientiously pious person who is particularly strict with himself, he should return it to its original owner.

❡ 11 This rule, namely that a tax collector is regarded as is a brigand, applies only if the collector is a heathen, or is self-appointed, or was appointed by the king but is not required to collect a fixed amount, and may take what he likes and leave what he likes. But if the king fixes a tax of, say, a third or a quarter (denar) or another fixed sum, and appoints to collect it on his behalf an Israelite known to be a trustworthy person who would not add to what was ordered by the king, this collector is not presumed to be a robber, for the king's decree has the force of law. Moreover, if one avoids paying such a tax, he is a transgressor, for he steals the king's property, whether the king be a heathen or an Israelite.

❡ 12 The same rule applies to cases where a king imposes as a tax on the citizenry, or on each person individually, a fixed annual amount, or imposes a fixed amount on each field, or decrees that if one breaks a specified law, he shall forfeit all his property to the palace, or decrees that if one is found in a field at harvest time, he shall pay the tax due on it whether he is the owner of the field or not, or makes some similar regulation. None of these cases is deemed robbery, nor is an Israelite who collects these levies on behalf of the king presumed to be a thief; rather he may well be a worthy person, provided only that he does not add, alter, or take anything for himself.

❨ 13 Similarly, if a king becomes angry with one of his servants or ministers among his subjects and confiscates his field or his court-yard, this is not deemed robbery and one is permitted to benefit from it. If one buys it from the king, he becomes its owner and the original owner cannot take it away from him. For the law of all kings permits them to confiscate all the property of those ministers with whom they are displeased, and the king has therefore canceled the owner's original right to it, so that the courtyard or field in question is regarded as ownerless, and if one buys it from the king, he becomes its lawful owner. But if a king takes the courtyard or field of one of the citizens, contrary to the laws he has promulgated, he is deemed a robber, and the original owner may recover it from anyone who buys it from the king.

❨ 14 The general rule is: any law promulgated by the king to apply to everyone and not to one person alone is not deemed robbery. But whatever he takes from one particular person only, not in accordance with a law known to everyone but by doing violence to this person, is deemed robbery. Consequently, when the king's treasurers or officers sell fields for the fixed tax due on such fields, their sale is valid. But the tax imposed on each individual may not be collected except from the person himself, and so, if they sell his field to recover the poll tax, it is not a legal sale unless the king's law permits such action.

Chapter 11

❨ 1 The return of lost property to an Israelite is a positive com-mandment, for Scripture says, "You shall surely return them to your brother" (Deut. 22:1). Moreover, if one sees the lost property of an Israelite and ignores it and leaves it, he transgresses a negative com-mandment in addition to disregarding a positive commandment, for Scripture says, "You shall not see your brother's ox (or his sheep go astray) and hide yourself from them" (ibid.). If he returns it, how-ever, he has fulfilled a positive commandment.

❨ 13 If one finds a sack or a basket, the rule is as follows: If he is a scholar or a respected elder who is not accustomed to taking such things in his hand, he need not concern himself with them. He must, however, examine his own conscience. If he would have taken these things back for himself had they belonged to him, he must also return them when they belong to another. But if he would not have overlooked his dignity even had they belonged to him, he need not return them when they belong to another.

If it is his custom to return similar articles in the country but not in town, and he finds them in town, he need not return them. If he finds them in the country, however, he must return them and see that they come into their owner's hands, even though he must enter into town with them and he is not accustomed to do this.

❲ 17   If one follows the good and upright path and does more than the strict letter of the law requires, he will return lost property in all cases, even if it is not in keeping with his dignity.

Chapter 13

❲ 1   If one finds lost property which he is obligated to return, he must advertise and let it be known, saying, "Let anyone who has lost property of such a kind come and identify it and take it . . ."

❲ 8   Formerly, if one found lost property, he would advertise it on three festivals. . . . Seven days after the last festival, he would advertise it a fourth time, to enable a listener to take a three-days' journey home, search among his belongings, return in three days, and find the advertiser proclaiming it on the seventh day.

❲ 9   After the Temple was destroyed, the sages decreed that if one finds lost property, he should advertise in synagogues and lecture rooms. However, when men of violence increased and went about saying that anything found belonged to the king, the sages decreed that a finder of lost property should tell his neighbors and friends, and that this would suffice.

WOUNDING AND DAMAGING

Chapter 1

❲ 1   If one wounds another, he must pay compensation to him for five effects of the injury, namely, damages, pain, medical treatment, enforced idleness, and humiliation. These five effects are all payable from the injurer's best property, as is the law for all who do wrongful damage.

❡ 5 How then do we know that when Scripture says, concerning limbs, "An eye for an eye," etc. (Ex. 21:24), it means compensation? It says in the context, "Stripe for stripe" (Ex. 21:25), and also says explicitly, "And if a man smite another with a stone or with his fist … he shall only pay for the loss of his time and shall cause him to be thoroughly healed" (Ex. 21:18–19). We thus learn from the word "for" (*tahat*) in the case of a "stripe" signifies compensation. The same conclusion applies to "for" in the case of the eye and the other limbs.

❡ 6 Although these rules appear plausible from the context of the Written Law, and were all made clear by Moses our Teacher from Mount Sinai, they have all come down to us as practical rules of law. For thus did our forebears see the law administered in the court of Joshua and in the court of Samuel, the Ramathite, and in every court ever set up from the time of Moses our Teacher until the present day.*

Chapter 3

❡ 5 If one insults another in speech or spits on another's clothes, he is exempt from paying compensation, but the court should institute preventive measures in this matter everywhere and at all times, as it sees fit. If one humiliates a scholar, the offender must pay him full compensation for humiliation, even if he humiliates him merely in speech. There is already a well-established decision that if one humiliates a scholar, even in speech, he is to be fined and made to pay thirty-five *denar* in gold, which is equal in weight to nine *sela* less a quarter; and we have a tradition that this fine may be enforced everywhere, both inside and outside the Land of Israel.

❡ 6 Cases of this kind occurred regularly in Spain. Some scholars used to forgo their right to claim, which was commendable of them, but at times one would claim and a compromise would be reached. The judges, however, used to say to the offender, "You are really obliged to give him a pound of gold."

❡ 7 Although if one humiliates ordinary persons by using derogatory speech he need not pay compensation, such action is considered a

*Note the emphasis on tradition rather than exegesis. Cf. Maimonides' Introduction; Book XIV, Rebels, ch. II; also our introduction, p. 13.

grave sin. Only a foolish scoundrel blasphemes and curses people, and the sages of old have said, "If one makes an honorable Israelite blanch by his words, he will have no share in the world to come."

Chapter 5

❡ 1 One is forbidden to wound either himself or another. Not only one who wounds another but even one who strikes a law-observing Israelite in the course of a quarrel, whether an adult or a minor, whether a man or a woman, transgresses a negative commandment contained in the verse, "He shall not exceed . . . to smite him" (Deut. 25:3). For if Scripture here warns against excess in lashing an offender, how much more does this warning apply to smiting an innocent person.

❡ 2 It is forbidden even to lift a hand against another, and if one does lift a hand against another, he is deemed wicked even if he does not actually strike him.

❡ 9 If one inflicts a personal injury on another, he may not be compared to one who damages another's property. For if one damages another's property, atonement is effected for him as soon as he pays whatever is required. But if one wounds another, atonement is not effected for him even if he has paid for all the five effects, or even if he has sacrificed all the rams of Nebaioth, for his sin is not forgiven until he begs forgiveness of the injured person and is pardoned.

❡ 10 The injured person, however, is forbidden to be harsh and to withhold forgiveness, for such behavior does not become a descendant of Israel. . . .

❡ 13 If one says to another, "Break So-and-So's articles, with the understanding that you are to be exempt," the offender is nevertheless liable for payment, just as if the first person had said to him, "Blind So-and-So's eye with the understanding that you are to be exempt." Yet even though it is the agent who must pay, the person who prompts him is his partner in wrongdoing and is an evil-doer, since he has in a way caused the blind to stumble and has encouraged a lawbreaker.

Chapter 8

❡ 9 It is forbidden to give either another's person or his property into the hand of a heathen, even if the other is wicked and a sinner and if he causes one distress and pain. If one gives another's person or his property into the hand of a heathen, he has no share in the world to come.

❡ 10 An informer may be killed anywhere, even at the present time when we do not try cases involving capital punishment, and it is permissible to kill him before he has informed. As soon as one says that he is about to inform against So-and-So's person or property, even a trivial amount of property, he surrenders himself to death. He must be warned and told, "Do not inform," and then if he is impudent and replies "Not so! I shall inform against So-and-So," it is a religious duty to kill him, and he who hastens to kill him acquires merit.

❡ 11 If the informer has carried out his intention and given information, it is my opinion that we are not allowed to kill him unless he is a confirmed informer, in which case he must be killed lest he inform against others. There are frequently cases in the cities of the Maghreb where informers who are known to reveal people's money are killed or are handed over to the heathen authorities to be executed, beaten, or imprisoned, as befits their crime.

Similarly, if one oppresses the community and troubles them, it is permissible to hand him over to the heathen authorities to be beaten, imprisoned, and fined. But if one merely distresses an individual, he must not be handed over.

Although the punishment of an informer is permitted, it is forbidden to destroy his property, for it belongs to his heirs.

MURDER AND PRESERVATION OF LIFE

Chapter 1

❡ 4 The court is warned against accepting ransom from a murderer, even if he offers all the money in the world and even if the avenger of blood agrees to let him go free. For the life of the murdered person is not the property of the avenger of blood but the property of God, and Scripture says, "Moreover, you shall take no ransom for the life of a murderer" (Num. 35:31). There is no offense about which the Law is so strict as it is about bloodshed, as it is said, "So shall you not pollute the land wherein you are; for blood, it pollutes the land ..." (ibid. 35:33).

Chapter 4

(8 If one commits murder without being seen by two witnesses at the same time, although they did see him one after the other; or if one commits murder in the presence of witnesses without first receiving a warning; or if the witnesses contradict each other in the cross-examination but not in the primary investigation—the rule in all such cases is that the murderer is put into a cell and fed on a minimum of bread and water until his stomach contracts and then he is given barley so that his stomach splits under the stress of sickness.

(9 This, however, is not done to other persons guilty of crimes involving the death penalty at the hand of the court; rather if one is condemned to death, he is put to death, and if he is not liable, he is allowed to go free. For although there are worse crimes than bloodshed, none causes such destruction to civilized society as bloodshed. Not even idolatry, nor immorality, nor desecration of the Sabbath, is the equal of bloodshed. For these are crimes between man and God, while bloodshed is a crime between man and man. If one has committed this crime, he is deemed wholly wicked, and all the meritorious acts he has performed during his lifetime cannot outweigh this crime or save him from judgment, as it is said, "A man that is laden with the blood of any person shall hasten his steps to the pit; none will support him" (Prov. 28:17). A lesson may be taken from Ahab, who worshiped idols and of whom it is said, "But there was none like Ahab" (I Kings 21:25). Yet when his sins and his merits were set in array before the God of all spirits (cf. Num. 16:22), the one sin that brought on him the doom of extermination and the weightiest of all his crimes was the blood of Naboth. For Scripture relates: "And there came forth the spirit and stood before the Lord" (I Kings 22:21); this was the spirit of Naboth, who was told, "You shall entice him and shall prevail also" (ibid. 22:22). Now the wicked Ahab did not commit murder himself but only brought it about. How much greater then is the crime of one who commits murder with his own hand!

Chapter 13

(1 If, on the road, one encounters a person whose animal is crouching under the weight of its burden, he is enjoined to unload the burden from the animal whether the burden is suited to it or too heavy for it. This is a positive commandment, for Scripture says, "You shall surely release it with him" (Ex. 23:5).

⟨ 2   One may not unload the animal and then leave the other person helpless and go away; rather he must help him raise the animal up and reload the burden onto it, for Scripture says, "You shall surely help him to lift them up again" (Deut. 22:4), which is an additional positive commandment. If one leaves the other helpless and neither unloads nor reloads, he disregards the positive commandments and transgresses a negative commandment, for Scripture says, "You shall not see your brother's ass," etc. (ibid.).

⟨ 3   If the passerby is a priest and the animal is crouching in a cemetery, he may not defile himself on its account, just as he may not defile himself in order to return lost property to its owner. Similarly, if one is an elder unaccustomed to loading or unloading, he is exempt, seeing that the act is not in keeping with his dignity.

⟨ 4   The general rule is as follows: In every case where if the animal were his own he would load or unload it, he must load or unload another's. But if one is pious and does more than the letter of the law demands, even if he is a prince of the highest rank, still if he sees another's animal crouching under its burden of straw or sticks or the like, he should help unload and reload.

⟨ 13   If one encounters two animals, one crouching under its burden and the other unburdened because the owner cannot find anyone to help him load, he is obligated to unload first to relieve the animal's suffering, and then to load the other. This rule applies only if the owners of the animals are both friends or both enemies (of the person who comes upon them). But if one is an enemy and the other a friend, he is obligated to load for the enemy first, in order to subdue his evil impulse.

⟨ 14   The enemy mentioned in the Law (cf. Ex. 23:5) does not mean a foreign enemy but an Israelite one. How can an Israelite have an Israelite enemy when Scripture says, "You shall not hate your brother in your heart" (Lev. 19:17)? The sages decreed that if one all alone sees another committing a crime and warns him against it and he does not desist, one is obligated to hate him until he repents and leaves his evil ways. Yet even if he has not yet repented and one finds him in difficulties with his burden, one is obligated to help him load or unload, and not leave him possibly to die. For the enemy might tarry because of his property and meet with danger, and the Torah is very solicitous for the lives of Israelites, whether of the wicked or of the righteous, since all Israelites acknowledge God and believe in the essentials of our religion. For it is said, "Say to them: As I live, says the Lord God, I have no pleasure in the death of the wicked but that the wicked turn from his way and live" (Ezek. 33:11).*

---

*This explains the inclusion of this chapter in the section on Murder and Preservation of Life.

*B*OOK XII is concerned not only with the modes of acquisition of property and other goods but also with the rights and responsibilities of ownership. Inasmuch as the subject matter is very practical and relevant—unaffected by the abnormality of Jewish political existence in exile—Maimonides shows himself to be especially attuned to post-Talmudic developments in the application of halakhic principles. Geonic ordinances and interpretations are carefully recorded and discussed; significant precedents and contemporary practices are mentioned.

The reader should note the long section concerning oral deception—verbal abuse, humiliation, hurting feelings—included in Sales, ch. XIV, where the more common, blatant forms of fraud and deception are reviewed. Chapter XVIII outlines an unusually stringent and, therefore, from the consumer's point of view, exceedingly fair, ethos for advertisement practices. Neighbors, ch. XII, is the classic illustration of how an ethical directive—a counsel of perfection—becomes formalized and standardized and generally binding. The interplay between the legal and the moral, the statutory requirement and the supererogatory aspiration, is effectively underscored in the concluding passage. Positive law is here seen as a springboard to the highest morality.

SALES

Chapter 14

¶ 12 Just as there is a law against fraud in buying and selling, so there is a law against deception by words, as it is said: "And you shall not wrong one another; but you shall fear your God; for I am the Lord your God" (Lev. 25:17), which refers to deception by words.

¶ 13 Thus if a man is a penitent one must not say to him, "Remember your former deeds." If he is a son of proselytes one must not say to him, "Remember the deeds of your fathers." If he is a proselyte and comes to study the Law one must not say to him, "Shall the mouth that ate unclean and forbidden food come and study the Law, which was uttered by the mouth of the Lord?" If he is afflicted with sickness and suffering or if he has buried his children one must not say to him, as his companions said to Job: "Is not your fear of God your confidence, and your hope the integrity of your ways? Remember, I pray you, who ever perished, being innocent?" (Job 4:6–7).

¶ 14 If assdrivers are seeking to buy produce one must not say to them, "Go to So-and-So," while knowing that the latter has never sold produce.

If a question is asked in a certain field of science, one must not say to him who is not versed in that science, "What will you say in this matter?" or "What is your opinion in this matter?"

It is thus in all similar cases.

¶ 15 Whoever defrauds a proselyte, whether in matters of money or by spoken words, transgresses three negative injunctions, as it is said: "And a stranger shall you not wrong" (Ex. 22:20), which refers to verbal over-reaching; "neither shall you oppress him" (ibid.), which refers to monetary over-reaching.

Hence we learn that he who over-reaches a proselyte (by words) transgresses three negative injunctions, to wit: "And you shall not wrong one another" (Lev. 25:17); "You shall not wrong one another" (*ibid.* 25:14); "And a stranger shall you not wrong" (Ex. 22:20).

❡ 16 Thus also, if one has over-reached the proselyte in matters of money he transgresses the following three negative injunctions: "You shall not wrong one another" (Lev. 25:14); "And you shall not wrong one another" (*ibid.* 25:17); "neither shall you oppress him" (Ex. 22:20).

❡ 17 But why is one, when deceiving a proselyte, guilty of transgressing the negative injunction referring to oral deception, even if he has committed a fraud in money matters and vice versa? Because Scripture has expressed both by the unqualified term of wronging; and in the negative injunction against deceiving a proselyte there is explicit reference to the two kinds of deception, *i.e.*, "shall you not wrong" and "neither shall you oppress."

❡ 18 Oral deception is more heinous than monetary fraud because restoration is possible in the latter while no restoration is possible in the former, and the latter concerns one's money while the former affects his person.

The verse "And you shall fear your God" (Lev. 25:17) is appended to the commandment against oral deception because it is a matter of the heart. Hence it may be inferred that in all matters of the heart Scripture says: "And you shall fear your God," and whosoever cries out to the Lord because of distress caused by oral deception is answered immediately, as it is said: "for I am the Lord" (*ibid.*).

Chapter 18

❡ 1 It is forbidden to deceive people in buying and selling or to deceive them by creating a false impression. A heathen and an Israelite are to be treated alike in this respect.

If one knows that an article he is selling has a defect he must inform the buyer about it.

It is forbidden to deceive people even by words.

❡ 2 One should not deck out a person or an animal or old vessels so that they appear new; but he may deck out the new ones by polishing, ironing, or beautifying them all they require.

❡ 3 One should not feed a man bran broth or the like to bloat him and thus make his face appear robust; nor should one paint his face with red clay or bloat his inward parts or soak his flesh in water. All similar acts are likewise forbidden.

One must not sell to a heathen meat of an animal not slaughtered according to ritual law under the impression that it is meat from an animal slaughtered according to ritual law, though to the heathen the two are the same.

Chapter 22

¶ 1 One cannot transfer title, whether by sale or by gift or by bequest of a dying person, to a thing which does not yet exist.

Thus if one says, "What this field will yield is sold to you," or "What this tree will yield is given to you," or "Give to So-and-So the young that this animal will bear," the transaction is not valid.

The same rule applies to all similar cases.

¶ 15 The rules of acquisition of things not yet in existence are different in the case of objects consecrated to the Temple in Jerusalem or in the case of the poor or in the case of vows from the rules that apply to common cases; for if a man says, "All that my animal bears will be consecrated for repair of the Temple in Jerusalem," or "It shall be forbidden to me to derive any benefit therefrom," or "I shall give it to charity," the rule is that though it cannot be consecrated now because it is not in existence, he must keep his word nevertheless, as it is said: "He shall do according to all that proceeds out of his mouth" (Num. 30:2).

¶ 16 Hence if a dying person enjoins us and says, "Whatever this tree brings forth shall be given to the poor," or "All the rent brought by this house shall go to the poor," the poor acquire title to these.

¶ 17 There are some Geonim who disagree with the above and say that the poor can acquire title only to those things that an ordinary man can and therefore cannot acquire title to a thing not in existence.

I, however, am not inclined to agree with this opinion, because while one is not under obligation to transfer any object, he is under obligation to fulfill a promise made to give to charity or to consecrate an object to the Temple, even as he is commanded to fulfill a vow, as we have explained in Laws Concerning Vows of Valuation.*

*See Book VI.

༄ ༅

ORIGINAL ACQUISITIONS AND GIFTS

Chapter 12

❨ 17   Perfectly righteous men and men of good works will not accept any gifts from men, but will put their trust in His Name, blessed be He, and not in human benefactors, as it has already been said: "But he that hates gifts shall live" (Prov. 15:27).

༄ ༅

NEIGHBORS

Chapter 12

❨ 5   Moreover, even if a man sells his land to another, the neighbor whose land is contiguous to the purchased land may repay the money to the purchaser and evict him thence. This purchaser whose land is not contiguous is considered as if he were an agent of the owner of the neighboring field.

This law of pre-emption applies, regardless of whether the other field is sold by the owner or by his agent or by the court. Even if the purchaser is a scholar, a neighbor, or a relation to the seller and the owner of the adjacent field is an ignorant person and not related, the latter has nevertheless priority and can evict the purchaser.

This rule obtains because it is said: "And you shall do what is right and good" (Deut. 4:18); and the sages have held that since the sale is the same, it is "good and right" that this place should be bought by the owner of the adjacent field rather than by an outsider.

❨ 13   If one sells to orphans the law of pre-emption does not apply because the "good and right" which results from kindness to them is greater than that which would redound to the owner of the adjacent land.

❨ 14   Thus, also, if one sells to a woman the law of pre-emption does not apply because it is not customary for a woman constantly to exert herself to buy; but now that she has bought it is a kindness to her to let the land remain with her.

Chapter 14

〔5 If one wishes to sell land and two people come, each saying, "I will buy it for this price," and neither of them is an adjacent neighbor, we hold as follows: if one is an urban resident and the other a rural resident the urban resident has priority. If one is a neighbor and the other a scholar the scholar has precedence. If a relation and a scholar, the scholar has precedence. If a neighbor and a relation, the neighbor has priority, because this too is included in the "good and right."

If one forestalls the other and buys it he acquires title to it, and the other, who would have had priority had they come together, cannot evict him, seeing that neither is an adjacent neighbor, for the sages have not enjoined priority in these instances except as a matter of piety, and it is becoming a devout spirit to act thus.

SLAVES

Chapter 1

〔7 It is forbidden for an Israelite who buys any Hebrew slave to make him do menial tasks which are assigned to slaves only, such as to make him carry his clothes after him to the bathhouse or take off his shoes, for it is said: "You shall not make him serve as a bondservant" (Lev. 25:39). He must treat him as a hired man, as it is said: "As a hired servant and as a settler, he shall be with you" (ibid. 25:40).

The Hebrew bondman, however, may cut the master's hair, wash his garment, and bake his dough. But the master should not make him an attendant at a public bath or a public barber or a public baker.

If that was his trade before he was sold he may follow it. He should not be taught a new trade, however, but be allowed to work at the same trade that he plied before.

This applies only to a Hebrew bondman who feels humiliated because he was sold into servitude. It is permitted, however, to make an Israelite who was not sold do the work of a slave inasmuch as he does that work of his own volition.

❡ 9 The master must treat his Hebrew male and female slaves as equals in regard to food, drink, clothing, and shelter, as it is said: "because he is well with you" (Deut. 15:16); i.e., you should not eat white bread and the slave black bread, you drink old wine and he new wine, you sleep on down feathers and he on straw, you reside in the city and he in the country, or you reside in the country and he dwell in the city, for it is further said: "He shall go out from you" (Lev. 25:41).

Hence the sages have said: He who buys a Hebrew bondman it is as if he had bought a master for himself.

One must treat his Hebrew slave as a brother, as it is said: "And over your brethren the children of Israel" (Lev. 25:46).

Nevertheless, the bondman must conduct himself as a slave in the work that he does do for his master.

Chapter 8

❡ 10 If a slave flees from a foreign land to the Land of Israel he is not restored to slavery; and concerning him does Scripture say: "You shall not deliver to his master a bondman that is escaped from his master to you" (Deut. 23:16); and he may demand of his master to write him a deed of manumission and to write against him a deed of indebtedness for his value until such a time as he shall have the means to pay him.

If the master refuses to free him the court releases him from his servitude and he may depart.*

❡ 11 This slave who flees to the Land of Israel has the status of proselyte, and concerning him Scripture has added another warning to one who would deceive him, because he is even more humble than the proselyte and with regard to him Scripture has specifically demanded: "He shall dwell with you, in your midst within one of your gates, where it likes him best; you shall not wrong him" (Deut. 23:17). This refers even to deception with words.

Hence you may learn that he who deceives this proselyte transgresses three negative commands, to wit: "You shall not wrong one

*See *Guide*, III, ch. 39.

another" (Lev. 25:17); "And a stranger shall you not wrong" (Ex. 22:20); and "You shall not wrong him" (Deut. 23:17). And he also transgresses "Neither shall you oppress him" (Ex. 22:20), as we have explained in the chapter pertaining to over-reaching.

Chapter 9

❡ 8   It is permitted to work a heathen slave with rigor. Though such is the rule, it is the quality of piety and the way of wisdom that a man be merciful and pursue justice and not make his yoke heavy upon the slave or distress him, but give him to eat and to drink of all foods and drinks.

The sages of old were wont to let the slave partake of every dish that they themselves ate of and to give the meal of the cattle and of the slaves precedence over their own. Is it not said: "As the eyes of slaves to the hand of their master, as the eyes of a female servant to the hand of her mistress" (Ps. 123:2)?

Thus also the master should not disgrace them by hand or by word, because Scriptural law has delivered them only to slavery and not to disgrace. Nor should he heap upon the slave oral abuse and anger, but should rather speak to him softly and listen to his claims. So it is also explained in the good paths of Job, in which he prided himself:

"If I did despise the cause of my manservant,
Or of my maidservant, when they contended with me . . .

Did not He that made me in the womb make him?
And did not One fashion us in the womb?" (Job 31:13, 15).

Cruelty and effrontery are not frequent except with heathen who worship idols. The children of our father Abraham, however, i.e., the Israelites, upon whom the Holy One, blessed be He, bestowed the favor of the Law and laid upon them statutes and judgments, are merciful people who have mercy upon all.*

Thus also it is declared by the attributes of the Holy One, blessed be He, which we are enjoined to imitate: "And His mercies are over all His works" (Ps. 145:9).

Furthermore, whoever has compassion will receive compassion, as it is said: "And He will show you mercy, and have compassion upon you, and multiply you" (Deut. 13:18).

*See Book V, Forbidden Intercourse, ch. XIV; Book VII, Gifts to the Poor, ch. X.

*T*HIS book, containing "laws of property concerned with the mutual transactions of people, such as loans, hire for wages, deposits," completes the codification of civil law. Its subject matter is more diffuse than that of Books XI and XII.

The selections from the Laws of Hiring focus upon aspects of labor relations, stressing the need for mutuality of trust and good will between employer and employee. The reader will presumably be interested in the discussion of such themes as prompt payment of wages, "moonlighting," and the equivalent of the "coffee break" or lunch period.

The relations of creditor and debtor are based on a combination of firm, impartial legal procedure with a concern for the dignity and sensitivities of the needy. While the rights of the creditor to collect his debt are carefully safeguarded, efforts are made to spare the debtor unnecessary humiliation. Chapter II is of obvious historical and juridical interest, illustrating the evolution of basic law in light of changing conditions.

The concluding section of Pleading should be studied in conjunction with the passages from Sanhedrin in Book XIV which emphasize the avoidance of fraud or deception even in procedural matters.

The idea that "charity begins at home" underlies the law which condemns those who transfer their property to strangers and ignore the rightful heirs (cf. *Guide, III, ch. 42*). In bolstering the legal-moral imperative, forbidding a father to discriminate among his sons lest this produce enmity and jealousy, Maimonides introduces an original application of the Biblical narrative.

The final passage, once again, moves in the realm of law and equity.

HIRING

Chapter 11

❲ 1 It is an affirmative commandment to give to the hired man his hire in time, for it is said, "In the same day you shall give him his hire" (Deut. 24:15). And he who delays payment until after the time when the hire is due transgresses a negative commandment. For it is said "Neither shall the sun go down upon it" (*ibid.*). But no lashes are to be administered for the transgression of this commandment since the transgressor is liable to pay. A man's hire, the hire for an animal, and the hire for utensils, all alike, must be paid in time, and if one delays payment until after the time when it is due he transgresses a negative commandment. In the case of a resident alien the affirmative commandment of "In the same day you shall give him his hire" applies, but no negative commandment is violated by a delay.

❲ 2 Whoever withholds the hire of a hired man is deemed as though he took away his livelihood from him. For it is said, "And he sets his soul upon it" (Deut. 24:15). And he transgresses four negative and one affirmative commandment, to wit: "You shall not oppress" (Lev. 19:13); "You shall not rob" (*ibid.*); "You shall not cause the wages of a hired man to abide with you all night until the morning" (*ibid.*); "The sun shall not go down upon it" (Deut. 24:15); and "In the same day you shall give him his hire" (*ibid.*).

What is the time when wages are due? A hireling for the day

collects his hire all night, and with respect to him it is said "You shall not cause the wages of a hired man to abide with you all night until the morning"; a hireling for the night collects all day, and with respect to him it is said "In the same day you shall give him his hire"; a hireling by the hour during the day collects all day; a hireling by the hour during the night collects all night; a hireling by the week, by the month, by the year, by the septennium if his term ends in the daytime, collects all day, and if in the nighttime, all night.

❴ 5 He who has withheld the hire of a hired man until after it was due is still bound to pay him immediately, even though he has transgressed an affirmative and a negative commandment; during the whole time in which he continues to withhold the hire from the hired man he transgresses an extra-Pentateuchal negative commandment. For it is said, "Say not to your neighbor, 'Go, and come again' " (Prov. 3:28).

Chapter 12

❴ 1 Whenever workers are working at anything which grows from the soil and has not been completely processed, whether severed from the soil or still attached to it, and their work constitutes a final processing, the employer is enjoined to allow them to eat of that at which they are working. For it is said "When you come into your neighbor's vineyard, then you may eat grapes until you have enough at your own pleasure. . . . When you come into your neighbor's standing corn, then you may pluck ears with your hand" (Deut. 23:25–26). From the oral tradition it has been learned that these passages of Scripture refer only to a man who was hired by the owner. For if he was not hired, who permitted him to come into his neighbor's vineyard or standing crops without his neighbor's consent? These passages can therefore be understood only thus: when you come into the domain of the owner to work you may eat of that at which you are working.

❴ 2 What is the difference between him who is working at that which is severed from the soil and him who is working at that which is attached to the soil? He who is working at that which is severed from the soil may eat thereof until it has been completely processed and is forbidden to eat thereof once it has been completely processed; while he who is working at that which is attached to the soil, such as a harvester of grain or a plucker of grapes, may not eat thereof until a stage of his work has been completed. If, for example, a hired man is plucking grapes, putting them in a basket until it is filled, shaking the contents of the basket out into some other place, returning, plucking grapes, and filling the basket again, he may not eat of the grapes until he has filled the basket. But by reason of the commandment relating to the restoration of lost property to its owner the sages have said: Workers may eat while walking from one row of vines to another and while returning from the wine press, in order that they should not neglect their work by sitting down to eat, but should rather eat in the midst of their work, while walking from one place to another, without neglecting their work.

❡ 3 He who neglects his work and eats, or eats not at the time when a stage of the work has been completed, transgresses a negative commandment. For it is said, "But you shall not move a sickle to your neighbor's standing corn" (Deut. 23:26). From the oral tradition it has been learned that this passage is to be interpreted thus: So long as you are occupied with reaping you must not move a sickle for your own eating. And so it is in all similar cases.

Similarly, a worker who carried off in his hands of that which he is working, or takes more than is required for his eating, giving it to others, transgresses a negative commandment. For it is said, "But you shall not put any in your vessel" (Deut. 23:25). However, no lashes are to be administered for the transgression of these two negative commandments because the transgressor is liable to pay.

❡ 14 If a worker, who was working together with his wife, children, and bondmen, had stipulated with the employer that neither he nor they should eat of that at which they were going to work, they may not eat thereof. This applies only to adults, because, possessing understanding, they may renounce their rights. But with respect to minors, one may not stipulate that they should not eat, because what they eat is neither their father's nor their employer's but belongs to heaven.

Chapter 13

❡ 6 The owner of the cow is permitted to withhold food from her in order that she should eat more of the grain which she is going to thresh, and the hirer of the cow is permitted to feed to her from the bundles of sheaves in order that she should not eat much from the grain she is threshing.

Similarly, an employer may give his workers wine to drink in order that they should not eat much of the grapes, and the workers may dip their bread in brine in order that they may eat much of the grapes.

But a worker may not do his own work at night and hire himself out for the day, or thresh with his cow in the evening and hire her out for the day; nor may he starve himself, giving away his own food to his children, because by doing so he weakens himself physically and mentally and renders himself incapable of exertion in his work, thus depriving the employer of what is due to him.

⟦ 7   Just as the employer is enjoined not to deprive the poor worker of his hire or withhold it from him when it is due, so is the worker enjoined not to deprive the employer of the benefit of his work by idling away his time, a little here and a little there, thus wasting the whole day deceitfully. Indeed, the worker must be very punctual in the matter of time, seeing that the sages were so solicitous in this matter that they exempted the worker from saying the fourth benediction of grace.

The worker must work with all his power, seeing that the just Jacob said, "And you know that with all my power I have served your father" (Gen. 31:6), and that he received his reward therefore in this world, too, as it is said, "And the man increased exceedingly" (ibid. 30:43).

CREDITOR AND DEBTOR

Chapter 1

⟦ 1   It is an affirmative commandment to lend to the poor of Israel. For it is written "If you lend money to any of My people, to the poor with you" (Ex. 22:24). From this passage one might infer that lending money to the poor is optional, but when we read in another passage "You shall surely lend him" (Deut. 15:8), we know that it is obligatory.*

*See Book VII, Gifts to the Poor, X, 7.

Lending money to the poor man is a more meritorious deed than giving charity to him who begs for it, for the one has already been driven to begging, while the other has not yet reached that stage.

Severe, indeed, is the censure of the Law against him who withholds a loan from the poor. For it is written, "Beware that there be not a base thought in your heart ... and your eye be evil against your needy brother, and you give him naught" (Deut. 15:9).

❨ 3 One is forbidden to appear before his debtor, nay even to pass before him, even though he does not make demand upon him—and, needless to say, if he does make demand upon him—lest he frighten or shame him.

Just as the creditor is forbidden to demand payment, so is the debtor forbidden to withhold from the creditor the money that is in his hands and to say to him "Go forth and come back again," provided he has the means of paying. For it is written, "Say not to your neighbor, 'Go, and come again' " (Prov. 3:28).

The debtor is also forbidden to borrow money and spend it unnecessarily or dissipate it, so that the creditor will not find anything from which to collect, even if the creditor be very rich. He who does this is classified as a wicked man. For it is written, "The wicked borrow, but pay not" (Ps. 37:21). And the sages have enjoined us: "Your fellow's property shall be as dear to you as your own" (Ethics of the Fathers 2:12).

Chapter 2

❨ 1 The rule of the Law is that when the creditor demands the debt an exemption is to be set apart for the debtor, if he has property, and the remainder is given to the creditor as we have stated. If no property belonging to the debtor is found, or if only such property as is exempt is found, the debtor may go free. He is to be neither imprisoned nor told, "Produce proof that you are poor," nor subjected to an oath, as the heathen are wont to judge. For it is written, "You shall not be to him as a creditor" (Ex. 22:24). The creditor is only told by the court "If you know of any property belonging to the debtor, go and levy upon it."

❨ 2 If the creditor claims that the debtor has property which he is concealing, and that it is in his house, it is not lawful either for the creditor or for the court's representative to enter the debtor's house, the Law being strict in this respect. For it is written, "You shall stand without" (Deut. 24:11). But the creditor may have the anathema proclaimed generally against him who has property and withholds it from the creditor.

When the first Geonim that arose after the compilation of the Gemara saw that deceivers had multiplied and that, consequently, all doors had become closed to would-be borrowers, they enacted the regulation that the debtor be subjected to a strict oath, akin to the Pentateuchal oath, while holding a sacred object: that he has nothing over and above his exemption, that he has not concealed anything in the hands of others, and that he has made no gift upon condition that it be returned to him. He is also to include in this oath a promise that whatever he may earn or whatever may come into his hands or possession as his own he will not spend on food, clothing, and the maintenance of his wife and children, or give it away to any person whatsoever, but will only take therefrom 30 days' food and 12 months' clothing, that is, food which is appropriate and clothing which is appropriate, not the food of gluttons and drunkards or that which is served before kings, and not the clothing of grandees and high officers, but that to which he is accustomed. And he must continually hand over to the creditor all surplus over and above his needs until the entire debt has been paid. And at the very beginning the anathema is to be proclaimed against him who knows of property, open or concealed, belonging to the debtor and does not notify the court.

Even now, after the above regulation has been enacted, neither the creditor nor the court's representative may enter the debtor's house for the purpose of making distraint, since the enactment was not intended to abolish an essential rule of the Law; the debtor himself must bring out his movables or say, "This or that is what I have." He is then allowed to keep what is properly to be kept by him and must turn the remainder over to the creditor and take the oath provided for by the above enactment. And so the courts of Israel rule everywhere.

If the debtor is seen to be in possession of property after he has taken the above oath, and he pleads, "The property belongs to others," or, "It was entrusted to me for the purpose of engaging in an enterprise on shares," no heed is to be paid to his plea unless he produces proof. So my teachers have ruled.

❪ 3 He who is required to take an oath that he has no property and that whatever he may earn he will turn over to his creditor, is not to be subjected to such an oath by each one of his creditors. For this oath is inclusive of all creditors and, moreover, it is an enactment of the later sages, which is not to be applied with strictness but with leniency.

❪ 4 If a man is generally reputed to be poor, honest, and living in integrity, the matter being manifest and known to the judge and to the majority of the people, and his creditor comes to subject him to an oath by virtue of the above-mentioned enactment, the creditor not being satisfied with the poverty of the debtor, but being desirous of tormenting him with this oath, of causing chagrin to him, and disgracing him in public, so as to take revenge of him or to force him to go to a heathen and borrow money or to take his wife's property and turn it over to him in order to be saved from this oath—it seems to me that a God-fearing judge is forbidden to subject the debtor to the oath, and that if he does cause him to swear, he renders null the negative commandment of the Law of "You shall not be to him as a creditor" (Ex. 22:24). Moreover, it is fitting for the judge to reprimand the creditor and to discomfit him because he is bearing ill will and walking in the hardness of his heart. For the Geonim made this enactment only because of the deceivers, and it is written, "Until you inquire about your brother" (Deut. 22:2)—"make inquiry about him, whether he is a deceiver or not a deceiver" (Mishnah, Bava Metzia 2:7). And since the man is generally reputed to be poor and not to be a deceiver, it is forbidden to subject him to the oath.

I also say that if the debtor is generally reputed to be a deceiver, and his ways in dealing with others are corrupt, and is also reputed to be a moneyed person but claims that he has nothing and is quick to swear, it is not proper for the judge to cause him to swear, but, if he has the power to do so, he should rather use compulsion against him, or declare him excommunicated, until he satisfies the creditor, since he is reputed to be a wealthy individual and since the satisfaction of a creditor is enjoined by the Law.

To put it generally: Everything the judge does in these matters with the intention of pursuing justice only, as we have been enjoined to pursue it, and not of tampering with the Law to the detriment of

one of the litigants, he is permitted to do, and, he will receive heavenly reward for it, provided always that his deeds are for the sake of
heaven.*

Chapter 4

❡ 7 Whoever writes a writing containing usury is deemed as
though he wrote, and called witnesses to attest, that he denied the
Lord, the God of Israel.

He who borrows or lends on usury in privacy is deemed as
though he denied the Lord, the God of Israel, and the Exodus from
Egypt. For it is written, "You shall not give your money upon interest" (Lev. 25:37), and this is followed by "I am the Lord your God,
who brought you forth out of the land of Egypt" (ibid. 25:38).

PLEADING

Chapter 16

❡ 9 One is forbidden to make a false plea in order to pervert justice
or to delay it. How is this to be understood? If a man has a debt of
one mina owing to him from his fellow, he must not claim two minas
in order to have his adversary make an admission with respect to one
mina and subject himself to liability to an oath.

If a man owed a mina to another and the creditor claimed two
minas, the debtor must not say to himself, "I will deny everything in
court and make an admission privately with respect to the one mina
in order not to become liable to an oath."

❡ 10 If three persons had a debt of one mina outstanding against
another who denied everything, it is not permissible for one to sue
and have the other two appear as witnesses and divide the proceeds
of the recovery. It is with respect to such matters and the like that
Scripture has admonished us, "Keep far from a false matter" (Ex.
23:7).

*See Book XIV, Sanhedrin, chs. XX–XXIV.

INHERITANCE

Chapter 6

❪ 11 He who gives away his property to a stranger, leaving out his heirs, incurs the displeasure of the sages, even though his heirs do not behave properly toward him. But such strangers acquire title to all the property given to them.

It is of the quality of piety that a pious man should not be a witness to a will by which a transfer of the inheritance from an heir is effected, even if it be from a son who is not of good behavior to his brother who is a wise man and of good behavior.

❪ 12 An apostate Israelite inherits his Israelite relatives. But if the courts see fit, in order not to lend encouragement to him, to deprive him of his property right, and penalize him that he should not inherit, they may do so. And if he has Israelite children, their apostate father's inheritance shall be given to them. Such is always the custom in the West.

❪ 13 The sages have ordained that a man, during his lifetime, should not make any distinction between his sons, even with respect to small matters, in order that they might not come to rivalry and jealousy even as Joseph and his brothers.

Chapter 11

❪ 1 If money was left to orphans by their father, it is not necessary to appoint a guardian. What, then, is to be done? A man is to be sought out who has landed property of the fairest quality, is trustworthy, versed in the Torah, and has never been subjected to excommunication, and the money is to be turned over to him by order of the court for the purpose of doing business therewith on condition that the orphans share in the profits but not in the losses, so that the orphans may benefit from the use of the money; if he has no landed property, he must give a pledge of broken lumps of gold which have no distinctive marks, and the court takes the pledge and gives him the money on condition that the orphans share in the profits but not in the losses.

And why should the court not take a pledge of gold utensils or of a gold bar? Because it may be that the utensils or the gold belong to others, who, after the death of the pledgor, would come, name the distinctive marks, and take the utensils or the bar, if the judge should happen to have knowledge that the pledgor was not reputed to be wealthy enough to own such a utensil or bar.

And at what ratio of the total profit shall the orphans' share be fixed? In accordance with the discretion of the judge; either one third of the profits, or one half thereof, or even one quarter, if the judge deems it to be to the advantage of the orphans.

If no man can be found who is willing to take the money on condition that the orphans do not share in the losses but only in the profits, some of the money may be spent to provide food for the orphans, until landed property shall have been purchased for the balance of the money and delivered to the guardian whom the court shall have appointed.

(12 Although the guardian is not required to render an account, as we have stated, he must make reckoning to himself privately with great care and beware of the Father of these orphans who rides upon the skies, as it is written, "Extol Him that rides upon the skies . . . a Father of the fatherless" (Ps. 68:5–6).

*T*HE last book is concerned primarily with the procedural aspects of law, the mechanics and dynamics of the judiciary, the role of authority, power, and discipline in the maintenance of the good society. Maimonides contended that "if a criminal is not punished, injurious acts will not be abolished . . . and none of those who design aggression will be deterred" (cf. Guide, III, ch. 41).

Note the following:

(1) The image of the judge, his moral and intellectual qualifications, his rights and responsibilities, and his creative role in administering justice; corruption in the administration of justice—in the appointment of judges—is condemned and abhorred and likened to idolatry (Sanhedrin, especially chs. II, III, XX, and XXIV).

(2) The portrayal of the king not only as a temporal sovereign endowed with vast powers and prerogatives, but as a spiritual leader committed to an exacting scale of values and ideals (Kings and Wars).

(3) The spelling out of the many implications and concrete applications of the central ethical imperative "Love your neighbor" (Mourning, ch. XIV).

(4) The suggestion, which was to play an important role in the

sixteenth century when the Jewish community in Safed was flourishing, that authoritative rabbinic ordination (semikhah) may be reinstated (Sanhedrin, VI, 11).

(5) The programmatic statement concerning the conciliatory treatment of contemporary Karaites (Rebels, III, 3).

(6) The description of the Messianic period, emphasizing its value as an instrument of intellectual achievement and spiritual elevation. The uncensored version of chapter XI, which accords Christianity and Islam a positive role in history, adds a new dimension to Maimonides' conception of the religious development of mankind.

SANHEDRIN

Chapter 1

❪ 1   It is a positive Biblical command to appoint judges and executive officials in every city and every district, as it is said: "Judges and officers shall you make in all your gates" (Deut. 16:18). "Judges" refers to the magistrates assigned to the court, before whom litigants appear. "Officers" refers to those who wield the rod and the lash. They stand before the judges; they make their rounds to the markets, squares, and shops, fixing prices, regulating weights, and correcting abuses. Their work is directed by the judges. Any person they find guilty of a misdemeanor is taken by them to court, and punishment corresponding to his offense is inflicted upon him.

❪ 3   How many regular tribunals are to be set up in Israel? How many members is each to comprise? First there is established a Supreme Court holding sessions in the sanctuary. This is styled "the Great Sanhedrin" and consists of seventy-one elders, as it is said: "Gather to Me seventy men of the elders of Israel" (Num. 11:16), with Moses at their head, as it is said "that they may stand there with you" (ibid.), thus making a tribunal of seventy-one. The one who excels in wisdom is appointed head of the tribunal. He is the presiding officer of the college and is always designated by the sages as Nasi. He occupies the place of Moses our Teacher. The most distinguished of the seventy is next in rank. He is seated to the right of the Nasi and is known as Av bet din. The other members are seated with them according to age and standing. The greater the knowledge a member possesses, the closer to the left of the Nasi is the seat assigned to him. They sit in the form of a semicircular threshing floor, so that the Nasi and Av bet din may see all of them.

In addition (to the Great Sanhedrin), two other tribunals, each numbering twenty-three members, are set up (in Jerusalem), one sitting at the entrance of the Temple Court and the other at the entrance of the Temple Mount.

Moreover, in each town with a population of one hundred and twenty and upward there is set up a Small Sanhedrin, meeting at the gate of the town, as it is said: "And establish justice in the gate" (Amos 5:15). How many are to make up the Small Sanhedrin? Twenty-three. The most learned among them is the presiding judge; the others are seated in the form of a semicircular threshing floor, so that the presiding judge is able to see them all.

Chapter 2

❨ 1 Only those are eligible to serve as members of the Sanhedrin—whether the Great or a Small Sanhedrin—who are wise men and understanding, that is, who are experts in the Torah and versed in many other branches of learning; who possess some knowledge of the general sciences such as medicine, mathematics, the calculation of cycles and constellations; and are somewhat acquainted with astrology, the arts of diviners, soothsayers, sorcerers, the superstitious practices of idolaters, and similar matters, so that they be competent to deal with cases requiring such knowledge.

Moreover, those who would qualify for membership in the Sanhedrin must be priests, Levites, and (lay) Israelites of good birth, worthy to marry (their daughters) into the priesthood, as it is said "that they may stand there with you" (Num. 11:16), implying, like you in wisdom, reverence, and lineage.

❨ 2 It is desirable that the Great Sanhedrin should have among its members priests and Levites, as it is said: "And you shall come to the priests, the Levites" (Deut. 17:9). If there are no priests and Levites available, the entire membership may be drawn from (lay) Israelites.

❨ 3 Neither a very aged man nor a eunuch is appointed to any Sanhedrin, since these are apt to be wanting in tenderness; nor is one who is childless appointed, because a member of the Sanhedrin must be a person who is sympathetic.

¶ 4   The king of Israel is not given a seat on the Sanhedrin, because it is forbidden to differ with him or to rebel against his word. But the High Priest may be given a seat, if he is fit for the office by reason of scholarship.

¶ 5   Although the kings of the House of David may not be given seats on the Sanhedrin, they judge others and are judged in a suit against them. But the kings of Israel may neither judge nor be judged, because they do not submit to the discipline of the Torah. (To sit in judgment on them) might lead to untoward consequences.

¶ 6   Just as the members of the court must be free from all suspicion with respect to conduct, so must they be free from all physical defects.

Every conceivable effort should be made to the end that all the members of that tribunal be of mature age, imposing stature, good appearance, that they be able to express their views in clear and well-chosen words, and be conversant with most of the spoken languages, in order that the Sanhedrin may dispense with the services of an interpreter.

¶ 7   In the case of a court-of-three, all the above-mentioned requirements are not insisted upon. Nevertheless it is essential that every one of the members thereof possess the following seven qualifications: wisdom, humility, fear of God, disdain of gain, love of truth, love of his fellow men, and a good reputation. All these prerequisites are explicitly set forth in the Torah. Scripture says "wise men and understanding" (Deut. 1:13), thus stating (that those chosen) must be men of wisdom; "and beloved of your tribes" (ibid.), that is, men with whom the spirit of their fellow creatures is pleased. What will earn for them the love of others? A good eye, a lowly spirit, friendly intercourse, and gentleness in speech and dealings with others.

Elsewhere it is said "men of valor" (Ex. 18:21), that is, men strong in the performance of the commandments, and strict with themselves, men who control their passions, whose character is above reproach, aye, whose youth is of unblemished repute. The phrase "men of valor" implies also stoutheartedness to rescue the oppressed from the hand of the oppressor, as it is said: "But Moses stood up and helped them" (Ex. 2:17). And just as Moses our Teacher was humble, so every judge should be humble. "Such as fear God" (Ex. 18:21)—this is to be understood literally; "hating gain" (ibid.), that is, they are not anxious about their own money and do not strive to accumulate wealth, for he that hastens after riches, want shall come upon him; "men of truth" (ibid.), that is, they pursue righteousness spontaneously and of their own accord; they love the truth, hate violence, and flee anything that savors of unrighteousness.

Chapter 3

❡ 7 The Divine Presence dwells in the midst of any competent Jewish tribunal. Therefore it behooves the judges to sit in court enwrapped (in fringed robes) in a state of fear and reverence and in a serious frame of mind. They are forbidden to behave frivolously, to jest, or to engage in idle talk. They should concentrate their minds on matters of Torah and wisdom.

❡ 8 A Sanhedrin, or king, or exilarch, who appoints to the office of judge one who is unfit for it (on moral grounds), or one whose knowledge of the Torah is inadequate to entitle him to the office, though the latter is otherwise a lovable person, possessing admirable qualities—whoever makes such an appointment transgresses a negative command, for it is said: "You shall not respect persons in judgment" (Deut. 1:17). It is learned by tradition that this exhortation is addressed to one who is empowered to appoint judges.

Said the rabbis: "Say not, 'So-and-So is a handsome man, I will make him judge; So-and-So is a man of valor, I will make him judge; So-and-So is related to me, I will make him judge; So-and-So is a linguist, I will make him judge.' If you do it, he will acquit the guilty and condemn the innocent, not because he is wicked, but because he is lacking in knowledge. Therefore Scripture says: 'You shall not respect persons in judgment.' "

The rabbis also said that he who appoints a judge unfit for his vocation is as though he had set up a pillar (for idol worship), for it is said: "Neither shall you set up a pillar, which the Lord your God hates" (ibid. 16:22). And if such an appointment is made in a place where scholars are available, it is as though he had planted an asherah, for it is said: "You shall not plant an asherah of any kind of tree beside the altar of the Lord your God" (ibid. 16:21).

Moreover, the injunction "You shall not make with Me gods of silver or gods of gold" (Ex. 20:23) has been interpreted by the sages to mean: gods who come into being through the influence of silver or gold, that is, a judge who owes his appointment to his wealth only.

❲ 9 It is forbidden to rise before a judge who procured the office he holds by paying for it. The rabbis bid us slight and despise him, regard the judicial robe in which he is enwrapped as the packsaddle of an ass.

❲ 10 It was the habit of the early sages to shun appointment to the position of judge. They exerted their utmost endeavors to avoid sitting in judgment unless they were convinced that there were no others so fit for the office as they, and that were they to persist in their refusal, the cause of justice would suffer. Even then they would not act in the capacity of judges until the people and the elders brought pressure upon them to do so.

Chapter 4

❲ 1 No one is qualified to act as judge, whether of the Great or a Small Sanhedrin or even of a court-of-three, unless he has been ordained by one who has himself been ordained. Moses our Teacher ordained Joshua by laying his hands upon him, as it is said: "And he laid his hands upon him, and gave him a charge" (Num. 27:23). He, likewise, ordained the seventy elders, and the Divine Presence rested upon them. The elders ordained others, who in turn ordained their successors. Hence there was an uninterrupted succession of ordained judges, reaching back to the tribunal of Joshua, indeed, to the tribunal of Moses our Teacher. It matters not whether one is ordained by the Nasi, or by a judge who has himself been ordained though he has never served as a member of the Sanhedrin.

❲ 2 What has been the procedure through the generations with regard to ordination? It has been effected not by the laying of hands upon the elder but by designating him by the title "Rabbi" and saying to him: "You are ordained and authorized to adjudicate even cases involving fines."

❲ 11 If there should be in all the Land of Israel but one man competent to ordain, he could invite two others to sit with him and proceed to ordain seventy men, either en masse or one after the other. He and the other seventy men would then constitute the Supreme Court and would thus be in a position to ordain other tribunals.

It seems to me that if all the wise men in the Land of Israel agreed to appoint judges and to ordain them, the ordination would be valid, empowering the ordained to adjudicate cases involving fines and to ordain others. If what we have said is true, the question arises: Why were the rabbis disturbed over the matter of ordination, apprehending the abolition of the laws involving fines? Because Israel is scattered and agreement on the part of all is impossible. If, however, there were one ordained by a man who had himself been ordained, no unanimity would be necessary. He would have the right to adjudicate cases involving fines because he would be an ordained judge. But this matter requires careful reflection.

Chapter 12

❨ 3   Once the witnesses say: "We gave him due warning and we know him," the court gives them a solemn charge. How are they charged in a capital case?

The court addresses them thus: "Perhaps what you are about to say is mere conjecture or hearsay, based on secondhand information, on what you heard from a trustworthy person. Perhaps you are unaware that we will in the course of the trial subject you to inquiry and query. Know that capital cases are unlike monetary cases. In a monetary case, one may make restitution and his offense is expiated; but in a capital case (the witness) is accountable for the blood of the man and the blood of his (potential) posterity until the end of time. Thus with respect to Cain it is said: 'The voice of your brother's bloods cries' (Gen. 4:10)—that is, his blood and the blood of his (potential) descendants. For this reason, but a single man was created, to teach us that if any man destroys a single life in the world, Scripture imputes it to him as though he had destroyed the whole world; and if any man preserves one life, Scripture ascribes it to him as though he had preserved the whole world. Furthermore, all human beings are fashioned after the pattern of the first man, yet no two faces are exactly alike. Therefore, every man may well say, 'For my sake the world was created.' And perhaps you will say, 'Why borrow this trouble?' It is said: 'He being a witness, whether he has seen or known, if he do not utter it, then he shall bear his iniquity' (Lev. 5:1). And perhaps you will say, 'Why should we incur guilt for the blood of this man?' It is written: 'And when the wicked perish, there is joy'(Prov. 11:10)."

If the witnesses stand by their evidence, the oldest of them is called and is subjected to inquiry and query, as will be set forth in the treatise on Evidence. If his testimony is unshaken, the second is called and examined likewise. Even if there are a hundred witnesses, each is subjected to inquiry and query. If their evidence tallies, the debate is opened with words of encouragement (to the accused), as has already been stated. He is advised not to be afraid of what the witnesses have said, if he knows that he is not guilty. Then the trial proceeds. If he is found not guilty, he is set free. If he is found guilty, he is held in custody till the following day. In the meantime the judges meet in pairs to study the case, eat but little and drink no wine at all; all night each judge discusses the case with his colleague or deliberates upon it by himself. The following day, early in the morning, they come to court. He who was in favor of acquittal says, "I was for acquittal and I hold to my opinion"; he who was for conviction says, "I was for conviction and hold to my opinion," or "I changed my opinion and am now for acquittal." Should there be any mistake as to the identity of those who were in favor of conviction or of acquittal for the same argument (deduced from two Scriptural verses) in which case the two count only as one, as has already been stated, the judges' clerks, who have a record of the reason given by each for his vote, call attention to this fact. The discussion is renewed. If (after the final vote is taken), the accused is found not guilty, he is set free. If it becomes necessary to add to the judges, the addition is made. If those for conviction are in the majority and the accused is pronounced liable, he is led forth to be executed.

The place of execution was outside the court, far away from it, as it is said: "Bring forth him that cursed without the camp" (Lev. 24:14). It seems to me that it was approximately six miles distant from the court, corresponding to the distance between the court of Moses our Teacher—the court located at the entrance of the Tent of Meeting—and the [outer limit of the] camp of Israel.

Chapter 18

《 6 ... It is a Scriptural decree that the court shall not put a man to death or flog him on his own admission (of guilt). This is done only on the evidence of two witnesses. It is true that Joshua condemned Achan to death on the latter's admission, and that David ordered the execution of the Amalekite stranger on the latter's admission. But those were emergency cases, or the death sentence pronounced in those instances was prescribed by the state law. The Sanhedrin, however, is not empowered to inflict the penalty of death or of flagellation on the admission of the accused. For it is possible that he was confused in mind when he made the confession. Perhaps he was one of those who are in misery, bitter in soul, who long for death, thrust the sword in their bellies, or cast themselves down from the roofs. Perhaps this was the reason that prompted him to confess to a crime he had not committed, in order that he might be put to death. To sum up the matter, the principle that no man is to be declared guilty on his own admission is a divine decree.*

Chapter 20

¶ 6 "You shall do no unrighteousness in judgment" (Lev. 19:15). This refers to the judge who perverts judgment, acquits the guilty, and condemns the innocent. It also refers to the judge who delays judgment, who discusses at undue length things that are obvious in order to annoy one of the parties to the suit. He too is included among the unrighteous.

¶ 7 A judge who is arrogant in decision, who hastens to give judgment before weighing it carefully in his mind, so that it be as clear to him as the sun, is foolish, wicked, and haughty. Therefore the rabbis enjoined, "Be deliberate in judgment" (Ethics of the Fathers 1:1). So too, Job said: "And the cause of him that I knew not I searched out" (Job 29:16).

¶ 8 Any judge who, when a suit is brought before him, seeks to deduce the decision in the case from an analogous case concerning which the law is known to him, and, though there is in the vicinity a greater scholar than he, refuses to go to consult him—such a judge belongs to the category of the wicked who are arrogant in decision. Touching such a judge, the rabbis said: "Evil upon evil will come upon him" (Yevamot 109b). For this and like attitudes betoken haughtiness and will lead to perversion of judgment.

"For she has cast down many wounded" (Prov. 7:26); this refers to a disciple who is not qualified and nevertheless renders decisions. "Yea, a mighty host are all her slain" (ibid.); this refers to a scholar who is qualified and refrains from rendering decisions. The last state-

---

*An example of Maimonides' attempt to fathom the reasons for "divine decrees" that defy explanation. See Book VIII, Trespass, VIII, 8; Guide, III, ch. 26.

ment applies only to one whose services are indispensable to the community. If, however, he refrains from rendering decisions because he knows that there is another man in the city who is competent to act as judge, he is praiseworthy. He who shuns the office of judge avoids enmity, robbery, and false swearing; and he who is arrogant in decision is foolish, wicked, and haughty.

❪ 9   A disciple is forbidden to give decisions in the presence of his teacher, unless there is a distance of three Persian miles between them—a distance corresponding to the space occupied by the camp of Israel.

❪ 10   Think not that the foregoing rules apply only to a case involving a large sum of money to be taken from one (litigant) and given to the other. At all times and in all respects, regard a suit entailing one thousand maneh and one entailing a perutah as of equal importance.

❪ 11   Judges do not meet to try a suit involving less than the value of a perutah. But, if they have met to consider a case involving the value of a perutah, the trial is completed even if the claim is reduced to less than the value of a perutah.

❪ 12   The judge who perverts judgment due to an Israelite transgresses one negative command, as it is said: "You shall do no unrighteousness in judgment" (Lev. 19:15). If the one thus wronged is a stranger, the judge transgresses two negative commandments, as it is said: "You shall not pervert the justice due to the stranger" (Deut. 24:17). If the one wronged is an orphan, the judge transgresses three negative commands, as it is said: "You shall not pervert the justice due to . . . the fatherless" (ibid.).

Chapter 21

❪ 1   A positive command enjoins upon the judge the duty to judge righteously, as it is said: "In righteousness shall you judge your neighbor" (Lev. 19:15). What is meant by a righteous judgment? It is a judgment marked by perfect impartiality to both litigants, not permitting one to state his case at length while telling the other to be brief, not to show courtesy to one and speak softly to him while frowning upon the other and addressing him harshly.

❪ 2   If one of the parties to a suit is well clad and the other ill clad, the judge should say to the former, "Either dress him like yourself before the trial is held or dress like him, then the trial will take place."

¶ 3 One of the litigants must not be allowed to be seated while the other is kept standing; but both should be standing. It is, however, within the discretion of the court to permit both to be seated. But one must not occupy a higher seat and the other a lower one; they are to be seated side by side. The latitude given to the judges to seat both litigants holds only while the case is still in the stage of discussion; once the case is completed, both must stand, for it is said: "And Moses sat to judge the people; and the people stood about Moses" (Ex. 18:13). When is the case to be regarded as completed? When the judges announce their decision saying, "So-and-So, you are innocent; So-and-So, you are guilty." This applies only to the litigants, but the witnesses must stand, as it is said: "Then both the men . . . shall stand" (Deut. 19:17).

¶ 4 If a scholar and an ignorant person come to court for a trial, the scholar is seated and the ignorant person is asked to take a seat. If the latter declines, the court does not insist (that he be seated). The scholar should not, however, come first and sit down before his teacher as though he would state his case to him. But if he has a set hour for study with him, he may come at the appointed time.

¶ 5 Since the close of the Talmud, it has become the practice of all courts associated with the academies to permit the parties to a lawsuit and the witnesses to be seated, in order to obviate strife. For we are powerless to maintain intact all the requirements of the law.

¶ 6 If the court has many cases on the docket, the case of an orphan is tried before that of a widow, as it is said: "Judge the fatherless, plead for the widow" (Is. 1:17); the case of a widow comes before that of a scholar, a scholar's before an illiterate's, the suit of a woman before that of a man, for the humiliation is greater in the case of a woman.

¶ 7 The judge is forbidden to hear the arguments of a litigant, aye, even a single statement made by him, before his opponent appears, or in the absence of his opponent, for it is said, "Hear the causes between your brethren" (Deut. 1:16). The judge who hears only one side, transgresses a negative command, as it is said: "You shall not accept a false report" (Ex. 23:1). This negative command implies also an admonition against listening to slander, indulging in it, and giving false testimony.

The litigant also is warned not to state his case to the court before his opponent arrives. Even to this and similar matters applies the injunction, "Keep far from a false matter" (*ibid.* 23:7).

¶ 8 The judge shall not hear the arguments from the mouth of an interpreter unless he knows the language spoken by the litigants and understands their arguments. If he is unable to speak their language fluently enough to address them, he may appoint an interpreter to advise them of the decision to set forth the reason for pronouncing one guilty and the other innocent.

¶ 9 It is imperative that the judge after hearing the arguments of both parties to the suit should repeat those arguments, as it is written: "And the king said: The one says, 'This is my son that lives, and your son is dead'" (I Kings 3:23). He must be satisfied in his mind that the decision he reached is correct and then give it.

¶ 10 How do we know that the judge should not express approval of the arguments of a litigant? It is said: "Keep far from a false matter" (Ex. 23:7). He should give his opinion and keep silent. Nor should he suggest to either suitor a line of argument. Even if he (the plaintiff) brought but one witness, the judge should not say to him, "We do not accept the testimony of one man." But he should address the defendant thus: "This man has testified against you." Perhaps the defendant would then admit the claim, saying, "The evidence given by him is true." The judge must therefore wait until the defendant says, "There is but one witness. I do not deem him trustworthy." This applies also to similar cases.

¶ 11 In the event the judge sees a point in favor of a litigant and finds that the latter is trying to bring out the point but is unable to formulate it, or the judge finds that the litigant is at pains to defend himself by a sound argument but that, agitated by fierce anger, the argument escapes him, or finds that as a result of an inferior mentality the litigant is confused, he is permitted to assist him somewhat by giving him a lead, in compliance with the exhortation, "Open your mouth for the dumb" (Prov. 31:8). But this matter requires due deliberation, for the judge must not appear as one who "plays the part of an advocate."

Chapter 22

❨ 4 It is commendable at the outset of a trial to inquire of the litigants whether they desire adjudication according to law or settlement by arbitration. If they prefer arbitration, their wish is granted. A court that always resorts to arbitration is praiseworthy. Concerning such a court, it is said: "Execute the justice of ... peace in your gates" (Zech. 8:16). What is the kind of justice which carries peace with it? Undoubtedly, it is arbitration. So too, with reference to David it is said: "And David executed justice and charity to all his people" (II Sam. 8:15). What is the kind of justice which carries charity with it? Undoubtedly, it is arbitration, i.e., compromise.

What has been said holds good only as long as the verdict has not yet been announced, in which case even if the judge has already heard the arguments of the litigants and knows in whose favor the verdict will be, it is commendable to effect an arbitration. But if the verdict has already been announced and the judge has said: "So-and-So, you are not guilty; So-and-So, you are guilty," he is not permitted to advise arbitration, but the law must take its course.

Chapter 23

❨ 1 "You shall take no gift" (Ex. 23:8). The purport of this prohibition is not to caution the judge against accepting a gift with the intention of perverting justice. Its purpose is to warn him not to accept a bribe even if he proposes to acquit the innocent and condemn the guilty. He who does it transgresses this negative command. To him too is addressed the admonition, "Cursed be he that takes a bribe" (Deut. 27:25). He is bound to return the bribe if the giver demands it.

❨ 2 The giver of a bribe, as well as the receiver, contravenes a negative command, as it is said: "Nor put a stumbling block before the blind" (Lev. 19:14).

❨ 3 Any judge who stays at home and magnifies his greatness in order to increase the perquisites of his attendants and clerks is classed with those who turn aside after gain. The sons of Samuel did it. Therefore it is written concerning them: "And they turned aside after lucre and took bribes" (I Sam. 8:3). Not only is a bribe of money forbidden but also a bribe of words.

It happened once that a judge was crossing a river on a small fishing boat, when a man stretched forth his hand and helped him get ashore. That man had a lawsuit, but the judge said to him, "I am disqualified from acting as judge in your suit."

It also happened that a man once removed a bird's feather from a judge's mantle; another man once covered spittle in front of a judge. In each of these instances, the judge said, "I am barred from trying your case."

There is also an incident on record of a man who presented to a priest, who was also a judge, a gift due to the priest. The judge said to the man, "I am ineligible to act as judge in your suit."

There is still another incident of a tenant farmer who, on Fridays, used to bring to the owner figs from the garden he was cultivating. On one occasion, however, he brought the figs on Thursday, because he had a lawsuit. The judge, however, said, "I am barred from acting as judge in your case," for though the figs were his, since the tenant brought them ahead of time, he was ineligible to try the case.

❬ 4 A judge who borrows things from others is ineligible to try a suit in which the man he borrows from is involved. This applies only to a judge who has nothing to lend in return. If, however, he is in possession of things to lend to others, he is qualified, for the man from whom he borrows may borrow things from him.

❬ 5 If a man takes payment for acting as judge, his decisions are null. This ruling obtains only if it is evident that the payment represents compensation for judicial services. But if he has an occupation in which he is engaged and two men come before him with a lawsuit, and he says to them, "Either procure me one who will attend to my work until I shall have adjudicated your case or remunerate me for loss of time," he is permitted to do so, provided that it is obvious that the payment is for loss of time only and no more and that the fee he receives is contributed equally by both parties to the suit and is given him in the presence of both. Under these circumstances he is permitted to accept payment.

❬ 6 A man is forbidden to act as judge for a friend even though the latter was not his groomsman, or is not his most intimate friend. Nor is he to act as judge for one whom he dislikes, although he is not his enemy, seeking his harm. It is essential that both parties to the suit should be alike in his estimation and affection. The judge who is unacquainted with the litigants and the life they lead is in the best conceivable position to render a righteous judgment.

❡ 7 Two scholars who dislike each other are forbidden to sit together in judgment, for this might lead to the rendering of a perverted judgment. Prompted by hostility, each will be inclined to refute the arguments of the other.

❡ 8 At all times a judge should think of himself as if a sword were suspended over his head and Gehenna gaping under him. He should know whom he is judging and before whom he is judging, and who will call him to account if he deviates from the line of truth, as it is written: "God stands in the congregation of God, in the midst of the judges" (Ps. 82:1); and it is also written: "Consider what you do; for you judge not for man, but for the Lord" (II Chron. 19:6).

❡ 9 A judge who does not render an absolutely true judgment causes the Divine Presence to depart from Israel. If he unlawfully expropriates money from one and gives it to another, the Holy One, blessed be He, will exact his life from him, for it is written: "And the Lord will despoil of life those that despoil them" (Prov. 22:23). A judge who, even for a single hour, renders absolutely true judgments is as though he had (helped to) set the world in order and cause the Divine Presence to dwell in Israel, as it is written: "God stands in the congregation of God" (Ps. 82:1).

Lest the judge say, "Why should I subject myself to this anxiety?" It is written: "He is with you in giving judgment" (II Chron. 19:6); the judge is to be guided only by what he sees with his eyes.

❡ 10 At all times while the litigants are before you regard them as guilty, on the presumption that there is no truth in the statements made by either of them, and be guided by what appears to you from the general drift of the arguments to be true. But when they have departed from your presence, regard them both as innocent, since they have acquiesced in the sentence passed by you, and judge each of them by the scale of merit.

Chapter 24

❡ 3 Whence do we derive that a judge who has reason to suspect one of the litigants of misrepresentation should not say, "I will decide the case according to the evidence and let the witnesses bear the responsibility"? Because it is said: "Keep far from a false matter"

(Ex. 23:7). How is he to proceed in such a case? Let him sedulously investigate the witnesses with the inquiries and queries to which witnesses in capital offenses are subjected. If after this thoroughgoing examination, he concludes [that there is nothing fraudulent about the suit, he gives his decision on the basis of the evidence. But if he has any scruples about it], suspecting dishonesty, or has no confidence in the witnesses, although he has no valid ground on which to disqualify them, or he is inclined to believe that the litigant is a subtle fraud, that the witnesses are honest men, giving their evidence in all innocence, but were led astray by the litigant, or if it appears to him from the whole tenor of the proceedings that some information is withheld, not brought into the open—in any of these or similar circumstances the judge is forbidden to render a decision. He should withdraw from the case and let another judge, who can without qualms of conscience pronounce judgment, handle it. For matters of this nature are committed to the heart, and Scripture says: "For the judgment is God's" (Deut. 1:17).

❴ 4 The court is empowered to flog him who is not liable to flagellation and to mete out the death penalty to him who is not liable to death. This extensive power is granted to the court not with the intention of disregarding the Law but in order to build a fence around it. Whenever the court sees that a command has fallen into general disuse, the duty devolves upon it to safeguard and strengthen the command in any way which in its judgment will achieve the desired result. But whatever measure it adopts is only a temporary one and does not acquire the force of a law, binding for all time to come.*

❴ 10 With regard to all these disciplinary measures, discretionary power is vested in the judge. He is to decide whether the offender deserves these punishments and whether the emergency of the hour demands their application. But whatever the expedient he sees fit to resort to, all his deeds should be done for the sake of heaven. Let not human dignity be light in his eyes; for the respect due to man supersedes a negative rabbinical command. This applies with even greater force to the dignity of the children of Abraham, Isaac, and Jacob, who adhere to the True Law. The judge must be careful not to do aught calculated to destroy their self-respect. His sole concern should be to enhance the glory of God, for whosoever dishonors the Torah

*See below, Rebels, II, 4.

is himself dishonored by men, and whosoever honors the Torah is himself honored by men. To honor the Torah means to follow its statutes and laws.

Chapter 25

❲ 1 It is forbidden to lead the community in a domineering and arrogant manner. One should exercise one's authority in a spirit of humility and reverence. The man at the head of the congregation who arouses excessive fear in the hearts of the members thereof for any but a religious purpose will be punished. It will not be given to him to have a son who will be a scholar, as it is written: "Men do therefore fear him; he will not see any (sons) that are wise of heart" (Job. 37:24).*

❲ 2 He is also forbidden to treat the people with disrespect, though they be ignorant. He should not force his way through the holy people (to get to his seat), for though they be uninformed and lowly, they are the children of Abraham, Isaac, and Jacob, of the hosts of God, brought forth out of Egypt with great power and with a mighty hand. He should bear patiently the cumbrance and burden of the community, as did Moses our Teacher, concerning whom it is said: "As a nursing father carries the sucking child" (Num. 11:12). It is also said: "And I charged your judges" (Deut. 1:16). This is an exhortation to the judge to bear patiently with the congregation, as does a nursing father bear with a sucking child. Consider Moses, the master prophet! We are told that no sooner did the Holy One, blessed be He, send him to Egypt than "He gave them (Moses and Aaron) a charge to the children of Israel" (Ex. 6:13), which sentence is interpreted by tradition that God said to Moses and Aaron, "You are to command Israel with the understanding that they will curse you, and cast stones at you" (Sifre, Num. 11:11).

❲ 3 Just as the judge is bidden to observe this command, so is the congregation bidden to accord respectful treatment to the judge, as it is said: "And I commanded you" (Deut. 1:18). This is an exhortation to the congregation to regard the judge with a feeling of reverence. The judge therefore must not make himself contemptible or indulge in frivolity.

*See Book I, Moral Dispositions, ch. II; Study, VI, 3; Book XIV, Kings, ch. II; Guide, I, ch. 54.

Chapter 26

❲ 1   He who curses a Jewish judge transgresses a negative command, for it is said: "You shall not revile the judges" (Ex. 22:27). So too, he who curses the Nasi, whether it be the head of the Great Sanhedrin or the king, transgresses a negative command, for it is said: "Nor curse a ruler of your people" (ibid.); aye, he who curses any Israelite is flogged, for it is said: "You shall not curse the deaf" (Lev. 19:14). Why does Scripture single out the deaf? To teach that cursing even one who neither hears nor is pained when cursed carries with it the penalty of flogging. It seems to me that he who curses a minor sensitive to affront is flogged, (for he is like the deaf).

EVIDENCE

Chapter 10

❲ 1   Transgressors are ineligible as witnesses by Biblical law, for it is said: "Put not your hand with the wicked to be an unrighteous witness" (Ex. 23:1). The traditional interpretation of this injunction is: "Accept not the wicked as a witness." Aye, if a competent witness knows that his fellow witness is a transgressor, but the judges do not know it, he is forbidden to join with him, even if the evidence is true, for by thus associating with him, the latter's testimony is accepted and the religiously competent man is in league with the wicked. It is hardly necessary to state that if the eligible witness knows that the other is a false witness, he is forbidden to give evidence, as it is said: "Put not your hand with the wicked."

Chapter 11

❲ 1   Whoever has no knowledge of the Scriptures, the Mishnah, and right conduct, has the status of a (potential) sinner and is, by rabbinical authority, ineligible as witness. The presumption is that a person on such a low level will commit most of the transgressions that assail him.

❲ 2   Therefore an am ha-aretz is not invited as witness, nor is his testimony accepted. If, however, he is known to be a person who is engaged in religious acts and the practice of benevolence, and leads a righteous life, so that "right conduct" may be ascribed to him, his testimony is accepted, even though he is ignorant, *i.e.*, is devoid of knowledge of the Scriptures and the Mishnah.

❲ 3 It follows therefore that every scholar is to be deemed eligible, unless he is found to be ineligible, and that every ignorant person is to be regarded as ineligible, unless it is known that he walks in the way of the righteous.

REBELS

Chapter 1*

❲ 1 The Great Sanhedrin of Jerusalem is the root of the Oral Law. The members thereof are the pillars of instruction; out of them go forth statutes and judgments to all Israel. Scripture bids us repose confidence in them, as it is said: "According to the law which they shall teach you" (Deut. 17:11). This is a positive command. Whoever believes in Moses our Teacher and his Law, is bound to follow their guidance in the practice of religion and to lean upon them.

❲ 2 Whoever does not act in accordance with their instruction transgresses a negative command, as it is said: "You shall not turn aside from the sentence which they shall declare to you, to the right hand, or to the left" (Deut. 17:11). The infraction of this negative command does not entail the penalty of flagellation, because this negative command was intended as a warning that the breach thereof involves a death sentence by the court; for any sage who defies their rulings is liable to death by strangulation, as it is said: "And the man that does presumptuously, in not hearkening ... even that man shall die" (*ibid.* 17:12). Whether the direction given by them is with regard to matters that they learned by tradition— matters that form the contents of the Oral Law—or with regard to

*See *Guide,* I, ch. 71; III, ch. 41.

rulings deduced by any of the hermeneutical rules by which the Torah is interpreted—rulings which they approved—or with regard to measures devised by them to serve as a fence about the Law—measures designed to meet the needs of the times, comprising decrees, ordinances, and customs; with regard to any of these three categories, obedience to the direction given by them is a positive command. Whoever disregards any of these transgresses a negative command. For Scripture says: "According to the law which they shall teach you" (ibid. 17:11); this refers to the ordinances, decrees, and customs which they promulgate in public in order to strengthen religion and stabilize the social order. "And according to the judgment which they shall tell you" (ibid.); this refers to the rulings derived by means of any of the exegetical principles by which the Scripture is expounded. "From the sentence which they shall declare to you" (ibid.); this refers to traditional matters, transmitted to them by preceding generations in unbroken succession.

❡ 3 So far as traditional laws are concerned, there never was any controversy. If there was any, we may be sure that the tradition does not date back to Moses our Teacher. As for rules derived by means of hermeneutical principles, if they received the sanction of all the members of the Great Sanhedrin, they were binding. If there was a difference of opinion among them, the Great Sanhedrin followed the majority, and decided the law in accordance with their opinion. This principle obtained also with respect to decrees, ordinances, and customs. If some felt that there was need for instituting a decree, for enacting an ordinance, or for discontinuing a practice, and others were of the opinion that there was no reason for the (new) decree or ordinance, or for the abandonment of the practice, they discussed the matter, followed the majority opinion, and acted accordingly.

❡ 4 So long as the Great Sanhedrin was in existence, there were no controversies in Israel. Whoever was in doubt with regard to a point of law consulted the local court. If the members thereof knew the law, they stated it; otherwise, the questioner together with the members of that court or their deputies went up to Jerusalem and submitted the question to the court that sat at the entrance of the Temple Mount. If the members thereof knew the answer, they stated it; otherwise, they all went to the court meeting at the entrance of the Court. If the members thereof knew the law, they stated it; otherwise, they all proceeded to the Hall of Hewn Stones, the seat of the

Great Sanhedrin, and put the question to that body. If the law concerning which they were all in doubt was known to the Great Sanhedrin, either from tradition or from the application of one of the principles by which Scripture is expounded, they stated it forthwith. If they were not certain of the law, they considered the question at the time when it was submitted to them, discussed it until they either reached a unanimous decision or put it to a vote and decided in accordance with the majority opinion, saying to the questioners, "This is the law," and the latter departed.

After the Great Sanhedrin ceased to exist, disputes multiplied in Israel: one declaring "unclean," giving a reason for his ruling; another declaring "clean," giving a reason for his ruling; one forbidding, the other permitting.

¶ 5 In case there is a difference of opinion between two scholars or two courts, one pronouncing "clean" what the other pronounces "unclean," one declaring "forbidden" what the other declares "permitted," and it is impossible to determine the correct decision, if the controversy is with regard to a Scriptural law, the more stringent view is followed; if it is with regard to a rabbinical law, the more lenient view is followed. This principle obtains in post-Sanhedric times, and obtained even at the time of the Sanhedrin if the case had not yet reached that tribunal. It obtains whether those who hold different views are contemporaries or live at different times.

Chapter 2

¶ 4 However, the court, even if it be inferior (to the former) is authorized to dispense for a time even with these measures. For these decrees are not to be invested with greater stringency than the commands of the Torah itself, which any court has the right to suspend as an emergency measure. Thus the court may inflict flagellation and other punishments, even in cases where such penalties are not warranted by the law if, in its opinion, religion will thereby be strengthened and safeguarded and the people will be restrained from disregarding the words of the Torah. It must not, however, establish the measure to which it resorts as a law binding upon succeeding generations, declaring, "This is the law."

So too, if, in order to bring back the multitudes to religion and save them from general religious laxity, the court deems it necessary to set aside temporarily a positive or a negative command, it may do so, taking into account the need of the hour. Even as a physician will amputate the hand or the foot of a patient in order to save his life, so the court may advocate, when an emergency arises, the temporary disregard of some of the commandments, that the commandments as a whole may be preserved. This is in keeping with what the early sages said: "Desecrate on his account one Sabbath that he be able to observe many Sabbaths" (Yoma 85b).

Chapter 3

❲ 1 He who repudiates the Oral Law is not to be identified with the rebellious elder spoken of in Scripture but is classed with the epicureans (whom any person has a right to put to death).

❲ 2 As soon as it is made public that he has repudiated the Oral Law, (he is cast into the pit and is not rescued from it), he is placed on a par with heretics, epicureans, those who deny the divine origin of Scripture, informers, and apostates—all of whom are ruled out of the community of Israel. No witnesses or previous warning or judges are required. (Whoever puts any of them to death fulfills a great precept, for he removes a stumbling block.)

❲ 3 This applies only to one who repudiates the Oral Law as a result of his reasoned opinion and conclusion, who walks lightmindedly in the stubbornness of his heart, denying first the Oral Law, as did Zadok and Boethus and all who went astray. But their children and grandchildren, who, misguided by their parents, were raised among the Karaites and trained in their views, are like a child taken captive by them and raised in their religion, whose status is that of an *anoos* (one who abjures the Jewish religion under duress), who, although he later learns that he is a Jew, meets Jews, observes them practice their religion, is nevertheless to be regarded as an *anoos*, since he was reared in the erroneous ways of his fathers. Thus it is with those who adhere to the practices of their Karaite parents. Therefore efforts should be made to bring them back in repentance, to draw them near by friendly relations, so that they may return to the strength-giving source, i.e., the Torah.

Chapter 6

❲ 1 The honoring of father and mother is a weighty positive command; so too, is reverence for them. The Bible attaches to the duty of honoring and revering parents an importance equal to that which it attaches to the duty of honoring and revering God. It is said: "Honor your father and your mother" (Ex. 20:12); and it is also written: "Honor the Lord with your substance" (Prov. 3:9). Concerning the duty due to parents, it is said: "You shall fear every man his mother and his father" (Lev. 19:3); and concerning duty to God, it is said: "You shall fear the Lord your God"(Deut. 6:13). We are enjoined to honor and revere them in the manner that we are enjoined to honor and revere His great Name.

❡ 7   To what lengths should the duty of honoring parents go? Even were they to take a purse of his, full of gold, and cast it in his presence into the sea, he must not shame them, manifest grief in their presence, or display any anger, but accept the divine decree without demur.

To what lengths should the duty of revering them go? Even if he is attired in costly garments, presiding over the congregation, and his parents come and rend his garments, strike him on the head, and spit in his face, he must not shame them. It behooves him to remain silent, to fear and revere the King, King of kings, who has thus decreed. For if a mortal king were to issue against him a decree, even more exasperating in character, he would be powerless to rebel against it, all the more so if the author of the decree is He who spoke and the world came into being in accordance with His will.

❡ 8   Although children are commanded to go to the above-mentioned lengths, the father is forbidden to impose too heavy a yoke upon them, to be too exacting with them in matters pertaining to his honor, lest he cause them to stumble. He should forgive them and close his eyes; for a father has the right to forgo the honor due him.

MOURNING

Chapter 1

❡ 1   It is a positive command to mourn for deceased relatives, as it is said: "And if I had eaten the sin-offering today, would it have been well-pleasing in the sight of the Lord?" (Lev. 10:19). According to Scriptural law, mourning is observed only on the first day, that is, the day of death, which is also the day of burial. Mourning on the other of the seven days is not of Biblical origin. For although we are told in the Bible: "And he (Joseph) made a mourning for his father seven days" (Gen. 50:10), when the Torah was given, the law was reinterpreted. It was Moses our Teacher who instituted seven days of mourning and seven days of feasting.

(2   When does the observance of mourning begin? From the time that the top stone closes the grave. But before the body is buried, the near of kin is not prohibited from doing any of the things a mourner is forbidden. For this reason, David washed and anointed himself before his deceased child was buried.

Chapter 4

(1   The Jewish practice with respect to the dead and their interment is as follows: they (who perform the last sacred offices) close his eyes; if his mouth is open, they bind up the jaws; after the body is washed, they stop up the organs of the lower extremities, rub him with divers spices, cut his hair, and dress him in an inexpensive shroud sewed with white linen thread. The rabbis introduced the custom of using as a shroud a rough cloth worth a zuz, in order not to shame the poor. They cover the face of the dead in order not to shame the poor whose faces have turned livid as a result of undernourishment.

(2   It is forbidden to bury the Nasi in a silk shroud or gold-embroidered garments, for this is arrogance, extravagance, and a heathen practice. The body is carried to the cemetery on the shoulder.

Chapter 13

(1   What procedure is followed in consoling mourners? After the body is buried, the mourners assemble and station themselves at the border of the cemetery. All who have escorted the dead stand around them, forming themselves into rows, row after row, each consisting of no fewer than ten people, excluding the mourners.

(2   The mourners stand on the left of the comforters, and all the comforters, one by one, pass by, saying to them, "Be you comforted of heaven." Then the mourners go home. On each of the seven days of mourning, condolence is tendered them, whether by the same visitors or new ones.

❪ 3 The mourner reclines in the most prominent place (when the meal of comfort is served). The comforters are permitted to sit only on the ground, as it is written: "So they sat down with him upon the ground" (Job 2:13), and they are not to say anything to him until he speaks first, as it is written: "And none spoke a word to him" (ibid.); Scripture continues: "After this opened Job his mouth" (ibid. 3:1) "... Then answered Eliphaz" (ibid. 4:1). As soon as he nods his head, the comforters are not permitted to stay any longer so that they fatigue him not.

❪ 4 If the deceased has left no near of kin to be comforted, ten worthy people come and sit in his place all the seven days of mourning and others come (to comfort them). If ten steady attendants are unavailable, the requisite number is supplied daily by those who volunteer their services. They come and sit in his place.

❪ 10 One should not weep for the dead more than three days or lament for him more than seven days. This obtains only in the case of the death of ordinary people, but in the case of scholars, the length of the period of weeping and lamentation is in proportion to their wisdom. But the weeping should not last longer than thirty days. For none is greater than was Moses our Teacher, yet it is said: "And the children of Israel wept for Moses ... thirty days; so the days of weeping in the mourning for Moses were ended" (Deut. 34:8); nor are memorial services to be held after twelve months. For none is greater in wisdom than was our teacher, the saint, yet memorial services for him were held only (for a period) of twelve months. So too, if the news of the demise of a sage is received after twelve months (of his death), no lamentation is made for him.

❪ 11 One should not indulge in excessive grief over one's dead, for it is said: "Weep not for the dead, neither bemoan him" (Jer. 22:10), that is to say, (weep not for him) too much, for that is the way of the world, and he who frets over the way of the world is a fool. What rule should one follow in case of bereavement? (The rule is:) Three days for weeping, seven days for lamenting, and thirty days for (abstaining) from cutting the hair and the other four things (forbidden to a mourner).

❪ 12 Whoever does not mourn the dead in the manner enjoined by the rabbis is cruel. (If one suffers bereavement,) one should be apprehensive, troubled, investigate his conduct, and return in repentance. If one of a company dies, all the members thereof should be troubled. During the first three days the mourner should think of himself as if a sword is resting upon his neck, from the third to the seventh day as if it is lying in the corner, thereafter as if it is moving toward him in the street.

Reflections of this nature will put him on his mettle, he will bestir himself and repent, for it is written: "You have stricken them, but they were not affected" (Jer. 5:3). He should therefore be wide awake and deeply moved.

Chapter 14

❨ 1   The following positive commands were ordained by the rabbis: visiting the sick; comforting the mourners; joining a funeral procession; dowering a bride; escorting departing guests; performing for the dead the last tender offices; acting as pallbearer; going before the bier; making lamentation (for the dead); digging a grave and burying the body; causing the bride and the bridegroom to rejoice; providing them with all their needs (for the wedding). These constitute deeds of lovingkindness performed in person and for which no fixed measure is prescribed. Although all these commands are only on rabbinical authority, they are implied in the precept: "And you shall love your neighbor as yourself" (Lev. 19:18), that is: what you would have others do to you, do to him who is your brother in the Law and in the performance of the commandments.

❨ 2   The reward for escorting strangers is greater than the reward for all the other commandments. It is a practice which Abraham our Father instituted, and the act of kindness which he exercised. He gave wayfarers food to eat and water to drink and escorted them. Hospitality to wayfarers is greater than receiving the Divine Presence, as it is said: "And he looked, and, lo, three men stood over against him, and when he saw them, he ran to meet them" (Gen. 18:2). But escorting guests is even greater than according them hospitality. Said the rabbis: "Whoever does not accompany guests is as though he would shed blood" (Sotah 46b).

❨ 3   A person may be compelled to escort a visitor, just as he is compelled to contribute to charity. The court used to provide escorts for itinerants. If it neglected to do so, it was accounted as if it had shed blood. Even if a person accompanies another the distance of four cubits a great reward is in store for him.*

*See Book VII, Gifts to the Poor.

How far is one bound to escort another? A teacher accompanies his pupil as far as the outskirts of the city; one accompanies one's equal up to the Sabbath limit; a pupil escorts his master a distance of a Persian mile; in the case of one's chief teacher, one is to escort him a distance of three Persian miles.

(4 All are in duty bound to visit the sick. Even a man of prominence must visit a less important person. The ill should be visited many times a day. The more often a person calls on the sick, the more praiseworthy he is, provided that he does not inconvenience the patient. He who visits the sick is as though he would take away part of his sickness and lighten his pain. Whoever does not call to see the sick is as though he would shed blood.

(5 A sick person should not be visited before the third day. If his illness came on suddenly and his condition is growing worse, he may be called on forthwith. He should not be visited either during the first three hours or during the last three hours of the day, because (during those hours) they who look after him are busy attending to his needs. Those who suffer from intestinal trouble or have eye trouble or headaches should not be visited, because it is hard for them to see callers.

(6 One who visits a sick person shall not sit upon the bed, or in a chair or on a bench or any elevated place, or above the head side of the patient, but should wrap himself up and sit below the head side, pray for his recovery, and depart.

(7 It seems to me that the duty of comforting mourners takes precedence over the duty of visiting the sick, because comforting mourners is an act of benevolence toward the living and the dead.

KINGS AND WARS

Chapter 1

(1 Three commandments—to be carried out on entering the Land of Israel—were enjoined upon Israel: to appoint a king, as it is said: "You shall in anywise set him king over you" (Deut. 17:15); to destroy the seed of Amalek, as it is said: "You shall blot out the remembrance of Amalek" (ibid. 25:19); and to build the Sanctuary, as it is said: "Even to His habitation shall you seek, and there you shall come" (ibid. 12:5).

¶ 2 The appointment of a king was to precede the war with Amalek, as it is written: "The Lord sent me to anoint you to be king over His people. . . . Now go and smite Amalek" (I Sam. 15:1, 3). The destruction of the seed of Amalek was to precede the erection of the sanctuary, as it is written: "And it came to pass, when the king dwelt in his house, and the Lord had given him rest from all his enemies round about, that the king said to Nathan the prophet: . . . I dwell in a house of cedar but the Ark of God dwells within curtains" (II Sam. 7:1–2).

Seeing that the setting up of a king was a commandment, why did the Holy One, blessed be He, look with disfavor upon the request (made by the people) of Samuel for a king? Because they asked it in a querulous spirit. Their request was prompted not by a desire to fulfill the commandment but by a desire to rid themselves of Samuel the prophet, as it is written: "For they have not rejected you, but they have rejected Me" (I Sam. 8:7).

Chapter 2

¶ 6 Just as Scripture accords great honor to the king and bids all pay him honor, so it bids him cultivate a humble and lowly spirit, as it is written: "And my heart is humbled within me" (Ps. 109:22). He must not exercise his authority in a supercilious manner, as it is said, "that his heart be not lifted up above his brethren" (Deut. 17:20). He should deal graciously and compassionately with the small and the great, conduct their affairs in their best interests, be wary of the honor of even the lowliest. When he addresses the public collectively, he shall use gentle language, as did David when he said: "Hear me, my brethren, and my people" (I Chron. 28:2). It is also written, "if you will be a servant to this people this day . . . then they will be your servants forever" (I Kings 12:7). At all times, his conduct should be marked by a spirit of great humility. None was greater than Moses our Teacher; yet he said: "And what are we? Your murmurings are not against us" (Ex. 16:8). He should put up with the cumbrances, burdens, grumblings, and anger of the people as a nursing father puts up with a sucking child. The Bible styles the king "shepherd" [as it is written], "to be shepherd over Jacob, His people" (Ps. 78:71). The way in which a shepherd acts is explicitly stated in the prophetic text: "Even as a shepherd that feeds his flock, that gathers the lambs in his arms, and carries them in his bosom and gently leads those that give suck" (Is. 40:11).

Chapter 3

❡ 1 As soon as the king ascends the throne, he must write a scroll of the Law for himself, in addition to the one which his ancestors have left him. He is to have it corrected by the court of seventy-one from the scroll in the Temple Court. If his father left him no scroll or it was lost, he must write two copies; one, the writing of which is obligatory upon every Jew, he shall place in his treasure-house, and the other is to be with him all the time, except when he enters the privy or bathhouse or any other place where it is improper to read it. When he goes forth to war, it shall be with him; when he returns (from war), it shall be with him; when he sits in judgment, it shall be with him; when he sits down to eat, it shall be before him, as it is said: "And it shall be with him, and he shall read therein all the days of his life" (Deut. 17:19).

❡ 5 The king is forbidden to drink to the point of intoxication, as it is written: "It is not for kings to drink wine" (Prov. 31:4). He shall be occupied day and night with the study of the Law and the needs of Israel, as it is said: "And it shall be with him, and he shall read therein all the days of his life" (Deut. 17:19).

❡ 6 So, too, he must not indulge in sexual excess. Even if he has only one wife, he shall not have frequent relations with her, as fools do, for it is written: "Give not strength to women" (Prov. 31:3). Scripture lays particular stress on (the danger) of his heart being turned away from God, as it is said, "that his heart turn not away" (Deut. 17:17); for his heart is the heart of the whole congregation of Israel. Therefore Scripture exhorts him more than any other Israelite to cleave to the Law, as it is said, "all the days of his life" (ibid. 17:19).

Chapter 4

❡ 1 It is within the province of the king to levy taxes upon the people for his own needs or for war purposes. He fixes the customs duties, and it is forbidden to evade them. He may issue a decree that whoever dodges them shall be punished either by confiscation of his property or by death, as it is written: "And you shall be his servants" (I Sam. 8:17). Elsewhere it is said: "All the people found therein shall be tributary to you, and shall serve you" (Deut. 20:11). From these verses we infer that the king imposes taxes and fixes customs duties and that all the laws enacted by him with regard to these and like matters are valid, for it is his prerogative to exercise all the authority set forth in the section relating to the King.

¶ 10 All the land he conquers belongs to him. He may give thereof to his servants and warriors as much as he wishes; he may keep thereof for himself as much as he wishes. In all these matters he is the final arbiter. But whatever he does should be done by him for the sake of heaven. His sole aim and thought should be to uplift the true religion, to fill the world with righteousness, to break the arm of the wicked, and to fight the battles of the Lord. The prime reason for appointing a king was that he execute judgment and wage war, as it is written: "And that our king may judge us, and go out before us, and fight our battles" (I Sam. 8:20).

Chapter 5

¶ 9 It is forbidden to emigrate from Palestine and go abroad, unless one goes to study the Law, or to marry a wife, or to rescue property from heathens, and then returns to Palestine. So, too, one may leave on business. But one is forbidden to make one's home abroad, unless there is a famine in Palestine so severe that a denar's worth of wheat is selling at two denar. This holds good only if money is available and food is high. But if food is cheap and money scarce and one is unable to earn it and has no savings, one may go to any place where one can make a living. But though one is permitted to emigrate, if one does, the act is not in conformity with the law of saintliness. Remember Mahlon and Chilion! They were the two great men of their generation. They left Palestine at a time of great distress; nevertheless, they incurred thereby the penalty of extinction.

¶ 10 The greatest of our sages used to kiss (the rocks) on the borders of the Land of Israel. They used to kiss the stones of the land and roll themselves in its dust, as it is written: "For your servants take pleasure in her stones, and love her dust" (Ps. 102:15).

([11   The rabbis said that the sins of him who lives in Palestine are forgiven, as it is written: "And the inhabitant shall not say: 'I am sick'; the people that dwell therein shall be forgiven their iniquity" (Is. 33:24). Even if one walks four cubits in it, one is assured of life in the world to come. So too, one who is buried there will obtain atonement; it is as though the place (where one lies) were an altar which effects atonement, as it is said: "And the land makes expiation for His people" (Deut. 32:43). In (forecasting) punishment, (the prophet) says: "And you yourself shall die in an unclean land" (Amos 7:17). There is no comparison between one whom Palestine receives while he is living and one whom it receives after his death; nevertheless the greatest among our wise men brought their dead there. Think of Jacob, our father, and of Joseph, the righteous!

([12   At all times one should live in Palestine even in a place the majority of whose population is heathen, and not live outside Palestine even in a place the majority of whose population is Jewish; for he who leaves Palestine is as though he would serve idolatry, as it is written: "For they have driven me out this day that I should not cleave to the inheritance of the Lord, saying: Go, serve other gods" (I Sam. 26:19). In (predicting) punishment, the prophet says: "Neither shall they enter into the Land of Israel" (Ezek. 13:9).

Just as it is forbidden to emigrate from Palestine to other lands, so it is forbidden to emigrate from Babylon to other lands, as it is written: "They shall be carried to Babylon, and there shall they be" (Jer. 27:22).

Chapter 7

([1   A priest is appointed to address the troops in time of war. He is anointed with the oil of anointment and is designated as "the priest anointed for war."

([2   Twice the priest anointed for war addresses the troops. Once he speaks to the men on the frontier when they are about to cross the border to give battle to the enemy. He says to them: "What man is there that has built a new house and has not dedicated it? . . . And what man is there that has planted a vineyard, and has not used the fruit thereof? . . . Let him go and return to his house," etc. (Deut. 20:5-7). Those who come under this category are to hold themselves ready for discharge when they hear the proclamation again. The second time he addresses them when they are arrayed for battle, saying to them: "Fear not, nor be alarmed, neither be affrighted at them" (Deut. 20:3).

❡ 3   When the battle lines are being drawn, getting ready to meet the enemy, the anointed priest mounts a platform and, facing the armed forces, says in Hebrew: "Hear, O Israel, draw nigh this day into battle against your enemies, let not your heart faint; fear not, nor be alarmed, neither be affrighted at them. For the Lord your God is He that goes with you, to fight for you against your enemies, to save you" (Deut. 20:3–4). Thus far the anointed priest speaks; another priest proclaims these words in a loud voice. The anointed priest then continues: "What man is there that has built a new house . . . and what man is there that has planted a vineyard . . . and what man is there that has betrothed a wife? . . . Let him go and return to his house" (ibid. 20:5–7). Thus far the anointed priest speaks; an officer proclaims these words in a loud voice. Then the officer, unprompted by the priest, continues: "What man is there that is fearful and fainthearted? . . ." (ibid. 20:8) and another officer proclaims these words to the armed forces.

❡ 15   "What man is there that is fearful and fainthearted?" (Deut. 20:8). This is to be understood literally, that is, the man who is not physically fit to join the ranks in battle. Once, however, he has joined the ranks, he should put his reliance upon Him who is the hope of Israel, their Savior in time of trouble. He should know that he is fighting for the oneness of God, risk his life, and neither fear nor be affrighted. Nor should he think of his wife or children, but, forgetting them and all else, concentrate on the war. He who permits his attention to be diverted during a battle and becomes disturbed, transgresses a negative command, as it is said: "Let not your heart faint, fear not, nor be alarmed, neither be affrighted at them" (ibid. 20:3). Moreover, he is accountable for the lives of all Israel. If he does not conquer (because) he did not fight with all his heart and soul, it is as though he had shed the blood of all, as it is said: "Lest his brethren's heart melt as his heart" (ibid. 20:8). This truth is brought out with notable clearness in the injunction of the prophet: "Cursed be he that does the work of the Lord with a slack hand, and cursed be he that keeps back his sword from blood" (Jer. 48:10).

He who fights with all his heart, without fear, with the sole intention of sanctifying the Name, is assured that no harm will befall him and no evil will overtake him. He will build for himself a lasting house in Israel, acquiring it for himself and his children forever, and will prove worthy of life in the world to come, as it is written: "For the Lord will certainly make my lord a sure house, because my lord fights the battles of the Lord; and evil is not found in you. . . . Yet the soul of my lord shall be bound in the bundle of life with the Lord your God" (I Sam. 25:28–29).

Chapter 8

❡ 10 Moses our Teacher bequeathed the Law and commandments to Israel, as it is said, "an inheritance of the congregation of Jacob" (Deut. 33:4), and to those of other nations who are willing to be converted (to Judaism), as it is said: "One law and one ordinance shall be both for you, and for the resident alien" (Num. 15:16). But no coercion to accept the Law and commandments is practiced on those who are unwilling to do so. Moreover, Moses our Teacher was commanded by God to compel all human beings to accept the commandments enjoined upon the descendants of Noah. Anyone who does not accept them is put to death. He who does accept them is invariably styled a resident alien. He must declare his acceptance in the presence of three associates. Anyone who has declared his intention to be circumcised and fails to do so within twelve months is treated like a heathen infidel.

❡ 11 A heathen who accepts the seven commandments and observes them scrupulously is a "righteous heathen," and will have a portion in the world to come, provided that he accepts them and performs them because the Holy One, blessed be He, commanded them in the Law and made known through Moses our Teacher that the observance thereof had been enjoined upon the descendants of Noah even before the Law was given. But if his observance thereof is based upon a reasoned conclusion he is not deemed a resident alien, or one of the pious of the Gentiles, but one of their wise men.*

Chapter 9

❡ 1 Six precepts were given to Adam: prohibition of idolatry, of blasphemy, of murder, of adultery, of robbery, and the command to establish courts of justice. Although there is a tradition to this

*See *Eight Chapters*, ch. VI; Letter to Hasdai.

effect—a tradition dating back to Moses our Teacher, and human reason approves of those precepts—it is evident from the general tenor of the Scriptures that he (Adam) was bidden to observe these commandments. An additional commandment was given to Noah: prohibition of (eating) a limb from a living animal, as it is said: "Only flesh with the life thereof, which is the blood thereof, shall you eat" (Gen. 9:4). Thus we have seven commandments. So it was until Abraham appeared who, in addition to the aforementioned commandments, was charged to practice circumcision. Moreover, Abraham instituted the Morning Service. Isaac set apart tithes and instituted the Afternoon Service. Jacob added to the preceding law (prohibiting) the sinew that shrank, and inaugurated the Evening Service. In Egypt Amram was charged to observe other precepts, until Moses came and the Law was completed through him.

Chapter 11

❨ 1 King Messiah will arise and restore the kingdom of David to its former state and original sovereignty. He will rebuild the sanctuary and gather the dispersed of Israel. All the ancient laws will be reinstituted in his days; sacrifices will again be offered; the Sabbatical and Jubilee years will again be observed in accordance with the commandments set forth in the Law.

He who does not believe in a restoration or does not look forward to the coming of the Messiah denies not only the teachings of the prophets but also those of the Law and Moses our Teacher, for Scripture affirms the rehabilitation of Israel, as it is said: "Then the Lord your God will turn your captivity, and have compassion upon you, and will return and gather you . . . if any of yours that are dispersed be in the uttermost parts of heaven . . . and the Lord your God will bring you into the land which your fathers possessed" (Deut. 30:3–5). These words stated in Scripture include all that the prophets said (on the subject). They recur in the section treating of Balaam. The prophecy in that section bears upon the two Messiahs: the first, namely, David, who saved Israel from the hand of their enemies; and the later Messiah, a descendant of David, who will achieve the final salvation of Israel. There it is said: "I see him, but not now" (Num. 24:17), this refers to David; "I behold him, but not nigh" (ibid.), this refers to King Messiah. "There shall step forth a star out of Jacob" (ibid.), this refers to David; "And a sceptre shall rise out of Israel" (*ibid.*), this refers to King Messiah. "And shall smite through the corners of Moab" (*ibid.*), this refers to David, for we are told: "And he smote Moab, and measured them with the line" (II Sam. 8:2); "And break down all the sons of Seth" (Num. 24:17), this refers to King Messiah, as it is written concerning him: "And his dominion shall be from sea to sea" (Zech. 9:10). "And Edom shall be a possession" (Num. 24:18), this refers to David, as it is written: "And all the Edomites became servants to David" (II Sam. 8:14); "And Seir shall be a possession" (Num. 24:18), this refers to (the days of) King Messiah, as it is written: "And saviors shall come up on Mount Zion to judge the mount of Esau" (Obad. 1:21).

❡ 2 So too, with reference to the cities of refuge, the Bible says: "And if the Lord your God enlarge your borders ... then you shall add three cities more for you" (Deut. 19:8–9)—a precept which has never been carried out. Yet, not in vain did the Holy One, blessed be He, give us this commandment. As for the prophetic utterances on the subject (of the Messiah), no citations are necessary, as all their books are full of this theme.

❡ 3 Do not think that King Messiah will have to perform signs and wonders, bring anything new into being, revive the dead, or do similar things. It is not so. Rabbi Akiva was a great sage, a teacher of the Mishnah, yet he was also the armor-bearer of Ben Kozba. He affirmed that the latter was King Messiah; he and all the wise men of his generation shared this belief until Ben Kozba was slain in (his) iniquity, when it became known that he was not (the Messiah). Yet the rabbis had not asked him for a sign or token. The general principle is: this Law of ours with its statutes and ordinances (is not subject to change). It is forever and all eternity; it is not to be added to or to be taken away from. (Whoever adds aught to it, or takes away aught from it, or misinterprets it, and strips the commandments of their literal sense is an impostor, a wicked man, and a heretic.)

❡ 4 If there arise a king from the House of David who meditates on the Torah, occupies himself with the commandments, as did his ancestor David, observes the precepts prescribed in the written and the Oral Law, prevails upon Israel to walk in the way of the Torah and to repair its breaches, and fights the battles of the Lord, it may be assumed that he is the Messiah. If he does these things and succeeds, rebuilds the sanctuary on its site, and gathers the dispersed of Israel, he is beyond all doubt the Messiah. He will prepare the whole world to serve the Lord with one accord, as it is written: "For then will I turn to the peoples a pure language, that they may all call upon the name of the Lord to serve Him with one consent" (Zeph. 3:9).

Chapter 12

❡ 1   Let no one think that in the days of the Messiah any of the laws of nature will be set aside, or any innovation be introduced into creation. The world will follow its normal course. The words of Isaiah: "And the wolf shall dwell with the lamb, and the leopard shall lie down with the kid" (Is. 11:6) are to be understood figuratively, meaning that Israel will live securely among the wicked of the heathens who are likened to wolves and leopards, as it is written: "A wolf of the deserts does spoil them, a leopard watches over their cities" (Jer. 5:6). They will all accept the true religion, and will neither plunder nor destroy, and together with Israel earn a comfortable living in a legitimate way, as it is written: "And the lion shall eat straw like the ox" (Is. 11:7). All similar expressions used in connection with the Messianic age are metaphorical. In the days of King Messiah the full meaning of those metaphors and their allusions will become clear to all.*

❡ 2   Said the rabbis: "The sole difference between the present and the Messianic days is delivery from servitude to foreign powers" (Sanhedrin 91b). To take the words of the prophets in their literal sense, it appears that the inauguration of the Messianic era will be marked by the war of Gog and Magog; that prior to that war, a prophet will arise to guide Israel and set their hearts aright, as it is written: "Behold, I will send you Elijah the prophet" (Mal. 3:23). He (Elijah) will come neither to declare the clean unclean, nor the unclean clean; neither to disqualify those who are presumed to be of legitimate descent, nor to pronounce qualified those who are presumed to be of illegitimate descent, but to bring peace in the world, as it is said: "And he shall turn the hearts of the fathers to the children" (ibid. 3:24).

Some of our sages say that the coming of Elijah will precede the advent of the Messiah. But no one is in a position to know the details of this and similar things until they have come to pass. They

*See Guide, III, ch. 11; also II, ch. 29.

are not explicitly stated by the prophets. Nor have the rabbis any tradition with regard to these matters. They are guided solely by what the Scriptural texts seem to imply. Hence there is a divergence of opinion on the subject. But be that as it may, neither the exact sequence of those events nor the details thereof constitute religious dogmas. No one should ever occupy himself with the legendary themes or spend much time on Midrashic statements bearing on this and like subjects. He should not deem them of prime importance, since they lead neither to the fear of God nor to the love of Him. Nor should one calculate the end. Said the rabbis: "Blasted be those who reckon out the end" (Sanhedrin 97b). One should wait (for his coming) and accept in principle this article of faith, as we have stated before.

❪ 3 In the days of King Messiah, when his kingdom will be established and all Israel will gather around him, their pedigrees will be determined by him through the Holy Spirit which will rest upon him, as it is written: "And he shall sit as a refiner and purifier ..." (Mal. 3:3). First he will purify the descendants of Levi, declaring: "This one, of good birth, is a priest; this one, of good birth, is a Levite." Those who are not of good birth will be demoted to the rank of (lay) Israelites, for it is written: "And the Tirshatha said to them that they should not eat of the most holy things, till there stood up a priest with Urim and Tummim" (Ezra 2:63). It is inferred therefrom that the genealogy of those considered to be of good lineage will be traced by means of the Holy Spirit, and those found to be of good birth will be made known. The descent of the Israelites will be recorded according to their tribes. He will announce: "This one is of such-and-such a tribe, and this one of such-and-such a tribe." But he will not say concerning those who are presumed to be of pure descent: "This is a bastard; this is a slave." For the rule is: once a family has been intermingled with others, it retains its status.

❪ 4 The sages and prophets did not long for the days of the Messiah that Israel might exercise dominion over the world, or rule over the heathens, or be exalted by the nations, or that it might eat and drink and rejoice. Their aspiration was that Israel be free to devote itself to the Law and its wisdom, with no one to oppress or disturb it, and thus be worthy of life in the world to come.

❪ 5 In that era there will be neither famine nor war, neither jealousy nor strife. Blessings will be abundant, comforts within the reach of all. The one preoccupation of the whole world will be to know the Lord. Hence Israelites will be very wise, they will know the things that are now concealed and will attain an understanding of their Creator to the utmost capacity of the human mind, as it is written: "For the earth shall be full of the knowledge of the Lord, as the waters cover the sea" (Is. 11:9).

The following is the uncensored version of the end of Kings, ch. XI.*

But if he does not meet with full success, or is slain, it is obvious that he is not the Messiah promised in the Torah. He is to be regarded like all the other wholehearted and worthy kings of the House of David who died and whom the Holy One, blessed be He, raised up to test the multitude, as it is written, "And some of them that are wise shall stumble, to refine among them, and to purify, and to make white, even to the time of the end; for it is yet for the time appointed" (Dan. 11:35).

Even of Jesus of Nazareth, who imagined that he was the Messiah, but was put to death by the court, Daniel had prophesied, as it is written, "And the children of the violent among your people shall lift themselves up to establish the vision; but they shall stumble" (Dan. 11:14). For has there ever been a greater stumbling than this? All the prophets affirmed that the Messiah would redeem Israel, save them, gather their dispersed, and confirm the commandments. But he caused Israel to be destroyed by the sword, their remnant to be dispersed and humiliated. He was instrumental in changing the Torah and causing the world to err and serve another besides God.

But it is beyond the human mind to fathom the designs of the Creator; for our ways are not His ways, neither are our thoughts His thoughts. All these matters relating to Jesus of Nazareth and the Ishmaelite (Mohammed) who came after him, only served to clear the way for King Messiah, to prepare the whole world to worship God with one accord, as it is written, "For then will I turn to the peoples

*Cf. *Epistle to Yemen.*

a pure language, that they may all call upon the name of the Lord to serve Him with one consent" (Zeph. 3:9). Thus the Messianic hope, the Torah, and the commandments have become familiar topics—topics of conversation (among the inhabitants) of the far isles and many peoples, uncircumcised of heart and flesh. They are discussing these matters and the commandments of the Torah. Some say, "Those commandments were true, but have lost their validity and are no longer binding"; others declare that they had an esoteric meaning and were not intended to be taken literally; that the Messiah has already come and revealed their occult significance. But when the true King Messiah will appear and succeed, be exalted and lifted up, they will forthwith recant and realize that they have inherited naught but lies from their fathers, that their prophets and forebears led them astray.

GUIDE OF THE PERPLEXED

INTRODUCTION TO GUIDE OF THE PERPLEXED

MEDIEVAL philosophy, whether Jewish, Muslim, or Christian, had many staple scholastic, and, often, purely technical concerns. It addressed itself to a wide range of unchanging problems—for example, in the realms of logic (problem of universals), psychology (nature of the soul), physics (matter, vacuum)—which cut across religious frontiers and had preoccupied philosophers since classical antiquity. It also had a panoply of applied problems and practical aspects; it concerned itself with problems of religious philosophy such as faith and reason, revelation, creation of the world, the nature of God and proofs for His existence, miracles, law, and ethics. It led, in addition, to a philosophic re-examination of religious practices and beliefs (e.g., prayer, providence).

The following chapters from the Guide have been selected to introduce the reader to some themes illustrating the impact of philosophy on religion—its challenges, its modes of thought and major tendencies, its suppositions, achievements, and goals. The dedication and introduction indicate the method and purposes of the book, underscoring the need for care and discretion, and arduous preparation; the student must patiently progress from logic, mathematics, and science, from all the liberal arts, to metaphysics—which is the queen of all studies. Maimonides suggests that perplexity is a noble result of the need to maintain the integrity and respectability of both religion and philosophy. The arraignment of the Mutakallimun and the forceful exposition of the differences between their philosophic approach and his own are basic for him. The identification of the rabbinic "Account of the Beginning" (Gen. 1) and "Account of the Divine Chariot" (Ezek. 1) with physics and metaphysics is, of course, crucial for his undertaking. It quickly becomes obvious that this identification is possible only on the basis of the correct interpretation—sometimes, indeed, the skillful decoding—of the parables and metaphors of the prophetic and rabbinic writings. The entire enterprise is subtle and complex and open-ended.

The reader should especially note:

(1) The limitations of the human intellect, the gradation of intellectual pursuits, and the difficulties of philosophical studies (Epistle Dedicatory; I, chs. 31–34);

(2) The ethical and ceremonial applications of the theory of divine attributes, particularly with regard to prayer (I, chs. 54 and 59; III, ch. 54);

(3) Prophecy and divine law and the special status of Mosaic prophecy (II, chs. 39–40);

(4) Theodicy and the problem of evil (III, ch. 12);

(5) Historic-rational explanation of the purpose of the Torah and its commandments (III, ch. 26 ff.);

(6) The confrontation between religious law with its insistence upon the necessity of action, and Aristotelian philosophy with its insistence upon the excellence and superiority of contemplation—a leitmotiv of medieval thought (e.g., I, ch. 1; III, chs. 27, 51, 52, and 54). Religious philosophy is punctuated with tensions between the active and contemplative life, withdrawal from and involvement in society, individual perfection and social ethics, and cognate problems.

Chapters 13–16, 25, and 27 of Part II provide an example of a full-fledged, philosophic discussion (on creation) and its implications for religious belief in general. Maimonides' critical attitude toward Aristotle is significant in this context. Demonstration of the fact that Aristotle was unable to extricate himself from certain intellectual impasses could serve as an effective antidote to a blind, unreasoned acceptance of Aristotelianism. Equally important is the stipulation that a religiously acceptable theory of creation must preserve God's freedom of action. Chapter 24 of Part III illustrates philosophical exegesis of a crucial Biblical theme—man's trials at the hands of God—and its application to the complex and perplexing problems of divine providence and human suffering. Together with Maimonides' outline of the history of philosophy which sustains the centrality of philosophy in religion (I, ch. 71), these discussions should give the reader some idea of the scope, method, and philosophic stance of the Guide. They should also make him appreciate the fact that there remains considerable doubt as to the proper interpretation of the Maimonidean philosophy.

An apology and a warning must accompany any attempt to anthologize the Guide, for Maimonides insisted that the sequence of the chapters and the context in which various philosophic arguments are introduced help the reader arrive at a proper understanding. I trust nevertheless that the following selections will tell their true story and reveal their genuine meaning to the thoughtful reader.

In the name of the Lord, God of the world (Gen. 21:33)

My honored pupil Rabbi *Joseph*, may *the* Rock guard *you*, son of *Rabbi Judah*, may *his repose be in Paradise*. When you came to me, having conceived the intention of journeying from the country farthest away in order to read texts under my guidance, I had a high opinion of you because of your strong desire for inquiry and because of what I had observed in your poems of your powerful longing for speculative matters. This was the case since your letters and compositions in rhymed prose came to me from Alexandria, before your grasp was put to the test. I said however: perhaps his longing is stronger than his grasp. When thereupon you read under my guidance texts dealing with the science of astronomy and prior to that texts dealing with mathematics, which is necessary as an introduction to astronomy, my joy in you increased because of the excellence of your mind and the quickness of your grasp. I saw that your longing for mathematics was great, and hence I let you train yourself in that science, knowing where you would end. When thereupon you read under my guidance texts dealing with the art of logic, my hopes fastened upon you, and I saw that you are one worthy to have the secrets of the prophetic books revealed to you so that you would consider in them that which perfect men ought to consider. Thereupon I began to let you see certain flashes and to give you certain indications. Then I saw that you demanded of me additional knowledge and asked me to make clear to you certain things pertaining to divine matters, to inform you of the intentions of the Mutakallimun in this respect, and to let you know whether their methods were demonstrative and, if not, to what art they belonged. As I also saw, you had already acquired some smattering of this subject from people other than myself; you were perplexed, as stupefaction had come over you; your noble soul demanded of you to "find out acceptable words" (Eccles. 12:10). Yet I did not cease dissuading you from this and enjoining upon you to approach matters in an orderly manner. My purpose in this was that the truth should be established in your mind according to the proper methods and that certainty should not come to you by accident. Whenever during your association with me a (Biblical) verse or some text of the sages was mentioned in which there was a pointer to some strange notion, I did not refrain from explaining it to you. Then when God decreed our separation and you betook yourself elsewhere, these meetings aroused in me a resolution that had slackened. Your absence moved me to compose this treatise, which I have composed for you and for those like you, however few they are. I have set it down in dispersed chapters. All of them that are written down will reach you where you are, one after the other. Be in good health.

PART ONE

INTRODUCTION TO PART ONE

THE first purpose of this treatise is to explain the meanings of certain terms occurring in books of prophecy. . . . It is not the purpose of this treatise to make its totality understandable to the vulgar or to beginners in speculation, nor to teach those who have not engaged in any study other than the science of the Law—I mean the legalistic study of the Law. For the purpose of this treatise and of all those like it is the science of Law in its true sense. Or rather its purpose is to give indications to a religious man for whom the validity of our Law has become established in his soul and has become actual in his belief—such a man being perfect in his religion and character, and having studied the sciences of the philosophers and come to know what they signify. The human intellect having drawn him on and led him to dwell within its province, he must have felt distressed by the externals of the Law and by the meanings of the above-mentioned equivocal, derivative, or amphibolous terms, as he continued to understand them by himself or was made to understand them by others. Hence he would remain in a state of perplexity and confusion as to whether he should follow his intellect, renounce what he knew concerning the terms in question, and consequently consider

236

that he has renounced the foundations of the Law. Or he should hold fast to his understanding of these terms and not let himself be drawn on together with his intellect, rather turning his back on it and moving away from it, while at the same time perceiving that he had brought loss to himself and harm to his religion. He would be left with those imaginary beliefs to which he owes his fear and difficulty and would not cease to suffer from heartache and great perplexity.

This treatise also has a second purpose: namely, the explanation of very obscure parables occurring in the books of the prophets, but not explicitly identified there as such. Hence an ignorant or heedless individual might think that they possess only an external sense, but no internal one. However, even when one who truly possesses knowledge considers these parables and interprets them according to their external meaning, he too is overtaken by great perplexity. But if we explain these parables to him or if we draw his attention to their being parables, he will take the right road and be delivered from this perplexity. That is why I have called this treatise the *Guide of the Perplexed*.

I do not say that this treatise will remove all difficulties for those who understand it. I do, however, say that it will remove most of the difficulties, and those of the greatest moment. A sensible man thus should not demand of me or hope that when we mention a subject, we shall make a complete exposition of it, or that when we engage in the explanation of the meaning of one of the parables, we shall set forth exhaustively all that is expressed in that parable. An intelligent man would be unable to do so even by speaking directly to an interlocutor. How then could he put it down in writing without becoming a butt for every ignoramus who, thinking that he has the necessary knowledge, would let fly at him the shafts of his ignorance? We have already explained in our legal compilations some general propositions concerning this subject and have drawn attention to many themes. Thus we have mentioned there that the "Account of the Beginning" is identical with natural science, and the "Account of the Divine Chariot" with divine science; and have explained the rabbinic saying: "The 'Account of the Divine Chariot' ought not to be taught even to one man, except if he be wise and able to understand by himself, in which case only the chapter headings may be transmitted to him" (Hagigah 11b, 13a). Hence you should not ask of me here anything beyond the chapter headings. And even those are not set down in order or arranged in coherent fashion in this treatise, but rather are scattered and entangled with other subjects that are to be clarified. For my purpose is that the truths be glimpsed and then again be concealed, so as not to oppose that divine purpose which one cannot possibly oppose and which has concealed from the vulgar among the people those truths especially requisite for His apprehension. As He has said: "The secret of the Lord is with them that fear Him" (Ps. 25:14). Know that with regard to natural matters as well, it is impossible to give a clear exposition when teaching some of their principles as they are. For you know the saying of the sages, may their memory be blessed: "The 'Account of the Beginning' ought not to be taught in the presence of two men" (Hagigah 11b). Now if someone explained all those matters in a book, he in effect would be teaching them to thousands of men. Hence these matters too occur in parables in the books of prophecy. The sages, may their memory be blessed, following the trail of these books, likewise have spoken of them in riddles and parables, for there is a close connection between these matters and the divine science, and they too are secrets of that divine science.

You should not think that these great secrets are fully and completely known to anyone among us. They are not. But sometimes truth flashes out to us so that we think that it is day, and then matter and habit in their various forms conceal it so that we find ourselves again in an obscure night, almost as we were at first. We are like someone in a very dark night over whom lightning flashes time and time again. Among us there is one for whom the lightning flashes time and time again, so that he is always, as it were, in unceasing light. Thus night appears to him as day. That is the degree of the great one among the prophets, to whom it was said: "But as for you, stand here by Me" (Deut. 5:28), and of whom it was said: "that the skin of his face sent forth beams" (Ex. 34:29), and so on. Among them there is one to whom the lightning flashes only once in the whole of his night; that is the rank of those of whom it is said: "They prophesied, but they did so no more" (Num. 11:25). There are others between whose lightning flashes there are greater or shorter intervals. Thereafter comes he who does not attain a degree in which his darkness is illumined by any lightning flash. It is illumined, however, by a polished body or something of that kind, stones or something else that give light in the darkness of the night. And even this small light that shines over us is not always there, but flashes and is hidden again, as if it were the "flaming sword which turned every way" (Gen. 3:24). It is in accord with these states that the degrees of the perfect vary. As for those who never even once see a light, but grope about in their night, of them it is said: "They know not, neither do they understand; they go about in the darkness" (Ps. 82:5). The truth, in spite of the strength of its manifestation, is entirely hidden from them, as is said of them: "And now men see not the light which is bright in the skies" (Job 37:21). They are the vulgar among the people. There is then no occasion to mention them here in this treatise.

Know that whenever one of the perfect wishes to mention, either orally or in writing, something that he understands of these secrets, according to the degree of his perfection, he is unable to explain with complete clarity and coherence even the portion that he has apprehended, as he could do with the other sciences whose teaching is generally recognized. Rather there will befall him when teaching another that which he had undergone when learning himself. I mean to say that the subject matter will appear, flash, and then be hidden again, as though this were the nature of this subject matter, be there much or little of it. For this reason, all the sages possessing knowledge of God the Lord, knowers of the truth, when they aimed at teaching something of this subject matter, spoke of it only in parables and riddles. They even multiplied the parables and made them different in species and even in genus. In most cases the subject to be explained was placed in the beginning or in the middle or at the end of the parable; this happened where a parable appropriate for the intended subject from start to finish could not be found. Sometimes the subject intended to be taught to him who was to be instructed was divided—although it was one and the same subject—among many parables remote from one another. Even more obscure is the case of one and the same parable corresponding to several subjects, its beginning fitting one subject and its ending another. Sometimes the whole is a parable referring to two cognate subjects within the particular species of science in question. The situation is such that the exposition of one who wishes to teach without recourse to parables and riddles is so obscure and brief as to make obscurity and brevity serve in place of parables and riddles. The men of knowledge and the sages are drawn, as it were, toward this purpose by the divine will just as they are drawn by their natural circumstances. Do you not see the following fact? God, may His mention be exalted, wished us to be perfected and the state of our societies to be improved by His laws regarding actions. Now this can come about only after the adoption of intellectual beliefs, the first of which being His apprehension, may He be exalted, according to our capacity. This, in its turn, cannot come about except through divine science, and this divine science cannot become actual except after a study of natural science. This is so since natural science borders on divine science, and its study precedes that of divine science in time as has been made clear to whoever has engaged in speculation on these matters. Hence God, may He be exalted, caused His book to open with the "Account of the Beginning," which, as we have made clear, is natural science. And because of the greatness and importance of the subject and because our capacity falls short of apprehending the greatest of subjects as it really is, we are told about those profound matters—which divine wisdom has deemed necessary to convey to us—in parables and riddles and in very obscure words. As (the sages) have said: "It is impossible to tell mortals of the power of the 'Account of the Beginning.' For this reason Scripture tells you obscurely: In the beginning God created (Gen. 1:1)," and so on.* They thus have drawn your attention to the fact that the above-mentioned subjects are obscure. You likewise know Solomon's saying: "That which was is far off, and exceeding deep; who can find it out?" (Eccles. 7:24). That which is said about all this is in equivocal terms so that the multitude might comprehend them in accord with the capacity of their understanding and the weakness of their representation, whereas the perfect man, who is already informed, will comprehend them otherwise.

We had promised in the *Commentary on the Mishnah* that we would explain strange subjects in the "Book of Prophecy" and in the "Book of Correspondence"—the latter being a book in which we promised to explain all the difficult passages in the Midrashim† where the external sense manifestly contradicts the truth and departs from the intelligible. They are all parables. However, when, many years ago, we began these books and composed a part of them, our beginning to explain matters in this way did not commend itself to us. For we saw that if we should adhere to parables and to concealment of what ought to be concealed, we would not be deviating from

---

*Cf. *Midrash Sheni, Ketuvim, Batei Midrashot,* IV.

†Maimonides uses here and subsequently the term *derashot.*

the primary purpose. We would, as it were, have replaced one individual by another of the same species. If, on the other hand, we explained what ought to be explained, it would be unsuitable for the vulgar among the people. Now it was to the vulgar that we wanted to explain the import of the Midrashim and the external meanings of prophecy. We also saw that if an ignoramus among the multitude of rabbanites should engage in speculation on these Midrashim, he would find nothing difficult in them, inasmuch as a rash fool, devoid of any knowledge of the nature of being, does not find impossibilities hard to accept. If, however, a perfect man of virtue should engage in speculation on them, he cannot escape one of two courses: either he can take the speeches in question in their external sense and, in so doing, think ill of their author and regard him as an ignoramus—in this there is nothing that would upset the foundations of belief; or he can attribute to them an inner meaning, thereby extricating himself from his predicament and being able to think well of the author whether or not the inner meaning of the saying is clear to him. With regard to the meaning of prophecy, the exposition of its various degrees, and the elucidation of the parables occurring in the prophetic books, another manner of explanation is used in this treatise. In view of these considerations, we have given up composing these two books in the way in which they were begun. We have confined ourselves to mentioning briefly the foundations of belief and general truths, while dropping hints that approach a clear exposition, just as we have set them forth in the great legal compilation, the *Mishneh Torah*.

My speech in the present treatise is directed, as I have mentioned, to one who has philosophized and has knowledge of the true sciences, but believes at the same time in the matters pertaining to the Law and is perplexed as to their meaning because of the uncertain terms and the parables. We shall include in this treatise some chapters in which there will be no mention of an equivocal term. Such a chapter will be preparatory for another, or it will hint at one of the meanings of an equivocal term that I might not wish to mention explicitly in that place, or it will explain one of the parables or hint at the fact that a certain story is a parable. Such a chapter may contain strange matters regarding which the contrary of the truth sometimes is believed, either because of the equivocality of the terms or because a parable is taken from the thing being represented or vice versa. . . .

INSTRUCTION WITH RESPECT TO THIS TREATISE

If you wish to grasp the totality of what this treatise contains, so
that nothing of it will escape you, then you must connect its chapters
one with another; and when reading a given chapter, your intention
must be not only to understand the totality of the subject of that
chapter, but also to grasp each word that occurs in it in the course of
the speech, even if that word does not belong to the intention of the
chapter. For the diction of this treatise has not been chosen at haphazard, but with great exactness and exceeding precision, and with
care to avoid failing to explain any obscure point. And nothing has
been mentioned out of its place, save with a view to explaining some
matter in its proper place. You therefore should not let your fantasies
elaborate on what is said here, for that would hurt me and be of no
use to yourself. You ought rather to learn everything that ought to be
learned and constantly study this treatise. For it then will elucidate
for you most of the obscurities of the Law that appear as difficult to
every intelligent man. I adjure—by God, may He be exalted!—every
reader of this treatise of mine not to comment upon a single word of
it and not to explain to another anything in it save that which has
been explained and commented upon in the words of the famous
sages of our Law who preceded me. But whatever he understands
from this treatise of those things that have not been said by any of
our famous sages other than myself should not be explained to
another; nor should he hasten to refute me, for that which he understood me to say might be contrary to my intention. He thus would
harm me in return for my having wanted to benefit him and would
"repay evil for good" (Ps. 38:21). All into whose hands it falls
should consider it well; and if it slakes his thirst, though it be on
only one point from among the many that are obscure, he should
thank God and be content with what he has understood. If, on the
other hand, he finds nothing in this treatise that might be of use to
him in any respect, he should think of it as not having been composed at all. If anything in it, according to his way of thinking,
appears to be in some way harmful, he should interpret it, even if in

a far-fetched way, in order to "pass a favorable judgment" (Ethics of the Fathers 1:6). For as we are enjoined to act in this way toward our vulgar ones, all the more should this be so with respect to our erudite ones and sages of our Law who are trying to help us to the truth as they apprehend it. I know that, among men generally, every beginner will derive benefit from some of the chapters of this treatise, though he lacks even an inkling of what is involved in speculation. A perfect man, on the other hand, devoted to Law and, as I have mentioned, perplexed, will benefit from all its chapters. How greatly will he rejoice in them and how pleasant will it be to hear them! But those who are confused and whose brains have been polluted by false opinions and misleading ways deemed by them to be true sciences, and who hold themselves to be men of speculation without having any knowledge of anything that can truly be called science, those will flee from many of its chapters. Indeed, these chapters will be very difficult for them to bear because they cannot apprehend their meaning and also because they would be led to recognize the falseness of the counterfeit money in their hands—their treasure and fortune held ready for future calamities. God, may He be exalted, knows that I have never ceased to be exceedingly apprehensive about setting down those things that I wish to set down in this treatise. For they are concealed things; none of them has been set down in any book—written in the religious community in these times of Exile—the books composed in these times being in our hands. How then can I now innovate and set them down? However, I have relied on two premises, the one being (the sages') saying in a similar case, "It is time to do something for the Lord" (Ps. 119:126), and so on;* the second being their saying, "Let all your acts be for the sake of heaven" (Ethics of the Fathers 2:7). Upon these two premises have I relied when setting down what I have composed in some of the chapters of this treatise.

To sum up: I am the man who when the concern pressed him and his way was straitened and he could find no other device by which to teach a demonstrated truth other than by giving satisfaction to a single virtuous man while displeasing ten thousand ignoramuses—I am he who prefers to address that single man by himself, and I do not heed the blame of those many creatures. For I claim to

---

*The verse continues as follows: "for they have infringed Your Law" (cf. Berakhot 63).

liberate that virtuous one from that into which he has sunk, and I shall guide him in his perplexity until he becomes perfect and he finds rest.

INTRODUCTION

One of seven causes should account for the contradictory or contrary statements to be found in any book or compilation.

The first cause: The author has collected the remarks of various people with differing opinions, but has omitted citing his authorities and has not attributed each remark to the one who said it. Contradictory or contrary statements can be found in such compilations because one of the two propositions is the opinion of one individual while the other proposition is the opinion of another individual.

The second cause: The author of a particular book has adopted a certain opinion that he later rejects; both his original and later statements are retained in the book.

The third cause: Not all the statements in question are to be taken in their external sense; some are to be taken in their external sense, while some others are parables and hence have an inner content. Alternatively, two apparently contradictory propositions may both be parables and when taken in their external sense may contradict, or be contrary to, one another.

The fourth cause: There is a proviso that, because of a certain necessity, has not been explicitly stated in its proper place; or the two subjects may differ, but one of them has not been explained in its proper place, so that a contradiction appears to have been said, whereas there is no contradiction.

The fifth cause arises from the necessity of teaching and making someone understand. For there may be a certain obscure matter that is difficult to conceive. One has to mention it or to take it as a premise in explaining something that is easy to conceive and that by rights ought to be taught before the former, since one always begins with what is easier. The teacher, accordingly, will have to be lax and, using any means that occur to him or gross speculation, will try to make that first matter somehow understood. He will not undertake to state the matter as it truly is in exact terms, but rather will leave it so in accord with the listener's imagination that the latter will understand only what he now wants him to understand. Afterward, in the appropriate place, that obscure matter is stated in exact terms and explained as it truly is.

The sixth cause: The contradiction is concealed and becomes evident only after many premises. The greater the number of premises needed to make the contradiction evident, the more concealed it is. It thus may escape the author, who thinks there is no contradiction between his two original propositions. But if each proposition is considered separately, a true premise being joined to it and the necessary conclusion drawn—and this is done to every conclusion: a true premise being joined to it and the necessary conclusion drawn—after many syllogisms the outcome of the matter will be that the two final conclusions are contradictory or contrary to each other. That is the kind of thing that escapes the attention of scholars who write books. If, however, the two original propositions are evidently contradictory, but the author has simply forgotten the first when writing down the second in another part of his compilation, this is a very great weakness, and that man should not be reckoned among those whose speeches deserve consideration.

The seventh cause: In speaking about very obscure matters it is necessary to conceal some parts and to disclose others. Sometimes in the case of certain dicta this necessity requires that the discussion proceed on the basis of a certain premise, whereas in another place necessity requires that the discussion proceed on the basis of another premise contradicting the first one. In such cases the vulgar must in no way be aware of the contradiction; the author accordingly uses some device to conceal it by all means. . . .

. . . Divergences that are to be found in this treatise are due to the fifth cause and the seventh. Know this, grasp its true meaning, and remember it very well so as not to become perplexed by some of its chapters.

And after these introductory remarks, I shall begin to mention the terms whose true meaning, as intended in every passage according to its context, must be indicated. This, then, will be a key permitting one to enter places the gates to which were locked. And when these gates are opened and these places are entered into, the souls will find rest therein, the eyes will be delighted, and the bodies will be eased of their toil and of their labor.

CHAPTER 1

Image (*tzelem*) and *likeness* (*demut*). People have thought that in the Hebrew language *image* denotes the shape and configuration of a thing. This supposition led them to the pure doctrine of the corporeality of God, on account of His saying: "Let us make man in our image, after our likeness" (Gen. 1:26). For they thought that God has a man's form, I mean his shape and configuration. The pure doctrine of the corporeality of God was a necessary consequence to be accepted by them. They accordingly believed in it and deemed that if they abandoned this belief, they would give the lie to the Biblical text; that they would even make the Deity to be nothing at all unless they thought that God was a body provided with a face and a hand, like them in shape and configuration. However, He is, in their view, bigger and more resplendent than they themselves, and the matter of which He is composed is not flesh and blood. As they see it, this is as far as one can go in establishing the separateness of God from other things. Now with respect to that which ought to be said in order to refute the doctrine of the corporeality of God and to establish His real unity—which can have no true reality unless one disproves His corporeality—you shall know the demonstration of all of this from this treatise. However, here, in this chapter, only an indication is given with a view to elucidating the meaning of *image* and *likeness*.

Now I say that in the Hebrew language the proper term designating the form that is well known among the multitude, namely, that form which is the shape and configuration of a thing, is *toar*. Thus Scripture says: "Beautiful in form (*toar*) and beautiful in appearance" (Gen. 39:6); "What form (*taoro*)* is he of?" (I Sam.

*From word *toar*.

28:14); "As the form (toar) of the children of a king" (Judges 8:18). This term is also applied to an artificial form; thus: "He marks its form [yeta'arehu] with a line, and he marks its form [yeta'arehu] with a compass" (Is. 44:13). Those terms are never applied to the Deity, may He be exalted; far and remote may this thought be from us. The term *image*, on the other hand, is applied to the natural form, I mean to the notion in virtue of which a thing is constituted as a substance and becomes what it is. It is the true reality of the thing in so far as the latter is that particular being. In man that notion is that from which human apprehension derives. It is on account of this intellectual apprehension that it is said of man: "In the image of God created He him" (Gen. 1:27). For this reason also, it is said: "You are contemptuous of their image" (Ps. 73:20). For *contempt* has for its object the soul, which is the specific form, not the shape and configuration of the parts of the body. I assert also that the reason why idols are called *images* lies in the fact that what was sought in them was the notion that was deemed to subsist in them, and not their shape and configuration. I assert similarly with regard to the Scriptural expression: "images of your emerods" (I Sam. 6:5). For what was intended by them was the notion of warding off the harm caused by the emerods, and not the shape of the emerods. If, however, there should be no doubt concerning the expressions "the images of your emerods" and *images* being used in order to denote shape and configuration, it would follow that *image* is an equivocal or amphibolous term applied to the specific form and also to the artificial form and to what is analogous to the two in the shapes and configurations of the natural bodies. That which was meant in the Scriptural dictum, "Let us make man in our image" (Gen. 1:26), was the specific form, which is intellectual apprehension, not the shape and configuration. We have explained to you the difference between *image* and *form*, and have explained the meaning of *image*.

As for the term *likeness* (demut), it is a noun derived from the verb *damah* (to be like), and it too signifies likeness in respect of a notion. For the Scriptural dictum, "I am like a pelican in the wilderness" (Ps. 102:7), does not signify that its author resembled the pelican with regard to its wings and feathers, but that his sadness was like that of the bird. In the same way in the verse, "Nor was any tree in the garden of God like it in beauty" (Ezek. 31:8), the likeness is with respect to the notion of beauty. Similarly the verses, "Their venom is in the likeness of the venom of a serpent" (Ps. 58:5), and "His likeness is that of a lion that is eager to tear in pieces" (Ps. 17:12), refer both of them to a likeness in respect of a notion and not with respect to a shape and a configuration. In the same way it is said, "the likeness of a throne ... the likeness of the throne" (Ezek. 1:26), the likeness referred to being in respect of elevation and sublimity, not in respect of a throne's square shape, its solidity, and the length of its legs, as wretched people think. A similar explanation should also be applied to the expression, "the likeness of the living creatures" (Ezek. 1:13). Now man possesses as his proprium something in him that is very strange as it is not found in anything else that exists under the sphere of the moon, namely, intellectual apprehension. In the exercise of this, no sense, no part of the body, none of the extremities are used; and therefore this apprehension was likened to the apprehension of the Deity, which does not require an instrument, although in reality it is not like the latter apprehension, but only appears so to the first stirrings of opinion. It was because of this something, I mean because of the divine intellect conjoined with man, that it is said of the latter that he is "in the image of God and in His likeness" (Gen. 1:26–27), not that God, may He be exalted, is a body and possesses a shape.

CHAPTER 2

Years ago a learned man propounded as a challenge to me a curious objection. It behooves us now to consider this objection and our reply invalidating it. However, before mentioning this objection and its invalidation, I shall make the following statement. Every Hebrew knew that the term *Elohim* is equivocal, designating the Deity, the angels, and the rulers governing the cities. Onkelos the Proselyte, peace be on him, has made it clear, and his clarification is correct, that in the dictum of Scripture, "And you shall be as Elohim, knowing good and evil" (Gen. 3:5), the last sense is intended. For he has translated: "And you shall be as rulers."

After thus having set forth the equivocality of this term, we shall begin to expound the objection. This is what the objector said: It is manifest from the clear sense of the Biblical text that the primary purpose with regard to man was that he should be, as the other animals are, devoid of intellect, of thought, and of the capacity to distinguish between good and evil. However, when he disobeyed, his disobedience procured him as its necessary consequence the great perfection peculiar to man, namely, his being endowed with the capacity that exists in us to make this distinction. Now this capacity is the noblest of the characteristics existing in us; it is in virtue of it that we are constituted as substances. Now it is a thing to be wondered at that man's punishment for his disobedience should consist in his being granted a perfection that he did not possess before, namely, the intellect. This is like the story told by somebody that a certain man from among the people disobeyed and committed great crimes, and in consequence was made to undergo a metamorphosis, becoming a star in heaven. This was the intent and the meaning of the objection, though it was not textually as we have put it.

Hear now the intent of our reply. We said: O you who engage in theoretical speculation using the first notions that may occur to you and come to your mind and who consider withal that you understand a book that is the guide of the first and the last men while glancing through it as you would glance through a historical work or a piece of poetry—when, in some of your hours of leisure, you leave off drinking and copulating—collect yourself and reflect, for things are not as you thought following the first notion that occurred to you, but rather as is made clear through reflection upon the following speech. For the intellect that God made overflow to man, and that is the latter's ultimate perfection, was that which Adam had been provided with before he disobeyed. It was because of this that it was said of him that he was created "in the image of God and in His likeness." It was likewise on account of it that he was addressed by God and given commandments, as it says: "And the Lord God commanded" (Gen. 2:16), and so on. For commandments are not given to beasts and beings devoid of intellect. Through the intellect one distinguishes between truth and falsehood, and that was found in (Adam) in its perfection and integrity. Fine and bad, on the other hand, belong to the things generally accepted as known, not to those cognized by the intellect. For one does not say: it is fine that heaven is spherical, and it is bad that the earth is flat; rather one says true and false with regard to these assertions. Similarly one expresses in our language the notions of truth and falsehood by means of the terms *emet* and *sheker*, and those of fine and bad by means of the terms *tov* and *ra*. Now man in virtue of his intellect knows *truth* from *falsehood*; and this holds good for all intelligible things. Accordingly when man was in his most perfect and excellent state, in accordance with his inborn disposition and possessed of his intellectual cognitions—because of which it is said of him: "You have made him but little lower than Elohim" (Ps. 8:6)—he had no faculty that was engaged in any way in the consideration of generally accepted things, and he did not apprehend them. So among these generally accepted things even that which is most manifestly bad, namely, uncovering the genitals, was not bad according to him, and he did not apprehend that it was bad. However, when he disobeyed and inclined toward his desires of the imagination and the pleasures of his corporeal senses— inasmuch as it is said: "that the tree was good for food and that it was a delight to the eyes" (Gen. 3:6)—he was punished by being deprived of that intellectual apprehension. He therefore disobeyed the commandment that was imposed upon him on account of his intellect and, becoming endowed with the faculty of apprehending generally accepted things, he became absorbed in judging things to be bad or fine. Then he knew how great his loss was, what he had been deprived of, and upon what a state he had entered. Hence it is said: "And you shall be like Elohim knowing good and evil"; and not: "knowing the false and the true," or "apprehending the false and the true." With regard to what is of necessity, there is no good and evil at all, but only the false and the true. Reflect on the dictum: "And the eyes of them both were opened, and they knew that they were naked" (Gen. 3:7). It is not said: "And the eyes of them both were opened, and they saw." For what was seen previously was exactly that which was seen afterward. There had been no membrane over the eye that was now removed, but rather he entered upon another state in which he considered as bad things that he had not seen in that light before. Know moreover that this expression, I mean, "to open," refers only to uncovering mental vision and in no respect is applied to the circumstance that the sense of sight has been newly acquired. Thus: "And God opened her eyes" (Gen. 21:19); "Then the eyes of the blind shall be opened" (Is. 35:5);

"Opening the ears, he hears not" (*ibid.* 42:20)—a verse that is analogous to its dictum, "That have eyes to see and see not" (Ezek. 12:2).

CHAPTER 17

Do not think that only the divine science should be withheld from the multitude. This holds good also for the greater part of natural science. In fact we have repeatedly set down for you our dictum: "The 'Account of the Beginning' ought not to be taught in the presence of two men." This is not only the case with regard to people adhering to Law, but also with regard to the philosophers and learned men of the various communities in ancient times. For they concealed what they said about the first principles and presented it in riddles. . . . Now as even those upon whom the charge of corruption would not be laid in the event of clear exposition used terms figuratively and resorted to teaching in similes, how much all the more is it incumbent upon us, the community of those adhering to Law, not to state explicitly a matter that is either remote from the understanding of the multitude or the truth of which as it appears to the imagination of these people is different from what is intended by us. Know this also.

CHAPTER 27

Onkelos the Proselyte was very perfect in the Hebrew and Syrian languages and directed his effort toward the abolition of the belief in God's corporeality. Hence he interprets in accordance with its meaning every attribute that Scripture predicates of God and that might lead toward the belief in corporeality.

CHAPTER 31

Know that the human intellect has objects of apprehension that it is within its power and according to its nature to apprehend. On the other hand, in that which exists there also are existents and matters that, according to its nature, it is not capable of apprehending in any way or through any cause; the gates of their apprehension are shut before it. There are also in that which exists things of which the intellect may apprehend one state while not being cognizant of other states. The fact that it apprehends does not entail the conclusion that it can apprehend all things—just as the senses have apprehensions but it is not within their power to apprehend at whatever distance the objects of apprehension may happen to be. Similarly with regard to all other bodily faculties, for the fact that a man is able to carry two hundred-weights does not mean that he is able to carry ten. The difference in capacity existing between the individuals of the species with regard to sensory apprehensions and all the other bodily faculties is manifest and clear to all men. However, it has a limit, inasmuch as these capacities cannot attain to every distance however far away nor to every degree however great it may happen to be. The identical rule obtains with regard to human intellectual apprehensions. There are great differences in capacity between the individuals of the species. This also is manifest and very clear to the men of knowledge. It may thus happen that whereas one individual discovers a certain notion by himself through his speculation, another individual is not able ever to understand that notion. Even if it were explained to him for a very long time by means of every sort of expression and parable, his mind would not penetrate to it in any way, but would turn back without understanding it. This difference in capacity is likewise not infinite, for man's intellect indubitably has a limit at which it stops. There are therefore things regarding which it has become clear to man that it is impossible to apprehend them. And he will not find that his soul longs for knowledge of them, inasmuch as he is aware of the impossibility of such knowledge and of there being no gate through which one might enter in order to attain it. Of this nature is our ignorance of the number of the stars of heaven and whether that number is even or odd, as well as our ignorance of the number of the species of living beings, minerals, plants, and other similar things.

On the other hand, there are things for the apprehension of which man will find that he has a great longing. The sway of the intellect endeavoring to seek for, and to investigate, their true reality exists at every time and in every group of men engaged in speculation. With regard to such things there is a multiplicity of opinions, disagreement arises between the men engaged in speculation, and doubts crop up; all this because the intellect is attached to an apprehension of these things, I mean to say because of its longing for them; and also because everyone thinks that he has found a way by means of which he will know the true reality of the matter. Now it is not within the power of the human intellect to give a demonstration of these matters. For in all things whose true reality is known through demonstration there is no tug of war and no refusal to accept a thing proven—unless indeed such refusal comes from an ignoramus who offers a resistance that is called resistance to demonstration. Thus you can find groups of people who dispute the doctrine that the earth is spherical and that the sphere has a circular motion and with regard to other matters of this kind. These folk do not enter into our purpose. The things about which there is this perplexity are very numerous in divine matters, few in matters pertaining to natural science, and nonexistent in matters pertaining to mathematics.

Alexander of Aphrodisias* says that there are three causes of disagreement about things. One of them is love of domination and love of strife, both of which turn man aside from the apprehension of truth as it is. The second cause is the subtlety and the obscurity of the object of apprehension in itself and the difficulty of apprehending it. And the third cause is the ignorance of him who apprehends and his inability to grasp things that it is possible to apprehend. That is what Alexander mentioned. However, in our times there is a fourth cause that he did not mention because it did not exist among them. It is habit and upbringing. For man has in his nature a love of, and an inclination for, that to which he is habituated. Thus you can see that the people of the desert—notwithstanding the disorderliness of their life, the lack of pleasures, and the scarcity of food—dislike the towns, do not hanker after their pleasures, and prefer the bad circum-

*Greek commentator of Aristotle.

stances to which they are accustomed to good ones to which they are not accustomed. Their souls accordingly would find no repose in living in palaces, in wearing silk clothes, and in the enjoyment of baths, ointments, and perfumes. In a similar way, man has love for, and the wish to defend, opinions to which he is habituated and in which he has been brought up and has a feeling of repulsion for opinions other than those. For this reason also man is blind to the apprehension of the true realities and inclines toward the things to which he is habituated. This happened to the multitude with regard to the belief in His corporeality and many other metaphysical subjects as we shall make clear. All this is due to people being habituated to, and brought up on, texts that it is an established usage to think highly of and to regard as true and whose external meaning is indicative of the corporeality of God and of other imaginings with no truth in them, for these have been set forth as parables and riddles. This is so for reasons that I shall mention further on.

Do not think that what we have said with regard to the insufficiency of the human intellect and its having a limit at which it stops is a statement made in order to conform to Law. For it is something that has already been said and truly grasped by the philosophers without their having concern for a particular doctrine or opinion. And it is a true thing that cannot be doubted except by an individual ignorant of what has already been demonstrated. We have put this chapter before others only with a view to its serving as an introduction to that which shall come after it.

CHAPTER 32

You who study my treatise know that something similar to what happens to sensory apprehensions happens likewise to intellectual apprehensions in so far as they are attached to matter. For when you see with your eye, you apprehend something that is within the power of your sight to apprehend. If, however, your eyes are forced to do something they are reluctant to do—if they are made to gaze fixedly and are set the task of looking over a great distance, too great for you to see, or if you contemplate very minute writing or a minute draw-

ing that is not within your power to apprehend—and if you force
your eye, in spite of its reluctance, to find out the true reality of the
thing, your eye shall not only be too weak to apprehend that which
you are unable to apprehend, but also too weak to apprehend that
which is within your power to apprehend. Your eye shall grow tired,
and you shall not be able to apprehend what you could apprehend
before having gazed fixedly and before having been given this task. A
similar discovery is made by everyone engaging in the speculative
study of some science with respect to his state of reflection. For if he
applies himself to reflection and sets himself a task demanding his
entire attention, he becomes dull and does not then understand even
that which is within his scope to understand. For the condition of all
bodily faculties is, in this respect, one and the same. Something sim-
lar can happen to you with regard to intellectual apprehensions. For
if you stay your progress because of a dubious point; if you do not
deceive yourself into believing that there is a demonstration with
regard to matters that have not been demonstrated; if you do not
hasten to reject and categorically to pronounce false any assertions
whose contradictories have not been demonstrated; if, finally, you do
not aspire to apprehend that which you are unable to apprehend—you will have achieved human perfection and attained the
rank of Rabbi Akiva, peace be on him, who "entered in peace and
went out in peace" (Hagigah 14b) when engaged in the theoretical
study of these metaphysical matters. If, on the other hand, you aspire
to apprehend things that are beyond your apprehension; or if you
hasten to pronounce false assertions, the contradictories of which
have not been demonstrated or that are possible, though very
remotely so—you will have joined Elisha Aher. That is, you will not
only not be perfect, but will be the most deficient among the
deficient; and it shall so fall out that you will be overcome by imaginings and by an inclination toward things defective, evil, and
wicked—this resulting from the intellect's being preoccupied and its
light's being extinguished. In a similar way, various species of delu-
sive imaginings are produced in the sense of sight when the visual
spirit is weakened, as in the case of sick people and of such as persist
in looking at brilliant or minute objects.

In this regard it is said: "Have you found honey? Eat so much
as is sufficient for you, lest you be filled therewith and vomit it"
(Prov. 25:16). In a similar way, the sages used this verse as a parable
that they applied to Elisha Aher. How marvelous is this parable,

inasmuch as it likens knowledge to eating, a meaning about which we have spoken (ch. 30). It also mentions the most delicious of foods, namely, honey. Now, according to its nature, honey, if eaten to excess, upsets the stomach and causes vomiting. Accordingly Scripture says, as it were, that in spite of its sublimity, greatness, and what it has of perfection, the nature of the apprehension in question—if not made to stop at its proper limit and not conducted with circumspection—may be perverted into a defect, just as the eating of honey may. For whereas the individual eating in moderation is nourished and takes pleasure in it, it all goes if there is too much of it. Accordingly Scripture does not say, "Lest you be filled therewith and loathe it," but rather says, "and vomit it." This notion is also referred to in Scripture in the dictum: "It is not good to eat much honey" (ibid. 25:27), and so on, as well as in the dictum, "Neither make yourself overwise; why should you destroy yourself?" (Eccles. 7:16). It likewise refers to this in the dictum: "Guard your foot when you go to the house of God" (ibid. 4:17), and so on. This is also referred to by David in the dictum: "Neither do I exercise myself in things too great or in things too marvelous for me (Ps. 131:1). The sages, too, intended to express this notion in their dictum: "Do not inquire about things that are too marvelous for you; do not investigate what is hidden from you; inquire into things that are permitted to you; you have no business with marvels" (Hagigah 13a). This means that you should let your intellect move about only within the domain of things that man is able to grasp. For in regard to matters that it is not in the nature of man to grasp, it is, as we have made clear, very harmful to occupy oneself with them. This is what the sages intended to signify by their dictum, "Whoever considers four things" and so on, completing the dictum by saying, "he who does not have regard for the honor of his Creator" (ibid. 11b), whereby they indicated what we have already made clear: namely, that man should not press forward to engage in speculative study of corrupt imaginings. When points appearing as dubious occur to him or the thing he seeks does not seem to him to be demonstrated, he should not deny and reject it, hastening to pronounce it false, but rather should persevere and thereby "have regard for the honor of his Creator." He should refrain and hold back. This matter has already become clear. The intention of these texts set down by the prophets and the sages is not, however, wholly to close the gate of speculation, and to deprive the intellect of the apprehension of things that it is possible to apprehend—as is thought by the ignorant and neglectful, who are pleased to regard their own deficiency and stupidity as perfection and wisdom, and the perfection and the knowledge of others as a deficiency and a defection from Law, and who thus "regard darkness as light and light as darkness" (Is. 5:20). Their purpose, in its entirety, rather is to make it known that the intellects of human beings have a limit at which they stop.

Do not criticize the terms applied to the intellect in this chapter and others. For the purpose here is to guide toward the intended notion and not to investigate the truth of the essence of the intellect; for other chapters are devoted to a precise account of this subject.

CHAPTER 33

Know that to begin with this science is very harmful, I mean the divine science. In the same way, it is also harmful to make clear the meaning of the parables of the prophets and to draw attention to the figurative senses of terms used in addressing people, figurative senses of which the books of prophecy are full. It behooves rather to educate the young and to give firmness to the deficient in capacity according to the measure of their apprehension. Thus he who is seen to be perfect in mind and to be formed for that high rank—that is to say, demonstrative speculation and true intellectual inferences— should be elevated step by step, either by someone who directs his attention or by himself, until he achieves his perfection. If, however, he begins with the divine science, it will not be a mere confusion in his beliefs that will befall him, but rather absolute negation. In my opinion an analogous case would be that of someone feeding a suckling with wheaten bread and meat and giving him wine to drink. He would undoubtedly kill him, not because these aliments are bad or unnatural for man, but because the child that receives them is too weak to digest them so as to derive a benefit from them. Similarly these true opinions were not hidden, enclosed in riddles, and treated by all men of knowledge with all sorts of artifice through which they could teach them without expounding them explicitly, because of something bad being hidden in them, or because they undermine the foundations of Law, as is thought by ignorant people who deem that they have attained a rank suitable for speculation. Rather have they been hidden because at the outset the intellect is incapable of receiving them; only flashes of them are made to appear so that the perfect man should know them. On this account they are called secrets and mysteries of the Torah, as we shall make clear. This is the cause of the fact that the "Torah speaks in the language of the sons of man,"* as we have made clear. This is so because it is presented in such a manner as to make it possible for the young, the women, and all the people to begin with it and to learn it. Now it is not within their power to understand these matters as they truly are. Hence they are confined to accepting tradition with regard to all sound opinions that are of such a sort that it is preferable that they should be pronounced true and with regard to all representations of this kind—and this in such a manner that the mind is led toward the existence of the objects of these opinions and representations but not toward grasping their essence as it truly is. When, however, a man grows perfect "and the mysteries of the Torah are communicated to him" (Hagigah 13a) either by somebody else or because he himself discovers them—inasmuch as some of them draw his attention to others—he attains a rank at which he pronounces the above-mentioned correct opinions to be true; and in order to arrive at this conclusion, he uses the veritable methods, namely, demonstration in cases where demonstration is possible or strong arguments where this is possible. In this way he represents to himself these matters, which had appeared to him as imaginings and parables, in their truth and understands their essence. Accordingly, the following speech of the sages has been repeated to you several times in our speech: "The 'Account of the Divine Chariot' ought not to be taught even to one man, except if he be wise and able to understand by himself," in which case "only the chapter headings may be transmitted to him." On this account one ought not to begin to teach this subject to anyone unless it be according to his capacity and then only under these two conditions; one of them being that the one who is to be taught is "wise," I mean that he has achieved knowledge of the sciences from which the premises of speculation derive; and the other, that he be full of understanding, intelligent, sagacious by nature, that he divine a notion even if it is only very slightly suggested to him in

*Yevamot 71a and Bava Metzia 31b.

a flash. This is the meaning of the dictum of the sages: "able to understand by himself."

I shall make clear to you the cause that prevents the instruction of the multitude in the veritable methods of speculation and that prevents their being taught to begin to grasp the essences of things as they are. I shall also explain to you that it is requisite and necessary that this should not be otherwise than thus. These explanations shall be made in the chapter following upon the present one. I shall then say:

CHAPTER 34

The causes that prevent the commencement of instruction with divine science, the indication of things that ought to be indicated, and the presentation of this to the multitude, are five.

The first cause is the difficulty, subtlety, and obscurity of the matter in itself. Thus Scripture says: "That which was is far off and exceeding deep; who can find it out?" (Eccles. 7:24). And it is said: "But wisdom, where shall it be found?" (Job 28:12). Now it is not fitting in teaching to begin with what is most difficult and obscure for the understanding. One of the parables generally known in our community is that likening knowledge to water. Now the sages, peace be on them, explained several notions by means of this parable; one of them being that he who knows how to swim brings up pearls from the bottom of the sea, whereas he who does not know, drowns. For this reason, no one should expose himself to the risks of swimming except he who has been trained in learning to swim.

The second cause is the insufficiency of the minds of all men at their beginnings. For man is not granted his ultimate perfection at the outset; for perfection exists in him only potentially, and in his beginnings he lacks this act. Accordingly it is said: "And man is born a wild ass" (Job 11:12). Nor is it necessarily obligatory in the case of every individual who is endowed with some thing in potency, that this thing should become actual. Sometimes it remains in its defective state either because of certain obstacles or because of paucity of training in what transforms that potentiality into actuality. Accordingly it is clearly said: "Not many are wise" (*ibid.* 32:9). The sages too have said: "I saw the people who have attained a high rank, and they were few."* For the obstacles to perfection are very many, and the objects that distract from it abound. When should he be able to achieve the perfect preparation and the leisure required for training so that what subsists in a particular individual in potency should be transformed into actuality?

The third cause lies in the length of the preliminaries. For man has in his nature a desire to seek the ends; and he often finds preliminaries tedious and refuses to engage in them. Know, however, that if an end could be achieved without the preliminaries that precede it, the latter would not be preliminaries, but pure distractions and futilities. Now if you would awaken a man—even though he were the dullest of all people—as one awakens a sleeping individual, and if you were to ask him whether he desired at that moment to have knowledge of the heavenly spheres, namely, what their number is and what their configuration, and what is contained in them, and what the angels are, and how the world as a whole was created, and what its end is in view of the arrangement of its various parts with one another, and what the soul is, and how it is created in time in the body, and whether the human soul can be separated from the body, and, if it can, in what manner and through what instrument and with what distinction in view, and if you put the same question to him with regard to other subjects of research of this kind, he would undoubtedly answer you in the affirmative. He would have a natural desire to know these things as they are in truth; but he would wish this desire to be allayed, and the knowledge of all this to be achieved by means of one or two words that you would say to him. If, however, you would lay upon him the obligation to abandon his occupation for a week's time until he should understand all this, he would not do it, but would be satisfied with deceptive imaginings through which his soul would be set at ease. He would also dislike being told that there is a thing whose knowledge requires many premises and a long time for investigation. You know that these matters are mutually connected; there being nothing in what exists besides God, may He be exalted, and the totality of the things He has made. For this totality includes everything comprised in what exists except only Him. There is, moreover, no way to apprehend Him except it be through the things He has made; for they are indicative of His exist-

*Sukkah 42b and Sanhedrin 43b.

ence and of what ought to be believed about Him, I mean to say, of what should be affirmed and denied with regard to Him. It is therefore indispensable to consider all beings as they really are so that we may obtain for all the kinds of beings true and certain premises that would be useful to us in our researches pertaining to the divine science.

How very many are the premises thus taken from the nature of numbers and the properties of geometrical figures from which we draw inferences concerning things that we should deny with respect to God, may He be exalted! And this denial is indicative to us of many notions. As for the matters pertaining to the astronomy of the spheres and to natural science, I do not consider that you should have any difficulty in grasping that those are matters necessary for the apprehension of the relation of the world to God's governance as this relation is in truth and not according to imaginings. There are also many speculative subjects that, although no premises can be obtained from them for the use of this science, nevertheless train the mind and procure it the habitus of drawing inferences and knowledge of the truth in matters pertaining to its essence. They also put an end to the confusion in most of the minds of those engaged in speculation, a confusion mistaking things that are accidental for those that are essential; hereby an end is also put to the perversion of opinions arising out of this confusion. All this is achieved in addition to the representation of these subjects as they really are, even if they in no way belong to the divine science. These subjects are also not devoid of utility in other points, namely, with respect to matters that lead up to that science. Accordingly, it is certainly necessary for whoever wishes to achieve human perfection to train himself at first in the art of logic, then in the mathematical sciences according to the proper order, then in the natural sciences, and after that in the divine science. We find many people whose mind stops short at one of these sciences; and sometimes even if their mind does not miss the mark, they are cut off by death while engaged in some preliminary study. Accordingly, if we never in any way acquired an opinion through following traditional authority and were not correctly conducted toward something by means of parables, but were obliged to achieve a perfect representation by means of essential definitions and by pronouncing true only that which is meant to be pronounced true in virtue of a demonstration—which would be impossible except after the above-mentioned lengthy preliminary studies—this state of affairs would lead to all people dying without having known whether there is a deity for the world, or whether there is not, much less whether a proposition should be affirmed with regard to Him or a defect denied. Nobody would ever be saved from this perdition except "one of a city or two of a family" (Jer. 3:14). As for the few solitary individuals that are "the remnant whom the Lord calls" (Joel 3:5), the perfection, which constitutes the end to be aimed at, is realized for them only after the above-mentioned preliminary studies.

Solomon has made it clear that the need for preliminary studies is a necessity and that it is impossible to attain true wisdom except after having been trained. For he says: "If the iron be blunt, and he does not whet the edge, then must he use more strength; but even more preparation is needed for wisdom" (Eccles. 10:10). And he also says: "Hear counsel and receive instruction, that you may be wise in your latter end" (Prov. 19:20). There is also a necessity of another kind for achieving knowledge of the preliminary studies. It arises from the fact that when a man seeks to obtain knowledge quickly, many doubts occur to him, and he moreover quickly understands objections—I mean to say the destruction of a particular doctrine, this being similar to the demolition of a building. Now the establishment of doctrines as true and the solution of doubts can only be grounded upon many premises taken from these preliminary studies. One engaged in speculation without preliminary study is therefore comparable to someone who walked on his two feet in order to reach a certain place and, while on his way, fell into a deep well without having any device to get out of there before he perishes. It would have been better for him if he had foregone walking and had quietly remained in his own place. In Proverbs, Solomon describes at length the state of lazy people and their incapacity—all this being a parable for the incapacity to seek knowledge of the sciences. Thus speaking of the desire of someone desirous to achieve his ends, but who, making no effort to achieve knowledge of the preliminary studies leading to these ends, does nothing else but desire, he says: "The desire of the slothful kills him; for his hands refuse to labor. He covets greedily all the day long; but the righteous gives and spares not" (Prov. 21:25–26). In these verses he says that the reason why the desire of the slothful kills him is to be found in the fact that he makes no effort and does not work with a view to that which would allay that desire; he has only an abundance of longing and nothing else, while he aspires to things for whose achievement he lacks the necessary instrument. It would be healthier for him if he renounced this desire. Consider now how the ending of the parable explains its beginning. For in his dictum, "but the righteous gives and spares not," the word "righteous" is not antithetical to "slothful" except according to the explanation we have propounded. For (Solomon) says that the just one among men is he who gives everything its due; he means thereby that he gives all his time to seeking knowledge and spares no portion of his time for anything else. He says, as it were: "But the righteous gives his days to wisdom and is not sparing of them"; which corresponds to his saying: "Give not your strength to women" (*ibid.* 31:3). Now the majority of the men of knowledge, I mean those generally known as men of knowledge, labor under this disease—I mean that which consists in seeking to achieve the ends and in speaking about them without having engaged in the studies preliminary to them. With some of them, their ignorance or their desire to have the first place goes so far as to cause them to disapprove of these preliminary studies, which they are incapable of grasping or are too lazy to seek to understand. Accordingly, they wish to show that these studies are harmful or useless. However, when one reflects, the truth of the matter is clear and manifest.

The fourth cause is to be found in the natural aptitudes. For it has been explained, or rather demonstrated, that the moral virtues are a preparation for the rational virtues, it being impossible to achieve true, rational acts—I mean perfect rationality—unless it be by a man thoroughly trained with respect to his morals and endowed with the qualities of tranquillity and quiet. There are, moreover, many people who have received from their first natural disposition a complexion of temperament with which perfection is in no way compatible. Such is the case of one whose heart is naturally exceedingly hot; for he cannot refrain from anger, even if he subject his soul to very stringent training. This is also the case of one whose testicles have a hot and humid temperament and are of a strong constitution and in whom the seminal vessels abundantly generate semen. For it is unlikely that such a man, even if he subject his soul to the most severe training, should be chaste. Similarly you can find among people rash and reckless folk whose movements, being very agitated and disordered, indicate a corruption of the complexion and a poor quality of the temperament, of which it is impossible to give an account. Perfection can never be perceived in such people. And to make an effort for their benefit in this matter is pure ignorance on the part of him who makes the effort. For this science, as you know, is not like the science of medicine or the science of geometry, and not everyone has the disposition required for it in the various respects we have mentioned. It is accordingly indubitable that preparatory moral training should be carried out before beginning with this science, so that man should be in a state of extreme uprightness and perfection; "For the perverse is an abomination to the Lord, but His secret is with the righteous" (Prov. 3:32). For this reason the teaching of this science to the young is disapproved of. In fact, it is impossible for them to absorb it because of the effervescence of their natures and of their minds being occupied with the flame of growth. When, however, this flame that gives rise to perplexity is extinguished, the young achieve tranquillity and quiet; and their hearts submit and yield with respect to their temperament. They then may call upon their souls to raise themselves up to this rank, which is that of the apprehension of Him, may He be exalted; I mean thereby the divine science that is designated as the "Account of the Divine Chariot." Accordingly Scripture says: "The Lord is near to them that are of a broken heart" (Ps. 34:19). And it says: "I dwell in the high and holy place, with him also that is of a contrite and humble spirit" (Is. 57:15), and so on.

The fifth cause is to be found in the fact that men are occupied with the necessities of the bodies, which are the first perfection; and more particularly if, in addition, they are occupied with taking care of a wife and of children; and even more especially if there is in them, superadded to that, a demand for the superfluities of life, which becomes an established habitus as a result of a bad conduct of life and bad customs. Things are so that if even a perfect man, as we have mentioned, were to occupy himself much with these necessary things and all the more if he were to occupy himself with unnecessary things, and if his desire for them should grow strong, he would find that his theoretical desires had grown weak and had been submerged. And his demand for them would slacken and become intermittent and inattentive. He accordingly would not grasp things that otherwise would have been within his power to grasp; or else he would grasp them with a confused apprehension, a mixture of apprehension and failure to apprehend.

In view of all these causes, these matters are only for a few solitary individuals of a very special sort, not for the multitude. For this reason, they should be hidden from the beginner, and he should be prevented from taking them up, just as a small baby is prevented from taking coarse foods and from lifting heavy weights.

CHAPTER 35

Do not think that all that we have laid down in the preceding chapters regarding the greatness and the hidden nature of the matter, the difficulty of apprehending it, and its having to be withheld from the multitude, refers also to the denial of the corporeality of God and to the denial of His being subject to affections. It is not so. For just as it behooves to bring up children in the belief, and to proclaim to the multitude, that God, may He be magnified and honored, is one and that none but He ought to be worshiped, so it behooves that they should be made to accept on traditional authority the belief that God is not a body; and that there is absolutely no likeness in any respect whatever between Him and the things created by Him; that His existence has no likeness to theirs. . . .

CHAPTER 54*

Know that the master of those who know, Moses our Teacher, peace be on him, made two requests and received an answer to both of them. One request consisted in his asking Him, may He be exalted, to let him know His essence and true reality. The second request, which he put first, was that He should let him know His attributes. The answer to the two requests that He, may He be exalted, gave him consisted in His promising him to let him know all His attributes, making it known to him that they are His actions, and teaching him that His essence cannot be grasped as it really is. Yet He drew his attention to a subject of speculation through which he can

*See *Mishneh Torah*, Book I, Moral Dispositions, ch. I.

apprehend to the furthest extent that is possible for man. For what
has been apprehended by (Moses), peace be on him, has not been
apprehended by anyone before him nor will it be apprehended by
anyone after him.

His request regarding the knowledge of (God's) attributes is
conveyed in his saying: "Show me now Your ways, that I may know
You" (Ex. 33:13), and so on. Consider the wondrous notions contained in this dictum. For his saying, "Show me now Your ways, that
I may know You," indicates that God, may He be exalted, is known
through His attributive qualifications; for when he would know the
"ways," he would know Him. Furthermore his saying, "That I may
find grace in Your sight" (ibid.), indicates that he who knows God
"finds grace in His sight" and not he who merely fasts and prays, but
everyone who has knowledge of Him. Accordingly, those who know
Him are those who are favored by Him and permitted to come near
Him, whereas those who do not know Him are objects of His wrath
and are kept far away from Him. For His favor and wrath, His nearness and remoteness, correspond to the extent of a man's knowledge
or ignorance. However, we have gone beyond the limits of the subject of this chapter. I shall accordingly return to the subject.

When (Moses) asked for knowledge of the attributes and asked
for forgiveness for the nation, he was given a (favorable) answer
with regard to their being forgiven. Then he asked for the apprehension of His essence, may He be exalted. This is what he means when
he says, "Show me, I pray You, Your glory" (Ex. 33:18), whereupon
he received a (favorable) answer with regard to what he had asked
for at first—namely, "Show me Your ways." For he was told: "I will
make all My goodness pass before you" (ibid. 33:19). In answer to
his second demand, he was told: "You can not see My face" (ibid.
33:20), and so on. This dictum—"all my goodness"—alludes to the
display to him of all existing things of which it is said: "And God
saw every thing that He had made, and, behold, it was very good"
(Gen. 1:31). By their display, I mean that he will apprehend their
nature and the way they are mutually connected so that he will know
how He governs them in general and in detail. This notion is indicated when it says: "He is trusted in all My house" (Num. 12:7);
that is, he has grasped the existence of all My world with a true and
firmly established understanding. For the opinions that are not correct are not firmly established. Accordingly, the apprehension of
these actions is an apprehension of His attributes, may He be

exalted, with respect to which He is known. The proof of the assertion that the thing, the apprehension of which was promised to him, was the actions of God, may He be exalted, is the fact that what was made known to him were simply pure attributes of action: "merciful and gracious, long-suffering . . ." (Ex. 34:6–7). It is then clear that the "ways"—for a knowledge of which he had asked and which, in consequence, were made known to him—are the actions proceeding from God, may He be exalted. The sages call them "characteristics" and speak of the "thirteen characteristics." This term, as they use it, is applied to moral qualities. Thus: "There are four characteristics among people who give charity . . . ; there are four characteristics among people who go to the house of learning . . ." (Ethics of the Fathers 5:13–14). This expression occurs frequently. The meaning here is not that He possesses moral qualities, but that He performs actions resembling the actions that in us proceed from moral qualities—I mean from aptitudes of the soul; the meaning is not that He, may He be exalted, possesses aptitudes of the soul. Scripture has restricted itself to mentioning only those "thirteen characteristics," although Moses apprehended "all His goodness"—I mean to say all His actions—because these are the actions proceeding from Him, may He be exalted, in respect of giving existence to men and governing them. This was Moses' ultimate object in his demand, the conclusion of what he says being: "That I may know You, to the end that I may find grace in Your sight and consider that this nation is Your people" (Ex. 33:13)—that is, a people for the government of which I need to perform actions that I must seek to make similar to Your actions in governing them.

It thus has become clear to you that the "ways" and the "characteristics" are identical. They are the actions proceeding from God, may He be exalted, in reference to the world. Accordingly, whenever one of His actions is apprehended, the attribute from which this action proceeds is predicated of Him, may He be exalted, and the name deriving from that action is applied to Him. For instance, one apprehends the kindness of His governance in the production of the embryos of living beings, the bringing of various faculties to existence in them and in those who rear them after birth—faculties that preserve them from destruction and annihilation and protect them against harm and are useful to them in all the doings that are necessary to them. Now actions of this kind proceed from us only after we feel a certain affection and compassion, and this is the meaning of mercy. God, may He be exalted, is said to be merciful, just as it is said, "As a father is merciful to his children" (Ps. 103:13), and it says, "And I will pity them, as a man pities his own son" (Mal. 3:17). It is not that He, may He be exalted, is affected and has compassion. But an action similar to that which proceeds from a father in respect to his child and that is attached to compassion, pity, and an absolute passion, proceeds from Him, may He be exalted, in reference to His holy ones, not because of a passion or a change. And just as when we give a thing to somebody who has no claim upon us, this is called grace in our language—as it says: "Grant them graciously" (Judges 21:22)—(so is the term applied to Him:) "Whom God has graciously given" (Gen. 33:5); "Because God has dealt graciously with me" (ibid. 33:11). Such instances are frequent. For He, may He be exalted, brings into existence and governs beings that have no claim upon Him with respect to being brought into existence and being governed. For this reason He is called gracious.

Similarly we find among His actions that proceed with regard to men great calamities overtaking certain individuals and destroying them, or some universal event annihilating whole tribes or even an entire region, exterminating the children and the children of the children, leaving in existence neither the products of the soil nor the offspring of living beings—for instance, submergence of land, earthquakes, destructive storms, military expeditions of one people against others in order to exterminate the latter by the sword and to efface all traces of them. Many of these actions would proceed from one of us in reference to another only because of a violent anger or a great hatred or a desire for vengeance. With reference to these actions He is called "jealous and avenging and keeping anger and wrathful" (Nah. 1:2), meaning that actions similar to those that proceed from us from a certain aptitude of the soul—namely, jealousy, holding fast to vengeance, hatred, or anger—proceed from Him, may He be exalted, because of the deserts of those who are punished, and not because of any passion whatever, may He be exalted above every deficiency. Similarly all (His) actions are such as resemble the actions proceeding from men on account of passions and aptitudes of the soul, but they by no means proceed from Him, may He be exalted, on account of a notion superadded to His essence.

The governor of a city, if he is a prophet, should acquire similarity to these attributes, so that these actions may proceed from him according to a determined measure and according to the deserts of the people who are affected by them and not merely because of his following a passion. He should not let loose the reins of anger nor let passion gain mastery over him, for all passions are evil; but, on the contrary, he should guard against them as far as this lies within the capacity of man. Sometimes, with regard to some people, he should be "merciful and gracious," not out of mere compassion and pity, but in accordance with what is fitting. Sometimes, with regard to some people, he should be "keeping anger and jealous and avenging" in accordance with their deserts, not out of mere anger; so he may order an individual to be burned without being angry and incensed with him and without hating him, because he perceives the deserts of that individual and considers the great benefit that many people will derive from the accomplishment of the action in question. Do you not see in the texts of the Torah, when it commanded the extermination of the seven nations and said, "you shall save alive nothing that breathes" (Deut. 20:16), that it immediately follows this by saying: "That they teach you not to do after all their abominations, which they have done to their gods and so you sin against the Lord your God?" (ibid. 20:18). Thus it says: do not think that this is hardheartedness or desire for vengeance. It is rather an act required by human opinion, which considers that everyone who deviates from the ways of truth should be put an end to and that all the obstacles impeding the achievement of the perfection that is the apprehension of Him, may He be exalted, should be interdicted. In spite of all this, it behooves that acts of mercy, forgiveness, pity, and commiseration should proceed from the governor of a city to a much greater extent than acts of retaliation. For the "thirteen characteristics" are all of them, with one exception, "characteristics of mercy"—the exception being: "visiting the iniquity of the fathers upon the children" (Ex. 34:7). For it says: "And that will by no means clear the guilty" (ibid.). The meaning is: and He will not utterly destroy—an interpretation deriving from the words: "And utterly destroyed, she shall sit upon the ground" (Is. 3:26). Know that his speech— "visiting the iniquity of the fathers upon the children"—only applies to the sin of idolatry in particular and not to any other sin. A proof of this is His saying in the Ten Commandments: "Unto the third and fourth generation of them that hate Me" (Ex. 20:5). For only an idolater is called hater: "for every abomination to the Lord, which He hates" (Deut. 12:31). He restricts Himself to the fourth generation only because the utmost of what man can see of his offspring is the fourth generation. Accordingly, when the people of an idolatrous city are killed, this means that an idolatrous old man and the offspring of the offspring of his offspring—that is, the child of the fourth generation—are killed. Accordingly, Scripture, as it were, predicated of Him that His commandments, may He be exalted, which undoubtedly are comprised in His actions, comprise the commandment to kill the offspring of idolaters, even if they are little children, together with the multitude of their fathers and grandfathers. We find this commandment continuously in the Torah in all passages. Thus he commands with regard to the city that has been led astray to idolatry: "Destroy it utterly and all that is therein" (ibid. 13:16)—all this being done with a view to blotting out traces that bring about necessarily great corruption, as we have made clear.

We have gone beyond the subject of this chapter; however, we have made clear why Scripture, in enumerating His actions, has confined itself here to those mentioned above, and that those actions are needed for the governance of cities. For the utmost virtue of man is to become like Him, may He be exalted, as far as he is able; which means that we should make our actions like unto His, as the sages made clear when interpreting the verse, "You shall be holy" (Lev. 19:2). They said: "He is gracious, so be you also gracious; He is merciful, so be you also merciful" (Sifre, Deut. 10:12). The purpose of all this is to show that the attributes ascribed to Him are attributes of His actions and that they do not mean that He possesses qualities.

CHAPTER 59*

... As everyone is aware that it is not possible, except through negation, to achieve an apprehension of that which is in our power to apprehend and that, on the other hand, negation does not give knowledge in any respect of the true reality of the thing with regard to which the particular matter in question has been negated—all men, those of the past and those of the future, affirm clearly that God, may He be exalted, cannot be apprehended by the intellects, and that none but He Himself can apprehend what He is, and that

*See Mishneh Torah, Book II, Prayer, ch. I.

apprehension of Him consists in the inability to attain the ultimate term in apprehending Him. Thus all the philosophers say: We are dazzled by His beauty, and He is hidden from us because of the intensity with which He becomes manifest, just as the sun is hidden to eyes that are too weak to apprehend it. This has been expatiated upon in words that it would serve no useful purpose to repeat here. The most apt phrase concerning this subject is the dictum occurring in the Psalms, "Silence is praise to You" (Ps. 65:2), which interpreted signifies: silence with regard to You is praise. This is a most perfectly put phrase regarding this matter. For of whatever we say intending to magnify and exalt, on the one hand we find that it can have some application to Him, may He be exalted, and on the other we perceive in it some deficiency. Accordingly, silence and limiting oneself to the apprehensions of the intellects are more appropriate— just as the perfect ones have enjoined when they said: "Commune with your own heart upon your bed, and be still" (Ps. 4:5).

You also know their famous dictum—would that all dicta were like it. I shall quote it to you textually, even though it is well remembered, so as to draw your attention to the various significations it expresses. They have said: "Someone who came into the presence of Rabbi Hanina said [in prayer]: God the Great, the Valiant, the Terrible, the Mighty, the Strong, the Tremendous, the Powerful. Thereupon [Rabbi Hanina] said to him: Have you finished all the praises of your Teacher? Even as regards the first three epithets [used by you] we could not have uttered them if Moses our Teacher had not pronounced them in the Law (Deut. 10:17) and if the men of the Great Synagogue had not [subsequently] come and established [their use] in prayer. And you come and say all this. What does this resemble? It is as if a mortal king who had millions of gold pieces were praised for possessing silver. Would this not be an offense to him?" (Berakhot 33b). Here ends the dictum of this perfect one. Consider in the first place his reluctance and unwillingness to multiply the affirmative attributes. Consider also that he has stated clearly that if we were left only to our intellects we should never have mentioned these attributes or stated a thing appertaining to them. Yet the necessity to address men in such terms as would make them achieve some representation—in accordance with the dictum of the sages: "The Torah speaks in the language of the sons of man" (Yevamot 71a; Bava Metzia 31b)—obliged resort to predicating of God their own perfections when speaking to them. It must then be our purpose to draw a line at using these expressions and not to apply them to Him except only in reading the Torah. However, as the men of the Great Synagogue, who were prophets, appeared in their turn and inserted the mention of these attributes in the prayer, it is our purpose to pronounce only these attributes when saying our prayers. According to the spirit, this dictum makes it clear that, as it happened, two necessary obligations determined our naming these attributes in our prayers: one of them is that they occur in the Torah, and the other is that the prophets in question used them in the prayer they composed. Accordingly, we should not have mentioned these attributes at all but for the first necessary obligation; and but for the second necessity, we should not have taken them out of their context and should not have had recourse to them in our prayers. As you continue to consider the attributes, it will become clear to you from this statement that we are not permitted in our prayers to use and to cite all the attributes ascribed to God in the books of the prophets. For [Rabbi Hanina] not only says: "If Moses our Teacher had not pronounced them, we could not have uttered them," but poses a second condition: "And if the men of the Great Synagogue had not [subsequently] come and established [their use] in prayer" (Berakhot 33b)—whereupon we are permitted to use them in our prayers.

Thus what we do is not like what is done by the truly ignorant who spoke at great length and spent great efforts on prayers that they composed and on sermons that they compiled and through which they, in their opinion, came nearer to God. In these prayers and sermons they predicate of God qualificative attributions that, if predicated of a human individual, would designate a deficiency in him. For they do not understand those sublime notions that are too strange for the intellects of the vulgar and accordingly took God, may He be magnified and glorified, for an object of study for their tongues; they predicated attributes of Him and addressed Him in all the terms that they thought permitted and expatiated at such length in this way that in their thoughts they made Him move on account of an affection. They did this especially when they found the text of a prophet's speech regarding these terms. Thereupon they had full license to bring forward texts that ought to be interpreted in every respect, and to take them according to their external meaning, to derive from them inferences and secondary conclusions, and to found upon them various kinds of discourses. This kind of license is frequently taken by poets and preachers or such as think that what they speak is poetry, so that the utterances of some of them constitute an absolute denial of faith, while other utterances contain such rubbish and such perverse imaginings as to make men laugh when they hear them, on account of the nature of these utterances, and to make them weep when they consider that these utterances are applied to God, may He be magnified and glorified. If I were not unwilling to set out the deficiencies of those who make these utterances, I should have quoted to you something of the latter in order that you should give heed to the points in which they may be impugned. However, the deficiencies in these utterances are most manifest to him who understands. It also behooves you to consider and say that in view of the fact that speaking ill and defamation are acts of great disobedience, how much all the more so is the loosening of the tongue with regard to God, may He be exalted, and the predicating of His qualificative attributions above which He is exalted. But I shall not say that this is an act of disobedience, but rather that it constitutes unintended obloquy and vituperation on the part of the multitude who listen to these utterances and on the part of the ignoramus who pronounces them. As for him who apprehends the deficiency of those speeches and yet uses those speeches, he belongs in my opinion to the category of people of whom it is said, "And the children of Israel did impute things that were not right to the Lord their God" (II Kings 17:9), and is said elsewhere, "And to utter error against the Lord" (Is. 32:6). Accordingly if you are one "who has regard for the honor of his Creator" (Hagigah 11b), you ought not to listen in any way to these utterances, let alone give expression to them and still less make up others like them. For you know the extent of the sin of him who "makes vituperative utterances against what is above" (Sukkah 53a; Taanit 25a). You accordingly ought not to set forth in any respect the attributes of God in an affirmative way— with a view, as you think, to magnifying Him—and ought not to go beyond that which has been inserted in the prayers and benedictions by the men of the Great Synagogue. For this is sufficient from the point of view of necessity; in fact, as Rabbi Hanina said, it is amply sufficient. But regarding the other attributes that occur in the books of the prophets and are recited during the perusal of these books, it is believed, as we have made clear, that they are attributes of action or that they indicate the negation of their nonexistence in God. This notion concerning them also should not be divulged to the vulgar.

For this kind of speculation is more suitable for the elite who consider that the magnification of God does not consist in their saying improper things but in their understanding properly.

Hereupon I shall return to completing the indications concerning the dictum of Rabbi Hanina and to giving it correct interpretation. He does not say, for example: "What does this resemble? It is as if a mortal king who had millions of gold pieces were praised for possessing one hundred pieces." For this example would have indicated that the perfections of Him, may He be exalted, while more perfect than the perfections that are ascribed to Him, still belong to the same species as the latter. As we have demonstrated, this is not so. But the wisdom manifest in this parable lies in his saying: "gold pieces and were praised for possessing silver." He says this in order to indicate that in God, may He be exalted, there is nothing belonging to the same species as the attributes that are regarded by us as perfections, but that all these attributes are deficiencies with regard to God, just as he made clear in this parable when he said: "Would this not be an offense to Him?" I have then already made it known to you that everything in these attributes that you regard as a perfection is a deficiency with regard to Him, may He be exalted, as it belongs to a species to which the things that are with us belong. Solomon, peace be on him, has rightly directed us with regard to this subject, in words that should be sufficient for us, when he said: "For God is in heaven and you upon the earth; therefore let your words be few" (Eccles. 5:1).

CHAPTER 71

Know that the many sciences devoted to establishing the truth regarding these matters that have existed in our religious community have perished because of the length of the time that has passed, because of our being dominated by the pagan nations, and because, as we have made clear, it is not permitted to divulge these matters to all people. For the only thing it is permitted to divulge to all people are the texts of the books. You already know that even the legalistic science of law was not put down in writing in the olden times because of the precept, which is widely known in the nation: "Words that I have communicated to you orally, you are not allowed to put down in writing" (Gittin 60b). This precept shows extreme wisdom with regard to the Law. For it was meant to prevent what has ultimately come about in this respect: I mean the multiplicity of opinions, the variety of schools, the confusions occurring in the expression of what is put down in writing, the negligence that accompanies what is written down, the divisions of the people who are separated into sects, and the production of confusion with regard to actions. All these matters should be within the authority of the Great Court of Law, as we have made clear in our juridical compilations and as the text of the Torah shows.* Now if there was insistence that the legalistic science of law should not, in view of the harm that would be caused by such a procedure, be perpetuated in a written compilation accessible to all the people, all the more could none of the mysteries of the Torah have been set down in writing and be made accessible to the people. On the contrary they were transmitted by a few men belonging to the elite, to a few of the same kind, just as I made clear to you from their saying: "The mysteries of the Torah may only be transmitted to a counsellor, wise in crafts" (Hagigah 14a), and so on. This was the cause that necessitated the disappearance of these great roots of knowledge from the nation. For you will not find with regard to them anything except slight indications and pointers occurring in the Talmud and the Midrashim. These are, as it were, a few grains belonging to the core, which are overlaid by many layers of rind, so that people were occupied with these layers of rind and thought that beneath them there was no core whatever.

As for that scanty bit of argument regarding the notion of the unity of God and regarding what depends on this notion, which you will find in the writings of some Geonim and in those of the Karaites, it should be noted that the subject matter of this argument was taken over by them from the Mutakallimun of Islam and that this bit is very scanty indeed if compared to what Islam has compiled on this subject. Also it has so happened that Islam first began to take this road owing to a certain sect, namely, the Mutazila, from whom our coreligionists took over certain things walking upon the road the Mutazila had taken. After a certain time another sect arose in Islam, namely, the Ashariyya, among whom other opinions arose. You will not find any of these latter opinions among our coreligionists. This

*Cf. *Mishneh Torah*, introduction; Deut. 17:8–12.

was not because they preferred the first opinion to the second, but because it so happened that they had taken over and adopted the first opinion and considered it a matter proven by demonstration.

As for the Andalusians (Spaniards) among the people of our nation, all of them cling to the affirmations of the philosophers and incline to their opinions, in so far as these do not ruin the foundation of the Law. You will not find them in any way taking the paths of the Mutakallimun. In many things concerning the scanty matter of which the later ones among them had knowledge, they have therefore approximately the same doctrine that we set forth in this treatise.

. . . There is no doubt that there are things that are common to all three of us, I mean the Jews, the Christians, and the Muslims: namely, the affirmation of the temporal creation of the world, the validity of which entails the validity of miracles and other things of that kind. As for the other matters that these two communities took the trouble to treat and were engrossed in—for instance, the study of the notion of trinity into which the Christians plunged* and the study of the Kalam into which certain sects of the Muslims plunged—so that they found it requisite to establish premises and to establish, by means of these premises that they had chosen, the conceptions into the study of which they had plunged and the notions that are peculiar to each of the two communities, having been established in it: these are things that we do not require in any respect whatever.

. . . When I studied the books of these Mutakallimun, as far as I had the opportunity—and I have likewise studied the books of the philosophers, as far as my capacity went—I found that the method of all of the Mutakallimun was one and the same in kind, though the subdivisions differed from one another. For the foundation of everything is that no consideration is due to how that which exists is, for it is merely a custom; and from the point of view of the intellect, it could well be different. Furthermore, in many places they follow the imagination and call it intellect. Thus when they propound the premises that we will let you hear, they found by their demonstrations the [affirmative] judgment that the world is created in time. And when it is thus established that the world is created in time, it is likewise undoubtedly established that it has a maker who has created

*See I, ch. 50.

it in time. Then they adduced arguments in favor of the inference that this maker is one; whereupon, basing themselves upon his being one, that he is not a body. This is the way of every Mutakallim from among the Muslims in anything concerning this subject. Thus also do those belonging to our community who imitate them and follow their ways. While the ways in which they adduce the arguments in favor of the inference as to, and propound the premises with regard to, the establishment of the temporal creation of the world or to the refutation of its pre-eternity, differ from one another, the universal thesis of all of them consists in the first place in the affirmation of the temporal creation of the world. And by means of its temporal creation, it is established as true that the deity exists.

Now when I considered this method of thought, my soul felt a very strong aversion to it, and had every right to do so. For every argument deemed to be a demonstration of the temporal creation of the world is accompanied by doubts and is not a cogent demonstration except among those who do not know the difference between demonstration, dialectics, and sophistic argument. As for those who know these arts, it is clear and evident to them that there are doubts with regard to all these proofs and that premises that have not been demonstrated have been used in them. The utmost power of one who adheres to a Law and who has acquired knowledge of true reality consists, in my opinion, in his refuting the proofs of the philosophers bearing on the eternity of the world. How sublime a thing it is when the ability is there to do it! And everyone who engages in speculation, who is perceptive, and who has acquired true knowledge of reality and does not deceive himself, knows that with regard to this question—namely the eternity of the world or its temporal creation—no cogent demonstration can be reached and that it is a point before which the intellect stops. . . .

PART TWO

CHAPTER 13

There are three opinions of human beings, namely, of all those who believe that there is an existent Deity, with regard to the eternity of the world or its production in time.

The first opinion, which is the opinion of all who believe in the Law of Moses our Teacher, is that the world as a whole—I mean to say, every existent other than God, may He be exalted—was brought into existence by God after having been purely and absolutely nonexistent, and that God, may He be exalted, had existed alone, and nothing else—neither an angel nor a sphere nor what subsists within the sphere. Afterward, through His will and His volition, He brought into existence out of nothing all the beings as they are, time itself being one of the created things. For time is consequent upon motion, and motion is an accident in what is moved. Furthermore, what is moved—that is, that upon the motion of which time is consequent—is itself created in time and came to be after not having been. Accordingly, one's saying: God "was" before He created the world—where the word "was" is indicative of time—and similarly all the thoughts that are carried along in the mind regarding the infinite duration of His existence before the creation of the world, are all of them due to a supposition regarding time or to an imagining of time and not due to the true reality of time. For time is undubitably an accident. According to us it is one of the created accidents, as are blackness and whiteness. And though it does not belong to the species of quality, it is nevertheless, generally stated, an accident necessarily following upon motion, as is made clear to whoever has understood the discourse of Aristotle on the elucidation of time and on the true reality of its existence. . . .

This is one of the opinions. And it is undoubtedly a basis of the Law of Moses our Teacher. And it is second to the basis that is the belief in the unity [of God]. Nothing other than this should come to your mind. It was Abraham our Father who began to proclaim in public this opinion to which speculation had led him. For this reason he made his proclamation "in the name of the Lord, God of the world" (Gen. 21:33);* he had also explicitly stated this opinion in saying: "Maker of heaven and earth" (Gen. 14:22).

The second opinion is that of all the philosophers of whom we have heard reports and whose discourses we have seen. They say that it is absurd that God would bring a thing into existence out of nothing. Furthermore, according to them, it is likewise not possible that a thing should pass away into nothing; I mean to say that it is not possible that a certain being, endowed with matter and form, should be generated out of the absolute nonexistence of that matter, or that it should pass away into the absolute nonexistence of that matter. To predicate of God that He is able to do this is, according to them, like predicating of Him that He is able to bring together two contraries in one instant of time, or that He is able to create something that is like Himself, may He be exalted, or to make Himself corporeal, or to create a square whose diagonal is equal to its side, and similar impossibilities. What may be understood from their discourse is that they say that just as His not bringing impossible things into existence does not argue a lack of power on His part—since what is impossible has a firmly established nature that is not produced by an agent and that consequently cannot be changed—it likewise is not due to lack of power on His part that He is not able to bring into existence a thing out of nothing, for this belongs to the class of all the impossible things. Hence they believe that there exists a certain matter that is eternal as the Deity is eternal; and that He does not exist without it,

*This is the invocation with which Maimonides begins each of the three parts of the *Guide of the Perplexed.*

nor does it exist without Him. They do not believe that it has the same rank in what exists as He, may He be exalted, but that He is the cause of its existence; and that it has the same relation toward Him as, for instance, clay has toward a potter or iron toward a smith; and that He creates in it whatever He wishes. Thus He sometimes forms out of it a heaven and an earth, and sometimes He forms out of it something else. The people holding this opinion believe that the heaven too is subject to generation and passing-away, but that it is not generated out of nothing and does not pass away into nothing. For it is generated and passes away just as the individuals that are animals are generated from existent matter and pass away into existent matter. The generation and passing-away of the heaven is thus similar to that of all the other existents that are below it.

The people belonging to this sect are in their turn divided into several sects. But it is useless to mention their various sects and opinions in this treatise. However, the universal principle held by this sect is identical with what I have told you. This is also the belief of Plato. For you will find that Aristotle in the *Akroasis* (*Physics*) relates of him that he, I mean Plato, believed that the heaven is subject to generation and passing-away. And you likewise will find his doctrine plainly set forth in his book to Timaeus. But he does not believe what we believe, as is thought by him who does not examine opinions and is not precise in speculation; he (the interpreter) imagines that our opinion and his (Plato's) opinion are identical. But this is not so. As for us, we believe that the heaven was generated out of nothing after a state of absolute nonexistence, whereas he believes that it has come into existence and has been generated from some other thing. This then is the second opinion.

The third opinion is that of Aristotle, his followers, and the commentators of his books. He asserts what also is asserted by the people belonging to the sect that has just been mentioned, namely, that something endowed with matter can by no means be brought into existence out of that which has no matter. He goes beyond this by saying that the heaven is in no way subject to generation and passing-away. His opinion on this point may be summed up as follows. He thinks that this being as a whole, such as it is, has never ceased to be and will never do so; that the permanent thing not subject to generation and passing-away, namely, the heaven, likewise does not cease to be; that time and motion are perpetual and everlasting and not subject to generation and passing-away; and also that the thing subject to generation and passing-away, namely, that which is beneath the sphere of the moon, does not cease to be. I mean to say that its first matter is not subject in its essence to generation and passing-away, but that various forms succeed each other in it in such a way that it divests itself of one form and assumes another. He thinks, furthermore, that this whole higher and lower order cannot be corrupted and abolished, that no innovation can take place in it that is not according to its nature, and that no occurrence that deviates from what is analogous to it can happen in it in any way. He asserts—though he does not do so textually, but this is what his opinion comes to—that in his opinion it would be an impossibility that will should change in God or a new volition arise in Him; and that all that exists has been brought into existence, in the state in which it is at present, by God through His volition; but that it was not produced after having been in a state of nonexistence. He thinks that just as it is impossible that the Deity should become nonexistent or that His essence should undergo a change, it is impossible that a volition should undergo a change in Him or a new will arise in Him. Accordingly, it follows necessarily that this being as a whole has never ceased to be as it is at present and will be as it is in the future eternity.

This is a summary and the truth of these opinions. They are the opinions of those according to whom the existence of the Deity for this world has been demonstrated. Those who have no knowledge of the existence of the Deity, may He be held sublime and honored, but think that things are subject to generation and passing-away through conjunction and separation due to chance and that there is no one who governs and orders being, are Epicurus, his following, and those like him, as is related by Alexander. It is useless for us to mention these sects. For the existence of the Deity has already been demonstrated, and there can be no utility in our mentioning the opinions of groups of people who built their doctrine upon a foundation the reverse of which has been demonstrated as true. Similarly it is useless for us to wish to prove as true the assertion of the people holding the second opinion, I mean that according to which the heaven is subject to generation and passing-away. For they believe in eternity; and there is, in our opinion, no difference between those who believe that heaven must of necessity be generated from a thing and pass away into a thing or the belief of Aristotle who believed that it is not subject to generation and corruption. For the purpose of every follower of the Law of Moses and Abraham our Father or of those who go the way of these two is to believe that there is nothing eternal in any way at all existing simultaneously with God; to believe also that the bringing into existence of a being out of nonexistence is for the Deity not an impossibility, but rather an obligation, as is deemed likewise by some of the men of speculation.

After we have expounded those opinions, I shall begin to explain and summarize the proofs of Aristotle in favor of his opinion and the motive that incited him to adopt it.

CHAPTER 14

I do not need to repeat in every chapter that I compiled this treatise for your benefit only because of my knowledge of your achievements. I do not need to set forth in every passage the text of the discourse of the philosophers, but only their intentions.* I shall not write at length, but only draw your attention to the methods that they aim at, as I did for you regarding the opinions of the Mutakallimun. I shall pay no attention to anyone who, besides Aristotle, has engaged in speculative discourse, for it is his opinions that ought to be considered. And if there are good grounds for refuting him or raising doubt with regard to these opinions as to some point on which we make a refutation or raise doubts, these grounds will be even firmer and stronger with respect to all others who disagreed with the fundamental principles of the Law. . . .

CHAPTER 15

My purpose in this chapter is to make it clear that Aristotle possesses no demonstration for the world being eternal, as he understands this.

*After listing (II, introduction) twenty-five premises or axioms which enable him to establish the existence of God, Maimonides notes: "I have already made it known to you that the purpose of this treatise is not to transcribe the books of the philosophers but to mention the proximate premises that are required for our purpose."

Moreover he is not mistaken with regard to this. I mean to say that he himself knows that he possesses no demonstration with regard to this point, and that the arguments and the proofs that he sets forth are merely such as occur to the mind and to which the soul inclines. Alexander [of Aphrodisias] thinks that they involve a lesser number of doubts. However, Aristotle cannot be supposed to have believed that these statements were demonstrations, for it was Aristotle who taught mankind the methods, the rules, and the conditions of demonstration.

What led me to speak of this is the fact that the latter-day followers of Aristotle believe that Aristotle has demonstrated the eternity of the world. Most of the people who believe themselves to philosophize follow Aristotle as an authority in this question and think that everything that he has mentioned constitutes a cogent demonstration as to which there can be no doubt. They regard it as disgraceful to disagree with him or to suppose that some concealed point or some false imagining in one of the issues has remained hidden from him. For this reason I thought that it was indicated to challenge them with regard to their opinion and to explain to them that Aristotle himself did not claim to have a demonstration in this question. Thus he says in the *Akroasis*: All the physicists preceding us believe that motion is not subject to generation and passing-away, except Plato, who believes that motion is subject to generation and passing-away, and the heaven too according to him is subject to generation and passing-away. This is literally what he says. Now it is certain that if there had been cogent demonstrations with regard to this question, Aristotle would not have needed to buttress his opinion by means of the fact that the physicists who preceded him had the same belief as he. Nor would he have needed to make all the assertions he makes in that passage concerning the vilification of those who disagree with him and the worthlessness of their opinion. For when something has been demonstrated, the correctness of the matter is not increased and certainty regarding it is not strengthened by the consensus of all men of knowledge with regard to it. Nor could its correctness be diminished and certainty regarding it be weakened even if all the people on earth disagreed with it. . . .

To sum up: Nothing in the methods that we have set forth in this chapter is capable either of establishing an opinion as correct or of proving it false or of arousing doubts with regard to it. And we have advanced the things we have only because we know that the majority of those who consider themselves as perspicacious, even though they have no understanding of anything in the sciences, decide simply that the world is eternal through acceptance of the authority of men celebrated for their science who affirm its eternity, whereas they reject the discourse of all the prophets, because their discourse does not use the method of scientific instruction, but that of imparting reports coming from God. Only a few favored by the intellect have been guided aright through this second method. As for what we desire in regard to the subject of the creation of the world according to the opinion of our Law, I shall speak of it in chapters that will follow.

CHAPTER 16

This is a chapter in which I shall explain to you what I believe with regard to this question. After that I shall give proofs for what we desire to maintain. I say then with regard to all that is affirmed by those Mutakallimun who think that they have demonstrated the newness of the world, that I approve of nothing in those proofs and that I do not deceive myself by designating methods productive of errors as demonstrations. If a man claims that he sets out to demonstrate a certain point by means of sophistical arguments, he does not, in my opinion, strengthen assent to the point he intends to prove, but rather weakens it and opens the way for attacks against it. For when it becomes clear that those proofs are not valid, the soul weakens in its assent to what is being proved. It is preferable that a point for which there is no demonstration remain a problem or that one of the two contradictory propositions simply be accepted. I have already set forth for your benefit the methods of the Mutakallimun in establishing the newness of the world, and I have drawn your attention to the points with regard to which they may be attacked. Similarly all that Aristotle and his followers have set forth in the way of proof of the eternity of the world does not constitute in my opinion a cogent demonstration, but rather arguments subject to grave doubts, as you shall hear. What I myself desire to make clear is that the world's being created in time, according to the opinion of our

Law—an opinion that I have already explained—is not impossible and that all those philosophic proofs from which it seems that the matter is different from what we have stated, all those arguments have a certain point through which they may be invalidated and the inference drawn from them against us shown to be incorrect. Now inasmuch as this is true in my opinion and inasmuch as this question—I mean to say that of the eternity of the world or its creation in time—becomes an open question, it should in my opinion be accepted without proof because of prophecy, which explains things to which it is not in the power of speculation to accede. For as we shall make clear, prophecy is not set at nought even in the opinion of those who believe in the eternity of the world.

After I have made it clear that what we maintain is possible, I shall begin to make it prevail likewise, by means of speculative proof, over any other affirmations; I refer to my making prevail the assertion of creation in time over the assertion of eternity. I shall make it clear that just as a certain disgrace attaches to us because of the belief in the creation in time, an even greater disgrace attaches to the belief in eternity. I shall now start to bring into being a method that shall render void the proofs of all those who prove by inference the eternity of the world.

CHAPTER 25

Know that our shunning the affirmation of the eternity of the world is not due to a text figuring in the Torah according to which the world has been produced in time. For the texts indicating that the world has been produced in time are not more numerous than those indicating that the Deity is a body. Nor are the gates of figurative interpretation shut in our faces or impossible of access to us regarding the subject of the creation of the world in time. For we could interpret them as figurative, as we have done when denying His corporeality. Perhaps this would even be much easier to do: we should be very well able to give a figurative interpretation of those texts and to affirm as true the eternity of the world, just as we have given a figurative interpretation of those other texts and have denied that He, may He be exalted, is a body.

Two causes are responsible for our not doing this or believing it. One of them is as follows. That the Deity is not a body has been demonstrated; from this it follows necessarily that everything that in its external meaning disagrees with this demonstration must be interpreted figuratively, for it is known that such texts are of necessity fit for figurative interpretation. However, the eternity of the world has not been demonstrated. Consequently in this case the texts ought not to be rejected and figuratively interpreted in order to make prevail an opinion whose contrary can be made to prevail by means of various sorts of arguments. This is one cause.

The second cause is as follows. Our belief that the Deity is not a body destroys for us none of the foundations of the Law and does not give the lie to the claims of any prophet. The only objection to it is constituted by the fact that the ignorant think that this belief is contrary to the text; yet it is not contrary to it, as we have explained, but is intended by the text. On the other hand, the belief in eternity the way Aristotle sees it—that is, the belief according to which the world exists in virtue of necessity, that no nature changes at all, and that the customary course of events cannot be modified with regard to anything—destroys the Law in its principle, necessarily gives the lie to every miracle, and reduces to inanity all the hopes and threats that the Law has held out, unless—by God!—one interprets the miracles figuratively also, as was done by the Islamic internalists (allegorists); this, however, would result in some sort of crazy imaginings.

If, however, one believed in eternity according to the second opinion we have explained—which is the opinion of Plato—according to which the heavens, too, are subject to generation and corruption, this opinion would not destroy the foundations of the Law and would be followed not by the lie being given to miracles, but by their becoming admissible. It would also be possible to interpret figuratively the texts in accordance with this opinion. And many obscure passages can be found in the texts of the Torah and others with which this opinion could be connected or rather by means of which it could be proved. However, no necessity could impel us to do this unless this opinion were demonstrated. In view of the fact that it has not been demonstrated, we shall not favor this opinion, nor shall we at all heed that other opinion, but rather shall take the texts according to their external sense and shall say: The Law has given us knowledge of a matter the grasp of which is not within our power, and the miracle attests to the correctness of our claims.

Know that with a belief in the creation of the world in time, all the miracles become possible and the Law becomes possible, and all questions that may be asked on this subject, vanish. Thus it might be said: Why did God give prophetic revelation to this one and not to that? Why did God give this Law to this particular nation, and why did He not legislate to the others? Why did He legislate at this particular time, and why did He not legislate before it or after? Why did He impose these commandments and these prohibitions? Why did He privilege the prophet with the miracles mentioned in relation to him and not with some others? What was God's aim in giving this Law? Why did He not, if such was His purpose, put the accomplishment of the commandments and the nontransgression of the prohibitions into our nature? If this were said, the answer to all these questions would be that it would be said: He wanted it this way; or His wisdom required it this way. And just as He brought the world into existence, having the form it has, when He wanted to, without our knowing His will with regard to this or in what respect there was wisdom in His particularizing the forms of the world and the time of its creation—in the same way we do not know His will or the exigency of His wisdom that caused all the matters, about which questions have been posed above, to be particularized. If, however, someone says that the world is as it is in virtue of necessity, it would be a necessary obligation to ask all those questions; and there would be no way out of them except through a recourse to unseemly answers in which there would be combined the giving the lie to, and the annulment of, all the external meanings of the Law with regard to which no intelligent man has any doubt that they are to be taken in their external meanings. It is then because of this that this opinion is shunned and that the lives of virtuous men have been and will be spent in investigating this question. For if creation in time were demonstrated—if only as Plato understands creation—all the overhasty claims made to us on this point by the philosophers would become void. In the same way, if the philosophers would succeed in demonstrating eternity as Aristotle understands it, the Law as a whole would become void, and a shift to other opinions would take place. I have thus explained to you that everything is bound up with this problem. Know this.

CHAPTER 27

I have already made it clear to you that the belief in the production of the world is necessarily the foundation of the entire Law. However, the belief in its passing-away after it has come into being and been generated is not, in our opinion, in any respect a foundation of the Law, and none of our beliefs would be hurt through the belief in its permanent duration. Perhaps you will say: Has it not been demonstrated that everything that comes into being passes away?; if then the world is generated it will pass away. Know then that this need not apply to us. For we do not assert that it has been generated according to the rule applying to the generation of the natural things that follow a natural order. For what is generated in accordance with the course of nature must of necessity pass away in accordance with the course of nature. For just as its nature had required that at first it should not exist in this particular way whereas after that it has come to exist in that way, it necessarily also requires that it should not exist in that way forever. For it is established as true that this mode of existence is not permanently attached to it by its nature. However, in view of our claim, based on the Law, that things exist and perish according to His will, may He be exalted, and not in virtue of necessity, it is not necessary for us to profess in consequence of that opinion that when He, may He be exalted, brings into existence a thing that had not existed, He must necessarily cause this existent to pass away. Rather does the matter inevitably depend on His will: if He wills, He causes the thing to pass away; and if He wills, He causes it to last; or it depends on what is required by His wisdom. It is accordingly possible that He should cause it to last for ever and ever and to endure as He Himself, may He be exalted, endures.

You know that while the sages state explicitly that the "throne of glory" has been created, they never say that it will become nonexistent. No prophet and no sage has ever been heard to say that the "throne of glory" will pass away or become nonexistent. Rather does the text of Scripture state that it will last forever. The same applies to the souls of the virtuous; for according to our opinion, they are created, but will never become nonexistent. According to certain opinions of those who follow the literal sense of the Midrashim, their bodies will also be in a state of perpetual felicity for ever and ever—an opinion resembling that of those whose belief as to the inhabitants of Paradise is generally known.

To sum up: Speculation obliges us to affirm that the passing-away of the world need not necessarily follow. Thus it only remains to examine this question in the light of the information imparted by the prophets and the sages. Have they given information that this world will without any doubt pass away, or have they not? Most of the vulgar among us believe that such information has been given and that all this world will pass away. However, I shall explain to you that this is not so, but that there are many texts that signify that it will last forever. All the passages from whose external sense it appears that the world will pass away, are most manifestly parables, as I shall explain. If, however, one of the externalists refuses to admit this and says that he must necessarily believe in the passing-away of the world, he should not be dealt with illiberally. However, he needs to be informed that the world's passing-away does not necessarily follow from the fact of its having been created in time, but that he believes in this, as he thinks, by way of accepting the veracity of the one who stated that parable, which he takes in its external sense. From the point of view of the Law, there is no harm in this in any respect whatever.

CHAPTER 29

. . . As the exposition has finally reached this point, we shall now put in a chapter that shall likewise give several indications as to texts concerned with the "Account of the Beginning." For the first purpose of this treatise is to explain what can be explained of the "Account of the Beginning" and of the "Account of the Divine Chariot." We shall put in this chapter after we have first set forth two preambles of general import. One of these is as follows: Not everything mentioned in the Torah concerning the "Account of the Beginning" is to be taken in its external sense as the vulgar imagine. For if the matter were such, the men of knowledge would not have been chary of divulging knowledge with regard to it, and the sages would not have expatiated on its being kept secret and on preventing the talk about it in the presence of the vulgar. For the external sense of these texts leads either to a grave corruption of the imagination and to giving vent to evil opinions with regard to the Deity, or to an absolute denial of the action of the Deity and to disbelief in the foundations of the Law. The correct thing to do is to refrain, if one lacks all knowledge of the sciences, from considering these texts merely with the imagination. One should not act like the wretched preachers and commentators who think that a knowledge of the interpretation of words is science and in whose opinion wordiness and length of speech add to perfection. On the other hand it is obligatory to consider them with what is truly the intellect after one has acquired perfection in the demonstrative sciences and knowledge of the secrets of the prophets. However, as I have explained several times in our *Commentary on the Mishnah*, none of those who know something of it should divulge it. And they say explicitly: "As from the beginning of the book up to here, the glory of God [requires] to conceal the thing" (Gen. Rabbah, ch. 9). They say it at the end of what is said concerning the sixth day [of the Beginning]. Thus what we have said has become clear. However, inasmuch as the divine commandment necessarily obliges everyone who has obtained a certain perfection to let it overflow toward others—as we shall make clear in the chapters on prophecy that follow—every man endowed with knowledge who has come to possess an understanding of something pertaining to these secrets, either through his own speculation or through being conducted toward this by a guide, must indubitably say something. It is, however, forbidden to be explicit about it. He must accordingly make the secret appear in flashes. Many such flashes, indications, and pointers occur in the sayings of some of the sages, but these sayings are mixed up with the sayings of others and with sayings of another kind. For this reason you will find that with regard to these mysteries, I mention the single saying on which the matter is based. . . .

CHAPTER 31

Perhaps it has already become clear to you what is the cause of the Law's establishing the Sabbath so firmly and ordaining "death by stoning" for breaking it. The master of the prophets has put people to death because of it. It comes third after the existence of the Deity and the denial of dualism. For the prohibition of the worship of anything except Him only aims at the affirmation of the belief in His unity. You know from what I have said that opinions do not last unless they are accompanied by actions that strengthen them, make them generally known, and perpetuate them among the multitude. For this reason we are ordered by the Law to exalt this day, in order that the principle of the creation of the world in time be established and universally known in the world through the fact that all people refrain from working on one and the same day. If it is asked: What is the cause of this? the answer is:"For in six days the Lord made" (Ex. 20:11).

For this commandment two different causes are given, corresponding to two different effects. In the first Decalogue, the cause for exalting the Sabbath is stated as follows: "For in six days the Lord made," and so on. In Deuteronomy (5:15), on the other hand, it is said: "And you shall remember that you were a slave in Egypt. Therefore the Lord your God commanded you to keep the sabbath day." This is correct. For the effect, according to the first statement, is to regard that day as noble and exalted. As it says: "Wherefore the Lord blessed the sabbath day, and hallowed it" (Ex. 20:11). This is the effect consequent upon the cause stated in the words: "For in six days," and so on. However, the order given us by the Law with regard to it and the commandment ordaining us in particular to keep it are an effect consequent upon the cause that we had been "slaves in Egypt" where we did not work according to our free choice and when we wished and where we had not the power to refrain from working. Therefore we have been commanded inactivity and rest so that we should conjoin the two things: the belief in a true opinion—namely, the creation of the world in time, which, at once and with the slightest of speculations, shows that the Deity exists—and the memory of the benefit God bestowed upon us by giving us rest "from under the burdens of the Egyptians" (Ex. 6:7). Accordingly, the Sabbath is, as it were, of universal benefit, both with reference to a true speculative opinion and to the well-being of the state of the body.

CHAPTER 39

... Hence, according to our opinion, there never has been a Law and there never will be a Law except the one that is the Law of Moses our Teacher. The explanation of this, according to what is literally stated in the prophetic books and is found in the tradition, is as follows. Not one of the prophets—such as the patriarchs, Shem, Eber, Noah, Methuselah, and Enoch—who came before Moses our Teacher, has ever said to a class of people: God has sent me to you and has commanded me to say to you such and such things; He has forbidden you to do such and such things and has commanded you to do such and such things. This is a thing that is not attested to by any text of the Torah and that does not figure in any true tradition. These men only received prophetic revelation from God according to what we have set forth. He who received a great overflow, as for instance Abraham, assembled the people and called them by the way of teaching and instruction to adhere to the truth that he had grasped. Thus Abraham taught the people and explained to them by means of speculative proofs that the world has but one Deity, that He has created all the things that are other than Himself, and that none of the forms and no created thing in general ought to be worshiped. This is what he instructed the people in, attracting them by means of eloquent speeches and by means of the benefits he conferred upon them. But he never said: God has sent me to you and has given me commandments and prohibitions. Even when the commandment of circumcision was laid upon him, his sons, and those who belonged to him, he circumcised them alone and did not use the form of a prophetic call to exhort the people to do this. Do you not see the text of the Torah referring to him that reads: "For I have known him" (Gen. 18:19), and so on.* Thus it is made clear that he acted only through injunction. Isaac, Jacob, Levi, Kohat, and Amram also addressed their call to the people in this way. You will find likewise that the sages say with reference to the prophets who came before him: "the court of justice of Eber, the court of justice of Methuselah, the school of Methuselah" (Gen. Rabbah, ch. 43). For all of them, peace be on them, were prophets who taught the people through being instructors, teachers, and guides, but did not say: "The Lord said to me: Speak to the sons of So-and-So." Things were like that before Moses our Teacher. As for Moses, you know what was said to him, what he said, and what all the people said to him: "This day we have seen that God does speak" (Deut. 5:21), and so on.

*The verse continues: "to the end that he may command his sons and his house after him, that they may keep the way of the Lord, to do righteousness and judgment."

As for the prophets from among us who came after Moses our Teacher, you know the text of all their stories and the fact that their function was that of preachers who called upon the people to obey the Law of Moses, threatened those who rejected it, and held out promises to those who were firm in observing it. We likewise believe that things will always be this way. As it says: "It is not in heaven" (*ibid.* 30:12), and so on; "for us and for our children for ever" (*ibid.* 29:28). And that is as it ought to be; for when a thing is as perfect as it is possible to be within its species, it is impossible that within that species there should be found another thing that does not fall short of that perfection either because of excess or deficiency. Thus in comparison with a temperament whose composition is of the greatest equibalance possible in the species in question, all other temperaments are not composed in accordance with this equibalance because of either deficiency or excess. Things are similar with regard to this Law, as is clear from its equibalance. For it says: "Just statutes and judgments" (*ibid.* 4:8); now you know the meaning of "just" is equibalanced. For these are manners of worship in which there is no burden and excess—such as monastic life and pilgrimage and similar things—nor a deficiency necessarily leading to greed and being engrossed in the indulgence of appetites, so that in consequence the perfection of man is diminished with respect to his moral habits and to his speculation—this being the case with regard to all the other nomoi of the religious communities of the past. When we shall speak in this treatise about the reasons accounting for the commandments, their equibalance and wisdom will be made clear to you in so far as this is necessary. For this reason it is said with reference to them: "The Law of the Lord is perfect" (Ps. 19:8). As for those who deem that its burdens are grievous, heavy, and difficult to bear—all of this is due to an error in considering them. I shall explain later on how easy they are in true reality according to the opinion of the perfect. For this reason it says: "What does the Lord your God require of you" (Deut. 10:12), and so on. And it says: "Have I been a wilderness to Israel?" (Jer. 2:31), and so on. However, all this refers to the virtuous, whereas in the opinion of those who are unjust, violent, and tyrannical, the existence of a judge who renders tyranny impossible is a most harmful and grievous thing. As for the greedy and the vile, the most grievous thing in their opinion is that which hinders their abandoning themselves to debauchery and punishes those who indulge in it. Similarly everyone who is deficient in any respect considers that a hindrance in the way of the vice that he prefers because of his moral corruption is a great burden. Accordingly, the facility or difficulty of the Law should not be estimated with reference to the passions of all the wicked, vile, morally corrupt men, but should be considered with reference to the man who is perfect among the people. For it is the aim of this Law that everyone should be such a man. Only that Law is called by us divine Law, whereas the other political regimens—such as the nomoi of the Greeks and the ravings of the Sabians and of others—are due, as I have explained several times, to the action of groups of rulers who were not prophets.

CHAPTER 40

It has been explained with utmost clarity that man is political by nature and that it is his nature to live in society. He is not like the other animals for which society is not a necessity. Because of the manifold composition of this species—for, as you know, it is the last one to have been composed—there are many differences between the individuals belonging to it, so that you can hardly find two individuals who are in any accord with respect to one of the species of moral habits, except in a way similar to that in which their visible forms may be in accord with one another.

... Now as the nature of the human species requires that there be those differences among the individuals belonging to it and as in addition society is a necessity for this nature, it is by no means possible that his society should be perfected except—and this is necessarily so—through a ruler who gauges the actions of the individuals, perfecting that which is deficient and reducing that which is excessive, and who prescribes actions and moral habits that all of them must always practice in the same way, so that the natural diversity is hidden through the multiple points of conventional accord and so that the community becomes well ordered. Therefore I say that the Law, although it is not natural, enters into what is natural. It is a part of the wisdom of the Deity with regard to the permanence of this species of which He has willed the existence, that He put it into its nature that individuals belonging to it should have the faculty of ruling. Among them there is the one to whom the regimen mentioned has been revealed by prophecy directly; he is the prophet or the bringer of the nomos. Among them there are also those who have the faculty to compel people to accomplish, observe, and actualize that which has been established by those two. They are a sovereign who adopts the nomos in question, and someone claiming to be a prophet who adopts the Law of the prophet—either the whole of it or a portion. His adopting a portion and abandoning another portion may be due either to this being easier for him or to his wishing out of jealousy to make people fancy that those matters came to him through a prophetic revelation and that with regard to them he does not follow somebody else. For among the people there are men who admire a certain perfection, take pleasure in it, have a passion for it, and wish that people should imagine that this perfection belongs to them, though they know that they possess no perfection. Thus you see that there are many who lay a claim to, and give out as their own, the poetry of someone else. This has also been done with regard to certain works of men of science and to particular points of many sciences. For an envious and lazy individual sometimes comes upon a thing invented by somebody else and claims that it was he who invented it. This has also happened with regard to the prophetic perfection. For we find people who laid a claim to prophecy and said things with regard to which there had never been at any time a prophetic revelation coming from God; thus, for instance, "Zedekiah son of Chenaanah" (cf. I Kings 22:11, 24). And we find other people who laid a claim to prophecy and said things that God has indubitably said—I mean things that had come through a prophetic revelation, but a prophetic revelation addressed to other people; thus, for instance, "Hananiah son of Azzur" (cf. Jer. 28:1 ff.). Accordingly, these men give out as their own the prophetic revelation in question and adorn themselves with it. The knowledge and discernment of all this are very clear. I shall explain this to you in order that the matter should not be obscure to you and so that you should have a criterion by means of which you will be able to distinguish between the regimens of nomoi that have been laid down, the regimens of the divine Law, and the regimens of those who took over something from the dicta of the prophets, raised a claim to it, and give it out as their own.

Concerning the nomoi* with respect to which those who have laid them down have stated clearly that these are nomoi that they have laid down by following their own thoughts, there is no need to adduce proofs for this, for with its being recognized by the adversary, no further evidence is needed. Accordingly, I only want to give you

*i.e., composed of man-made laws.

knowledge concerning the regimens with regard to which the claim is made that they are prophetic; some of them are truly prophetic—I mean divine—while others are nomoi, and others again are plagiarisms.

Accordingly, if you find a Law the whole end of which and the whole purpose of the chief thereof, who determined the actions required by it, are directed exclusively toward the ordering of the city and of its circumstances and the abolition in it of injustice and oppression; and if in that Law attention is not at all directed toward speculative matters, no heed is given to the perfecting of the rational faculty, and no regard is accorded to opinions being correct or faulty—the whole purpose of that Law being, on the contrary, the arrangement, in whatever way this may be brought about, of the circumstances of people in their relations with one another and provision for their obtaining, in accordance with the opinion of that chief, a certain something deemed to be happiness—you must know that that Law is a nomos* and that the man who laid it down belongs, as we have mentioned, to the third class, I mean to say to those who are perfect only in their imaginative faculty.

If, on the other hand, you find a Law all of whose ordinances are due to attention being paid, as was stated before, to the soundness of the circumstances pertaining to the body and also to the soundness of belief—a Law that takes pains to inculcate correct opinions with regard to God, may He be exalted in the first place, and with regard to the angels, and that desires to make man wise, to give him understanding, and to awaken his attention, so that he should know the whole of that which exists in its true form—you must know that this guidance comes from Him, may He be exalted, and that this Law is divine.

It remains for you to know whether he who lays claim to such a guidance is a perfect man to whom a prophetic revelation of that guidance has been vouchsafed, or whether he is an individual who lays claim to these dicta, having plagiarized them. The way of putting this to a test is to consider the perfection of that individual, carefully to examine his actions, and to study his way of life. The strongest of the indications you should pay attention to is constituted by his renunciation of, and contempt for, the bodily pleasures, for this is the first of the degrees of the people of science and, all the more, of the prophets. . . .

*In this context, a law promulgated by a legislator who was not a prophet.

INTRODUCTION TO PART THREE

W E HAVE already made it clear several times that the chief aim of this treatise is to explain what can be explained of the "Account of the Beginning" and the "Account of the Divine Chariot," with a view to him for whom this treatise has been composed. We have already made it clear that these matters belong to the mysteries of the Torah, and you know that the sages blame those who divulge the mysteries of the Torah. They have already made it clear that the reward of him who conceals the mysteries of the Torah, which are clear and manifest to the men of speculation, is very great. At the conclusion of Pesahim (119a), when speaking of the signification of the dictum—"For her gain shall be for them that dwell before the Lord, to eat their fill, and *limekhasse atik*" (Is. 23:18)—they say: "For him who covers the things revealed by the Ancient of Days, namely, the mysteries of the Torah." Understand the extent of that toward which they give guidance, if you are of those that understand. They have already made it clear how secret the "Account of the Divine Chariot" was and how foreign to the mind of the multitude. And it has been made clear that even that portion of it that becomes clear to him who has been given access to the understanding of it, is subject to a legal prohibition against its being taught and explained except orally to one man having certain stated qualities, and even to that one only the chapter headings may be mentioned. This is the reason why the knowledge of this matter has ceased to exist in the entire religious community, so that nothing great or small remains of it. And it had to happen like this, for this knowledge was only transmitted from one chief to another and has never been set down in writing. If this is so, what stratagem can I use to draw attention toward that which may have appeared to me as indubitably clear, manifest, and evident in my opinion, according to what I have understood in these matters? On the other hand, if I had omitted setting down something of that which has appeared to me as clear, so that that knowledge would perish when I perish, as is inevitable, I should have considered that conduct as extremely cowardly with regard to you and everyone who is perplexed. It would have been, as it were, robbing one who deserves the truth of the truth, or begrudging an heir his inheritance. And both those traits are blameworthy. On the other hand, as has been stated before, an explicit exposition of this knowledge is denied by a legal prohibition, in addition to that which is imposed by judgment. In addition to this there is the fact that in that which has occurred to me with regard to these matters, I followed conjecture and supposition; no divine revelation has come to me to teach me that the intention in the matter in question was such and such, nor did I receive what I believe in these matters from a teacher. But the texts of the prophetic books and the dicta of the sages, together with the speculative premises that I possess, showed me that things are indubitably so and so. Yet it is possible that they are different and that something else is intended. Now rightly guided reflection and divine aid in this matter have moved me to a position, which I shall describe. Namely, I shall interpret to you that which was said by Ezekiel the prophet, in such a way that anyone who heard that interpretation would think that I do not say anything over and beyond what is indicated by the text, but that it is as if I translated words from one language to another or summarized the meaning of the external sense of the speech. On the other hand, if that interpretation is examined with a perfect care by him for whom this treatise is composed and who has understood all its chapters—every chapter in its turn—the whole matter, which has become clear and manifest to me, will become clear to him so that nothing in it will remain hidden from him. This is the ultimate term that it is possible to attain in combining utility for everyone with abstention from explicit statements in teaching anything about his subject—as is obligatory.

After this introduction has preceded, apply your mind to the chapters that will follow concerning this great, noble, and sublime subject, which is "a stake upon which everything hangs and a pillar upon which everything is supported."*

CHAPTER 8

. . . For if it so happens that the matter of a man is excellent and suitable, neither dominating him nor corrupting his constitution, that matter is a divine gift. To sum up: it is easy, as we have mentioned, to control suitable matter. If it is unsuitable, it is not impossible for someone trained to quell it. For this reason Solomon—both he and others—inculcated all these exhortations. Also the commandments and prohibitions of the Law are only intended to quell all the impulses of matter. It behooves him who prefers to be a human being in truth, not a beast having the shape and configuration of a human being, to endeavor to diminish all the impulses of matter— such as eating, drinking, copulation, anger, and all the habits consequent upon desire and anger—to be ashamed of them, and to set for them limits in his soul. . . .

You know the severe prohibition that obtains among us against obscene language.† This also is necessary. For speaking with the tongue is one of the properties of a human being and a benefit that is granted to him and by which he is distinguished. As it says: "Who has made man's mouth?" (Ex. 4:11). And the prophet says: "The Lord God has given me the tongue of them that are taught" (Is. 50:4). Now this benefit granted us with a view to perfection in order that we learn and teach should not be used with a view to the greatest deficiency and utter disgrace, so that one says what the ignorant and sinful Gentiles say in their songs and their stories, suitable for them but not for those to whom it has been said: "And you

*Cf. Is. 22:23–24 and Judges 16:26.

†Cf. Ketuvot 8b and Shabbat 33a.

shall be to Me a kingdom of priests, and a holy nation" (Ex. 19:6). And whoever has applied his thought or his speech to some of the stories concerning that sense which is a disgrace to us, so that he thought more about drink or copulation than is needful or recited songs about these matters, has made use of the benefit granted to him, applying and utilizing it to commit an act of disobedience with regard to Him who has granted the benefit and to transgress His orders. He is like those of whom it is said: "And I multiplied to her silver and gold, which they used for Baal" (Hos. 2:10). I can also give the reason why this our language is called "the holy language." It should not be thought that this is, on our part, an empty appellation or a mistake; in fact it is indicative of true reality. For in this holy language no word at all has been laid down in order to designate either the male or the female organ of copulation, nor are there words designating the act itself that brings about generation, the sperm, the urine, or the excrements. No word at all designating, according to its first meaning, any of these things has been laid down in the Hebrew language, they being signified by terms used in a figurative sense and by allusions. It was intended thereby to indicate that these things ought not to be mentioned and consequently that no terms designating them should be coined.

CHAPTER 12

Often it occurs to the imagination of the multitude that there are more evils in the world than there are good things. As a consequence, this thought is contained in many sermons and poems of all the religious communities, which say that it is surprising if good exists in the temporal, whereas the evils of the temporal are numerous and constant. This error is not found only among the multitude, but also among those who deem that they know something.

Razi* has written a famous book, which he has entitled *Divine*

*Maimonides refers here to Abu Bakr Muhammad Ibn Zakariyya al-Razi, who died sometime between 923 and 932. Razi (the Rhazes of the Latins) was a famous physician and a philosopher who attacked religion based on prophetic revelation. Only fragments of the book mentioned by Maimonides have come down to us.

Things. He filled it with the enormity of his ravings and his ignorant notions. Among them there is a notion that he has thought up, namely, that there is more evil than good in what exists; if you compare man's well-being and his pleasures in the time span of his well-being with the pains, the heavy sufferings, the infirmities, the paralytic afflictions, the wretchedness, the sorrows, and the calamities that befall him, you find that his existence—he means the existence of man—is a punishment and a great evil inflicted upon him. He began to establish this opinion by inductively examining these misfortunes, so as to oppose all that is thought by the adherents of the truth regarding the beneficence and manifest munificence of the Deity and regarding His being, may He be exalted, the absolute good and regarding all that proceeds from Him being indubitably an absolute good. The reason for this whole mistake lies in the fact that this ignoramus and those like him among the multitude consider that which exists only with reference to a human individual. Every ignoramus imagines that all that exists exists with a view to his individual sake; it is as if there were nothing that exists except him. And if something happens to him that is contrary to what he wishes, he makes the trenchant judgment that all that exists is an evil. However, if man considered and represented to himself that which exists and knew the smallness of his part in it, the truth would become clear and manifest to him. For this extensive raving entertained by men with regard to the multitude of evils in the world is not said by them to hold good with regard to the angels or with regard to the spheres and the stars or with regard to the elements and the minerals and the plants composed of them or with regard to the various species of animals, but their whole thought only goes out to some individuals belonging to the human species. If someone has eaten bad food and consequently was stricken with leprosy, they are astonished how this great ill has befallen him and how this great evil exists. They are also astonished when one who frequently copulates is stricken blind, and they think it a marvelous thing the calamity of blindness that has befallen such a man and other such calamities.

Now the true way of considering this is that all the existent individuals of the human species and, all the more, those of the other species of the animals are things of no value at all in comparison with the whole that exists and endures. It has made this clear, saying: "Man is like vanity" (Ps. 144:4), and so on. "Man, that is a worm; and the son of man, that is a maggot" (Job 25:6). "How much less in them that dwell in houses of clay" (ibid. 4:19), and so on. "Be-

hold, the nations are as a drop of a bucket" (Is. 40:15), and so on.
There are also all the other passages figuring in the texts of the books
of the prophets concerning this sublime and grave subject, which is
most useful in giving man knowledge of his true value, so that he
should not make the mistake of thinking that what exists is in existence only for the sake of him as an individual. According to us, on
the other hand, what exists is in existence because of the will of its
Creator; and among the things that are in existence, the species of
man is the least in comparison to the superior existents—I refer to
the spheres and the stars. As far as comparison with the angels is
concerned, there is in true reality no relation between man and
them. Man is merely the most noble among the things that are subject to generation, namely, in this our nether world; I mean to say
that he is the noblest thing that is composed of the elements.
Withal his existence is for him a great good and a benefit on the part
of God because of the properties with which He has singled him out
and perfected him. The greater part of the evils that befall its individuals are due to the latter, I mean the deficient individuals of the
human species. It is because of our own deficiencies that we lament
and call for aid. We suffer because of evils that we have produced
ourselves of our free will; but we attribute them to God, may He be
exalted above this; just as He explains in His book, saying: "Is corruption His? No; His children's is the blemish" (Deut. 32:5), and so
on. Solomon, too, has explained this, saying: "The foolishness of
man perverts his way; and his heart frets against the Lord" (Prov.
19:3). The explanation of this lies in the fact that all the evils that
befall man fall under one of three species.

The first species of evil is that which befalls man because of the
nature of coming-to-be and passing-away, I mean to say because of
his being endowed with matter. Because of this, infirmities and paralytic afflictions befall some individuals either in consequence of their
original natural disposition, or they supervene because of changes occurring in the elements, such as corruption of the air or a fire from
heaven and a landslide. We have already explained that divine
wisdom has made it obligatory that there should be no coming-to-be
except through passing-away. Were it not for the passing-away of the
individuals, the coming-to-be relating to the species would not continue. Thus that pure beneficence, that munificence, that activity
causing good to overflow, are made clear. He who wishes to be endowed with flesh and bones and at the same time not be subject to

impressions and not to be attained by any of the concomitants of matter merely wishes, without being aware of it, to combine two contraries, namely, to be subject to impressions and not to be subject to them. For if he were not liable to receive impressions, he would not have been generated, and what exists of him would have been one single individual and not a multitude of individuals belonging to one species. . . .

The evils of the second kind are those that men inflict upon one another, such as tyrannical domination of some of them over others. These evils are more numerous than those belonging to the first kind, and the reasons for that are numerous and well known. The evils in question also come from us. However, the wronged man has no device against them. At the same time, there is no city existing anywhere in the whole world in which evil of this kind is in any way widespread and predominant among the inhabitants of that city; but its existence is also rare—in the cases, for instance, when one individual surprises another individual and kills him or robs him by night. This kind of evil becomes common, reaching many people, only in the course of great wars; and such events too do not form the majority of occurrences upon the earth taken as a whole.

The evils of the third kind are those that are inflicted upon any individual among us by his own action; this is what happens in the majority of cases, and these evils are much more numerous than those of the second kind. All men lament over evils of this kind; and it is only seldom that you find one who is not guilty of having brought them upon himself. He who is reached by them deserves truly to be blamed. To him one may say what has been said: "This has been to you of your own doing" (Mal. 1:9). It has also been said: "He does it that would destroy his own soul" (Prov. 6:32). Solomon has said about evils of this kind: "The foolishness of man perverts his way" (ibid. 19:3), and so on. He also has explained with reference to evils of this kind that they are done by man to himself; his dictum being: "Behold, this only have I found, that God made man upright; but they have sought out many thoughts" (Eccles. 7:29); these thoughts are those that have been vanquished by these evils. About this kind it has also been said: "For affliction comes not forth from the dust, neither does trouble spring out of the ground" (Job 5:6). Immediately afterward it is explained that this sort of evil is brought into existence by man, for it is said: "For man is born to trouble" (ibid. 5:7), and so on. This kind is consequent upon all vices, I mean concupiscence for eating, drinking, and copulation, and doing these things with excess in regard to quantity or irregularly or when the quality of the foodstuffs is bad. For this is the cause of all corporeal and psychical diseases and ailments. With regard to the diseases of the body, this is manifest. With regard to the diseases of the soul due to this evil regimen, they arise in two ways: In the first place, through the alteration necessarily affecting the soul in consequence of the alteration of the body, the soul being a corporeal faculty—it having already been said that the moral qualities of the soul are consequent upon the temperament of the body. And in the second place, because of the fact that the soul becomes familiarized with, and accustomed to, unnecessary things and consequently acquires the habit of desiring things that are unnecessary either for the preservation of the individual or for the preservation of the species; and this desire is something infinite. For whereas all necessary things are restricted and limited, that which is superfluous is unlimited. If, for instance, your desire is directed to having silver plate, it would be better if it were of gold; some have crystal plate; and perhaps plate is procured that is made out of emeralds and rubies, whenever these stones are to be found. Thus every ignoramus who thinks worthless thoughts is always sad and despondent because he is not able to achieve the luxury attained by someone else. In most cases such a man exposes himself to great dangers, such as arise in sea voyages and the service of kings; his aim therein being to obtain these unnecessary luxuries. When, however, he is stricken by misfortunes in these courses he has pursued, he complains about God's decree and predestination and begins to put the blame on the temporal and to be astonished at the latter's injustice in not helping him to obtain great wealth, which would permit him to procure a great deal of wine so as always to be drunk and a number of concubines adorned with gold and precious stones of various kinds so as to move him to copulate more than he is able so as to experience pleasure—as if the end of existence consisted merely in the pleasure of such an ignoble man.

The error of the multitude has arrived at the point where they impute to the Creator deficiency of power because of His having produced that which exists and endowed it with a nature entailing, according to their imagination, these great evils; inasmuch as this nature does not help every vicious man to achieve the satisfaction of his vice so that his corrupt soul should reach the term of its demand, which, according to what we have explained, has no limit. On the other hand, men of excellence and knowledge have grasped and understood the wisdom manifested in that which exists, as David has set forth, saying: "All the paths of the Lord are mercy and truth to those that keep His covenant and His testimonies" (Ps. 25:10). By this he says that those who keep to the nature of that which exists, keep the commandments of the Law, and know the ends of both, apprehend clearly the excellency and the true reality of the whole. For this reason they take as their end that for which they were intended as men, namely, apprehension. And because of the necessity of the body, they seek what is necessary for it, "bread to eat, and raiment to put on" (Gen. 28:20), without any luxury. If one restricts oneself to what is necessary, this is the easiest of things and may be obtained with a very small effort. Whatever in it that is seen as difficult and hard for us is due to the following reason: when one endeavors to seek what is unnecessary, it becomes difficult to find even what is necessary.

For the more frequently hopes cling to the superfluous, the more onerous does the matter become; forces and revenues are spent for what is unnecessary and that which is necessary is not found. You ought to consider the circumstances in which we are placed with regard to its being found. For the more a thing is necessary for a living being, the more often it may be found and the cheaper it is. On the other hand, the less necessary it is, the less often it is found and it is very expensive. Thus, for instance, the necessary for man is air, water, and food. But air is the most necessary, for nobody can be without it for a moment without perishing. As for water, one can remain without it for a day or two. Accordingly, air is indubitably easier to find and cheaper than water. Water is more necessary then food, for certain people may remain, if they drink and do not eat, for four or five days without food. Accordingly, in every city you find water more frequently and at a cheaper price than food. Things are similar with regard to foodstuffs; those that are most necessary are easier to find at a given place and cheaper than the unnecessary. Regarding musk, amber, rubies, and emeralds, I do not think that anyone of sound intellect can believe that man has strong need for them unless it be for medical treatment; and even in such cases, they and other similar things can be replaced by numerous herbs and earths. . . .

CHAPTER 24

The subject of trial is also very difficult; it is one of the greatest difficulties of the Law. The Torah mentions it in six passages, as I shall make clear to you in this chapter. What is generally accepted among people regarding the subject of trial is this: God sends down calamities upon an individual, without their having been preceded by a sin, in order that his reward be increased. However, this principle is not at all mentioned in the Torah in an explicit text. And there is in the Torah only one passage among the six whose external meaning suggests such a notion; I shall explain its meaning. The principle of the Law that runs counter to this opinion is that contained in His dictum, may He be exalted: "A God of faithfulness and without iniquity" (Deut. 32:4). Nor do all the sages profess this opinion of the multitude, for they say sometimes: "There is no death without sin and no suffering without transgression" (Shabbat 55a). And this is the opinion that ought to be believed by every adherent of the Law who is endowed with intellect, for he should not ascribe injustice to God, may He be exalted above this, so that he believes that Zayd is innocent of sin and is perfect and that he does not deserve what befell him. However, the external meaning of the trials mentioned in the Torah in the passages in question is that they took place in order to test and to receive information so that one could know the degree of faith or the degree of obedience of the individual or nation in question. And this is the great difficulty, especially in the story of the binding of Isaac, which was known only to God and to the two individuals involved, to one of whom it was said: "For now I know that you fear God" (Gen. 22:12). It is the same with regard to its dictum: "For the Lord your God tries you out, to know whether you do love the Lord" (Deut. 13:4), and so on. And also with regard to its dictum: "To know what was in your heart" (*ibid.* 8:2), and so on. Now I will resolve all these difficulties for you.

Know that the aim and meaning of all the trials mentioned in the Torah is to let people know what they ought to do or what they must believe. Accordingly, the notion of a trial consists as it were in a certain act being done, the purpose being not the accomplishment of that particular act, but the latter's being a model to be imitated and followed. Thus the interpretation of its dictum—"To know whether you do love" (*ibid.* 13:4)—is not: in order that God should know that, for He already knew it; but the meaning resembles that of its dictum—"To know that I am the Lord that does sanctify you" (Ex. 31:13)—the meaning of which is: in order that the religious communities should know. In the same manner (Scripture) says (Deut. 13:2 ff.): If a man claiming prophecy arise and if you see his suggestions tend to make one believe in the truth of his claim, know that God wished to make known hereby to the religious communities the extent of your certitude with regard to His Law, may He be exalted, and your apprehension of its true reality; and also to make known that you do not let yourselves be deceived by the deceptions of a deceiver and that your faith in God cannot be disturbed. This will be a support for everyone who seeks the truth, for he will seek out the beliefs that are so firm that when one has them one pays no attention to the man who tries to compete through working a miracle. For this man issues a call to believe in impossible things, whereas a competition as to miracles is only useful when something possible is claimed, as we have made clear in *Mishneh Torah*.

After it has been made clear that the meaning of "to know" here is: in order that people should know, the same can be said with regard to its dictum concerning manna: "That He might afflict you to try you out, to know what was in your heart, whether you would keep His commandments, or no" (*ibid.* 8:2). The meaning of this is: in order that the religious communities should know this and that it should be generally accepted throughout the world that those who wholly devote themselves to His service, may He be exalted, are provided by Him with food in an unthought-of way. The same notion is expressed when manna is spoken of on the occasion when it first came down: "That I may try them out, whether they will walk in My Torah, or no" (Ex. 16:4); which means: in order that everyone should consider this and should see whether being devoted to His service is useful and sufficient or not sufficient. As for what is said (in Scripture) for the third time again concerning manna—namely, "Who fed you in the wilderness with manna, which your fathers knew not, that He might afflict you, and that He might try you out, to do you good at your latter end" (Deut. 8:16)—it may suggest that God sometimes makes an individual suffer in order that his reward be greater. But this is not the truth of the matter. For this dictum has one of two meanings: One of them is the notion concerning manna repeatedly expressed in the first and second dictum, namely:

in order that it should be known whether being devoted to God does or does not suffice as far as food is concerned and gives relief from fatigue and weariness. Or *nassotekha* (try you out) may mean: to accustom you, this being an interpretation that can refer to its dictum: "is not accustomed [*nisstah*] to set the sole of her foot" (*ibid.* 28:56), and so on. It is as if it said that He, may He be exalted, has first accustomed you to misery in the desert in order to make your well-being greater when once you came into the land. And this is true, for to pass from weariness to rest is more pleasant than to be constantly at rest. And it is known that but for their misery and weariness in the desert, they would not have been able to conquer the land and to fight. The Torah literally states this: "For God said: Lest peradventure the people repent when they see war, and they return to Egypt. But God led the people about, by the way of the wilderness of the Sea of Reeds" (Ex. 13:17-18). For prosperity does away with courage, whereas a hard life and fatigue necessarily produce courage—this being the good that, according to the story in question, will come "at their latter end" (Deut. 8:16).

As for its dictum, "For God is come to try you out" (Ex. 20:17), it expresses the same notion as the one stated in Deuteronomy concerning a man claiming "to prophesy in the name of an idol: For the Lord your God tries you out" (Deut. 13:4), the meaning of which we have made clear. He told them similarly here at the Gathering at Mount Sinai: Be not afraid; this great gathering that you have seen has taken place only in order that you acquire certitude through sight, so that if, in order to make publicly known the extent of your faith, "the Lord your God tried you out with a false prophet" (*ibid.*) who would call upon you to demolish what you have heard, you should remain firm and keep your feet from stumbling. For if I had come to you as a prophet, as you had thought, and I had said to you what had been said to me without your hearing it for yourselves, it would have been possible for you to fancy that what is told by another is true even if that other had come to you with something contradicting what has been made known to you; this is what could have happened if you had not heard it at this gathering.

As for the story of Abraham at the binding (of Isaac), it contains two great notions that are fundamental principles of the Law. One of these notions consists in our being informed of the limit of love for God, may He be exalted, and fear of Him—that is, up to what limit they must reach. For in this story he was ordered to do something that bears no comparison either with sacrifice of property or with sacrifice of life. In truth it is the most extraordinary thing that could happen in the world, such a thing that one would not imagine that human nature was capable of it. Here there is a sterile man having an exceeding desire for a son, possessed of great property and commanding respect, and having the wish that his progeny should become a religious community. When a son comes to him after his having lost hope, how great will be his attachment to him and love for him! However, because of his fear of Him, who should be exalted, and because of his love to carry out His command, he holds this beloved son as little, gives up all his hopes regarding him, and hastens to slaughter him after a journey of days. For if he had chosen to do this immediately, as soon as the order came to him, it would have been an act of stupefaction and disturbance in the absence of exhaustive reflection. But his doing it days after the command had come to him shows that the act sprang from thought, correct understanding, consideration of the truth of His command, may He be exalted, love of Him, and fear of Him. No other circumstance should be put forward, nor should one opt for the notion that he was in a state of passion. For Abraham our Father did not hasten to slaughter Isaac because he was afraid that God would kill him or make him poor, but solely because of what is incumbent upon men—namely, to love Him and fear Him, may He be exalted— and not, as we have explained in several passages, for any hope of a reward or for fear of punishment. Accordingly, the angel said to him: "For now I know that you fear God" (Gen. 22:12): meaning that through the act because of which the term fearing God is applied to you, all men will know what the limits of the fear of the Lord are. Know that this notion is corroborated and explained in the Torah, in which it is mentioned that the final end of the whole of the Torah, including its commandments, prohibitions, promises, and narratives, is one thing only—namely, fear of Him, may He be exalted. This is referred to in its dictum: "If you will not take care to observe all the words of this Law that are written in this book, that you may fear this glorious and awesome Name" (Deut. 28:58). This is one of the two notions aimed at in the binding.

The second notion consists in making known to us the fact that the prophets consider as true that which comes to them from God in a prophetic revelation. For it should not be thought that what they hear or what appears to them in a parable is not certain or is commingled with illusion just because it comes about in a dream and in a vision, as we have made clear, and through the intermediary of the imaginative faculty. Accordingly, (Scripture) wished to make it known to us that all that is seen by a prophet in a vision of prophecy is, in the opinion of the prophet, a certain truth, that the prophet has no doubts in any way concerning anything in it, and that in his opinion its status is the same as that of all existent things that are apprehended through the senses or through the intellect. A proof for this is the fact that (Abraham) hastened to slaughter, as he had been commanded, "his son, his only son, whom he loved" (Gen. 22:2), even though this command came to him in a dream or in a vision. For if a dream of prophecy had been obscure for the prophets, or if they had doubts or incertitude concerning what they apprehended in a vision of prophecy, they would not have hastened to do that which is repugnant to nature, and (Abraham's) soul would not have consented to accomplish an act of so great an importance if there had been a doubt about it.

In truth it was fitting that this story, I mean the binding, should come to pass through the hand of Abraham and in regard to someone like Isaac. For Abraham our Father was the first to make known the belief in Unity, to establish prophecy, and to perpetuate this opinion and draw people to it. It says: "For I have known him, to the end that he may command his children and his household after him, that they may keep the way of the Lord, to do righteousness and judgment" (Gen. 18:19). Thus, just as they followed his correct and useful opinions, namely, those that were heard from him, so ought one to follow the opinions deriving from his actions and especially from this action through which he validated the fundamental principle affirming the truth of prophecy and made known to us the ultimate end toward which the fear and love of God may reach.

It is in this way that the meaning of trials should be understood. And it should not be believed that God, may He be exalted, wants to test and try out a thing in order to know that which He did not know before....

CHAPTER 26

Just as there is disagreement among the men of speculation among the adherents of Law whether His works, may He be exalted, are consequent upon wisdom or upon the will alone without being intended toward any end at all, there is also the same disagreement among them regarding our Laws, which He has given to us. Thus, there are people who do not seek for them any cause at all, saying that all Laws are consequent upon the will alone. There are also people who say that every commandment and prohibition in these Laws is consequent upon wisdom and aims at some end, and that all Laws have causes and were given in view of some utility. It is, however, the doctrine of all of us—both of the multitude and of the elite—that all the Laws have a cause, though we ignore the causes for some of them and we do not know the manner in which they conform to wisdom. With regard to this the texts of the Bible are clear: "righteous statutes and judgments" (Deut. 4:8); "The judgments of the Lord are true, they are righteous altogether" (Ps. 19:10).

About the statutes designated as *hukkim**—for instance those concerning the "mingled stuff, meat in milk," and "the sending of the goat"†—(the sages) make literally the following statement: "Things which I have prescribed for you, about which you have not the permission to think, which are criticized by Satan and refuted by the Gentiles" (Yoma 67b). They are not believed by the multitude of the sages to be things for which there is no cause at all and for which one must not seek an end. For this would lead, according to what we have explained, to their being considered as frivolous actions. On the contrary, the multitude of the sages believe that there indubitably is a cause for them—I mean to say a useful end—but that it is hidden from us either because of the incapacity of our intellects or the deficiency of our knowledge. Consequently there is, in their opinion, a cause for all the commandments; I mean to say that any particular commandment or prohibition has a useful end. In the case of some of them, it is clear to us in what way they are useful—as in the case of the prohibition of killing and stealing. In the case of others, their utility is not clear—as in the case of the interdiction of the "first products" (Lev. 19:23) (of trees) and of (sowing) "the vineyard with diverse seeds" (Deut. 22:9). Those commandments whose utility is clear to the multitude are called *mishpatim* (judgments), and those whose utility is not clear to the multitude are called *hukkim* (statutes). The sages always say with regard to the verse: "For it is no vain thing" (*ibid.* 32:47)—"And if it is vain, it

*This Hebrew term is sometimes interpreted as designating those religious laws that have no (or no obvious) explanation in terms of human reason.

†Cf. Deut. 22:11; Ex. 23:19; Lev. 16:10 and 21.

is because of you";* meaning that this legislation is not a vain matter without a useful end and that if it seems to you that this is the case with regard to some of the commandments, the deficiency resides in your apprehension. You already know the tradition that is widespread among us according to which the causes for all the commandments, with the exception of that concerning the red heifer, were known to Solomon; and also their dictum that God hid the causes for the commandments in order that they should not be held in little esteem, as happened to Solomon with regard to the three commandments whose causes are made clear.†

All their dicta proceed according to this principle, and the texts of the (Scriptural) books indicate it. However, I found in *Bereshit Rabbah* (ch. 44) a text of the sages from which it appears when one first reflects on it that some of the commandments have no other cause than merely to prescribe a law, without there having been in view in them any other end or any real utility. This is their dictum in that passage: "What does it matter to the Holy One, blessed be He, that animals are slaughtered by cutting their neck in front or in the back? Say therefore that the commandments were only given in order to purify the people. For it is said: 'The word of the Lord is purified' (Ps. 18:31)." Though this dictum is very strange and has no parallel in other dicta, I have interpreted it, as you will hear, in such a manner that we shall not abandon the views of all their dicta and we shall not disagree with a universally agreed upon principle, namely, that one should seek in all the Laws an end that is useful in regard to being: "For it is no vain thing" (Deut. 32:47). He says: "I said not to the seed of Jacob: Seek Me for nothing; I, the Lord, speak righteousness, I declare things that are right" (Is. 45:19).

What everyone endowed with a sound intellect ought to believe on this subject is what I shall set forth to you: The generalities of the commandments necessarily have a cause and have been given because of a certain utility; their details are that in regard to which it was said of the commandments that they were given merely for the sake of commanding something. For instance the killing of animals because of the necessity of having good food is manifestly useful, as we shall make clear (III, ch. 48). But the prescription that they should be killed through having the upper and not the lower part of their throat cut, and having their esophagus and windpipe severed at one particular place is, like other prescriptions of the same kind, im-

*Palestinian Talmud, Pe'ah, I; Ketuvot, VIII.
†See *Book of Commandments*, number 365.

posed with a view to purifying the people. The same thing is made clear to you through their example: "Slaughtered by cutting their neck in front or in the back" (Gen. Rabbah, ch. 44). I have mentioned this example to you merely because one finds in their text: "Slaughtered by cutting their neck in front or in the back." However, if one studies the truth of the matter, one finds it to be as follows: As necessity occasions the eating of animals, the commandment was intended to bring about the easiest death in an easy manner. For beheading would only be possible with the help of a sword or something similar, whereas a throat can be cut with anything. In order that death should come about more easily, the condition was imposed that the knife should be sharp. The true reality of particulars of commandments is illustrated by the sacrifices. The offering of sacrifices has in itself a great and manifest utility, as I shall make clear. But no cause will ever be found for the fact that one particular sacrifice consists in a lamb and another in a ram and that the number of the victims should be one particular number. Accordingly, in my opinion, all those who occupy themselves with finding causes for something of these particulars are stricken with a prolonged madness in the course of which they do not put an end to an incongruity, but rather increase the number of incongruities. Those who imagine that a cause may be found for suchlike things are as far from truth as those who imagine that the generalities of a commandment are not designed with a view to some real utility.

Know that wisdom rendered it necessary—or, if you will, say that necessity occasioned—that there should be particulars for which no cause can be found; it was, as it were, impossible in regard to the Law that there should be nothing of this class in it. In such a case the impossibility is due to the circumstances that when you ask why a lamb should be prescribed and not a ram, the same question would have to be asked if a ram had been prescribed instead of a lamb. But one particular species had necessarily to be chosen. The same holds for your asking why seven lambs and not eight have been prescribed. For a similar question would have been put if eight or ten or twenty had been prescribed. However, one particular number had necessarily to be chosen. This resembles the nature of the possible, for it is certain that one of the possibilities will come to pass. And no question should be put why one particular possibility and not another comes to pass, for a similar question would become necessary if another possibility instead of this particular one had come to pass. Know this notion and grasp it. The constant statements of (the sages) to the effect that there are causes for all the commandments, as well as the opinion that the causes were known to Solomon, have in view the utility of a given commandment in a general way, not an examination of its particulars.

This being so, I have seen fit to divide the 613 commandments into a number of classes, every one of which comprises a number of commandments belonging to one kind or akin in meaning. I shall inform you of the cause of every one of these classes, and I shall show their utility about which there can be no doubt and to which there can be no objection. Then I shall return to each of the commandments comprised in the class in question and I shall explain to you the cause of it, so that only very few commandments will remain whose cause has not been clear to me up to now. Some of the particulars of, and conditions for, some of the commandments have also become clear to me, and it is possible to give their causes. You will hear all this. However, I shall not be able to clarify to you all this giving of causes before I set before you, as a preliminary, a number of chapters in which I will include premises that are useful as an introduction for the purpose I have in mind. These are the chapters with which I will begin now.

CHAPTER 27

The Law as a whole aims at two things: the welfare of the soul and the welfare of the body. As for the welfare of the soul, it consists in the multitude's acquiring correct opinions corresponding to their respective capacity. Therefore some of them (namely, the opinions) are set forth explicitly and some of them are set forth in parables. For it is not within the nature of the common multitude that its capacity should suffice for apprehending that subject matter as it is. As for the welfare of the body, it comes about by the improvement of their ways of living one with another. This is achieved through two things. One of them is the abolition of their wronging each other. This is tantamount to every individual among the people not being permitted to act according to his will and up to the limits of his power, but being forced to do that which is useful to the whole. The second thing consists in the acquisition by every human individual of moral qualities that are useful for life in society so that the affairs of the city may be ordered. Know that as between these two aims, one is indubitably greater in nobility, namely, the welfare of the soul—I mean the procuring of correct opinions—while the second aim—I mean the welfare of the body—is prior in nature and time. The latter aim consists in the governance of the city and the well-being of the states of all its people according to their capacity. This second aim is the more certain one, and it is the one regarding which every effort has been made precisely to expound it and all its particulars. For the first aim can only be achieved after achieving this second one. For it has already been demonstrated that man has two perfections: a first perfection, which is the perfection of the body, and an ultimate perfection, which is the perfection of the soul. The first perfection consists in being healthy and in the very best bodily state, and this is only possible through his finding the things necessary for him whenever he seeks them. These are his food and all the other things needed for the governance of his body, such as a shelter, bathing, and so forth. This cannot be achieved in any way by one isolated individual. For an individual can only attain all this through a political association, it being already known that man is political by nature. His ultimate perfection is to become rational in actu, I mean to have an intellect in actu; this would consist in his knowing everything concerning all the beings that it is within the capacity of man to know in accordance with his ultimate perfection. It is clear that to this ultimate perfection there do not belong either actions or moral qualities and that it consists only of opinions toward which speculation has led and that investigation has rendered compulsory. It is also clear that this noble and ultimate perfection can only be achieved after the first perfection has been achieved. For a man cannot represent to himself an intelligible even when taught to understand it and all the more cannot become aware of it of his own accord, if he is in pain or is very hungry or is thirsty or is hot or is very cold. But once the first perfection has been achieved it is possible to achieve the ultimate, which is indubitably more noble and is the only cause of permanent preservation.

The true Law then, which as we have already made clear (II, ch. 39) is unique—namely, the Law of Moses our Teacher—has come to bring us both perfections, I mean the welfare of the states of people in their relations with one another through the abolition of reciprocal wrongdoing and through the acquisition of a noble and excellent character. In this way the preservation of the population of the country and their permanent existence in the same order become possible, so that every one of them achieves his first perfection; I mean also the soundness of the beliefs and the giving of correct opinions through which ultimate perfection is achieved. The letter of the Torah speaks of both perfections and informs us that the end of this Law in its entirety is the achievement of these two perfections. For He, may He be exalted, says: "And the Lord commanded us to do all these statutes, to fear the Lord our God, for our good always, that He might preserve us alive, as it is at this day" (Deut. 6:24). Here He puts the ultimate perfection first because of its nobility; for, as we have explained, it is the ultimate end. It is referred to in the dictum: "For our good always." You know already what (the sages) have said interpreting His dictum: "That it may be well with you, and that you may prolong your days" (*ibid.* 22:7). They said: "That it may be well with you in a world in which everything is well and that you may prolong your days in a world the whole of which is long" (Kiddushin 39b; Hullin 142a). Similarly the intention of His dictum here, "For our good always," is this same notion: I mean the attainment of "a world in which everything is well and (the whole of which is) long." And this is perpetual preservation. On the other hand, His dictum, "That He might preserve us alive, as it is at this day," refers to the first and corporeal preservation, which lasts for a certain duration and which can only be well ordered through political association, as we have explained.

CHAPTER 28

Among the things to which your attention ought to be directed is that you should know that in regard to the correct opinions through which the ultimate perfection may be obtained, the Law has communicated only their end and made a call to believe in them in a summary way—that is, to believe in the existence of the Deity, may He be exalted, His unity, His knowledge, His power, His will, and His eternity. All these points are ultimate ends, which can be made clear in detail and through definitions only after one knows many opinions. In the same way the Law also makes a call to adopt certain beliefs, belief in which is necessary for the sake of political welfare. Such, for instance, is our belief that He, may He be exalted, is violently angry with those who disobey Him and that it is therefore necessary to fear Him and to dread Him and to take care not to diso-bey. With regard to all the other correct opinions concerning the whole of being—opinions that constitute the numerous kinds of all the theoretical sciences through which the opinions forming the ulti-mate end are validated—the Law, albeit it does not make a call to di-rect attention toward them in detail as it does with regard to (the opinions forming ultimate ends), does do this in summary fashion by saying: "To love the Lord."* You know how this is confirmed in the dictum regarding love: "With all your heart, and with all your soul, and with all your might" (Deut. 6:5). We have already explained in *Mishneh Torah* that this love becomes valid only through the appre-hension of the whole of being as it is and through the consideration of His wisdom as it is manifested in it. We have also mentioned there the fact that the sages call attention to this notion.

What results from what we have now stated as a premise regard-ing this subject is that whenever a commandment, be it a prescrip-tion or a prohibition, requires abolishing reciprocal wrongdoing, or urging to a noble moral quality leading to a good social relationship, or communicating a correct opinion that ought to be believed either on account of itself or because it is necessary for the abolition of re-ciprocal wrongdoing or for the acquisition of a noble moral quality, such a commandment has a clear cause and is of a manifest utility. No question concerning the end need be posed with regard to such commandments. For no one was ever so perplexed for a day as to ask why we were commanded by the Law that God is one, or why we were forbidden to kill and to steal, or why we were forbidden to exer-cise vengeance and retaliation, or why we were ordered to love each other. The matters about which people are perplexed and opinions disagree—so that some say that there is no utility in them at all ex-cept the fact of mere command, whereas others say that there is a utility in them that is hidden from us—are the commandments from whose external meaning it does not appear that they are useful ac-cording to one of the three notions we have mentioned: I mean to say that they neither communicate an opinion nor inculcate a noble quality nor abolish reciprocal wrongdoing. Apparently these com-mandments are not related to the welfare of the soul, as they do not communicate a belief, or to the welfare of the body, as they do not communicate rules useful for the governance of the city or for the governance of the household. Such, for instance, are the prohibi-

*Deut. 11:13, 22; 19:9; 30:6, 16, 20.

tions of the "mingled stuff," of the "mingling" (of diverse species), and of "meat in milk," and the commandment "concerning the covering of blood, the heifer whose neck was broken," and the "firstling of an ass,"* and others of the same kind. However, you will hear my explanation for all of them and my exposition of the correct and demonstrated causes for them all with the sole exception—as I have mentioned to you—of details and particular commandments. I shall explain that all these and others of the same kind are indubitably related to one of the three notions referred to—either to the welfare of a belief or to the welfare of the conditions of the city, which is achieved through two things: abolition of reciprocal wrongdoing and acquisition of excellent characters.

Sum up what we have said concerning beliefs as follows: In some cases a commandment communicates a correct belief, which is the one and only thing aimed at—as, for instance, the belief in the unity and eternity of the Deity and in His not being a body. In other cases the belief is necessary for the abolition of reciprocal wrongdoing or for the acquisition of a noble moral quality—as, for instance, the belief that He, may He be exalted, has a violent anger against those who do injustice, according to what is said: "And My wrath shall wax hot, and I will kill" (Ex. 22:23), and so on, and as the belief that He, may He be exalted, responds instantaneously to the prayer of someone wronged or deceived: "And it shall come to pass, when he cries to Me, that I will hear; for I am gracious" (ibid. 22:26).

CHAPTER 29

It is well known that Abraham our Father was brought up in the religious community of the Sabians,† whose doctrine it is that there is no Deity but the stars. When I shall have made known to you in this chapter their books, translated into Arabic, which are in our hands today, and their ancient chronicles and I shall have revealed to you through them their doctrine and histories, it will become clear to

*Cf. Lev. 17:13; Deut. 21:1–9; Ex. 13:13.

†The term is used by Maimonides to designate the pagans.

you from this that they explicitly asserted that the stars are the deity and that the sun is the greatest deity. They also said that the rest of the seven stars are deities, but that the two luminaries are the greatest of them. You will find that they explicitly say that the sun governs the upper and the lower world. They say it in these very terms. And you will find that they mention in those books and those chronicles the story of Abraham our Father, and they say literally what follows: When Ibrahim, who was brought up in Kutha, disagreed with the community and asserted that there was an agent other than the sun, various arguments were brought forward against him. In these arguments they set forth the clear and manifest activities of the sun in what exists. Thereupon he, they mean Abraham, told them: You are right; it is like an axe in the hands of a carpenter. Then they mention a part of his argumentation, peace be on him, against them. At the conclusion of the story they mention that the king put Abraham our Father into prison, and that, being in prison, he persevered for days and days in arguing against them. Thereupon the king became afraid that he would ruin his polity and turn the people away from their religions and banished him toward Syria after having confiscated all his property. This is what they relate. You will find this story set forth in this manner in *The Nabatean Agriculture*.* They do not mention what is related in our true traditions, and the prophetic revelation that came to him. For they tax him with lying because of his disagreeing with their corrupt opinion. I have no doubt that in view of the fact that he, may peace be upon him, disagreed with the doctrine of all men, these erring men reviled, blamed, and belittled him. Accordingly, because he bore this for the sake of God, may He be exalted, and preferred truth to his reputation, he was told: "And I will bless them that bless you, and him that curses you will I curse; and in you shall all the families of the earth be blessed" (Gen. 12:3). And in point of fact his activity has resulted, as we see today, in the consensus of the greater part of the population of the earth in glorifying him and considering themselves as blessed through his memory, so that even those who do not belong to his progeny pretend to descend from him. No one is antagonistic to him or ignorant of his greatness except the remnants of this religious community that has perished, remnants that survive in the extremities of the earth, as for instance the infidels among the Turks in the extreme

*A supposedly ancient Sabian book.

North and the Hindus in the extreme South. These are the remnants of the religious community of the Sabians, for this was a religious community that extended over the whole earth.

The utmost attained by the speculation of those who philosophized in those times consisted in imagining that God was the spirit of the sphere and that the sphere and the stars are a body of which the Deity, may He be exalted, is its spirit. Abu Bakr Ibn al-Saigh (Ibn Bajja) has mentioned this in the commentary on the *Akroasis*.* Therefore all the Sabians believed in the eternity of the world, since in their opinion heaven is the deity.

They deem Adam to have been an individual born of male and female like the other human individuals, but they glorify him and say that he was a prophet, the envoy of the moon, who called people to worship the moon, and that there are compilations of his on the cultivation of the soil. Similarly the Sabians say that Noah was a cultivator of the soil and that he did not approve of the worship of idols. Therefore you will find that all the Sabians blame Noah and say that he never worshiped an idol. . . . Their purpose in mentioning Adam and everything they ascribe to him is to fortify their doctrine concerning the eternity of the world so that it should follow that the stars and the sphere are the deity.

However, when the "pillar of the world" (Abraham) grew up and it became clear to him that there is a separate Deity that is neither a body nor a force in a body and that all the stars and the spheres were made by Him, and he understood that the fables upon which he was brought up were absurd, he began to refute their doctrine and to show up their opinions as false; he publicly manifested his disagreement with them and called "in the Name of the Lord, God of the world" (Gen. 21:33)—both the existence of the Deity and the creation of the world in time by that Deity being comprised in that call.

In conformity with these opinions, the Sabians set up statues for the planets, golden statues for the sun and silver ones for the moon, and distributed the minerals and the climes between the planets, saying that one particular planet was the deity of one particular clime. And they built temples, set up the statues in them, and thought that the forces of the planets overflowed toward these statues and that consequently these statues talked, had understanding, gave prophetic revelation to people—I mean, the statues—and made known to peo-

---

*i.e., Aristotle's *Physics*.

ple what was useful to them. Similarly they said of the trees, which were assigned to the various planets, that when one particular tree was set apart for one particular planet, planted with a view to the latter, and a certain treatment was applied to it and with it, the spirit of that planet overflowed toward that tree, gave prophetic revelation to people, and spoke to them in sleep. You will find all this set forth literally in their books, to which I shall draw your attention. These were the prophets of Baal and the prophets of Asherah that are mentioned in our texts; among them these opinions became so firm that "they forsook the Lord" (Is. 1:4) and called: "O Baal, answer us" (I Kings 18:26). All this came about because of these opinions being generally accepted, ignorance being widespread and the world then often being given to raving concerning imaginings of this kind. Accordingly, such opinions developed among them that some of them became "soothsayers, enchanters, sorcerers, charmers, consulters with familiar spirits, wizards, and necromancers" (cf. Deut. 18:10–11). We have already made it clear in our great compilation, *Mishneh Torah*, that Abraham our Father began to refute these opinions by means of arguments and feeble preaching, conciliating people and drawing them to obedience by means of benefits. Then Moses our Teacher received prophetic inspiration; thereupon he perfected the purpose in that he commanded killing these people, wiping out their traces, and tearing out their roots: "You shall break down their altars" (Judges 2:2),* and so on, and forbade following those ways of theirs in anything: "And you shall not walk in the customs of the nation" (Lev. 20:23), and so on. You know from texts of the Torah figuring in a number of passages that the first intention of the Law as a whole is to put an end to idolatry, to wipe out its traces and all that is bound up with it, even its memory as well as all that leads to any of its works—as, for instance, familiar spirits and a wizard and making to pass through fire, a diviner, a soothsayer, an enchanter, a sorcerer, a charmer, and a necromancer—and to warn against doing anything at all similar to their works and, all the more, against repeating the latter. It is explicitly stated in the text of the Torah that everything that was regarded by them as worship of their gods and as a way of coming near to them, is hateful and odious to God. This is stated in His saying: "For every abomination to the Lord, which He hates, have they done to their gods" (Deut. 12:31). You will find that in their books, about which I shall give you infor-

---

*Cf. Ex. 34:13; Deut. 7:5.

mation, they mention that under certain circumstances they offer to the sun, their highest deity, seven beetles, seven mice, and seven bats. This alone is sufficient to arouse disgust in human nature. Consequently, all the commandments that are concerned with the prohibition against idolatry and everything that is connected with it or leads toward it or may be ascribed to it, are of manifest utility, for all of them are meant to bring about deliverance from these unhealthy opinions that turn one's attention away from all that is useful with regard to the two perfections toward the crazy notions in which our fathers and forefathers were brought up: "Your fathers dwelt of old time on the other side of the river, even Terah, the father of Abraham and the father of Nachor; and they served other gods" (Josh. 24:2). It is about these notions that the truthful prophets have said: "For they walked after vain things that do not profit."* How great then is the utility of every commandment that delivers us from this great error and brings us back to the correct belief: namely, that there is a Deity who is the Creator of all this; and it is He who ought to be worshiped and loved and feared and not the things that are deemed to be gods; and that to come near to this true Deity and to obtain His good will, nothing is required that is fraught with any hardship whatever, the only things needed being love of Him and fear of Him and nothing else. For these two are, as we shall explain, the end of divine worship: "And now, Israel, what does the Lord your God require of you" (Deut. 10:12), and so on. We shall exhaust this subject in the sequel.

I shall now return to my purpose and say that the meaning of many of the laws became clear to me and their causes became known to me through my study of the doctrines, opinions, practices, and cult of the Sabians, as you will hear when I explain the reasons for the commandments that are considered to be without cause. I shall mention to you the books from which all that I know about the doctrines and opinions of the Sabians will become clear to you so that you will know for certain that what I say about the reasons for these laws is correct.

The most important book about this subject is *The Nabatean Agriculture* translated by Ibn Wahshiyya.† In a future chapter I shall

---

*This quotation amalgamates two passages: I Sam. 12:21 and Jer. 2:8.

†Abu Bakr Ahmad Ibn Ali Ibn Wahshiyya seems to have been the author of this work, which he passed off as a translation from the Chaldean. The work appeared in 904.

let you know why the Sabians treated their doctrines and agriculture
in the same work. This book is filled with the ravings of the idolaters
and with notions to which the souls of the vulgar incline and by
which they are captivated—I mean the actions of talismans, practices
with a view to causing spirits to descend, demons, and ghouls living
in deserts. In this book are also included extraordinary ravings laughed
at by the intelligent, which are thought to deprecate the manifest
miracles through which the people of the earth know that there is a
Deity governing the people of the earth; as it says: "That you may
know that the earth is the Lord's" (Ex. 9:29); and: "That I am the
Lord in the midst of the earth" (ibid. 8:18). . . .

In that book it is related that an individual from among the
prophets of idolatry, named Tammuz, called upon a king to worship
the seven planets and the twelve signs of the Zodiac. Thereupon that
king killed him in an abominable manner. It is narrated that on the
night of his death all the statues from the various countries of the
earth assembled in the temple in Babylon, near the great golden
statue, which was the statue of the sun. This statue was suspended
between heaven and earth. And it came to a stop in the middle of
the temple, while all the other statues surrounded it. Then it began
to eulogize Tammuz and to relate what had happened to him, and
all the statues wept and lamented during the whole of the night. In
the morning, however, the statues flew away and returned to their
temples in the various countries of the earth. And this became an enduring traditional custom to lament and weep over Tammuz on the
first day of the month of Tammuz. The women weep over him and
eulogize him. Consider then and understand and see what were the
opinions of the people in those times. For this story of Tammuz is
very ancient among the Sabians. And from this book you will understand most of the ravings, practices, and festivals of the Sabians.

As for the story they tell about Adam and the serpent and the
tree of the knowledge of good and evil, a story that also alludes to
unusual clothing, take great care not to be confused in your intellect
in such a way as to have the notion that what they say is a thing that
has ever happened to Adam or to somebody else. For it is by no
means a story concerning something real. With very little reflection
it will become clear to you that all that they set forth in this fable is
absurd and that it is a story that they put out after the promulgation
of the Torah. For when the Torah had become generally known
among the religious communities and they had heard the external

meaning of the "Account of the Beginning," taking the whole of it according to its external meaning, they concocted this story in order that inexperienced people should listen to it and be so deceived as to think that the world is eternal and that the story described in the Torah happened the way they tell it. Even though a man like you does not have to have his attention drawn to this point—as you have already acquired such sciences as will prevent your mind from becoming attached to the fables of the Sabians and the ravings of the Chasdeans and Chaldeans who are devoid of all science that is truly a science—I have warned against this in order to safeguard others, for the multitude frequently incline to regarding fables as the truth. . . .

The knowledge of these opinions and practices is a very important chapter in the exposition of the reasons for the commandments. For the foundation of the whole of our Law and the pivot around which it turns, consists in the effacement of these opinions from the minds and of these monuments from existence. With respect to their effacement from the minds, it says: "Lest your heart be deceived" (Deut. 11:16); "Whose heart turns away this day" (ibid. 29:17); and with respect to their effacement from existence, it says: "You shall break down their altars . . . and hew down their groves" (ibid. 7:5); "And destroy their name out of that place" (ibid. 12:3). These two purposes are reiterated in a number of passages. For this is the first intention extending over the whole of the Law, as is made known to us by the sages in their transmitted commentary on His dictum, may He be exalted: "Even all that the Lord has commanded you by the hand of Moses" (Num. 15:23). For they say: "Herefrom you may learn that everyone who professes idolatry, disbelieves in the Torah in its entirety; whereas he who disbelieves in idolatry, professes the Torah in its entirety."* Cognize this.

CHAPTER 30

When you consider these ancient and unhealthy opinions, it will become clear to you that among all men it was an accepted view that

*Sifre, Num. 15:23; Horayot 8a; Kiddushin 40a.

through the worship of stars the earth becomes populated and the soil fertile. Their men of knowledge, as well as the ascetics and the men of piety among them, preached this to the people and taught them that agriculture, on which the existence of man depends, can only be perfected and succeed according to wish if you worship the sun and the stars; if you anger them through disobedience, the land will become barren and devastated. In their books they say that Jupiter had been angry with the wildernesses and the deserts and that they therefore lacked water and lacked trees and were inhabited by ghouls. They had a very great esteem for the peasants and the cultivators of the soil because of their being engaged in cultivating the earth, an occupation that conforms to the will of the stars and pleases them. The reason why the idolaters had a great esteem for oxen was the utility of the latter in agriculture. They even said that it was not permitted to kill them because force was joined in them to handiness for man in agriculture; the oxen only acted thus and submitted to man in spite of their force because the gods were pleased with their work in agriculture. Inasmuch as these opinions were generally accepted, (the idolaters) connected idolatry with agriculture, the latter being necessary for the subsistence of man and of most animals. Accordingly, the priests of idolatry preached to the people during their assemblies in the temples and fortified in their minds the notion that through the practices of this cult, rains would fall, the trees would bear fruit, and the land would become fertile and populous. Consider what they say in *The Nabatean Agriculture* in the passage on the vineyard; you will find there the following text of the Sabians: All the ancient sages have said and the prophets have commanded and prescribed to play on musical instruments before the statues during festivals. They said—and they were truthful—that the gods were pleased with this and accorded the best reward to those who acted thus. They multiplied the promises concerning this—promising, that is, a prolongation of life, a warding off of calamities, the disappearance of infirmities, the fertility of the sowing, and the thriving of the fruits. The text of the Sabians continues up to here.

Now inasmuch as these notions were generally accepted so that they were regarded as certain, and as God, may He be exalted, wished in His pity for us to efface this error from our minds and to take away fatigue from our bodies through the abolition of these tiring and useless practices and to give us Laws through the instrumentality of Moses our Teacher, the latter informed us in His name, may He be exalted, that if the stars and the planets were worshiped, their worship would be a cause for the rain ceasing to fall, for the land being devastated and producing nothing, for the fruit of the trees falling off, for misfortunes attending circumstances, for infirmities befalling the bodies, and for a shortening of lives. These are the intentions of the words of the convenant, which the Lord made. You will find that this intention is reiterated in the whole of the Torah: I mean that it is a necessary consequence of the worship of the stars that rains will cease to fall, that the land will be devastated, that circumstances will become bad, that the bodies will suffer from diseases, and that lives will be short; whereas a necessary consequence of the abandonment of their worship and the adoption of the worship of God will be rainfall, the fertility of the land, good circumstances, health of the body, and length of life. This is the contrary of what was preached by the idolaters to the people in order that they worship idols. For the foundation of the Law consists in putting an end to this opinion and effacing its traces, as we have explained.

CHAPTER 31

There is a group of human beings who consider it a grievous thing that causes should be given for any law; what would please them most is that the intellect would not find a meaning for the commandments and prohibitions. What compels them to feel thus is a sickness that they find in their souls, a sickness to which they are unable to give utterance and of which they cannot furnish a satisfactory account. For they think that if those laws were useful in this existence and had been given to us for this or that reason, it would be as if they derived from the reflection and the understanding of some intelligent being. If, however, there is a thing for which the intellect could not find any meaning at all and that does not lead to something useful, it indubitably derives from God; for the reflection of man would not lead to such a thing. It is as if, according to these people of weak intellects, man were more perfect than his Maker; for man speaks and acts in a manner that leads to some intended end, whereas the Deity does not act thus, but commands us to do things that are not useful to us and forbids us to do things that are not harmful to us. But He is far exalted above this; the contrary is the case—the whole purpose consisting in what is useful for us, as we have explained on the basis of its dictum: "For our good always, that He might preserve us alive, as it is at this day" (Deut. 6:24). And it says: "Which shall hear all these statutes and say: Surely this great community is a wise and understanding people" (*ibid.* 4:6). Thus it states explicitly that even all the statutes will show to all the nations that they have been given with wisdom and understanding. Now if there is a thing for which no reason is known and that does not either procure something useful or ward off something harmful, why should one say of one who believes in it or practices it that he is wise and understanding and of great worth? And why should the religious communities think it a wonder? Rather things are indubitably as we have mentioned: every commandment from among these 613 commandments exists either with a view to communicating a correct opinion, or to putting an end to an unhealthy opinion, or to communicating a rule of justice, or to warding off an injustice, or to endowing men with a noble moral quality, or to warning them against an evil moral quality. Thus all (the commandments) are bound up with three things: opinions, moral qualities, and political civic actions. We do not count speeches as one of these things since the speeches that the Law enjoins or forbids belong in part to the class of civic actions, and in part are meant to cause opinions, and in part are meant to cause moral qualities. Therefore we have limited ourselves here, in giving reasons for every law, to these three classes.

CHAPTER 32

If you consider the divine actions—I mean to say the natural actions—the Deity's wily graciousness and wisdom, as shown in the creation of living beings, in the gradation of the motions of the limbs, and the proximity of some of the latter to others, will through them become clear to you. Similarly His wisdom and wily graciousness, as shown in the gradual succession of the various states of the

whole individual, will become clear to you. The brain is an example
of the gradation of the motions and the proximity of the limbs of an
individual: for its front part is soft, very soft indeed, whereas its pos-
terior part is more solid. The spinal marrow is even more solid and
becomes more and more solid as it stretches on. The nerves are
organs of sensation and of motion. Accordingly, the nerves required
only for apprehension by the senses or for motion that presents but
little difficulty, like the motions of the eyelids and of the jaws, proceed from the brain, whereas the motions required for moving the
limbs proceed from the spinal marrow. As, however, it is impossible
for a nerve, in view of its softness—even for a nerve proceeding from
the spinal marrow—to move an articulation, the matter was wilily
and graciously arranged as follows: the nerves are ramified into fibers,
and the latter, having been filled with flesh, became muscles. Thereupon the nerve, having overpassed the extremity of the muscle, having become more solid, and having been commingled with fragments
of ligaments, becomes a tendon. The tendon joins and adheres to the
bone; and thereupon, because of this gradation, the nerve is capable
of moving a limb. I mentioned only this one example to you because
it is the most obvious of the wonders explained in the treatise "On
the Utilities of the Parts of the Body," all of which wonders are
clear, manifest, and well known to those who consider them with a
penetrating mind. Similarly the Deity made a wily and gracious
arrangement with regard to all the individuals of the living beings
that suck. For when born, such individuals are extremely soft and
cannot feed on dry food. Accordingly, breasts were prepared for them
so that they should produce milk with a view to their receiving
humid food, which is similar to the composition of their bodies, until
their limbs gradually and little by little become dry and solid.

Many things in our Law are due to something similar to this
very governance on the part of Him who governs, may He be glorified and exalted. For a sudden transition from one opposite to
another is impossible. And therefore man, according to his nature, is
not capable of abandoning suddenly all to which he was accustomed.
As therefore God sent Moses our Teacher to make out of us "a kingdom of priests and a holy nation" (Ex. 19:6)—through the knowledge of Him, may He be exalted, accordingly to what He has
explained, saying: "To you it was shown that you might know"
(Deut. 4:35), and so on; "Know this day, and lay it to your heart"
(ibid. 4:39), and so on—so that we should devote ourselves to His
worship according to what He said: "And to serve Him with all your

heart" (*ibid.* 11:13), and: "And you shall serve the Lord your God" (Ex. 23:25), and: "And Him shall you serve" (Deut. 13:5); and as at that time the way of life generally accepted and customary in the whole world and the universal service upon which we were brought up consisted in offering various species of living beings in the temples in which images were set up, in worshiping the latter, and in burning incense before them—the pious ones and the ascetics being at that time, as we have explained, the people who were devoted to the service of the temples consecrated to the stars: His wisdom, may He be exalted, and His gracious ruse, which is manifest in regard to all His creatures, did not require that He give us a Law prescribing the rejection, abandonment, and abolition of all these kinds of worship. For one could not then conceive the acceptance of (such a Law), considering the nature of man, which always likes that to which it is accustomed. At that time this would have been similar to the appearance of a prophet in these times who, calling upon the people to worship God, would say: "God has given you a Law forbidding you to pray to Him, to fast, to call upon Him for help in misfortune. Your worship should consist solely in meditation without any works at all." Therefore He, may He be exalted, suffered the above-mentioned kinds of worship to remain, but transferred them from created or imaginary and unreal things to His own name, may He be exalted, commanding us to practice them with regard to Him, may He be exalted. Thus He commanded us to build a Temple for Him: "And let them make Me a Sanctuary" (Ex. 25:8); to have an altar for His name: "An altar of earth you shall make to Me" (*ibid.* 20:24); to have the sacrifice offered up to Him: "When any man of you brings an offering to the Lord" (Lev. 1:2); to bow down in worship before Him; and to burn incense before Him. And He forbade the performance of any of these actions with a view to someone else: "He that sacrifices to the gods shall be utterly destroyed" (Ex. 22:19), and so on; "For you shall bow down to no other god" (*ibid.* 34:14). And He singled out priests for the service of the Sanctuary, saying: "That they may minister to Me in the priest's office" (*ibid.* 28:14). And because of their employment in the Temple and the sacrifices in it, it was necessary to fix for them dues that would be sufficient for them; namely, the dues of the Levites and the priests. Through this divine ruse it came about that the memory of idolatry was effaced and that the grandest and true foundation of our belief—namely, the existence and oneness of the Deity—was firmly established, while at the same time the souls had no feeling of repugnance and were not repelled because of the abolition of modes of worship to which they were accustomed and than which no other mode of worship was known at that time.

I know that on thinking about this at first your soul will necessarily have a feeling of repugnance toward this notion and will feel aggrieved because of it; and you will ask me in your heart and say to me: How is it possible that none of the commandments, prohibitions, and great actions—which are very precisely set forth and prescribed for fixed seasons—should be intended for its own sake, but for the sake of something else, as if this were a ruse invented for our benefit by God in order to achieve His first intention? What was there to prevent Him, may He be exalted, from giving us a Law in accordance with His first intention and from procuring us the capacity to accept this? In this way there would have been no need for the things that you consider to be due to a second intention. Hear then the reply to your question that will put an end to this sickness in your heart and reveal to you the true reality of that to which I have drawn your attention. It is to the effect that the text of the Torah tells a quite similar story, namely, in its dictum: "God led them not by the way of the land of the Philistines, although it was near. . . . But God led the people about, by the way of the wilderness of the Sea of Reeds" (ibid. 13:17–18). Just as God perplexed them in anticipation of what their bodies were naturally incapable of bearing—turning them away from the high road toward which they had been going, toward another road so that the first intention should be achieved—so did He in anticipation of what the soul is naturally incapable of receiving, prescribe the laws that we have mentioned so that the first intention should be achieved, namely, the apprehension of Him, may He be exalted, and the rejection of idolatry. For just as it is not in the nature of man that, after having been brought up in slavish service occupied with clay, bricks, and similar things, he should all of a sudden wash off from his hands the dirt deriving from them and proceed immediately to fight against "the children of Anak" (Num. 13:28), so is it also not in his nature that, after having been brought up upon very many modes of worship and of customary practices, which the souls find so agreeable that they become as it were a primary notion, he should abandon them all of a sudden. And just as the Deity used a gracious ruse in causing them to wander perplexedly in the desert until their souls became courageous—it being well known that life in the desert and lack of comforts for the body necessarily develop courage whereas the opposite circumstances necessarily develop cowardice—and until, moreover, people were born who were not accustomed to humiliation and servitude—all this having been brought about by Moses by means of divine commandments: "At the commandment of the Lord they encamped, and at the commandment of the Lord they journeyed, at the commandment of the Lord by the hand of Moses" (*ibid.* 9:23)—so did this group of laws derive from a divine grace, so that they should be left with the kind of practices to which they were accustomed and so that consequently the belief, which constitutes the first intention, should be validated in them.

As for your question: What was there to prevent God from giving us a Law in accordance with His first intention and from procuring us the capacity to accept this?—you lay yourself open to an inference from this second question. For one may say to you: What was there to prevent God from making them march "by the way of the land of the Philistines" and procuring them the capacity to engage in wars so that there should be no need for this roundabout way with "the pillar of cloud by day and the pillar of fire by night?" (Ex. 13:22). Also you lay yourself open to a third question as an inference, a question regarding the reason for the detailing of promises and threats with regard to the whole Law. One may say to you: Inasmuch as God's first intention and His will are that we should believe in this Law and that we should perform the actions prescribed by it, why did He not procure us the capacity always to accept this intention and to act in accordance with it, instead of using a ruse with regard to us, declaring that He will procure us benefits if we obey Him and will take vengeance on us if we disobey Him and performing in deed all these acts of benefiting and all these acts of vengeance? For this too is a ruse used by Him with regard to us in order to achieve His first intention with respect to us. What was there to prevent Him from causing the inclination to accomplish the acts of obedience willed by Him and to avoid the acts of disobedience abhorred by Him, to be a natural disposition fixed in us?

There is one and the same general answer to all these three questions and to all the others that belong to the same class: Though all miracles change the nature of some individual being, God does not change at all the nature of human individuals by means of miracles. Because of this great principle it says: "O that they had such an heart as this" (Deut. 5:26), and so on. It is because of this that there are commandments and prohibitions, rewards and punishments. We have already explained this fundamental principle by giving its proofs in a number of passages in our compilations. We do not say this because we believe that the changing of the nature of any human individual is difficult for Him, may He be exalted. Rather is it possible and fully within the capacity of God. But according to the foundations of the Law, of the Torah, He has never willed to do it, nor shall He ever will it. For if it were His will that the nature of any human individual should be changed because of what He, may He be exalted, wills from that individual, sending of prophets and all giving of a Law would have been useless.

I return to my subject and I say that, as this kind of worship—I mean the sacrifices—pertain to a second intention, whereas invocation, prayer, and similar practices and modes of worship come closer to the first intention and are necessary for its achievement, a great difference has been made between the two kinds. For one kind of worship—I mean the offering of sacrifices—even though it was done in His name, may He be exalted, was not prescribed to us in the way it existed at first; I mean to say in such a way that sacrifices could be offered in every place and at every time. Nor could a temple be set up in any fortuitous place, nor could any fortuitous man offer the sacrifice: "Whosoever would, he consecrated him" (I Kings 13:33). On the contrary, He forbade all this and established one single house (as the Temple), "To the place which the Lord shall choose" (Deut. 12:26), so that sacrifices should not be offered elsewhere: "That you offer not your burnt-offerings in every place that you see" (ibid. 12:13). Also only the offspring of one particular family can be priests. All this was intended to restrict this kind of worship, so that only the portion of it should subsist whose abolition is not required by His wisdom. On the other hand, invocation and prayers are made in every place and by anyone whoever he may be. This also applies to the fringes, the doorposts, and the phylacteries and other similar modes of worship. Because of the notion I have revealed to you, people are frequently blamed in the books of the prophets because of their zeal for sacrifices, and it is explained to them that they are not the object of a purpose sought for its own sake and that God can dispense with them. Thus Samuel says: "Has the Lord as great delight in burnt-offerings and sacrifices, as in hearkening to the voice of the Lord?" (I Sam. 15:22), and so on. And Isaiah says: "To what purpose is the multitude of your sacrifices to Me? says the Lord" (Is. 1:11), and so on. And Jeremiah says: "For I spoke not to your fathers, nor commanded them in the day that I brought them out of the land of Egypt, concerning burnt-offerings and sacrifices; but this thing commanded I them, saying: Hearken to My voice, and I will be your God, and you shall be My people" (Jer. 7:22–23). This dictum has been regarded as difficult by everyone whose words I have seen or heard. They say: How can Jeremiah say of God that He has given us no injunctions "concerning burnt-offerings and sacrifices," seeing that the greater part of the commandments are concerned with these things? However, the purpose of the dictum is as I have explained to you. For he says that the first intention consists only in your apprehending Me and not worshiping someone other than Me: "And I will be your God, and you shall be My people." Those laws concerning sacrifices and repairing to the Temple were given only for the sake of the realization of this fundamental principle. It is for the sake of that principle that I transferred these modes of worship to My name, so that the trace of idolatry be effaced and the fundamental principle of My unity be established. You, however, came and abolished this end, while holding fast to what has been done for its sake. For you have doubted of My existence: "They have belied the Lord, and said: It is not He" (ibid. 5:12). And you have committed "idolatry: And burn incense to Baal, and walk after other gods . . . and come to the house" (ibid. 7:9–10), and so on. And still you continue to repair to the Temple of the Lord, offering sacrifices, which are things that have not been intended in the first intention.

I have another way of interpreting this verse; it too leads to the very same purpose that we have mentioned. It has been made clear both in the (Scriptural) text and in the tradition that in the first legislation given to us there was nothing at all "concerning burnt-offerings and sacrifices." You ought not to occupy yourself with "the passover of Egypt"* for the reason for this is clear and evident, as we shall set forth. Moreover, this happened in the land of Egypt, whereas the laws referred to in the verse in question are those that have been given to us after the exodus from Egypt. For this reason Jeremiah makes the following restriction in that verse: "In the day that I brought them out of the land of Egypt." For the first command given after the exodus from Egypt was the one given to us in Marah, namely, His saying to us there: "If you will diligently hearken to the voice of the Lord your God" (Ex. 15:26), and so on. "There He made for them a statute and a judgment" (ibid. 15:25),

---

*Cf. Ex. 12:21 and 26–27, according to which the killing of a lamb in sacrifice was already prescribed in Egypt.

and so on. And the correct tradition says: "The Sabbath and the civil laws were prescribed at Marah."* Accordingly, the statute referred to is the Sabbath, and the judgment consists in the civil laws, that is, in the abolition of mutual wrongdoing. And this is, as we have explained, the first intention: I mean the belief in correct opinions, namely, in the creation of the world in time. For you already know that the foundation of the law addressed to us concerning the Sabbath is its contribution in fortifying this principle, as we have explained in this treatise. Besides the correctness of the beliefs, the intention also included the abolition of mutual wrongdoing among men. Accordingly, it is already clear to you that in the first legislation there was nothing at all concerning burnt-offerings and sacrifices, for, as we have mentioned, these belong to the second intention. The very notion expressed by Jeremiah is also set forth in Psalms by way of blame to the whole religious community because of its being at that time ignorant of the first intention and not distinguishing between it and the second intention. The psalmist says: "Hear, O My people, and I will speak; O Israel, and I will testify against you: God, your God, am I. I will not reprove you for your sacrifices and your burnt-offerings, to have been continually before Me. I will take no bullock out of your house, nor he-goats out of your fold" (Ps. 50:7–9). Whenever this notion is repeated, this is what is aimed at thereby. Understand this thoroughly and reflect upon it.

CHAPTER 34

Among the things that you likewise ought to know is the fact that the Law does not pay attention to the isolated. The Law was not given with a view to things that are rare. For in everything that it wishes to bring about, be it an opinion or a moral habit or a useful work, it is directed only toward the things that occur in the majority of cases and pays no attention to what happens rarely or to the damage occurring to the unique human being because of this way of determination and because of the legal character of the governance. For the Law is a divine thing; and it is your business to reflect on the natural things in which the general utility, which is included in

*Shabbat 87b; Sanhedrin 56b.

them, nonetheless necessarily produces damages to individuals, as is clear from our discourse and the discourse of others. In view of this consideration also, you will not wonder at the fact that the purpose of the Law is not perfectly achieved in every individual and that, on the contrary, it necessarily follows that there should exist individuals whom this governance of the Law does not make perfect. For not everything that derives necessarily from the natural specific forms is actualized in every individual. Indeed, all things proceed from one Deity and one agent and "have been given from one shepherd" (Eccles. 12:11). The contrary of this is impossible, and we have already explained (III, ch. 15) that the impossible has a stable nature that never changes. In view of this consideration, it also will not be possible that the laws be dependent on changes in the circumstances of the individuals and of the times, as is the case with regard to medical treatment, which is particularized for every individual in conformity with his present temperament. On the contrary, governance of the Law ought to be absolute and universal, including everyone even if it is suitable only for certain individuals and not suitable for others; for if it were made to fit individuals, the whole would be corrupted and you would make out of it something that varies.* For this reason, matters that are primarily intended in the Law ought not to be dependent on time or place; but the decrees ought to be absolute and universal, according to what He, may He be exalted, says: "As for the congregation, there shall be one statute (*hukkah*) for you" (Num. 15:15). However, only the universal interests, those of the majority, are considered in them, as we have explained.

After I have set forth these premises, I shall begin to explain what I have intended to explain.

CHAPTER 35

With a view to this purpose, I have divided all the commandments into fourteen classes.

The first class comprises the commandments that are fundamental opinions. They are those that we have enumerated in Laws of the

*See, for example, Shabbat 35b.

Basic Principles of the Torah [*Hilkhot Yesodei ha-Torah*].* Repentance and fasts also belong, as I shall explain, to this class. With respect to inculcating opinions that are correct and that are useful for belief in the Law, one should not say, what is their utility? as we have explained.

The second class comprises the commandments concerned with the prohibition of idolatry. They are those that we have enumerated in Laws Concerning Idolatry [*Hilkhot Avodah Zarah*]. Know that the prohibitions regarding garments of diverse sorts, first products (of trees), and (sowing) the vineyard with diverse seeds, also belong to this class, as shall be explained. The reason for this class is also well known. For all of them are meant to validate the true opinions and to make the multitude cling to them throughout the ages.

The third class comprises the commandments concerned with improvement of the moral qualities. They are those that we have enumerated in Laws Relating to Moral Disposition and Ethical Conduct [*Hilkhot Deot*]. It is well known that through fine moral qualities human association and society are perfected, which is necessary for the good order of human circumstances.

The fourth class comprises the commandments concerned with giving alms, lending, bestowal of gifts, and matters that are connected with this—as for instance estimations and anathemas,† the ordinances concerning loans and slaves, and all the commandments that we have enumerated in the Book of Seeds [*Sefer Zeraim*] with the exception of those treating of the mingling (of diverse species) and the first products (of trees). The reason for all these is manifest, for they are equally useful in turn to all men. For one who is rich today will be poor tomorrow, or his descendants will be poor; whereas one who is poor today will be rich tomorrow, or his son will be rich.

The fifth class comprises the commandments concerned with prohibiting wrongdoing and aggression. They are those included in our compilation in the Book of Torts [*Sefer Nezikin*]. The utility of this class is manifest.

The sixth class comprises the commandments concerned with punishments, as for instance laws concerning thieves and robbers and laws concerning false witnesses—in fact most of the matters we have

---

*This and the other titles referred to in this chapter are parts of Maimonides' legal compilation, *Mishneh Torah*.

†*i.e.*, vows that can be redeemed and those that cannot.

enumerated in the Book of Judges [*Sefer Shofetim*]. The utility of this is clear and manifest, for if a criminal is not punished, injurious acts will not be abolished in any way and none of those who design aggression will be deterred. No one is as weak-minded as those who deem that the abolition of punishments would be merciful on men. On the contrary, this would be cruelty itself on them as well as the ruin of the order of the city. On the contrary, mercy is to be found in His command, may He be exalted: "Judges and officers shall you make in all your gates" (Deut. 16:18).

The seventh class comprises the laws of property concerned with the mutual transactions of people, such as loans, hire for wages, deposits, buying, selling, and other things of this kind. Inheritance also belongs to this group. These are the commandments that we have enumerated in the Books of Acquisition and Judgments [*Sefer Kinyan ve-Mishpatim*]. The utility of this class is clear and manifest. For these property associations are necessary for people in every city, and it is indispensable that rules of justice should be given with a view to these transactions and that these transactions be regulated in a useful manner.

The eighth class comprises the commandments concerning the days in which work is forbidden, I mean Sabbaths and festivals. Scripture has explained the reason of each of these days and has mentioned the cause for each of them, which may consist either in the intention to inculcate a certain opinion or to procure a rest for the body or in both these things, as we shall explain later on.

The ninth class comprises all the other practices of worship prescribed to everybody, such as prayer and recitation of *Shema* and the other things we have enumerated in the Book of Adoration [*Sefer Ahavah*] with the exception of circumcision. The utility of this class is manifest, for it is wholly composed of works that fortify opinions concerning the love of the Deity and what ought to be believed about Him and ascribed to Him.

The tenth class comprises the commandments concerned with the Sanctuary and its utensils and servants. These are the commandments that we have enumerated in a portion of the Book of Service [*Sefer Avodah*]. We have already set forth in the foregoing the utility of this class of commandments.

The eleventh class comprises the commandments concerned with the sacrifices. These are the majority of the commandments that we have enumerated in the Book of Service and the Book of

Sacrifices [*Sefer Korbanot*]. We have already set forth in the fore-going the utility of the legislation with regard to the sacrifices in general and the necessity for it in those times.

The twelfth class comprises the commandments concerned with things unclean and clean. The purpose of all of them is in general to make people avoid entering the Sanctuary, so that it should be considered as great by the soul and feared and venerated, as I shall explain.

The thirteenth class comprises the commandments concerned with the prohibition of certain foods and what is connected therewith. These are the commandments that we have enumerated in the Laws Concerning Forbidden Foods [*Hilkhot Maakhalot Asurot*]. The (commandments concerning) vows and the state of the Nazirites belong to this class. The purpose of all this is, as we have explained in the *Commentary on the Mishnah* in the introduction to Avot, to put an end to the lusts and licentiousness manifested in seeking what is most pleasurable and to taking the desire for food and drink as an end.

The fourteenth class comprises the commandments concerned with the prohibition of certain sexual unions. They are those that we have enumerated in the Book of Women [*Sefer Nashim*] and in Laws Concerning Prohibited Sexual Relations [*Hilkhot Issurei Biah*]. The interbreeding of beasts belongs to this class. The purpose of this too is to bring about a decrease of sexual intercourse and to diminish the desire for mating as far as possible, so that it should not be taken as an end, as is done by the ignorant, according to what we have explained in the *Commentary on the Mishnah* (Avot). Circumcision also belongs to this class.

It is known that all the commandments are divided into two groups: "transgressions between man and his fellow man and transgressions between man and God" (Yoma 85b). Among the classes we have differentiated and enumerated, the fifth, sixth, seventh, and a portion of the third, belong to the group devoted to the relation between man and his fellow man, while all the other classes deal with the relation between man and God. For every commandment, whether it be a prescription or a prohibition, whose purpose it is to bring about the achievement of a certain moral quality or of an opinion or the rightness of actions, which only concerns the individual himself and his becoming more perfect, is called by the sages a commandment dealing with the relation between man and God, even though in reality it sometimes may affect relations between man and his fellow man. But this happens only after many intermediate steps and through comprehensive considerations, and it does not lead from the beginning to harming a fellow man. Understand this.

After I have made known the reasons for these classes of commandments, I shall return to examining the commandments belonging to each class, namely, those of which it may be fancied that they have no utility or that they constitute a decree that cannot be comprehended by the intellect in any way. And I shall explain the reasons for them and in what respect they are useful, making an exception only for those few whose purpose I have not grasped up to this time.

CHAPTER 36

The commandments comprised in the first class, which are the opinions that we have enumerated in Laws of the Basic Principles of the Torah, have all of them a manifest cause. If you consider them one by one, you discover the correctness of this opinion and its being a demonstrable matter. Similarly all the encouragement to learning and teaching and the fortifying assurances with regard to them figuring therein, are of manifest utility; for if knowledge is not achieved, no right action and no correct opinion can be achieved. There is also a manifest utility in honoring the bearers of the Law; for if a great veneration is not accorded to them in the souls, their voice will not be listened to when they give guidance regarding opinions and actions. Within this commandment—I mean its dictum, "You shall rise up before the hoary head" (Lev. 19:32)—is also included the injunction to be invested with the moral quality of modesty.

To this class also belongs the commandment addressed to us to swear in His name and the prohibition addressed to us against breaking one's oath and swearing in vain. All this has a manifest reason; for it is intended to glorify Him, may He be exalted. Accordingly, these are actions necessitating a belief in His greatness.

In the same way the commandment given to us to call upon Him, may He be exalted, in every calamity—I mean its dictum "Then you shall sound an alarm with the trumpets" (Num. 10:9)— likewise belongs to this class. For it is an action through which the correct opinion is firmly established that He, may He be exalted, apprehends our situations and that it depends upon Him to improve them if we obey, and to make them ruinous if we disobey; we should not believe that such things are fortuitous and happen by chance. This is the meaning of its dictum, "And if you walk with Me in the way of chance" (Lev. 26:21), by which it means: If you consider that the calamities with which I cause you to be stricken are to be borne as a mere chance, I shall add for you to this supposed chance its most grievous and cruel portion. This is the meaning of its dictum: "And if you walk with Me in the way of chance, then I will walk with you in the way of a furious chance" (*ibid.* 26:27–28). For their belief that this is chance contributes to necessitating their persistence in their corrupt opinions and unrighteous actions, so that they do not turn away from them; thus it says: "You have stricken them, but they were not affected" (Jer. 5:3). For this reason we have been commanded to invoke Him, may He be exalted, and to turn rapidly toward Him and call out to Him in every misfortune.

It is manifest that repentance also belongs to this class, I mean to the opinions without the belief in which the existence of individuals professing a Law cannot be well ordered. For an individual cannot but sin and err, either through ignorance—by professing an opinion or a moral quality that is not preferable in truth—or else because he is overcome by desire or anger. If then the individual believed that this fracture can never be remedied, he would persist in his error and sometimes perhaps disobey even more because of the fact that no stratagem remains at his disposal. If, however, he believes in repentance, he can correct himself and return to a better and more perfect state than the one he was in before he sinned. For this reason there are many actions that are meant to establish this correct and very useful opinion, I mean the confessions,* the sacrifices in expiation of negligence and also of certain sins committed intentionally, and the fasts. The general characteristic of repentance from any sin consists in one's being divested of it. And this is the purpose of this opinion. Thus the utility of all these things is become manifest.

*Cf. Lev. 5:5; 16:21.

CHAPTER 51

This chapter that we bring now does not include additional matter over and above what is comprised in the other chapters of this treatise. It is only a kind of a conclusion, at the same time explaining the worship as practiced by one who has apprehended the true realities peculiar only to Him after he has obtained an apprehension of what He is; and it also guides him toward achieving this worship, which is the end of man, and makes known to him how providence watches over him in this habitation until he is brought over to the "bundle of life."*

I shall begin the discourse in this chapter with a parable that I shall compose for you. I say then: The ruler is in his palace, and all his subjects are partly within the city and partly outside the city. Of those who are within the city, some have turned their backs upon the ruler's habitation, their faces being turned another way. Others seek to reach the ruler's habitation, turn toward it, and desire to enter it and to stand before him, but up to now they have not yet seen the wall of the habitation. Some of those who seek to reach it have come up to the habitation and walk around it searching for its gate. Some of them have entered the gate and walk about in the antechambers. Some of them have entered the inner court of the habitation and have come to be with the king, in one and the same place with him, namely, in the ruler's habitation. But their having come into the inner part of the habitation does not mean that they see the ruler or speak to him. For after their coming into the inner part of the habitation, it is indispensable that they should make another effort; then they will be in the presence of the ruler, see him from afar or from nearby, or hear the ruler's speech or speak to him.

Now I shall interpret to you this parable that I have invented. I say then: Those who are outside the city are all human individuals who have no doctrinal belief, neither one based on speculation nor one that accepts the authority of tradition—such individuals as the furthermost Turks found in the remote North, the Negroes found in

*Cf. I Sam. 25:29. According to the commentators, these words refer to eternal life.

the remote South, and those who resemble them from among them that are with us in these climes. The status of those is like that of irrational animals. To my mind they do not have the rank of men, but have among the beings a rank lower than the rank of man but higher than the rank of the apes. For they have the external shape and lineaments of a man and a faculty of discernment that is superior to that of the apes.

Those who are within the city, but have turned their backs upon the ruler's habitation, are people who have opinions and are engaged in speculation, but who have adopted incorrect opinions either because of some great error that befell them in the course of their speculation or because of their following the traditional authority of one who had fallen into error. Accordingly, because of these opinions, the more these people walk the greater is their distance from the ruler's habitation. And they are far worse than the first. They are those concerning whom necessity at certain times impels killing them and blotting out the traces of their opinions lest they should lead astray the ways of others.

Those who seek to reach the ruler's habitation and to enter it, but never see the ruler's habitation, are the multitude of the adherents of the Law, I refer to the ignoramuses who observe the commandments.

Those who have come up to the habitation and walk around it are the jurists who believe true opinions on the basis of traditional authority and study the Law concerning the practices of divine service, but do not engage in speculation concerning the fundamental principles of religion and make no inquiry whatever regarding the rectification of belief.

Those who have plunged into speculation concerning the fundamental principles of religion, have entered the antechambers. People there indubitably have different ranks. He, however, who has achieved demonstration, to the extent that that is possible, of everything that may be demonstrated; and who has ascertained in divine matters, to the extent that that is possible, everything that may be ascertained; and who has come close to certainty in those matters in which one can only come close to it—has come to be with the ruler in the inner part of the habitation.

Know, my son, that as long as you are engaged in studying the mathematical sciences and the art of logic, you are one of those who walk around the house searching for its gate as (the sages) have said resorting to a parable: "Ben Zoma is still outside" (Hagigah 15a). If, however, you have understood the natural things, you have entered the habitation and are walking in the antechambers. If, however, you have achieved perfection in the natural things and have understood divine science, you have entered in the ruler's place into the inner court and are with him in one habitation. This is the rank of the men of science; they, however, are of different grades of perfection.

There are those who set their thought to work after having attained perfection in the divine science, turn wholly toward God, may He be cherished and held sublime, renounce what is other than He, and direct all the acts of their intellect toward an examination of the beings with a view to drawing from them proof with regard to Him, so as to know His governance of them in whatever way it is possible. These people are those who are present in the ruler's council. This is the rank of the prophets. Among them there is he who because of the greatness of his apprehension and his renouncing everything that is other than God, may He be exalted, has attained such a degree that it is said of him, "And he was there with the Lord" (Ex. 34:28), putting questions and receiving answers, speaking and being spoken to, in that holy place. And because of his great joy in that which he apprehended, "he did neither eat bread nor drink water" (ibid.). For his intellect attained such strength that all the gross faculties in the body ceased to function. I refer to the various kinds of the sense of touch. Some prophets could only see, some of them from close by and some from afar, as (a prophet) says: "From afar the Lord appeared to me" (Jer. 31:3). The various degrees of prophecy have already been discussed by us. Let us now return to the subject of this chapter, which is to confirm men in the intention to set their thought to work on God alone after they have achieved knowledge of Him, as we have explained. This is the worship peculiar to those who have apprehended the true realities; the more they think of Him and of being with Him, the more their worship increases.

As for someone who thinks and frequently mentions God, without knowledge, following a mere imagining or following a belief adopted because of his reliance on the authority of somebody else, he is to my mind outside the habitation and far away from it and does not in true reality mention or think about God. For that thing which is in his imagination and which he mentions in his speech does not correspond to any being at all and has merely been invented by his imagination, as we have explained in our discourse concerning the attributes. This kind of worship ought only to be engaged in after intellectual conception has been achieved. If, however, you have apprehended God and His acts in accordance with what is required by the intellect, you should afterward engage in totally devoting yourself to Him, endeavor to come closer to Him, and strengthen the bond between you and Him—that is, the intellect. Thus it says: "To you it was shown, that you might know that the Lord" (Deut. 4:35), and so on; and it says: "Know this day, and lay it to your heart" (ibid. 4:39), and so on; and it says, "Know that the Lord He is God" (Ps. 100:3). The Torah has made it clear that this last worship to which we have drawn attention in this chapter can only be engaged in after apprehension has been achieved; it says: "To love the Lord your God, and to serve Him with all your heart and with all your soul" (Deut. 11:13). Now we have made it clear several times that love is proportionate to apprehension. After love comes this worship to which attention has also been drawn by (the sages) who said: "This is the worship in the heart."* In my opinion it consists in setting thought to work on the first intelligible and in devoting oneself exclusively to this as far as this is within one's capacity. Therefore you will find that David exhorted Solomon and fortified him in these two things, I mean his endeavor to apprehend Him and his endeavor to worship Him after apprehension has been achieved. He said: "And you, Solomon my son, know the God of your father and serve him. . . . If you seek Him, He will be found of you" (I Chron. 28:9), and so on. The exhortation always refers to intellectual apprehensions, not to imagination; for thought concerning imaginings is not called knowledge but "that which comes into your mind" (Ezek. 20:32). Thus it is clear that after apprehension, total devotion to Him and the employment of intellectual thought in constantly loving Him should be aimed at. Mostly this is achieved in solitude and isolation. Hence every excellent man stays frequently in solitude and does not meet anyone unless it is necessary.

A call to attention. We have already made it clear to you that that intellect which overflowed from Him, may He be exalted, toward us is the bond between us and Him. You have the choice: if you wish to strengthen and to fortify this bond, you can do so; if, however, you wish gradually to make it weaker and feebler until you cut it, you can also do that. You can only strengthen this bond by

*Taanit 2a; Palestinian Talmud, Berakhot, IV.

employing it in loving Him and in progressing toward this, just as we have explained. And it is made weaker and feebler if you busy your thought with what is other than He. Know that even if you were the man who knew most the true reality of the divine science, you would cut that bond existing between you and God if you would empty your thought of God and busy yourself totally in eating the necessary or in occupying yourselves with the necessary. You would not be with Him then, nor He with you. For that relation between you and Him is actually broken off at that time. It is for this reason that excellent men begrudge the times in which they are turned away from Him by other occupations and warn against this, saying: "Do not let God be absent from your thought" (Shabbat 149a). And David says, "I have set the Lord always before me; because He is at my right hand, I shall not bend down" (Ps. 16:8), he means to say: I do not empty my thought of Him, and it is as if He were my right hand from which, because of the rapidity of its motion, my attention is not distracted even for an instant, and therefore I do not bend down—that is, I do not fall.

Know that all the practices of the worship, such as reading the Torah, prayer, and the performance of the other commandments, have only the end of training you to occupy yourself with His commandments, may He be exalted, and not with that which is other than He. If, however, you pray merely by moving your lips while facing a wall, and at the same time think about your buying and selling, or if you read the Torah with your tongue while your heart is set upon the building of your habitation and does not consider what you read; and similarly in all cases in which you perform a commandment merely with your limbs—as if you were digging a hole in the ground or hewing wood in the forest—without reflecting either upon the meaning of that action or upon Him from whom the commandment proceeds or upon the end of the action, you should not think that you have achieved the end. Rather you will then be similar to those of whom it is said: "You are near in their mouth, and far from their reins" (Jer. 12:2).

From here on I will begin to give you guidance with regard to the form of this training so that you should achieve this great end. The first thing that you should cause your soul to hold fast to is that, while reciting the Shema prayer, you should empty your mind of everything and pray thus. You should not content yourself with being intent while reciting the first verse of Shema and saying the first benediction. When this has been carried out correctly and has been practiced consistently for years, cause your soul, whenever you read or listen to the Torah, to be constantly directed—the whole of you and your thought—toward reflection on what you are listening to or reading. When this too has been practiced consistently for a certain time, cause your soul to be in such a way that your thought is always quite free of distraction and gives heed to all that you are reading of the other discourses of the prophets and even when you read all the benedictions, so that you aim at meditating on what you are uttering and at considering its meaning. If, however, while performing these acts of worship, you are free from distraction and not engaged in thinking upon any of the things pertaining to this world, cause your soul—after this has been achieved—to occupy your thought with things necessary for you or superfluous in your life, and in general with worldly things, while you eat or drink or bathe or talk with your wife and your small children, or while you talk with the common run of people. Thus I have provided you with many and long stretches of time in which you can think all that needs thinking regarding property, the governance of the household, and the welfare of the body. On the other hand, while performing the actions imposed by the Law, you should occupy your thought only with what you are doing, just as we have explained. When, however, you are alone with yourself and no one else is there and while you lie awake upon your bed, you should take great care during these precious times not to set your thought to work on anything other than that intellectual worship consisting in nearness to God and being in His presence in that true reality that I have made known to you and not by way of affections of the imagination. In my opinion this end can be achieved by those of the men of knowledge who have rendered their souls worthy of it by training of this kind.

And there may be a human individual who, through his apprehension of the true realities and his joy in what he has apprehended, achieves a state in which he talks with people and is occupied with his bodily necessities while his intellect is wholly turned toward Him, may He be exalted, so that in his heart he is always in His presence, may He be exalted, while outwardly he is with people, in the sort of way described by the poetical parables that have been invented for these notions: "I sleep, but my heart wakes; it is the voice of my beloved that knocks" (Song of Songs 5:2), and so on. I do not say that this rank is that of all the prophets; but I do say that this is the rank of Moses our Teacher, of whom it is said: "And Moses alone shall come near to the Lord; but they shall not come near" (Ex. 24:2); and of whom it is said: "And he was there with the Lord" (*ibid.* 34:28); and to whom it was said, "But as for you, stand here by Me" (Deut. 5:28). All this according to what we have explained regarding the meaning of these verses. This was also the rank of the patriarchs, the result of whose nearness to Him, may He be exalted, was that His name became known to the world through them: "The God of Abraham, the God of Isaac, and the God of Jacob . . . this is My name for ever" (Ex. 3:15). Because of the union of their intellects through apprehension of Him, it came about that He made a lasting covenant with each of them: "Then I will remember My covenant with Jacob" (Lev. 26:42), and so on. For in those four, I mean the patriarchs and Moses our Teacher, union with God—I mean apprehension of Him and love of Him—became manifest, as the texts testify. Also the providence of God watching over them and over their posterity was great. Withal they were occupied with governing people, increasing their fortune, and endeavoring to acquire property. Now this is to my mind a proof that they performed these actions with their limbs only, while their intellects were constantly in His presence, may He be exalted. It also seems to me that the fact that these four were in a permanent state of extreme perfection in the eyes of God, and that His providence watched over them continually even while they were engaged in increasing their fortune—I mean while they tended their cattle, did agricultural work, and governed their household—was necessarily brought about by the circumstance that in all these actions their end was to come near to Him, may He be exalted; and how near! For the end of their efforts during their life was to bring into being a religious community that would know and worship God. "For I have known him, to the end that he may command" (Gen. 18:19), and so on. Thus it has become clear to you that the end of all their efforts was to spread the doctrine of the unity of the Name in the world and to guide people to love Him, may He be exalted. Therefore this rank befitted them, for these actions were pure worship of great import. This rank is not a rank that, with a view to the attainment of which, someone like myself may aspire for guidance. But one may aspire to attain that rank which was mentioned before this one through the training that we described. One must beseech God that He remove the obstructions that separate us from Him, even though most of them come from us, as we have explained in certain chapters of this treatise: "Your iniquities have separated between you and your God" (Is. 59:2). . . .

The result is that when a perfect man is stricken with years and approaches death, this apprehension increases very powerfully, joy over this apprehension and a great love for the object of apprehension become stronger, until the soul is separated from the body at that moment in this state of pleasure. Because of this the sages have indicated with reference to the deaths of Moses, Aaron, and Miriam that the three of them died by a kiss. They said (Bava Batra 17a) that the dictum (of Scripture), "And Moses the servant of the Lord died there in the land of Moab by the mouth of the Lord" (Deut. 34:5), indicates that he died by a kiss. Similarly it is said of Aaron: ". . . by the mouth of the Lord, and died there" (Num. 33:38). And they said of Miriam in the same way: "She also died by a kiss." But with regard to her it is not said, "by the mouth of the Lord"; because she was a woman, the use of the figurative expression was not suitable with regard to her.* Their purpose was to indicate that the three of them died in the pleasure of this apprehension due to the intensity of passionate love. In this dictum the sages, may their memory be blessed, followed the generally accepted poetical way of expression that calls the apprehension that is achieved in a state of intense and passionate love for Him, may He be exalted, a kiss, in accordance with its dictum: "Let him kiss me with the kisses of his mouth" (Song of Songs 1:2), and so on. (The sages), may their memory be blessed, mention the occurrence of this kind of death, which in true reality is salvation from death, only with regard to Moses, Aaron, and Miriam. The other prophets and excellent men are beneath this degree; but it holds good for all of them that the apprehension of their intellects becomes stronger at the separation, just as it is said: "And your righteousness shall go before you; the glory of the Lord shall be at your rear" (Is. 58:8). After having reached this condition of enduring permanence, that intellect remains in one and the same state, the impediment that sometimes screened him off having been removed. And he will remain permanently in that state of intense pleasure, which does not belong to the genus of bodily pleasures, as we have explained in our compilations and as others have explained before us.

Bring your soul to understand this chapter, and direct your efforts to the multiplying of those times in which you are with God

*See Moed Katan 28b.

or endeavoring to approach Him and to decreasing those times in which you are with other than He and in which you make no efforts to approach Him. This guidance is sufficient in view of the purpose of this treatise.

CHAPTER 52

Man does not sit, move, and occupy himself when he is alone in his house, as he sits, moves, and occupies himself when he is in the presence of a great king; nor does he speak and rejoice while he is with his family and relatives, as he speaks in the king's council. Therefore he who chooses to achieve human perfection and to be in true reality a man of God must give heed and know that the great king who always accompanies him and cleaves to him is greater than any human individual, even if the latter be David and Solomon. This king who cleaves to him and accompanies him is the intellect that overflows toward us and is the bond between us and Him, may He be exalted. Just as we apprehend Him by means of that light which He caused to overflow toward us—as it says, "In Your light do we see light" (Ps. 36:10)—so does He by means of this selfsame light examine us; and because of it, He, may He be exalted, is constantly with us, examining from on high: "Can any hide himself in secret places that I shall not see him?" (Jer. 23:24). Understand this well. Know that when perfect men understand this, they achieve such humility, such awe and fear of God, such reverence and such shame before Him, may He be exalted—and this in ways that pertain to true reality, not to imagination—that their secret conduct with their wives and in latrines is like their public conduct with other people. This, as you will find, was the way of our most renowned sages with their wives: "One uncovers a handbreadth and covers up a handbreath" (Nedarim 20a–b). They also said: "Who is modest? Whoever behaves by night as he behaves by day" (Berakhot 62a). You know already that they forbade (Kiddushin 31a) "walking about with an erect carriage because (of the Biblical dictum), 'The whole earth is full of His glory' " (Is. 6:3); all this being intended firmly to establish the notion that I have mentioned to you, that we are always before

Him, may He be exalted, and walk about to and fro while His Indwelling is with us. And the greatest among the sages avoided uncovering their heads, because man is covered about by the Indwelling. They also spoke little for this reason. We have already given in the *Commentary on Avot** the explanation that was needed concerning the habit of speaking but little: "For God is in heaven and you upon the earth; therefore let your words be few" (Eccles. 5:1).

This purpose to which I have drawn your attention is the purpose of all the actions prescribed by the Law. For it is by all the particulars of the actions and through their repetition that some excellent men obtain such training that they achieve human perfection, so that they fear, and are in dread and in awe of God, may He be exalted, and know who it is that is with them and as a result act subsequently as they ought to. He, may He be exalted, has explained that the end of the actions prescribed by the whole Law is to bring about the passion of which it is correct that it be brought about, as we have demonstrated in this chapter for the benefit of those who know the true realities. I refer to the fear of Him, may He be exalted, and the awe before His command. It says: "If you will not take care to observe all the words of this Law that are written in this book, that you may fear this glorious and fearful Name, the Lord your God" (Deut. 28:58). Consider how it is explicitly stated for your benefit that the intention of "all the words of this Law" is one end, namely, "that you may fear the Name," and so on. The fact that this end is achieved through actions, you can learn from its dictum in this verse: "If you will not take care to observe." For it has already been made clear that this refers to actions prescribed by commandments and prohibitions. As for the opinions that the Torah teaches us—namely, the apprehension of His being and His unity, may He be exalted—these opinions teach us love, as we have explained several times. You know to what extent the Torah lays stress upon love: "With all your heart, and with all your soul, and with all your might" (*ibid.* 6:5). For these two ends, namely, love and fear, are achieved through two things: love through the opinions taught by the Law, which include the apprehension of His being as He, may He be exalted, is in truth; while fear is achieved by means of all actions prescribed by the Law, as we have explained. Understand this summary.

**Commentary on the Mishnah*, Avot 1:17.

CHAPTER 53

This chapter includes an interpretation of the meaning of three terms that we have need of interpreting: namely, *hesed* (lovingkindness), *mishpat* (judgment), and *tzedakah* (righteousness).

We have already explained in the *Commentary on Avot* that the meaning of *hesed* is excess in whatever matter excess is practiced. In most cases, however, it is applied to excess in beneficence. Now it is known that beneficence includes two notions, one of them consisting in the exercise of beneficence toward one who has no right at all to claim this from you, and the other consisting in the exercise of beneficence toward one who deserves it, but in a greater measure than he deserves it. In most cases the prophetic books use the word *hesed* in the sense of practicing beneficence toward one who has no right at all to claim this from you. Therefore every benefit that comes from Him, may He be exalted, is called *hesed*. Thus it says: "I will make mention of the lovingkindness (*hasdei*) of the Lord" (Is. 63:7). Hence this reality as a whole—I mean that He, may He be exalted, has brought it into being—is *hesed*. Thus it says: "The world is built up in lovingkindness (*hesed*)" (Ps. 89:3), the meaning of which is: the building-up of the world is lovingkindness. And He, may He be exalted, says in an enumeration of His attributes: "And abundant in lovingkindness" (Ex. 34:6).

The word *tzedakah* is derived from *tzedek*, which means justice; justice being the granting to everyone who has a right to something, that which he has a right to, and giving to every being that which corresponds to his merits. But in the books of the prophets, fulfilling the duties imposed upon you with regard to others is not called *tzedakah* in conformity with the first sense. For if you give a hired man his wages or pay a debt, this is not called *tzedakah*. On the other hand, the fulfilling of duties with regard to others imposed upon you on account of moral virtue, such as remedying the injuries of all those who are injured, is called *tzedakah*. Therefore it says with reference to the returning of a pledge to the poor: "And it shall be *tzedakah* to you" (Deut. 24:13). For when you walk in the way of the moral virtues, you do justice to your rational soul, giving her the due that is her right. And because every moral virtue is called *tzedakah*, it says: "And he believed in the Lord, and it was accounted to him as *tzedakah*" (Gen. 15:6). I refer to the virtue of faith. This applies likewise to His dictum, may He be exalted: "And it shall be *tzedakah* to us if we take care to observe" (Deut. 6:25), and so on.

As for the word *mishpat*, it means judgment concerning what ought to be done to one who is judged, whether in the way of conferring a benefit or of punishment.

Thus it has been summarized that *hesed* is applied to beneficence taken absolutely; *tzedakah*, to every good action performed by you because of a moral virtue with which you perfect your soul; and *mishpat* sometimes has as its consequence punishment and sometimes the conferring of a benefit. When refuting the doctrine of divine attributes, we have already explained that every attribute by which God is described in the books of the prophets is an attribute of action. Accordingly, He is described as *Hasid* (one possessing lovingkindness)* because He has brought the all into being; as *Tzaddik* (righteous)† because of His mercy toward the weak—I refer to the governance of the living being by means of its forces; and as *Judge*‡ because of the occurrence in the world of relative good things and of relative great calamities, necessitated by judgment that is consequent upon wisdom. The Torah uses all three terms: "Shall the *Judge* of all the earth . . ." (Gen. 18:25); "*Tzaddik* (righteous) and upright is He" (Deut. 32:4); "And abundant in *hesed* (lovingkindness)" (Ex. 34:6). In interpreting the meaning of these terms, it was our purpose to prepare the way for the chapter that we shall bring after this one.

CHAPTER 54

The term *wisdom* (*hokhmah*) is applied in Hebrew in four senses. It is applied to the apprehension of true realities, which have for their end the apprehension of Him, may He be exalted. It says: "But wisdom, where shall it be found?" (Job 28:18), and so on. It says: "If you seek her as silver" (Prov. 2:4), and so on. This usage is fre-

---

*A word deriving from the same verbal root as *hesed*.

†A word deriving from the same verbal root as *tzedakah*.

‡*Shofet*, a word deriving from the same verbal root as *mishpat*.

quent. The term is applied to acquiring arts, whatever the art might be: "And every wise-hearted among you" (Ex. 35:10); "And all the women that were wise-hearted" (*ibid.* 35:25). It is applied to acquiring moral virtues: "And teach his elders wisdom" (Ps. 105:22); "Is wisdom with aged men?" (Job 12:12)—for the thing that is acquired through mere old age is a disposition to achieve moral virtues. It is applied to the aptitude for stratagems and ruses: "Come, let us deal wisely with them" (Ex. 1:10). According to this meaning it says: "And fetched there a wise woman" (II Sam. 14:2), meaning thereby that she had an aptitude for stratagems and ruses. In this sense it is said: "They are wise to do evil" (Jer. 4:22). It is possible that the meaning of wisdom in Hebrew indicates aptitude for stratagems and the application of thought in such a way that the stratagems and ruses may be used in achieving either rational or moral virtues, or in achieving skill in a practical art, or in working evil and wickedness. It has, accordingly, become plain that the term wise can be applied to one possessing the rational virtues, to one possessing the moral virtues, to everyone skilled in a practical art, and to one possessing ruses in working evil and wickedness. According to this explanation, one who knows the whole of the Law in its true reality is called wise in two respects: in respect of the rational virtues comprised in the Law and in respect of the moral virtues included in it. But since the rational matter in the Law is received through tradition and is not demonstrated by the methods of speculation, the knowledge of the Law came to be set up in the books of the prophets and the sayings of the sages as one separate species and wisdom, in an unrestricted sense, as another species. It is through this wisdom, in an unrestricted sense, that the rational matter that we receive from the Law through tradition, is demonstrated. All the texts that you find in the (Scriptural) books that extol wisdom and speak of its wonder and of the rarity of those who acquire it—"Not many are wise" (Job 32:9); "But wisdom, where shall it be found?" (*ibid.* 28:12), and so on; and many other texts of this kind—treat of that wisdom which teaches us to demonstrate the opinions of the Torah. This is also frequent in the sayings of the sages; I mean that they set up the knowledge of the Torah as one separate species and wisdom as another species. They say of Moses our Teacher: "He was father in wisdom, father in the Torah, father among the prophets" (Megillah 13a). And with reference to its dictum concerning Solomon, "And he was wiser than all men" (I Kings 5:11), they say: "Not (wiser) than Moses" (Rosh

Hashanah 21b); for the dictum, "than all men," means: than his contemporaries. Therefore you will find that it mentions "Heman and Calcol and Darda, the sons of Mahol" (I Kings 5:11), who were celebrated then as wise men. The sages mention likewise that man is required first to obtain knowledge of the Torah, then to obtain wisdom, then to know what is incumbent upon him with regard to the legal science of the Law—I mean the drawing of inferences concerning what one ought to do. And this should be the order observed: The opinions in question should first be known as being received through tradition; then they should be demonstrated; then the actions through which one's way of life may be ennobled, should be precisely defined. This is what they literally say regarding man's being required to give an account with respect to these three matters in this order. They say: "When man comes to judgment, he is first asked: Have you fixed certain seasons for the study of the Torah? Have you ratiocinated concerning wisdom? Have you inferred one thing from another?" (Shabbat 31a). It has thus become clear to you that, according to them, the science of the Torah is one species and wisdom is a different species, being the verification of the opinions of the Torah through correct speculation. After we have made all these preliminary remarks, hear what we shall say:

The ancient and the modern philosophers have made it clear that the perfections to be found in man consist of four species. The first and the most defective, but with a view to which the people of the earth spend their lives, is the perfection of possessions—that is, of what belongs to the individual in the manner of money, garments, tools, slaves, land, and other things of this kind. A man's being a great king also belongs to this species of perfection. Between this perfection and the individual himself there is no union whatever; there is only a certain relation, and most of the pleasure taken in the relation is purely imaginary. I refer to one's saying: This is my house; this is my slave; this money is mine; these are my soldiers. For if he considers his own individual self, he will find that all this is outside his self and that each of these possessions subsists as it is by itself. Therefore when the relation referred to has been abolished, there is no difference between an individual who has been a great king and the most contemptible of men, though nothing may have changed in any of the things that were attributed to him. The philosophers have explained that the endeavor and the efforts directed by man toward this kind of perfection are nothing but an effort with a view to something purely imaginary, to a thing that has no permanence. And even if these possessions should remain with him permanently during the whole of his life, he would by no means thereby achieve perfection in his self.

The second species has a greater connection than the first with the individual's self, being the perfection of the bodily constitution and shape—I refer to that individual's temperament being most harmonious, his limbs well proportioned and strong as they ought to be. Neither should this species of perfection be taken as an end, for it is a corporeal perfection and does not belong to man qua man, but qua animal; for man has this in common with the lowest animals. Moreover, even if the strength of a human individual reached its greatest maximum, it would not attain the strength of a strong mule, and still less the strength of a lion or an elephant. The end of this perfection consists, as we have mentioned, in man's transporting a heavy burden or breaking a thick bone and in other things of this kind, from which no great utility for the body may be derived. Utility for the soul is absent from this species of perfection.

The third species is a perfection that to a greater extent than the second species subsists in the individual's self. This is the perfection of the moral virtues. It consists in the individual's moral habits having attained their ultimate excellence. Most of the commandments serve no other end than the attainment of this species of perfection. But this species of perfection is likewise a preparation for something else and not an end in itself. For all moral habits are concerned with what occurs between a human individual and someone else. This perfection regarding moral habits is, as it were, only the disposition to be useful to people; consequently it is an instrument for someone else. For if you suppose a human individual is alone, acting on no one, you will find that all his moral virtues are in vain and without employment and unneeded, and that they do not perfect the individual in anything; for he only needs them and they again become useful to him in regard to someone else.

The fourth species is the true human perfection; it consists in the acquisition of the rational virtues—I refer to the conception of intelligibles, which teach true opinions concerning the divine things. This is in true reality the ultimate end; this is what gives the individual true perfection, a perfection belonging to him alone; and it gives him permanent perdurance; through it man is man. If you consider each of the three perfections mentioned before, you will find that

356 GUIDE OF THE PERPLEXED

they pertain to others than you, not to you, even though, according
to the generally accepted opinion, they inevitably pertain both to you
and to others. This ultimate perfection, however, pertains to you
alone, no one else being associated in it with you in any way: "They
shall be only your own" (Prov. 5:17), and so on. Therefore you
ought to desire to achieve this thing, which will remain permanently
with you, and not weary and trouble yourself for the sake of others,
O you, who neglect your own soul so that its whiteness has turned
into blackness through the corporeal faculties having gained dominion over it—as is said in the beginning of the poetical parables that
have been coined for these notions; it says: "My mother's sons were
incensed against me; they made me keeper of the vineyards; but
mine own vineyard have I not kept" (Song of Songs 1:6). It says on
this very same subject: "Lest you give your splendor to others, and
your years to the cruel" (Prov. 5:9).

The prophets too have explained to us and interpreted to us the
self-same notions—just as the philosophers have interpreted them—
clearly stating to us that neither the perfection of possession nor the
perfection of health nor the perfection of moral habits is a perfection
of which one should be proud or that one should desire; the perfection of which one should be proud and that one should desire is
knowledge of Him, may He be exalted, which is the true science.
Jeremiah says concerning these four perfections: "Thus says the
Lord: Let not the wise man glory in his wisdom, neither let the
mighty man glory in his might, let not the rich man glory in his
riches; but let him that glories, glory in this, that he understands and
knows Me" (Jer. 9:22–23). Consider how he mentioned them
according to the order given them in the opinion of the multitude.
For the greatest perfection in their opinion is that of "the rich man
in his riches," below him "the mighty man in his might," and below
him "the wise man in his wisdom." (By the expression, "the wise
man in his wisdom") he means him who possesses the moral virtues;
for such an individual is also held in high esteem by the multitude,
to whom the discourse in question is addressed. Therefore these perfections are arranged in this order. The sages apprehended from this
verse the very notions we have mentioned and have explicitly stated
that which I have explained to you in this chapter: namely, that the
term wisdom (hokhmah), used in an unrestricted sense and regarded
as the end, means in every place the apprehension of Him, may He
be exalted; that the possession of the treasures acquired, and com-

peted for, by man and thought to be perfection are not a perfection; and that similarly all the actions prescribed by the Law—I refer to the various species of worship and also the moral habits that are useful to all people in their mutual dealings—that all this is not to be compared with this ultimate end and does not equal it, being but preparations made for the sake of this end. Hear verbatim a text of theirs dealing with all these notions; it is a text in *Bereshit Rabbah*. It is said there: "One Scriptural dictum says: 'And all things desirable are not to be compared to her' (Prov. 8:11). Another Scriptural dictum says: 'And all things you can desire are not to be compared to her' (*ibid.* 3:15). The expression 'things desirable,' refers to commandments and good actions; while 'things you can desire,' refers to precious stone and pearls. Neither 'things desirable' nor 'things you can desire' are to be compared to her, but let him that glories, glory in this, that he understands and knows Me" (Gen. Rabbah, ch. 35 *in fine*). Consider how concise is this saying, how perfect is he who said it, and how he left out nothing of all that we have mentioned and that we have interpreted and led up to at length.

As we have mentioned this verse and the wondrous notions contained in it, and as we have mentioned the saying of the sages about it, we will complete the exposition of what it includes. For when explaining in this verse the noblest ends, he does not limit them only to the apprehension of Him, may He be exalted. For if this were his purpose, he would have said; "But let him that glories, glory in this, that he understands and knows Me," and have stopped there; or he would have said: "that he understands and knows Me that I am One"; or he would have said: "that I have no figure," or that "there is none like Me," or something similar. But he says that one should glory in the apprehension of Myself and in the knowledge of My attributes, by which he means His actions, as we have made clear with reference to its dictum: "Show me now Your ways" (Ex. 33:13), and so on. In this verse he makes it clear to us that those actions that ought to be known and imitated are lovingkindness, judgment, and righteousness. He adds another corroborative notion through saying, "in the earth"—this being a pivot of the Law. For matters are not as the overbold opine who think that His providence, may He be exalted, terminates at the sphere of the moon and that the earth and that which is in it are neglected: "The Lord has forsaken the earth" (Ezek. 9:9). Rather is it as has been made clear to us by the Teacher of those who know: "That the earth is the Lord's" (Ex. 9:29). He means to say that His providence also extends over the earth in the way that corresponds to what the latter is, just as His providence extends over the heavens in the way that corresponds to what they are. This is what he says: "That I am the Lord who exercises lovingkindness, judgment, and righteousness, in the earth" (Jer. 9:23). Then he completes the notion by saying: "For in these things I delight, says the Lord." He means that it is My purpose that there should come from you "lovingkindness, righteousness, and judgment in the earth" in the way we have explained with regard to the thirteen attributes: namely, that the purpose should be assimilation to them and that this should be our way of life. Thus the end that he sets forth in this verse may be stated as follows: It is clear that the perfection of man that may truly be gloried in is the one acquired by him who has achieved, in a measure corresponding to his capacity, apprehension of Him, may He be exalted, and who knows His providence extending over His creatures as manifested in the act of bringing them into being and in their governance as it is. The way of life of such an individual, after he has achieved this apprehension, will always have in view loving-kindness, righteousness, and judgment, through assimilation to His actions, may He be exalted, just as we have explained several times in this treatise.

This is the extent of what I thought fit that we should set down in this treatise; it is a part of what I consider very useful to those like you. I hope for you that through sufficient reflection you will grasp all the intentions I have included therein, with the help of God, may He be exalted; and that He will grant us "and all (the people) of Israel, being fellows," that which He has promised us: "Then the eyes of the blind shall be opened, and the ears of the deaf shall be unstopped" (Is. 45:5). "The people that walked in darkness have seen a great light; they that dwelt in the land of the shadow of death, upon them has the light shined" (ibid. 9:1).

AMEN

God is very near to everyone who calls,
If he calls truly and has no distractions;
He is found by every seeker who searches for Him,
If he marches toward Him and goes not astray.

OTHER WRITINGS

EIGHT CHAPTERS

MAIMONIDES' view of Pirke Avot (Ethics of the Fathers) as a special treatise on the therapy of the soul, showing the way to perfection and happiness, determined the nature of his introduction to this section of the Mishnah. Its ultimate concern is the exploration and affirmation of human freedom. This presupposes the need to regulate one's passions and appetites, for all action must be free, volitional, and self-determining if it is to be meaningful and responsible. It follows that one who hopes to regulate the soul must be acquainted with the faculties of the soul, just as the physician must know the parts of the body; hence the description of the soul and its faculties in Chapter I. Chapter II insists that thoughts—like actions—are also subject to control and, if appropriate, censure. In other words, virtues are twofold: ethical and intellectual. A soul that produces bad and dishonorable actions or thoughts is sick and needs healing—and that is why Maimonides frequently draws the parallel between medical doctors and physicians of the soul (Chapter III).

Chapter IV delineates the theory of the "golden mean," which is the state of a healthy soul. The reader should be attentive to the many problems which Maimonides encounters in trying to define virtue as the mean between two unacceptable extremes. Noteworthy is the description of the Torah as a delicately constructed system of moderation and spirituality, obviating the need for extremism or asceticism. The rationale for many laws is established in the light of this principle. Maimonides is most emphatic in his repudiation of the monastic ethos—a theme of great importance for medieval history. The polemical thrust of his exposition—rebuffing those Jews who seek heightened spirituality in non-Jewish modes of mysticism and asceticism—is quite pronounced. Chapter VI revolves around the question of autonomy and heteronomy in morality: who is the perfect person—the one who is good by nature and inclination, or the one who subdues his passions and forces himself to be good? Chapter VIII analyzes the role of human freedom.

FOREWORD

We have already explained in the introduction to this work (i.e., the Commentary on the Mishnah) the reason the author of the Mishnah had for putting this treatise (Avot) in this Order (Nezikin).* We have also mentioned the great benefit that is to be derived from this treatise, and have promised many times in preceding passages to discuss certain important points at some length in commenting upon it. For, although the contents of the treatise seem clear and easy to understand, yet to carry out all that it contains is not a simple matter for everybody. Moreover, not all of its contents is intelligible without ample comment, withal that it leads to great perfection and true happiness. For these reasons, I have deemed it advisable here to go into a more lengthy discussion. Besides, our rabbis of blessed memory have said, "He who wishes to be saintly, let him practice the teachings of Avot" (Bava Kamma 30a). Now, there is nothing that ranks so high with us as saintliness, unless it be prophecy, and it is saintliness that paves the way to prophecy; as our rabbis of blessed memory said, "Saintliness leads to holy inspiration" (Avodah Zarah 20b). Thus, their words make it clear that the putting into practice of the teachings of this tractate leads one to

---

*The reason was to underscore the special importance of judicial ethics, the exceptional integrity and unflagging morality of the wise men, inasmuch as the latter's behavior is a model for others.

prophecy. I shall later expound the truth of this assertion, because upon it depends a number of ethical principles.

Further, I deem it fit to preface the commentary on the respective *halakhot* proper by some useful chapters, from which the reader may learn certain basic principles which may later serve as a key to what I am going to say in the commentary. Know, however, that the ideas presented in these chapters and in the following commentary are not of my own invention; neither did I think out the explanations contained therein, but I have gleaned them from the words of the wise occurring in the Midrashim, in the Talmud, and in other of their works, as well as from the words of the philosophers, ancient and recent, and also from the works of various authors, as one should accept the truth from whatever source it proceeds.* Sometimes, I may give a statement in full, word for word in the author's own language, but there is no harm in this, and it is not done with the intention of glorifying myself by presenting as my own something that was said by others before me, since I have just confessed (my indebtedness to others), even though I do not say "So-and-So said," which would necessitate useless prolixity. Sometimes, too, the mentioning of the name of the authority drawn upon might lead one who lacks insight to believe that the statement quoted is faulty, and wrong in itself, because he does not understand it. Therefore, I prefer not to mention the authority, for my intention is only to be of service to the reader and to elucidate for him the thoughts hidden in this tractate. I shall now begin the chapters, which, in accordance with my intention, are to serve here as an introduction, which is to consist of eight chapters.

CHAPTER I: CONCERNING THE HUMAN SOUL
AND ITS FACULTIES

Know that the human soul is one, but that it has many diversified activities. Some of these activities have, indeed, been called souls, which has given rise to the opinion that man has many souls, as was the belief of the physicians, with the result that the most distinguished of them states in the introduction of his book that there are

*See *Mishneh Torah*, Book III, Sanctification of the New Moon, XVII, 24.

three souls, the physical, the vital, and the psychical. These activities are falled *faculties* and *parts*, so that the phrase "parts of the soul," frequently employed by philosophers, is commonly used. By the word "parts," however, they do not intend to imply that the soul is divided into parts as are bodies, but they merely enumerate the different activities of the soul as being parts of a whole, the union of which makes up the soul.

You know that the improvement of the moral qualities is brought about by the healing of the soul and its activities. Therefore, just as the physician, who endeavors to cure the human body, must have a perfect knowledge of it in its entirety and its individual parts, just as he must know what causes sickness that it may be avoided, and must also be acquainted with the means by which a patient may be cured, so, likewise, he who tries to cure the soul, wishing to improve the moral qualities, must have a knowledge of the soul in its totality and its parts, must know how to prevent it from becoming diseased, and how to maintain its health. . . .

I say that the soul has five faculties: the nutritive (also known as the "growing" faculty), the sensitive, the imaginative, the appetitive, and the rational. . . .

The faculty of sensation consists of the five well-known senses of seeing, hearing, tasting, smelling, and feeling. . . .

The imagination is that faculty which retains impressions of things perceptible to the mind, after they have ceased to affect directly the senses which conceived them. This faculty, combining some of these impressions and differentiating among others, can construct new ideas which it has in fact never perceived, and which it could not possibly have perceived. For instance, one may imagine an iron ship floating in the air, or a man whose head reaches the heaven and whose feet rest on the earth, or an animal with a thousand eyes, and many other similar impossibilities which the imagination may construct and endow with an existence that is fanciful. In this regard, the Mutakallimun have fallen into grievous and pernicious error, as a result of which their false theories form the cornerstone of a sophistical system which divides things into the necessary, the possible, and the impossible; so that they believe, and have led others to believe, that all creations of the imagination are possible, not having in mind, as we have stated, that this faculty may attribute existence to that which cannot possibly exist.

The appetitive is that faculty by which a man desires, or loathes a thing, and from which there arise the following activities: the pursuit of an object or flight from it, inclination and avoidance, anger and affection, fear and courage, cruelty and compassion, love and hate, and many other similar psychic qualities. . . .

Reason, that faculty peculiar to man, enables him to understand, reflect, acquire knowledge of the sciences, and to discriminate between proper and improper actions.

CHAPTER II: CONCERNING THE TRANSGRESSIONS
OF THE FACULTIES OF THE SOUL AND THE
DESIGNATION OF THOSE FACULTIES WHICH ARE
THE SEAT OF THE VIRTUES AND THE VICES

Know that transgressions and observances of the Law have their origin only in two of the faculties of the soul, namely, the sensitive and the appetitive, and that to these two faculties alone are to be ascribed all transgressions and observances. The faculties of nutrition and imagination do not give rise to observance or transgression, for in connection with neither is there any conscious or voluntary act. That is, man cannot consciously suspend their functions, nor can he curtail any one of their activities. The proof of this is that the functions of both these faculties, the nutritive and the imaginative, continue to be operative when one is asleep, which is not true of any other of the soul's faculties.

As regards the rational faculty, uncertainty prevails (among philosophers), but I maintain that observance and transgression may also originate in this faculty, in so far as one believes a true or a false doctrine, though no action which may be designated as an observance or a transgression results therefrom.

Now, as for the virtues, they are of two kinds, moral and intellectual, with the corresponding two classes of vices. The intellectual virtues belong to the rational faculty. They are (1) wisdom, which is the knowledge of the direct and indirect causes of things based on a previous realization of the existence of those things, the causes of which have been investigated; (2) reason, consisting of (a) inborn, theoretical reason, that is, axioms, (b) the acquired intellect, which we need not discuss here, and (c) sagacity and intellectual cleverness, which is the ability to perceive quickly, and to grasp an idea without delay, or in a very short time. The vices of this faculty are the antitheses or the opposites of these virtues.

Moral virtues belong only to the appetitive faculty to which that of sensation in this connection is merely subservient. The virtues of this faculty are very numerous, being moderation (i.e., fear of sin), liberality, honesty, meekness, humility, contentedness, (which the rabbis call "wealth," when they say [Ethics of the Fathers 4:1], "Who is truly wealthy? He who is contented with his lot"), courage, (faithfulness), and other virtues akin to these. The vices of this faculty consist of a deficiency or of an exaggeration of these qualities.

CHAPTER III: CONCERNING THE DISEASES OF THE SOUL

The ancient maintained that the soul, like the body, is subject to good health and illness. The soul's healthful state is due to its condition, and that of its faculties, by which it constantly does what is right, and performs what is proper, while the illness of the soul is occasioned by its condition, and that of its faculties, which results in its constantly doing wrong, and performing actions that are improper. The science of medicine investigates the health of the body. Now, just as those who are physically ill imagine that, on account of their vitiated tastes, the sweet is bitter and the bitter is sweet—and likewise fancy the wholesome to be unwholesome—and just as their desire grows stronger and their enjoyment increases for such things as dust, coal, very acidic and sour foods, and the like—which the healthy loathe and refuse, as they are not only not beneficial even to the healthy, but possibly harmful—so those whose souls are ill, that is the wicked and the morally perverted, imagine that the bad is good, and that the good is bad. The wicked man, moreover, continually longs for excesses which are really pernicious, but which, on account of the illness of his soul, he considers to be good. Likewise, just as when people, unacquainted with the science of medicine, realize that they are sick, and consult a physician, who tells them what they must do, forbidding them to partake of that which they imagine beneficial, and prescribing for them things which are unpleasant and bitter, in order that their bodies may become healthy, and that they may again choose the good and spurn the bad, so those whose souls become ill should consult the sages, the moral physicians, who will advise them against indulging in those evils which they (the morally ill) think are good, so that they may be healed by that art of which I shall speak in the next chapter, and through which the moral qualities are restored to their normal condition. But, if he who is morally sick be not aware of his illness, imagining that he is well, or, being aware of it, does not seek a remedy, his end will be similar to that of one, who, suffering from bodily ailment yet continuing to indulge himself, neglects to be cured, and who in consequence surely meets an untimely death.

Those who know that they are in a diseased state, but nevertheless yield to their inordinate passions, are described in the truthful Law which quotes their own words, "Though I walk in the stubbornness of my heart, in order that the indulgence of the passions may appease the thirst for them" (Deut. 29:18). This means that, while intending to quench one's thirst, one may on the contrary intensify it. He who is ignorant of his illness is spoken of in many places by Solomon, who says, "The way of the fool is straight in his own eyes, but he who hearkens to counsel is wise" (Prov. 12:15). This means that he who listens to the counsel of the sage is wise, for the sage teaches him the way that is actually right and not the one that he (the morally ill) erroneously considers to be such. Solomon also says, "There is many a way which seems even before a man; but its ends are ways to death" (ibid. 4:19). Again, in regard to these who are morally ill, in that they do not know what is injurious from that which is beneficial, he says, "The way of the wicked is like darkness; they do not know against what they stumble" (ibid. 14:12).*

The art of healing the diseases of the soul will, however, form the subject-matter of the fourth chapter.

CHAPTER IV: CONCERNING THE CURE OF THE DISEASES OF THE SOUL

Good deeds are such as are equibalanced, maintaining the mean between two equally bad extremes, the too much and the too little. Virtues are psychic conditions and dispositions which are midway

*See Mishneh Torah, Book I, Moral Dispositions, II, 1.

between two reprehensible extremes, one of which is characterized by an exagggeration, the other by a deficiency. Good deeds are the product of these dispositions. To illustrate, abstemiousness is a disposition which adopts a mid-course between inordinate passion and total insensibility to pleasure. Abstemiousness, then, is a proper rule of conduct, and the psychic disposition which gives rise to it is an ethical quality; but inordinate passion, the extreme of excess, and total insensibility to enjoyment, the extreme of deficiency, are both absolutely pernicious. The psychic dispositions, from which these two extremes, inordinate passion and insensibility, result—the one being an exaggeration, the other a deficiency—are alike classed among moral imperfections.

Likewise, liberality is the mean between miserliness and extravagance; courage, between recklessness and cowardice; dignity, between haughtiness and loutishness; humility, between arrogance and self-abasement; contentedness, between avarice and slothful indifference; and benevolence, between meanness and prodigality. (Since definite terms do not exist in our language with which to express these latter qualities, it is necessary to explain their content, and tell what the philosophers meant by them. A man is called benevolent whose whole intention is to do good to others by personal service, by money, or advice, and with all his power, but without meanwhile bringing suffering or disgrace upon himself. That is the medium line of conduct. The mean man is one who does not want others to succeed in anything, even though he himself may not thereby suffer any loss, hardship, or injury. That is the one extreme. The prodigal man, on the contrary, is one who willingly performs the above-mentioned deeds, in spite of the fact that thereby he brings upon himself great injury, or disgrace, terrible hardship, or considerable loss. That is the other extreme.) Gentleness is the mean between irascibility and insensibility to shame and disgrace; and modesty, between impudence and shamefacedness. (The explanation of these latter terms, gleaned from the sayings of our sages [may their memory be blessed!] seems to be this. In their opinion, a modest man is one who is very bashful, and therefore modesty is the mean. This we gather from their saying, "A shamefaced man cannot learn" [Ethics of the Fathers 2:5]. They also assert, "A modest man is worthy of Paradise" [ibid. 5:20], but they do not say this of a shamefaced man. Therefore, I have thus arranged them.) So it is with the other qualities. One does not necessarily have to use conventional terms for these qualities, if only the ideas are clearly fixed in the mind.

It often happens, however, that men err as regards these qualities, imagining that one of the extremes is good, and is a virtue. Sometimes, the extreme of the too much is considered noble, as when temerity is made a virtue, and those who recklessly risk their lives are hailed as heroes. Thus, when people see a man, reckless to the highest degree, who runs deliberately into danger, intentionally tempting death, and escaping only by mere chance, they laud such a one to the skies and say that he is a hero. At other times, the opposite extreme, the too little, is greatly esteemed, and the coward is considered a man of forbearance; the idler, as being a person of a contented disposition; and he, who by the dullness of his nature is callous to every joy, is praised as a man of moderation (that is, one who eschews sin). In like manner, profuse liberality and extreme lavishness are erroneously extolled as excellent characteristics. This is, however, an absolutely mistaken view, for the really praiseworthy is the medium course of action to which everyone should strive to adhere, always weighing his conduct carefully, so that he may attain the proper mean.

Know, moreover, that these moral excellences or defects cannot be acquired, or implanted in the soul except by means of the frequent repetition of acts resulting from these qualities, which, practiced during a long period of time, accustoms us to them. If these acts performed are good ones, then we shall have gained a virtue; but if they are bad, we shall have acquired a vice. Since, however, no man is born with an innate virtue or vice, as we shall explain in Chapter VIII, and, as everyone's conduct from childhood up is undoubtedly influenced by the manner of living of his relatives and countrymen, his conduct may be in accord with the rules of moderation; but, then again, it is possible that his acts may incline toward either extreme, as we have demonstrated, in which case, his soul becomes diseased. In such a contingency, it is proper for him to resort to a cure exactly as he would were his body suffering from an illness. So, just as when the equilibrium of the physical health is disturbed and we note which way it is tending in order to force it to go in exactly the opposite direction until it shall return to its proper condition, and, just as when the proper adjustment is reached we cease this operation and have recourse to that which will maintain the proper balance, in exactly the same way must we adjust the moral equilibrium. Let us take, for example, the case of a man in whose soul there has developed a disposition (of great avarice) on account of which he deprives himself (of every comfort in life), and which, by the way, is one of

the most detestable of defects, and an immoral act, as we have
shown in this chapter. If we wish to cure this sick man, we must not
command him merely (to practice) deeds of generosity, for that
would be as ineffective as a physician trying to cure a patient consumed by a burning fever by administering mild medicines, which
treatment would be inefficacious. We must, however, induce him to
squander so often, and to repeat his acts of profusion so continuously until that propensity which was the cause of his avarice has
totally disappeared. Then, when he reaches that point where he is
about to become a squanderer we must teach him to moderate his
profusion, and tell him to continue with deeds of generosity, and
watch with due care lest he relapse either into lavishness or niggardli-
ness.

If, on the other hand, a man is a squanderer, he must be
directed to practice strict economy and to repeat acts of niggardli-
ness. It is not necessary however, for him to perform acts of avarice as many times as the mean man should those of profusion. This
subtle point, which is a canon and secret of the science of medicine,
tells us that it is easier for a man of profuse habits to moderate them
to generosity, than it is for a miser to become generous. Likewise, it
is easier for one who is apathetic (and eschews sin) to be excited to
moderate enjoyment, than it is for one, burning with passion, to curb
his desires. Consequently, the licentious man must be made to practice restraint more than the apathetic man should be induced to
indulge his passions; and, similarly, the coward requires exposure to
danger more frequently than the reckless man should be forced to
cowardice. The mean man needs to practice lavishness to a greater
degree than should be required of the lavish to practice meanness.
This is a fundamental principle of the science of curing moral ills.

On this account, the saintly ones were not accustomed to cause
their dispositions to maintain an exact balance between the two
extremes, but deviated somewhat, by way of (caution and) restraint,
now to the side of exaggeration, now to that of deficiency. Thus, for
instance, abstinence would incline to some degree toward excessive
denial of all pleasures; valor would approach somewhat toward
temerity; generosity to lavishness; modesty to extreme humility, and
so forth. This is what the rabbis hinted at, in their saying, "Do more
than the strict letter of the law demands" (Bava Metzia 35a).

When, at times, some of the pious ones deviated to one extreme
by fasting, keeping nightly vigils, refraining from eating meat or

drinking wine, renouncing sexual intercourse, clothing themselves in woolen and hairy garments, dwelling in the mountains, and wandering about in the wilderness, they did so partly as a means of restoring the health of their souls, as we have explained above, and partly because of the immorality of the townspeople. When the pious saw that they themselves might become contaminated by association with evil men or by constantly seeing their actions, fearing that their own morals might become corrupt on account of contact with them, they fled to the wildernesses far from their society, as the prophet Jeremiah said, "Oh that some one would grant me in the wilderness the dwelling of a wanderer, and I would quit my people and abandon them; for they are all adulterers, a troop of faithless evildoers" (Jer. 9:1). When the ignorant observed saintly men acting thus, not knowing their motives, they considered their deeds virtuous in and of themselves; and so, blindly imitating their acts, thinking thereby to become like them, they chastised their bodies with all kinds of afflictions, imagining that they had acquired perfection and moral worth, and that by this means man would approach nearer to God, as if He hated the human body and desired its destruction. It never occurred to them, however, that these actions were bad and resulted in moral imperfection of the soul. Such men can only be compared to one ignorant of the art of healing who sees skillful physicians curing patients at the point of death by administering (purgatives known in Arabic as) colocynth, scammony, aloe, and the like, and depriving them of food, and foolishly concludes that since these things cure sickness, they must be all the more efficacious in preserving health or prolonging life. If a person should take these things constantly and treat himself as a sick person, he would really become ill. Likewise, those who are spiritually well but have recourse to remedies will undoubtedly become morally ill.

The perfect Law which leads us to perfection—as one who knew it well testifies by the words, "the Law of the Lord is perfect restoring the soul; the testimonies of the Lord are faithful making wise the simple" (Ps. 19:9)—recommends none of these things (such as self-torture, flight from society, etc.). On the contrary, it aims at man's following the path of moderation in accordance with the dictates of nature, eating, drinking, enjoying legitimate sexual intercourse, all in moderation, and living among people in honesty and uprightness, but not dwelling in the wilderness or in the mountains, or clothing oneself in garments of hair and wool, or afflicting the body. The Law even warns us against these practices if we interpret it according to what tradition tells us is the meaning of the passage concerning the Nazirite, "And he (the priest) shall make an atonement for him because he has sinned against the soul" (Num. 6:11). The rabbis ask, "Against what soul has he sinned? Against his own soul, because he has deprived himself of wine. Is this not then a conclusion a minori ad majus? If one who deprives himself merely of wine must bring an atonement, how much more incumbent is it upon one who denies himself every enjoyment."*

By the words of our prophets and of the sages of our Law, we see that they were bent upon moderation and the care of their souls and bodies in accordance with what the Law prescribes and with the answer which God gave through His prophet to those who asked whether the fast day once a year should continue or not. They asked Zechariah, "Shall I weep in the fifth month with abstinence as I have done already these many years?" (Zech. 7:3). His answer was, "When you fasted and mourned in the fifth and in the seventh (month) already these seventy years, did you at all fast for Me, yes for Me? And if you do eat and if you do drink are you not yourselves those that eat and yourselves those that drink?" (ibid. 7:5). After that, he enjoined upon them justice and virtue alone, not fasting, when he said to them, "Thus has said the Lord of hosts. Execute justice and show kindness and mercy every man to his brother" (ibid. 7:9). He said further, "Thus has said the Lord of hosts, the fast of the fourth, and the fast of the fifth, and the fast of the seventh, and the fast of the tenth (month) shall become to the house of Judah gladness and joy and merry festivals; only love truth and peace" (ibid. 8:19). Know that by "truth" the intellectual virtues are meant, for they are immutably true, as we have explained in Chapter II, and that by "peace" the moral virtues are designated, for upon them depends the peace of the world.

But to resume. Should those of our coreligionists—and it is of them alone that I speak—who imitate the followers of other religions, maintain that when they torment their bodies, and renounce every joy, they do so merely to discipline the faculties of their souls by inclining somewhat to the one extreme, as is proper and in accordance with our own recommendations in this chapter, our answer is that they are in error, as I shall now demonstrate. The Law did not lay down its prohibitions or enjoin its commandments except for just

*Nazir 19a, 22a; Taanit 11a; Bava Kamma 91b; Nedarim 10a.

this purpose, namely, that by its disciplinary effects we may persistently maintain the proper distance from either extreme. For the restrictions regarding all the forbidden foods, the prohibitions of illicit intercourse, the forewarning against prostitution, the duty of performing the legal marriage rites—which, nevertheless, does not permit intercourse at all times, as, for instance, during the period of menstruation and after childbirth, besides its being otherwise restricted by our sages and entirely interdicted during the daytime, as we have explained in the tractate Sanhedrin—all of these God commanded in order that we should keep entirely distant from the extreme of the inordinate indulgence of the passions, and, even departing from the exact medium, should incline somewhat toward self-denial, so that there may be firmly rooted in our souls the disposition for moderation.

Likewise, all that is contained in the Law concerning the giving of tithes, the gleaning of the harvest, the forgotten sheaves, the single grapes, and the small bunches in the vineyards for the poor, the law of the Sabbatical year and of the Jubilee, the giving of charity according to the wants of the needy one, all these approach the extreme of lavishness to be practiced in order that we may depart far from its opposite, stinginess, and thus, nearing the extreme of excessive prodigality, there may become instilled in us the quality of generosity. If you should test most of the commandments from this point of view, you would find that they are all for the discipline and guidance of the faculties of the soul. Thus, the Law forbids revenge, the bearing of a grudge, and blood-revenge by saying, "You shall not avenge nor bear any grudge" (Lev. 19:18); "you shall surely unload with him" (the ass of him who hates you) (Ex. 23:5); "you shall surely help him to lift them up again" (your brother's ass or ox which has fallen by the way) (Deut. 22:4). These commandments are intended to weaken the force of wrath or anger. Likewise, the command, "You shall surely bring them back" (your brother's ox or lamb which has gone astray) (ibid. 22:1), is meant to remove the disposition of avarice. Similarly, "Before the hoary head shall you rise up, and honor the face of the old man" (Lev. 19:32), "Honor your father and your mother" etc. (Ex. 22:12), "You shall not depart from the sentence which they may tell you" etc. (Deut. 17:11), are intended to do away with boldness, and to produce modesty. Then in order to keep away from the other extreme, i.e., of excessive bashfulness, we are told, "You shall indeed rebuke your neighbor," etc.

(Lev. 19:17), "You shall not fear him" (the false prophet), etc. (Deut. 18:22), so that excessive bashfulness, too, should disappear in order that we pursue the medium course. Should, however, anyone—who would without doubt be foolish if he did so—try to enforce these commands with additional rigor, as, for instance, by prohibiting eating and drinking more than does the Law, or by restricting connubial intercourse to a greater degree, or by distributing all of his money among the poor, or using it for sacred purposes more freely than the Law requires, or by spending it entirely upon sacred objects and upon the sanctuary, he would indeed be performing improper acts, and would be unconsciously going to either one or the other extreme, thus forsaking completely the proper mean. In this connection, I have never heard a more remarkable saying than that of the rabbis, found in the Palestinian Talmud in the ninth chapter of the treatise Nedarim, where they greatly blame those who bind themselves by oaths and vows, in consequence of which they are fettered like prisoners. The exact words they use are, "Said Rabbi Iddai, in the name of Rabbi Isaac, 'Do you not think that what the Law prohibits is sufficient for you that you must take upon yourself additional prohibitions?'" (IX, 1).*

From all that we have stated in this chapter, it is evident that it is man's duty to aim at performing acts that observe the proper mean, and not to desist from them by going to one extreme or the other, except for the restoration of the soul's health by having recourse to the opposite of that from which the soul is suffering. He who is acquainted with the science of medicine, for instance, upon noting the least sign of a change for the worse in his health does not remain indifferent to it, but prevents the sickness from increasing to a degree that will require recourse to violent remedies. Similarly, when a man feels that one of his limbs has become affected, he carefully nurses it, refraining from things that are injurious to it, and applying every remedy that will restore it to its healthy condition, or at least keep it from getting worse. In like manner, the moral man will constantly examine his characteristics, weigh his deeds, and daily investigate his psychic condition; and if, at any time, he finds his soul deviating to one extreme or another, he will immediately hasten to apply the proper remedy, and not suffer an evil aptitude to acquire strength, as we have shown, by a constant repetition of that evil action which it occasioned. He is, likewise, bound to be mindful of

*See *Mishneh Torah*, Book I, Moral Dispositions, III, 1.

his defects, and constantly to endeavor to remedy them, as we have said above, for it is impossible for any man to be free from all faults. Philosophers tell us that it is most difficult and rare to find a man who, by his nature, is endowed with every perfection, moral as well as mental. This thought is expressed often in the prophetical books. as, "Behold, in His servants He puts no trust, and His angels He charges with folly" (Job 4:18), "How can man be justified with God? or how can be pure one that is born of woman?" (*ibid.* 25:4), and Solomon says of mankind in general, "For no man is so righteous upon earth that he should do always good, and never sin" (Eccles. 7:20).

You know also, that God said to our teacher Moses, the master of former and later ages, "Because you have not confided in Me, to sanctify Me" (Num. 20:12), "Because you rebelled against My order at the waters of Meribah" (*ibid.* 20:24), "Because you did not sanctify Me" (Deut. 32:51). All this (God said) although the sin of Moses consisted merely in that he departed from the moral mean of patience to the extreme of wrath in so far as he exclaimed, "Hear now you rebels," etc. (Num. 20:10), yet for this God found fault with him that such a man as he should show anger in the presence of the entire community of Israel, where wrath is unbecoming. This was a profanation of God's name, because men imitated the words and conduct of Moses, hoping thereby to attain temporal and eternal happiness. How could he, then, allow his wrath free play, since it is a pernicious characteristic, arising, as we have shown, from an evil psychic condition? The divine words, "You have rebelled against My order" are, however, to be explained as follows. Moses was not speaking to ignorant and vicious people, but to an assembly, the most insignificant of whose women, as the sages put it, were on a plane with (the prophet) Ezekiel, the son of Buzi.* So, when Moses said or did anything, they subjected his words or actions to the most searching examination. Therefore, when they saw that he waxed wrathful, they said, "He has no moral imperfection, and if he did not know that God is angry with us for demanding water and that we have stirred up the wrath of God, he would not have been angry with us." However, we do not find that when God spoke to Moses about this matter He was angry. On the contrary, He said, "Take the staff ... and give drink to the congregation and their cattle" (Num. 20:8).

*Mekhilta, Ex. 15:2.

We have, indeed, digressed from the subject of this chapter, but have, I hope, satisfactorily solved one of the most difficult passages of Scripture concerning which there has been much arguing in the attempt to state exactly what the sin was which Moses committed. Let what others have said be compared with our opinion and the truth will surely prevail.

Now, let me return to my subject. If a man will always carefully discriminate as regards his actions, directing them to the medium course, he will reach the highest degree of perfection possible to a human being, thereby approaching God, and sharing in His happiness. This is the most acceptable way of serving God which the sages, too, had in mind when they wrote the words, "He who orders his course aright is worthy of seeing the salvation of God, as it is said, 'To him that orders his course aright, will I show the salvation of God!' (Ps. 50:23). Do not read *vesam* but *vesham derekh*."* *Shumah* means "weighing" and "valuation." This is exactly the idea which we have explained in this chapter.

This is all we think necessary to be said on this subject.

CHAPTER VI: CONCERNING THE DIFFERENCE
BETWEEN THE SAINTLY (OR HIGHLY ETHICAL)
MAN AND HIM WHO (SUBDUES HIS PASSIONS
AND) HAS SELF-RESTRAINT

Philosophers maintain that though the man of self-restraint performs moral and praiseworthy deeds, yet he does them desiring and craving all the while for immoral deeds, but, subduing his passions and actively fighting against a longing to do those things to which his faculties, his desires, and his psychic disposition excite him, succeeds, though with constant vexation and irritation, in acting morally. The saintly man, however, is guided in his actions by that to which his inclination and disposition prompt him, in consequence of which he acts morally from innate longing and desire. Philosophers unanimously agree that the latter is superior to, and more perfect than, the one who has to curb his passions, although they add that it is possi-

*Sotah 5b; Moed Katan 5a.

ble for such a one to equal the saintly man in many regards. In general, however, he must necessarily be ranked lower in the scale of virtue, because there lurks within him the desire to do evil, and though he does not do it, the fact that his inclinations are all in that direction nevertheless signifies the presence of an immoral psychic disposition. Solomon, also, entertained the same idea when he said, "The soul of the wicked desires evil" (Prov. 21:10), and, in regard to the saintly man's rejoicing in doing good, and the discontent experienced by him who is not innately righteous, when required to act justly, he says, "It is bliss to the righteous to do justice, but torment to the evildoer" (ibid. 21:15). This is manifestly an agreement between Scripture and philosophy.

When, however, we consult the rabbis on this subject, it would seem that they consider him who desires iniquity and craves for it (but does not do it), more praiseworthy and perfect than the one who feels no torment at refraining from evil; and they even go so far as to maintain that the more praiseworthy and perfect a man is, the greater is his desire to commit iniquity and the more irritation does he feel at having to desist from it. This they express by saying, "Whosoever is greater than his neighbor has likewise greater evil inclinations" (Sukkah 52a). Again, as if this were not sufficient, they even go so far as to say that the reward of him who overcomes his evil inclination is commensurate with the torture occasioned by his resistance, which thought they express by the words, "According to the labor is the reward" (Ethics of the Fathers 5:23). Furthermore, they command that man should conquer his desires, but they forbid one to say, "I, by my nature, do not desire to commit such and such a transgression, even though the Law does not forbid it." Rabbi Simeon ben Gamaliel summed up this thought in the words, "Man should not say, 'I do not want to eat meat together with milk; I do not want to wear clothes made of a mixture of wool and linen; I do not want to enter into an incestuous marriage,' but he should say, 'I do indeed want to, yet I must not, for my Father in heaven has forbidden it.' "*

At first blush, by a superficial comparison of the sayings of the philosophers and the rabbis, one might be inclined to say that they contradict one another. Such, however, is not the case. Both are correct and, moreover, are not in disagreement in the least, as the evils which the philosophers term such—and of which they say that he

*Sifra, Lev. 20:26.

who has no longing for them is more to be praised than he who
desires them but conquers his passion—are things which all people
commonly agree are evils, such as the shedding of blood, theft, robbery, fraud, injury to one who has done no harm, ingratitude, contempt for parents, and the like. The prescriptions against these are
called commandments, about which the rabbis said, "If they had not
already been written in the Law, it would be proper to add them"
(Yoma 67b). Some of our later sages, who were infected with the
unsound principles of the Mutakallimun, called these rational laws.*
There is no doubt that a soul which has the desire for and lusts after
the above-mentioned misdeeds, is imperfect; that a noble soul has
absolutely no desire for any such crimes and experiences no struggle
in refraining from them. When, however, the rabbis maintain that he
who overcomes his desire has more merit and a greater reward (than
he who has no temptation), they say so only in reference to laws that
are ceremonial prohibitions. This is quite true, since, were it not for
the Law, they would not at all be considered transgressions. Therefore, the rabbis say, that man should permit his soul to entertain the
natural inclination for these things, but that the Law alone should
restrain him from them. Ponder over the wisdom of these men of
blessed memory manifest in the examples they adduce. They do not
declare, "Man should not say, 'I have no desire to kill, to steal and to
lie, but I have a desire for these things, yet what can I do, since my
Father in heaven forbids it!' " No, the instances they cite are all
from the ceremonial law, such as partaking of meat and milk
together, wearing clothes made of wool and linen, and entering into
consanguineous marriages. These and similar enactments are what
God called "My statutes," which, the rabbis say, are "statutes which I
(God) have enacted for you, which you have no right to subject to
criticism, which the nations of the world attack and which Satan
denounces, as for instance, the statutes concerning the red heifer, the
scapegoat, and so forth" (Yoma 67b). Those transgressions, however,
which the later sages called rational laws are termed commandments,
as the rabbis explained.†

It is now evident from all that we have said, what the transgressions are for which, if a man have no desire at all, he is on a higher
plane than he who has a longing, but controls his passion for them;
and it is also evident what the transgressions are of which the oppo-

*See *Guide*, introduction; III, ch. 26.
† See *Mishneh Torah*, Book VIII, Trespass, VIII, 8.

site is true. It is an astonishing fact that these two classes of expressions should be shown to be compatible with one another, but their content points to the truth of our explanation.

CHAPTER VIII: CONCERNING THE NATURAL
DISPOSITION OF MAN

It is impossible for man to be born endowed by nature from his very birth with either virtue or vice, just as it is impossible that he should be born skilled by nature in any particular art. It is possible, however, that through natural causes he may from birth be so constituted as to have a predilection for a particular virtue or vice, so that he will more readily practice it than any other. For instance, a man whose natural constitution inclines toward dryness, whose brain matter is clear and not overloaded with fluids, finds it much easier to learn, remember, and understand things than the phlegmatic man whose brain is encumbered with a great deal of humidity. But, if one who inclines constitutionally toward a certain excellence is left entirely without instruction, and if his faculties are not stimulated, he will undoubtedly remain ignorant. On the other hand, if one by nature dull and phlegmatic, possessing an abundance of humidity, is instructed and enlightened, he will—though with difficulty, it is true—gradually succeed in acquiring knowledge and understanding. In exactly the same way, he whose blood is somewhat warmer than is necessary has the requisite quality to make of him a brave man. Another, however, the temperament of whose heart is colder than it should be, is naturally inclined toward cowardice and fear, so that if he should be taught and trained to be a coward, he would easily become one. If, however, it be desired to make a brave man of him, he can without doubt become one, provided he receive the proper training which would require, of course, great exertion.

I have entered into this subject so you may not believe the absurd ideas of astrologers, who falsely assert that the constellation at the time of one's birth determines whether one is to be virtuous or vicious, the individual being thus necessarily compelled to follow out a certain line of conduct. We, on the contrary, are convinced that our

Law agrees with Greek philosophy, which substantiates with convincing proofs the contention that man's conduct is entirely in his own hands. No compulsion is exerted upon man, and no external influence is brought to bear that would constrain him to be either virtuous or vicious. Of course, as we have said above, a man may be by nature so constituted as to find it easy or hard, as the case may be, to do a certain thing; but that he must necessarily do, or refrain from doing, a certain thing is absolutely untrue. Were a man compelled to act according to the dictates of predestination, then the commands and prohibitions of the Law would become null and void and the Law would be completely false, since man would have no freedom of choice in what he does. Moreover, it would be useless, in fact absolutely in vain, for man to study, to instruct, or attempt to learn an art, as it would be entirely impossible for him, on account of the external force compelling him, according to the opinion of those who hold this view, to keep from doing a certain act, from gaining certain knowledge, or from acquiring a certain characteristic. Reward and punishment, too, would be pure injustice, both as regards man towards man, and as between God and man. Suppose, under such conditions, that Simeon should kill Reuben. Why should the former be punished, seeing that he was constrained to do the killing, and Reuben was predestined to be slain? How could the Almighty, who is just and righteous, chastise Simeon for a deed which it was impossible for him to leave undone, and which, though he strove with all his might, he would be unable to avoid? If such were the true state of affairs, all precautionary measures, such as building houses, providing means of subsistence, fleeing when one fears danger, and so forth, would be absolutely useless, for that which is decreed beforehand must necessarily happen. This theory is, therefore, positively unsound, contrary to reason and common sense, and, by attributing injustice to God (far be it from Him!), subversive of the fundamental principles of religion. In reality, the undoubted truth of the matter is that man has full sway over all his actions. If he wishes to do a thing, he does it; if he does not wish to do it, he need not, without any external compulsion controlling him. Therefore, God commanded man, saying, "See I have set before you this day life and good, death and evil . . . therefore choose life" (Deut. 30:15), giving us, as regards these, freedom of choice. Consequently, punishment is inflicted upon those who disobey, and reward granted to the obedient, as it is said, "If you will hearken," and "If you will not hearken" (Deut. 11:27–28). Learning and teaching are also necessary, according to the commands, "You shall teach them to your children" (*ibid.* 11:19), "and you shall learn them and observe to do them" (*ibid.* 5:1), and, similarly, all the other passages referring to the study of the commandments. It is also necessary to take all the precautionary measures laid down in the Law, such as "You shall make a battlement for your roof, that you bring not blood upon your house" (*ibid.* 22:8), "lest he die in the battle" (*ibid.* 20:5, 7), "wherein shall he sleep?" (Ex. 22:26), and "no man shall take to pledge the lower or the upper millstone" (Deut. 24:6), and many other passages in regard to precautions found in the Torah and the Prophets.

The statement found in the sayings of the rabbis, "All is in the power of God except the fear of God"* is, nevertheless, true, and in accord with what we have laid down here. Men are, however, very often prone to err in supposing that many of their actions, in reality the result of their own free will, are forced upon them, as, for instance, marrying a certain woman, or acquiring a certain amount of money. Such a supposition is untrue. If a man espouses and marries a woman legally, then she becomes his lawful wife, and by his marrying her he has fulfilled the divine command to increase and multiply. God, however, does not decree the fulfillment of a commandment. If, on the other hand, a man has consummated with a woman an unlawful marriage, he has committed a transgression. But God does not decree that a man shall sin. Again, suppose a man robs another of money, steals from him, or cheats him, and then uttering a false oath, denies it; if we should say that God had destined that this sum should pass into the hands of the one and out of the possession of the other, God would be preordaining an act of iniquity. Such, however, is not the case. Rather, all of man's actions are subject to his free will and undoubtedly comply with or transgress God's commands; for, as has been explained in Chapter II, the commands and prohibitions of the Law refer only to those actions which man has absolute free choice to perform or not to perform. Moreover, to this faculty of the soul (i.e., the freedom of the will) "the fear of God" is subservient, and is, in consequence, not predestined by God but, as we have explained, is entirely in the power of the human free will. By the word "all," the rabbis meant to designate only natural

*Berakhot 33b; Niddah 16b; Megillah 25a.

phenomena which are not influenced by the will of man, as whether a person is tall or short, whether it is rainy or dry, whether the air is pure or impure, and all other such things that happen in the world which have no connection with man's conduct.

In making this assertion that obedience or disobedience to the Law of God does not depend upon the power or will of God, but solely upon that of man himself, the sages followed the dictum of Jeremiah, who said, "Out of the mouth of God there comes neither the bad nor the good" (Lam. 3:38). By the words "the bad" he meant vice, and by "the good," virtue; and, accordingly, he maintains that God does not preordain that any man should be vicious or virtuous. Since this is so, it behooves man to mourn and weep over the sins and the transgressions he has committed, as he has sinned of his own free will in accordance with what the prophet says, "Wherefore should a living man mourn? Let every man mourn because of his sins" (ibid. 3:39). He continues, then, to tell us that the remedy for this disease is in our own hands, for, as our misdeeds were the result of our own free will, we have, likewise, the power to repent of our evil deeds, and so he goes on to say, "Let us search through and investigate our ways, and let us return to the Lord. Let us lift up our heart with our hands to God in the heavens" (ibid. 3:40–41).

The theory generally accepted by people and found in rabbinical and prophetical writings, that man's sitting and rising and all of his movements are governed by the will and desire of God, is true only in one respect. For instance, when a stone is thrown into the air and falls to the ground, it is correct to say that the stone fell in accordance with the will of God, for it is true that God decreed that the earth and all its elements should be the center of attraction, so that when any part of it is is thrown into the air, it is attracted back to the center. Similarly, all particles of fire ascend according to God's will, which preordained that fire should go upward. But it is wrong to suppose that when a certain part of the earth is thrown upward God wills at that very moment that it should fall. The Mutakallimun are, however, of a different opinion in this regard, for I have heard them say that the Divine Will is constantly at work, decreeing everything from time to time.* We do not agree with them, but believe that the Divine Will ordained everything at creation and that all things, at all times, are regulated by the laws of nature and run their natural

---

*This is a denial of natural law. See Commentary on the Mishnah, Avot 5:6.

course in accordance with what Solomon said, "As it was so it will ever be, as it was made so it continues, and there is nothing new under the sun" (Eccles. 1:9). This occasioned the sages to say that all miracles which deviate from the natural course of events, whether they have already occurred or, according to promise, are to take place in the future, were foreordained by the Divine Will during the six days of creation, nature being then so constituted that those miracles which were to happen really did afterward take place. Then, when such an occurrence happens at its proper time, it may have been regarded as an absolute innovation, whereas in reality it was not.

The rabbis expatiate upon this subject in Midrash Kohelet and in other writings, one of their statements in reference to this matter being, "Everything follows its natural course."* In everything that they said, you will always find that the rabbis (peace be unto them!) avoided referring to the Divine Will as determining a particular event at a particular time. When, therefore, they said that man rises and sits down in accordance with the will of God, their meaning was that, when man was first created, his nature was so determined that rising up and sitting down were to be optional to him; but they did not mean that God wills at any special moment that man should or should not get up, as He determines at any given time that a certain stone should or should not fall to the ground. The sum and sub- stance of the matter is, then, that you should believe that just as God willed that man should be upright in stature, broadchested, and have fingers, likewise did He will that man should move or rest of his own accord, and that his actions should be such as his own free will dictates to him without any outside influence or restraint, which fact God clearly states in the truthful Law, which elucidates this problem when it says, "Behold, the man is become as one of us to know good and evil" (Gen. 3:22). The Targum, in paraphrasing this passage, explains the meaning of the words *mimmennu ladaat tov vara*. Man has become the only being in the world who possesses a characteristic which no other being has in common with him. What is this charac- teristic? It is that by and of himself man can distinguish between good and evil and do that which he pleases with absolutely no re- straint. Since this is so, it would have even been possible for him to have stretched out his hand and, taking of the tree of life, to have eaten of its fruit, and thus live forever.

*Avodah Zarah 54b.

Since it is an essential characteristic of man's makeup that he should of his own free will act morally or immorally, doing just as he chooses, it becomes necessary to teach him the ways of righteousness, to command and exhort him, to punish and reward him according to his deserts. It behooves man also to accustom himself to the practice of good deeds until he acquires the virtues corresponding to those good deeds; and, furthermore, to abstain from evil deeds so that he may eradicate the vices that may have taken root in him. Let him not suppose that his characteristics have reached such a state that they are no longer subject to change, for any one of them may be altered from the good to the bad and vice versa; and, moreover, all in accordance with his own free will. To confirm this theory, we have mentioned all these facts concerning the observances and the transgressions of the Law. . . .

There is one thing more relating to this problem about which we must say a few words in order to treat in a comprehensive manner the subject matter of this chapter Although I had not intended at all to speak of it, necessity forces me to do so. This topic is the prescience of God. It is with an argument based on this notion that our views are opposed by those who believe that man is predestined by God to do good or evil and that man has no choice as to his conduct since his volition is dependent upon God. The reason for their belief they base on the following statement. "Does God know or does He not know that a certain individual will be good or bad? If you say He knows, then it necessarily follows that man is compelled to act as God knew beforehand he would act, otherwise God's knowledge would be imperfect. If you say that God does not know in advance, then great absurdities and destructive religious theories will result." Listen, therefore, to what I shall tell you, reflect well upon it, for it is unquestionably the truth.

It is, indeed, an axiom of the science of the divine, i.e., metaphysics, that God (may He be blessed!) does not know by means of knowledge and does not live by means of life. Therefore He and His knowledge may not be considered two different things in the sense that this proposition is true of man; for man is distinct from knowledge, and knowledge from man, in consequence of which they are two different things. If God knew by means of knowledge, He would necessarily be a plurality and the primal essence would be composite, that is, consisting of God Himself, the knowledge by which He knows, the life by which He lives, the power by which He has strength, and similarly of all His attributes. I shall only mention one argument, simple and easily understood by all, though there are strong and convincing arguments and proofs that solve this difficulty. It is manifest that God is identical with His attributes and His attributes with Him, so that it may be said that He is the knowledge, the knower, and the known, and that He is the life, the living, and the source of His own life, the same being true of His other attributes. This conception is very hard to grasp and you should not hope to understand it thoroughly by two or three lines in this treatise. There can only be imparted to you a vague idea of it.

Now, in consequence of this important axiom, the Hebrew language does not allow the expression *Hé Adonai* (the life of God) as it does *Hé Faraoh* (the life of Pharaoh), where the word *hé* (in the construct state) is related to the following noun, for the thing possessed and the possessor (in this case) are two different things. Such a construction cannot be used in regard to the relation of a thing to itself. Since the life of God is His essence, and His essence is His life, not being separate and distinct from each other, the word "life," therefore, cannot be put in the construct state, but the expression *Hai Adonai* (the living God) is used, the purpose of which is to denote that God and His life are one.*

Another accepted axiom of metaphysics is that human reason cannot fully conceive God in His true essence, because of the perfection of God's essence and the imperfection of our own reason, and because His essence is not due to causes through which it may be known. Furthermore, the inability of our reason to comprehend Him may be compared to the inability of our eyes to gaze at the sun, not because of the weakness of the sun's light, but because that light is more powerful than that which seeks to gaze into it. Much that has been said on this subject is self-evident truth.

From what we have said, it has been demonstrated also that we cannot comprehend God's knowledge, that our minds cannot grasp it all, for He is His knowledge, and His knowledge is He. This is an especially striking idea, but those (who raise the question of God's knowledge of the future) fail to grasp it to their dying day. They are, it is true, aware that the divine essence, as it is, is incomprehensible, yet they strive to comprehend God's knowledge, so that they may know it, but this is, of course, impossible. If the human reason could

*See *Mishneh Torah*, Book I, Basic Principles, II, 10; Repentance, V, 5.

grasp His knowledge, it would be able also to define His essence, since both are one and the same, as the perfect knowledge of God is the comprehension of Him as He is in His essence, which consists of His knowledge, His will, His life, and all His other majestic attributes. Thus, we have shown how utterly futile is the pretension to define His knowledge. All that we can comprehend is that just as we know that God exists, so are we cognizant of the fact that He knows. If we are asked, "What is the nature of God's knowledge?," we answer that we do not know any more than we know the nature of His true existence. Scripture finds fault, moreover, with him who tries to grasp the truth of the divine existence, as we see by the words, "Can you by searching find out God? Can you find out the Almighty to perfection?" (Job 11:7).

Reflect, then, upon all that we have said; that man has control over his actions, that it is by his own determination that he does either right or wrong without, in either case, being controlled by fate, and that, as a result of this divine commandment, teaching, preparation, reward, and punishment are proper. Of this there is absolutely no doubt. As regards, however, the character of God's knowledge, how He knows everything, this is, as we have explained, beyond the reach of human ken.

This is all that we purposed saying in this chapter, and it is now time to bring our words to an end and begin the interpretation of this treatise to which these eight chapters are an introduction.

*T*HE following passages were selected because of their intrinsic, substantive interest, illustrating as they do the scope and purpose of this commentary as well as the range of hermeneutical techniques and historical-philosophical concerns. In addition, the thoughtful reader may be especially enlightened concerning the all-pervasive problem of continuity and change in the thought of Maimonides, because many of these passages demonstrate the extent to which ideas elaborated in the Mishneh Torah and Guide are already present here embryonically or allusively. Successive analysis of certain passages, extracted from different works composed over a period of three decades, should enable the reader to evaluate the methodological merit and legitimacy of relying upon an early work like this to resolve problems in the later works.

Some of the axial themes treated are: reward and punishment; the relation of ethical and intellectual virtues; pride and humility; free will; the rule of the golden mean and necessary exceptions to this rule; the economic self-sufficiency of the scholar; law and ethics; the relation of the individual to society. The remarks on the origins of Karaism are significant. One invariably notices the ubiquitous emphasis on the pursuit of wisdom.

The repeated references in the text to the Eight Chapters—
the introduction to this part of his Commentary on the Mishnah—
demonstrate beyond doubt that Maimonides considered that work to
be an integral part of the entire commentary and not a special philosophical excursus of interest only to a restricted audience.

CHAPTER 1

*I   Moses received the Torah at Sinai and transmitted it to Joshua,
and Joshua to the Elders . . . .*

I   In our introduction to this treatise (*i.e.* the *Commentary on the
Mishnah*) we have elucidated how the form of the tradition evolved.
The only intention here is to explain the words of the saintly men
and the moralists in order to stimulate the acquisition of some of the
attributes from them—those whose benefit is great. Here we shall
prolong in cautioning against some of the vices, for their detriment is
great. As for the rest, I shall only define words and some of the subjects, for except for a few of them, their meanings are clear.

*III   Antigonos of Sokho received the tradition from Simeon the
Righteous. He used to say: "Be not like servants who serve the
master upon the condition of receiving a gift, but be like servants
who serve the master not upon the condition of receiving a gift. And
let the fear of Heaven be upon you."*

III   The benevolence that a man will bestow upon one to whom he
does not owe a favor would be termed a *gift*. Indeed, he would do
this by way of kindness and graciousness, as in the instance where a
man will say to his servant, or to his minor son, or to his wife, "Do
such and such for me and I shall give you a *denar* or two"—this constitutes the difference between a gift and a wage, for a wage is what
is given as a matter of legal obligation.

This saintly man said (to his disciples): "You should not serve
the Lord, may He be blessed, upon the condition that He be benef-
icent to you and bestow kindness upon you, and thus expect a
reward and serve Him for its sake. Rather, serve Him as servants who
do not expect a beneficence or an act of kindness." By means of this

he intended that they should serve out of love—as we stated in the tenth chapter of Sanhedrin. Nevertheless, he did not exempt them from (the obligation to serve Him out of) fear, and he said that although you serve Him out of love do not utterly forsake fear; (therefore his statement,) "And let the fear of Heaven be upon you." For the precept concerning fear was mentioned in the Torah, as it was said, "Fear the Lord your God . . . (Deut. 6:13). And the sages said: "Serve out of love, serve out of fear"; and they said, "One who serves out of love will not forget a thing of what he was commanded to do, and one who serves out of fear will not do a thing against which he was cautioned." For fear has an important function in the negative precepts, certainly in the precepts whose rationale rests on revelation alone.*

This sage had two disciples, one named Zadok and the other named Boethus. When they heard him deliver this statement, they departed from him. The one said to his colleague, "Behold, the master expressly stated that man has neither reward nor punishment, and there is no expectation at all." (They said this) because they did not understand his intention. The one lent support to his colleague and they departed from the community and forsook the Torah.

A sect banded around the one, and another sect around his colleague. The sages termed them "Sadducees and Boethusians." Since they were unable to consolidate the masses according to what they perceived of the faith—for this evil belief divided the consolidated, it would certainly not consolidate the divided—they feigned belief in the matter (of the written Torah) because they could not falsify it before the multitude. For had they brought it forth from their mouths, meaning to say, (their disbelief in) the words of the Torah, they would have killed them. Therefore, each said to his party that he believes in the Torah but disputes the tradition since it is not authentic. (They said) this in order to exempt themselves from the precepts of the tradition and the decrees and ordinances inasmuch as they could not thrust aside everything, the written (Torah) and the tradition. Moreover, the path for interpretation was broadened for them. Since the interpretation became a matter of their choice, each, according to his intention, could be lenient in what he might wish or be stringent in what he might wish. (This was possible) because he did not believe at all in the fundamental principle. They, however,

*See *Mishneh Torah*, Book I, Repentance, ch. X; *Commentary on Helek*; *Book of Commandments*, number 3.

sought to deceive in matters which were accepted by only some people.

From the time that these evil sects went forth, they have been termed "Karaites" in these lands*—meaning to say, Egypt. However, their appellation according to the sages is "Sadducees and Boethusians." They are the ones who began to contest the tradition and to interpret all the passages (of the Torah) according to what appeared to them without at all hearkening to a sage; the reverse of what the One to be blessed stated, ". . . according to the Torah which they shall instruct you and according to the judgment which they shall tell you, you shall do, you shall not turn aside either to the right or to the left from the sentence which they shall declare to you" (Deut. 17:11).

> XVII   Simeon, his son, said: "All my days I have grown up among the sages, and I have found nothing better for a person than silence. The expounding is not the fundamental point, but the practice. And all who multiply words occasion sin."

XVII   The sage has said, "In the multitude of words there lacks not trespass . . ." (Prov. 10:19). The reason for this is that the multitude of words (contains words that) are additional, superfluous, and sinful, as I shall presently explain. For when a man multiplies words he will assuredly trespass, since it is impossible that there would not be among his words a word that is not proper to utter. Of the signs of wise men is a lessening of words, and of the signs of fools is a multitude of words, as it is said, ". . . and a fool's voice through a multitude of words" (Eccles. 5:2). The sages have said that a lessening of words is evidence of the high station of the parents and that a man is of pure lineage. They said: "In Babylon, silence is the mark of pure lineage" (Kiddushin 71b).†

I say that according to the requirement of the Torah, speech should be classified into five categories: 1) Prescribed, 2) Cautioned Against (or Prohibited), 3) Rejected, 4) Desired, 5) Permitted.

The first category is the prescribed, namely, studying the Torah, teaching it, and studying its rabbinic learning. This is an obligatory positive precept, as it is said, ". . . and speak of them . . ." (Deut. 6:7), and it is equivalent to all the precepts. What was stated as admonition with regard to study is so extensive that this treatise cannot contain part of it.

*See *Mishneh Torah*, introduction, end.
†See *Mishneh Torah*, Book I, Moral Dispositions, II, 4–5.

The second category is the prohibited and cautioned-against speech, such as bearing false witness, speaking falsehood, talebearing, and cursing. The teachings of the Torah offer guidance regarding this category; similarly, obscene speech and slander.

The third category is the rejected speech which has no benefit in it to man for his soul—purporting neither to transgression nor to rebelliousness, such as most of the discussions of the multitude regarding what has happened and what was, what are the customs of a certain king in his palace, how was So-and-So's death caused, or how did a certain person become rich. The sages term these discussions "idle talk." Saintly men personally persevered to forsake this category of speech. It was said of Rav, the disciple of Rabbi Hiyya, that in all his days he never indulged in idle talk. Also pertaining to this category, where a man will denounce virtue or laud vice, be they moral or intellectual.

The fourth category is the desired, namely, speech that is in praise of the intellectual virtues or the moral virtues and simultaneously in denunciation of either of the two types of vices. (As an example,) to bestir the soul to virtues through prose and poetry and to preclude it from vices through those means themselves. Thus, to praiseworthy men and to extol their virtues in order that their customs will appear good in the sight of men that they may walk in their ways; and to denounce evil men for their vices in order that their deeds and memory will be condemned in the sight of men that they may remove from them and will not conduct themselves according to their customs. This category, meaning to say, learning the noble attributes and removing from the base attributes, would be termed derekh eretz—proper conduct.

The fifth category is the permitted, namely, speech concerning what specifically applies to man—one's business interest, livelihood, food, drink, clothing, and the rest of what one requires. This is permitted, it is neither desired nor rejected. However, if he wishes, he may speak what he might wish concerning it; and if he wishes, he need not speak. Pertaining to this category, a man is praised when he lessens words in it. Moralists are cautioned against multiplying words in it. However, the prohibited and the rejected require neither an admonition nor an exhortation, for it is proper to keep absolutely silent on it.

Concerning the prescribed and the desired—were a man able to speak of it all his days, it would be excellent. However, one needs to be cautious of two things. The first of them—that his deeds be consistent with his words, as they said: "Pleasant are the words that emanate from the mouth of one who practices them"; and it was to this subject that he referred when he said, "The expounding is not the fundamental point, but the practice." The sages say to the righteous that he should teach the virtues, as they said: "Expound, because it becomes you to expound"; and the prophet said, "Rejoice in the Lord, you who are righteous; praise is comely for the upright . . ." (Ps. 33:1). The other matter is brevity. One should strive to multiply the subjects with few words, and that the reverse should not be the case—and it is, as they said: "One should always instruct his students by way of brevity."

Know, that poetical compositions, in whichever language they may be, should be examined with regard to their themes (in order to determine) whether they follow a manner of speech which we classified. Indeed, I explained this even though this is clear, inasmuch as I have seen elders and saintly men of our coreligionists when they were at a wine banquet, such as a wedding or some other occasion, and were a man to wish to recite an Arabic poem, even if the theme of that poem were the praise of courage or generosity, and it is of the category of the Desired, or the praises of wine, they would protest this with every manner of protest, for in their opinion it is not permitted to listen to it. However, were the bard to recite any manner of Hebrew poem, they would not protest it, and it would not be evil in their sight despite there being in those words (themes that pertain to) the Cautioned Against or the Rejected. This is utter folly; since speech shall be neither forbidden, nor permitted, nor desired, nor rejected, nor prescribed in its utterance from the standpoint of the language utilized, but from the standpoint of its subject.* For if the theme of that poem were virtue, it would be required to recite it in whichever language it may be. If, however, the purpose of that poem were vice, in whichever language it may be, it is prohibited to recite it.

I also have an addendum pertaining to this. For were there two poems, both having the same theme—arousing the power of lust, praising it, and causing the soul to rejoice in it—it is vice, and it is of the category of rejected speech because it stimulates and bestirs a base attribute, as was made clear from our words in the fourth chapter. However, were one of the two poems Hebrew, and the other Arabic or some other non-Hebrew language, listening to the Hebrew and articulating it would be more objectionable according to the

*A similar idea is expressed in *Mishneh Torah*, Book II, Shema, III, 5.

Torah due to the exaltedness of the language, for it should only be utilized for noble purposes*—certainly (its use would be prohibited) if it were combined with it by inserting in it a verse from the Torah or from the Song of Songs associated with that theme. For then it departs from the category of the Rejected to the category of the Prohibited and the Cautioned Against, for the Torah prohibited making the words of prophecy into forms of song dealing with vices and unseemly matters.

CHAPTER 2

IV   Hillel said: "Do not separate yourself from the community, and do not be sure of yourself until the day of your death. . . ."

IV   In the fourth chapter we have made known that one should not separate from the community except in accordance with their (i.e., its members') corruption, as we explained it there.†

V   The empty man does not fear sin, the ignorant man cannot be saintly. . . .

V   "The empty man" is one who does not have either wisdom or (moral) attributes. "The ignorant man" is one who does not have intellectual virtues but has some moral virtues.‡

X   Rabbi Eliezer said: "Let your friend's honor be dear to you as your own; be not easy to provoke; and repent one day before your death. . . ."

X   "Be not easy to provoke" (means) do not ready yourself to anger and fury. They have hyperbolized in denouncing anger and fury, and the severest among their teachings is their statement: "Everyone who is given to anger is as if he worships an idol" (Shabbat 105b). They juxtaposed this with the statement, "Neither let there be a strange god in you (i.e., anger) nor shall you bow down to a foreign god (i.e., idolatry)" (Ps. 81:10), meaning to say that the two matters are equal.**

*See *Guide*, III, ch. 8.
†See *Mishneh Torah*, Book I, Moral Dispositions, VI, 1.
‡See *Guide*, III, ch. 54.
**See *Mishneh Torah*, Book I, Moral Dispositions, II, 3.

"And repent one day before your death." One does not know when one will die—perhaps today, perhaps tomorrow; thus let all one's days be in repentance.*

> XII   Rabbi Yose said: "Let your friend's property be dear to you as your own; prepare yourself to study Torah, for it is not yours by inheritance; and let all your deeds be for the sake of Heaven."

XII   In the eighth chapter we have explained the meaning of pre-disposition and predilection, (viz.) that it is necessary for man to prepare himself for (the acquisition of) virtues. In the fifth chapter we explained the meaning of his statement, "and let all your deeds be for the sake of Heaven."†

> XV   Rabbi Tarfon said: "The day is short, the task is great, and the master of the house is urgent."

XV   This is a parable concerning the brevity of years, the great amount of wisdom (to be acquired) and man's slothfulness in seeking it, despite the great amount of recompense for it, and despite the multitude of the Torah's admonitions and its exhortations to seek wisdom and learning.

CHAPTER 3

> IX   Rabbi Hanina ben Dosa said: "Everyone whose fear of sin precedes his wisdom, his wisdom endures. Whereas everyone whose wisdom precedes his fear of sin, his wisdom will not endure." He used to say: "Everyone whose deeds exceed his wisdom, his wisdom endures. Whereas everyone whose wisdom exceeds his deeds, his wisdom will not endure."

IX   Behold, this matter is also agreed upon by the philosophers: when the habit of (moral) virtues precedes wisdom until it will be a firm trait, and afterward one were to study wisdom which would stimulate him toward those good qualities, he would increase in

---

*Op. cit., Repentance, VII, 2.
†See Mishneh Torah, Book I, Moral Dispositions, III, 3.

delight and love of wisdom and in determination to add to it, since it would bestir him toward what was habituated. However, when evil traits precede, and afterward one were to study, wisdom would preclude him from what he would desire through habit. Wisdom would be burdensome to him and he would forsake it.*

> XV   All is foreseen yet the authority is given, and the world is judged by goodness, and everything is (reckoned) according to the multitude of the deed.

XV   This statement incorporates very important matters, and it is fitting that this statement be attributed to Rabbi Akiva. This is its explanation in brief, and it is offered on condition that you are aware of everything that was previously stated in the introductory chapters. He said, "Everything that is in the world is known before Him, may He be blessed, and He is conscious of it, as it was said, 'All is foreseen.'" Subsequently, he said, "Do not think that since He is cognizant of deeds, predetermination would be (logically) imperative"; that is to say that man would be coerced in his deeds with regard to any deed. Such is not the case; rather, the authority is in the power of man in what he may do, as it was said, "Yet the authority is given," meaning to say that every man is given authority, as we explained in the eighth chapter.†

(With reference to . . . "and the world is judged by goodness,") he said that the judgment of the Lord, may He be blessed, with men is indeed through kindness and goodness and not according to the judgment that is fitting for them. As the One to be blessed made clear from His ways, He said, ". . . long-suffering and abundant in kindness and truth . . ." (Ex. 34:6), and our rabbis, may their memory be blessed, said: "Long-suffering to the righteous and to the wicked" (Eruvin 22a); and the prophet said, "The Lord is good to all . . ." (Ps. 145:9).‡

(With reference to ". . . and everything is [reckoned] according to the multitude of the deed,") subsequently, he said that virtues will not be attained by a man according to the magnitude of the deed, but according to the multitude of the number of the deeds. That is, that virtues will indeed be attained by repeating the good

*See, in light of this, Guide, III, ch. 27 ff.; Mishneh Torah, Book I, Basic Principles, IV, 13.

†See Mishneh Torah, Book I, Repentance, ch. V; Eight Chapters.

‡See Mishneh Torah, Book XII, Slaves, IX, 8; Guide, I, ch. 54.

deeds many times. With this (method) he will attain a firm trait—and not when a man performs a single major act of the good acts, for through this alone he will not attain a firm trait. The illustration of this: When a man gave to one who is deserving a thousand gold pieces all at once, (that is,) to one man, and he did not give anything to another man, he will not achieve the attribute of generosity through this single major deed, just as it is attained by one who contributed a thousand gold pieces in a thousand instances, and gave all of those gold pieces from the standpoint of generosity. Inasmuch as this one repeated the practice of generosity a thousand times, he attained a firm trait, whereas that one, in only one instance was his soul powerfully stimulated toward a good act, and thereafter it (i.e., the stimulus) ceased from him. Thus, according to the Torah, the recompense for one who redeemed a captive for one hundred *denars*, or dealt charitably toward a poor man to the extent of one hundred *denars* which was sufficient for his need, is not on a par with the recompense for one who redeemed ten captives, or fulfilled the need of ten poor men, each to the extent of ten *denars*. It is with this (illustration) that the analogy is made, and this is the meaning of his statement, ". . . according to the multitude of the deed," not, however, "according to the magnitude of the deed."*

CHAPTER 4

IV   Rabbi Levitas of Yavneh said: "Be exceedingly humble in spirit. . . ."

IV   In the introductory chapters we have explained and noted that modesty is of the moral virtues, and it is midway between pride and humbleness of spirit, and it has no other appellation except "modesty." Pride, however, has many appellations in the Hebrew language: "arrogant," "conceited," "proud," and "exalted." Of the appellations applied by the sages, may their memory be blessed, there are: "insolent," "haughty," and "overbearing." But over against these is "humbleness of spirit."

In the fourth chapter we have explained that, from the stand-

*See *Mishneh Torah*, Book I, Moral Dispositions, I, 7; *Eight Chapters*, ch. IV.

point of a precautionary measure, a man should incline a bit toward one of the extremes so that he will stand at the median of deeds. However, with regard to this attribute alone among all the rest, meaning to say, with regard to pride, the rabbis tended all the way to the extreme of deficiency; that is, they inclined completely to humbleness of spirit in order that they would not leave any room for pride in their souls.*

> V Rabbi Ishmael (his son) said: "One who learns in order to teach is afforded the opportunity to learn and to teach. Whereas one who learns in order to practice is afforded the opportunity to learn, to teach, to observe, and to practice." Rabbi Zadok said: "Do not fashion it into a crown with which to magnify yourself, nor into a spade with which to dig." Thus Hillel used to say, "And he who makes use of the crown will perish." Hence you may deduce: whoever derives benefit from the words of the Torah removes his life from the world.

V After I decided that I would not discuss this counsel because it is clear, and also because of my awareness that my teachings concerning it would not appeal to most of the great sages of the Torah, and perhaps to all of them, I revoked my decision and I shall discuss it without regard to either previous or current authorities.

Know that this which he said, "that you shall not fashion the Torah into a spade with which to dig," is to say, do not consider it an implement with which to earn a livelihood; and he explained and said that everyone who will derive benefit in this world through the honor of the Torah removes his life from the world, meaning, from the life of the world to come. People distorted this obvious language and they cast it (i.e., the correct meaning) behind their backs, and they depended upon the literal meanings of the words, for they did not understand them; therefore, I shall explain them. They established portions for themselves which devolved upon individuals and upon communities, and by means of utter folly they brought people to think that this is obligatory, and that it is proper that they aid scholars and students and men who are engaged in the Torah and for whom the Torah represents their craft. All this is in error. We will not find in the Torah nor in the teachings of the sages a teaching which will verify it, nor a basis upon which it will be supported at all.

For were we to reflect upon the teachings of our rabbis, may their memory be blessed, with regard to them we will not find that

---

*See *Mishneh Torah*, Book I, Moral Dispositions, II, 3.

they requested money from people, nor did they collect money for honored and esteemed academies, nor for Exilarchs, nor for their judges, nor for disseminators of the Torah, nor for any of the great nor for the rest of the people of the folk. Instead, we will find in every generation, in all their communities, that among them there were poor in the extreme of poverty, as well as very wealthy in the extreme of wealth. Far be it from me to suspect that those generations were not kind and charitable. For indeed, had that poor man stretched forth his hand to take, they would have filled his house with gold and pearls, but he was unwilling. Instead, he was content with his work through which he was supported, whether in abundance or in scarcity, and he spurned what people possessed because the Torah precluded him from this.

You are aware that Hillel the Elder was a wood hewer and he used to study under Shemaiah and Avtalyon, and he was poor in the extreme of poverty. His station was pre-eminent as you are aware from his disciples who were compared to Moses, Aaron, and Joshua, and the least significant among his disciples was Rabbi Yohanan ben Zakkai. The discerning have no doubt that, had he instructed the people of his generation (that it was proper for him) to derive benefit from them, they would not have allowed him to hew wood. And Rabbi Hanina ben Dosa for whom a Heavenly Voice went forth and proclaimed, "The entire world is sustained only because of My son Hanina, and as for My son Hanina, he is satisfied with a kav of carobs from one Sabbath eve to the next"—he did not request from people. And Karna was a judge in the Land of Israel and he was a water drawer. When litigants would come before him he used to say, "Give me one who will draw water in my place," or, "Give me (an amount) sufficient for (the loss incurred by) my idleness and I will judge for you."

The Israelites of their generation were neither cruel nor unkind. Nor do we find a sage of the needy sages who denounced the people of his generation because they did not enrich him. Far be it from them. Instead, they themselves were saintly men, believers in the truth for its own sake, and they believed in the Lord, may He be blessed, and in the Torah of Moses through which man will merit the life of the world to come, and they did not allow themselves to request money from people. They understood that taking it constituted a profanation of the Name in the sight of the multitude, inasmuch as they would think that the Torah is merely another trade through which a man may earn a livelihood, and it would be despised in their sight, thus he who does this ". . . contemned the word of the Lord. . . "

Indeed, those who are bold to dispute the truth and the plain passages, and who are overt in taking people's money either with their consent or against their consent, have led astray by means of the incidents that will be found in the Gemara regarding persons who have bodily impairments, or regarding elderly people who are advanced in years so that it is impossible for them to perform work. For they have no recourse but to take money from others; for if not, what shall they do—are they to die? The Torah did not command this.*

> VI   Rabbi Yose said: "Whoever honors the Torah is himself honored by mankind. Whereas whoever dishonors the Torah is himself dishonored by mankind."

VI   "The honor of the Torah"—that is when one displays zealousness in practicing it, and he will honor the sages who sustain it, and the books which they authored on it. Thus, dishonoring the Torah is the opposite of the three.†

> VIII   He used to say: "Do not judge alone, for there is none who may judge alone save One. . . ."

VIII   The Torah permitted a man who is a publicly acknowledged expert to judge alone, as we explained in Sanhedrin. However, this (allowance) is a teaching of the Torah, and he partly cautioned against it here from the standpoint of ethics and not from the standpoint of a prohibition.

CHAPTER 5

> VI   Ten things were created on the eve of Sabbath at twilight, and these are they: the mouth of the earth, the mouth of the well, the mouth of the donkey, the bow, the manna, the rod, the Shamir, the letters, the writing, and the tablets. Some say also the evil

*See *Mishneh Torah*, Book I, Study, III, 10–11.

†See *Mishneh Torah*, Book II, Sefer Torah, X, 11; Book XIV, Sanhedrin, XXIV, 10.

spirits, the grave of Moses, and the ram of Abraham our Father. Some say also the tongs made with tongs.

VI   "Also the tongs made with tongs"—who made the first? In the eighth chapter we mentioned to you that they (*i.e.*, the sages) did not believe in the periodic change of the Divine Will. Rather, (they believed) that at the beginning of the fashioning of the phenomena, He instituted into nature that through them there would be fashioned all that would be fashioned. Whether the phenomenon which would be fashioned would be frequent, namely, a natural phenomenon, or would be an infrequent change, namely, a sign, they are all equal. Therefore, they said that (at twilight) on the sixth day He instituted into the nature of the earth that Korah and his company would sink (into it), and concerning the well, that it would bring forth the water, and concerning the donkey, that it would speak, and similarly for the rest.*

XXIII   *Ben Hé Hé said: "According to the suffering is the reward."*

XXIII   And Ben Hé Hé said, "Your recompense shall be according to what you will suffer in the (study of the) Torah."† They said: "The only segment of wisdom that will endure is what you will learn through travail, toil, and awe of the teacher."‡

*See *Guide,* II, ch. 29.
†See *Eight Chapters,* ch. VI.
‡See *Mishneh Torah,* Book I, Study, III, 12; IV, 5.

*T*AKING his cue from the underlying text which refers to those who have a share in the world to come, Maimonides describes five views concerning the nature of the world to come, i.e., the ultimate bliss which awaits the deserving, righteous person. He emphasizes sharply—as he does also in the Mishneh Torah, Book I, Repentance, ch. X—that the only genuine motive for all religious behavior is disinterested love of God with no craving for any reward whatsoever.

Inasmuch as the primary source of information about these matters is the aggadah, Maimonides analyzes three possible methods for the interpretation of aggadic texts—it is worthwhile to compare this with the Guide, II, ch. 29 and III, ch. 43. He rejects the views both of those who blithely and unqualifiedly accept aggadah as literal exegesis and of those who ridicule it because of its apparent folly and deficiency; he insists upon the need for rationalistic, allegorical interpretation in order to preserve the credibility and respectability of Judaism (see Guide, III, ch. 31). This outer-directed motif, the imperative to project a favorable and attractive image of Judaism, is boldly underscored.

The text concludes with the enumeration of the Thirteen Principles upon which Judaism is based—the common beliefs and commitments of "all Israelites." This systematic formulation of a specific number of basic principles of belief provided the impetus for the creation of an extensive literature on dogma and triggered a long, sometimes acrimonious debate concerning the role of dogma in Judaism.

THE MISHNAH

> All Jews have a share in the world to come, as it is said, "Your people also shall be all righteous, they shall inherit the land forever; the branch of My planting, the work of My hands wherein I glory" (Is. 60:21). But these have no share in the world to come: one who says that the resurrection of the dead is not taught in the Torah; one who says that the Torah is not from heaven; and the atheist. Rabbi Akiva adds: one who reads the apocryphal books or who utters charms over a wound saying, "I will put none of the diseases upon you which I have put upon the Egyptians, for I am the Lord that heals you" (Ex. 15:26). Abba Saul adds: the one who pronounces the letters of the Tetragrammaton.

I must speak now of the great fundamental principles of our faith. Know that the masters of Torah hold differing opinions concerning the good which will come to a person as a result of fulfilling the commandments which God commanded us through Moses our Teacher. As a consequence of their different understanding of the problem, they also hold widely different opinions concerning the evil which the transgressor suffers. So much confusion has invaded their opinions that it is almost impossible to find anyone whose opinion is uncontaminated by error.

One group thinks that the expected good is the Garden of Eden, a place in which one eats and drinks without any physical work or effort. They also believe that there houses are made of precious stones, beds of silk, rivers flow with wine and fragrant oils, and many other things of that sort. This group believes that the evil is Gehenna, a place of raging fire, in which bodies are burned and agonies of all sorts are inflicted upon men. Their descriptions of these afflictions are told at great length. This group adduces proof for their opinions from the words of our sages and from passages in the Scripture whose literal meaning seems either wholly or largely compatible with what they say.

A second group asserts that the good for which we hope is the Days of the Messiah, in whose time all men will be angels, and all of them will live forever. They will be giants in stature and will grow in number and strength until they have occupied the entire world forever. The Messiah will, with the help of God, live forever. They also believe that in those days the earth will bring forth garments woven, bread baked, and many other impossible things. In this view, the evil is that a man may not be alive in those days and may not merit the privilege of seeing them. This group also adduces proof from many statements found in the writings of our sages and from Biblical verses whose literal meaning seems to agree either wholly or partly with what they say.

A third group holds that the good for which we hope is the resurrection of the dead. By this they mean that a man will live after his death and return to his family and dear ones to eat and drink and never die again. According to this opinion the evil is that a man may not live after his death among those who are resurrected. Here, too, proof is adduced from many sayings that are found in the words of the sages and from Biblical verses whose literal meaning seem to teach this, wholly or in part.

A fourth view holds that the goal of fulfilling the commandments is the achievement of bodily peace and mundane success like fertile lands, extensive possessions, many children, health, peace, and security. They also believe that there will be a Jewish king who will rule over those who oppressed us. The evil that will overtake us if we deny the Torah is the opposite of these, as in our present exile. Those who hold this opinion likewise find support for their views in verses of Torah, particularly the curses, and from other passages in Scripture.

A fifth group—and a large one—combines the opinions of all the others. They assert that the ultimate hope is that the Messiah will come, that he will resurrect the dead, who will enter the Garden of Eden where they will eat and drink in perfect health forever.

However, concerning this strange world to come, you will rarely find anyone to whom it occurs to think about it seriously or to adopt it as a fundamental doctrine of our faith, or to inquire what it really means, whether the world to come is the ultimate good or whether some other possibility is. Nor does one often find persons who distinguish between the ultimate good itself and the means which lead to the ultimate good. What everybody always wants to know, both the masses and the learned, is how the dead will arise. They want to know whether they will be naked or clothed, whether they will rise in the same shrouds with which they were buried, with the same embroidery, style, and beauty of sewing, or in a plain garment which just covers their bodies. Or they ask whether, when the Messiah comes, there will still be rich men and poor men, weak men and strong men, and other similar questions.

You, however, who read this book thoughtfully, must understand the analogy which I am about to draw for you. Prepare your mind to understand what I tell you about all this. Imagine a small child who has been brought to his teacher so that he may be taught the Torah, which is his ultimate good because it will bring him to perfection. However, because he is only a child and because his understanding is deficient, he does not grasp the true value of that good, nor does he understand the perfection which he can achieve by means of Torah. Of necessity, therefore, his teacher, who has acquired greater perfection than the child, must bribe him to study by means of things which the child loves in a childish way. Thus, the teacher may say, "Read and I will give you some nuts or figs; I will give you a bit of honey." With this stimulation the child tries to read. He does not work hard for the sake of reading itself, since he does not understand its value. He reads in order to obtain the food. Eating these delicacies is far more important to him than reading, and a greater good to him. Therefore, although he thinks of study as work and effort, he is willing to do it in order to get what he wants, a nut or a piece of candy. As the child grows and his mind improves, what was formerly important to him loses its importance, while other things become precious. The teacher will stimulate his desire for whatever he wants then. The teacher may say to the child, "Read and I will give you beautiful shoes or nice clothes." Now the child will apply himself to reading for the sake of new clothes and not for the sake of study itself. He wants the garment more than the Torah. This coat will be the end which he hopes to achieve by reading. As his intelligence improves still more and these things, too, become unimportant to him, he will set his desire upon something of greater value. Then his teacher may say to him, "Learn this passage or this chapter, and I will give you a denar or two." Again he will try to read in order to receive the money, since money is more important to him than study. The end which he seeks to achieve through his study is to acquire the money which has been promised him. When his understanding has so improved that even this reward has ceased to be valuable to him, he will desire something more honorable. His teacher may say to him then, "Study so that you may become the president of a court, a judge, so that people will honor you and rise before you as they honor So-and-So." He will then try hard to read in order to attain his new goal. His final end then will be to achieve the honor, the exaltation, and the praise which others might confer upon him.

Now, all this is deplorable. However, it is unavoidable because of man's limited insight, as a result of which he makes the goal of wisdom something other than wisdom itself, and assumes that the purpose of study is the acquisition of honor, which makes a mockery of truth. Our sages called this learning not for its own sake. They had in mind the kind of person who performs the commandments and energetically studies Torah not for their own intrinsic worth but with some other purpose in view. Our sages warned against this and said, "Do not make the Torah a crown for self-glorification or a spade with which to dig" (Ethics of the Fathers 4:7). They hinted at what I have just explained to you, that the end of wisdom is neither to acquire honor from other men nor to earn more money. One ought not to busy oneself with God's Torah in order to earn one's living by it; nor should the end of studying wisdom be anything but knowing it. The truth has no other purpose than knowing that it is truth. Since the Torah is truth, the purpose of knowing it is to do it. A good man must not wonder, "If I perform these commandments, which are virtues, and if I refrain from these transgressions, which are vices which God commanded us not to do, what will I get out of it?" This is precisely what the child does when he asks, "If I read, what will you give me?" The child is answered in some such way because, when we know his limited understanding and his desire for something other than a real goal, we answer him on the level of his folly, as it is said in Proverbs 26:5: "Answer the fool according to his folly."

Our sages have already warned us about this. They said that one should not make the goal of one's service of God or of doing the commandments anything in the world of things. Antigonos of Sokho—a man who had achieved perfection and grasped the truth of things—meant precisely this when he said: "Do not be like the servants who serve their master for the sake of receiving a reward, but be like servants who serve their master without expecting a reward" (Ethics of the Fathers 1:3). He meant by this that one should believe the truth for the sake of the truth. We say of such a man that he serves out of love. To him the sages have applied the verse: "His profound desire is in God's commandments" (Ps. 112:1). Rabbi Eliezer added: "... in His commandments, but not in the reward of His commandments" (Avodah Zarah 19a).*

All of this is clear proof of what we have said. A passage from the *Sifre* makes the point even better. "Should you be tempted to say, 'I will study Torah in order to become rich, or in order to be called Rabbi, or in order to receive a reward in the world to come,' Scripture says (Deut. 11:13): 'To love the Lord your God'—whatever you do, do it only out of love." It has now been made quite clear to you that this is what the Torah means and our sages make fundamental. Only a disturbed fool whose mind is deranged by folly and by fantasy will refuse to recognize this truth.

Abraham our Father achieved this level; he served God out of love. We, too, must be aroused to move in this direction. However, our sages knew that this is a very difficult goal to achieve and that not every man could achieve it. One may understand the goal and still reject it, failing to apprehend that it is a principle of faith. Men do not do anything except to achieve profit or to avoid loss. Most men would regard any other action as useless and meaningless.

Under these circumstances it is hard to say to one who is studying Torah, "Do certain things and refrain from doing certain other things but not out of fear of divine punishment and not in order to acquire a reward." This is an exceedingly difficult thing to do because most men have not achieved such truth that they are able to be like Abraham our Father. Therefore, in order that the masses stay faithful and do the commandments, it was permitted to tell them that they might hope for a reward and to warn them against transgressions out of fear of punishment. It was hoped that they might be urged to strengthen their intentions so that they would ultimately grasp the truth and the way toward perfection, just like the child in the analogy which I cited above. It was for this reason that the sages charged Antigonos of Sokho with indiscretion. They had him in mind when they said, "O wise ones, be careful with your words" (Ethics of the Fathers 1:11). The masses, after all, lose nothing when they do the

*See *Guide*, III, ch. 54.

commandments out of fear of punishment and out of hope for reward, since they are not perfect. It is good for them insofar as it strengthens and habituates them in loyalty to what the Torah requires. Out of this effort they may be awakened to the knowledge of the truth and serve God out of love. This is what the sages meant when they said, "A man ought always to labor in the Torah, even if not for its own sake! For doing it not for its own sake, he may come to do it for its own sake" (Pesahim 50b).

You must know that the words of the sages are differently interpreted by three groups of people.

The first group is the largest one. I have observed them, read their books, and heard about them. They accept the teachings of the sages in their simple literal sense and do not think that these teachings contain any hidden meaning at all. They believe that all sorts of impossible things must be. They hold such opinions because they have not understood science and are far from having acquired knowledge. They possess no perfection which would rouse them to insight from within, nor have they found anyone else to stimulate them to profounder understanding. They, therefore, believe that the sages intended no more in their carefully emphatic and straightforward utterances than they themselves are able to understand with inadequate knowledge. They understand the teachings of the sages only in their literal sense, in spite of the fact that some of their teachings, when taken literally, seem so fantastic and irrational that if one were to repeat them literally, even to the uneducated, let alone to sophisticated scholars, their amazement would prompt them to ask how anyone in the world could believe such things true, much less edifying.

The members of this group are poor in knowledge. One can only regret their folly. Their very effort to honor and to exalt the sages in accordance with their own meager understanding actually humiliates them. As God lives, this group destroys the glory of the Torah and extinguishes its light, for they make the Torah of God say the opposite of what it intended. For He said in His perfect Torah, "The nations who hear of these statutes shall say: Surely this great nation is a wise and understanding people" (Deut. 4:6). But this group expounds the laws and the teachings of our sages in such a way that when the other peoples hear them they say that this little people is foolish and ignoble.*

*See *Guide*, III, ch. 31.

The worst offenders are preachers who preach and expound to the masses what they themselves do not understand. Would that they keep silent about what they do not know, as it is written: "If only they would be utterly silent, it would be accounted to them as wisdom" (Job 13:5). Or they might at least say, "We do not understand what our sages intended in this statement, and we do not know how to explain it." But they believe they do understand, and they vigorously expound to the people what they think rather than what the sages really said. They, therefore, give lectures to the people on the tractate Berakhot and on this present chapter, and other texts, expounding them word-for-word according to their literal meaning.*

The second group is also a numerous one. It, too, consists of persons who, having read or heard the words of the sages, understand them according to their simple literal sense and believe that the sages intended nothing else than what may be learned from their literal interpretation. Inevitably, they ultimately declare the sages to be fools, hold them up to contempt, and slander what does not deserve to be slandered. They imagine that their own intelligence is of a higher order than that of the sages, and that the sages were simpletons who suffered from inferior intelligence. The members of this group are so pretentiously stupid that they can never attain genuine wisdom. Most of those who have stumbled into this error are involved with medicine or astrology. They regard themselves as cultivated men, scientists, critics, and philosophers. How remote they are from true humanity compared to real philosophers! They are more stupid than the first group; many of them are simply fools.

This is an accursed group, because they attempt to refute men of established greatness whose wisdom has been demonstrated to competent men of science. If these fools had worked at science hard enough to know how to write accurately about theology and similar subjects both for the masses and for the educated, and if they understood the relevance of philosophy, then they would be in a position to understand whether the sages were in fact wise or not, and the real meaning of their teachings would be clear to them.

There is a third group. Its members are so few in number that it is hardly appropriate to call them a group, except in the sense in which one speaks of the sun as a group (or species) of which it is the only member. This group consists of men to whom the greatness of

*See *Guide*, II, ch. 29.

our sages is clear. They recognize the superiority of their intelligence from their words which point to exceedingly profound truths. Even though this third group is few and scattered, their books teach the perfection which was achieved by the authors and the high level of truth which they had attained. The members of this group understand that the sages knew as clearly as we do the difference between the impossibility of the impossible and the existence of that which must exist. They know that the sages did not speak nonsense, and it is clear to them that the words of the sages contain both an obvious and a hidden meaning. Thus, whenever the sages spoke of things that seem impossible, they were employing the style of riddle and parable which is the method of truly great thinkers. For example, the greatest of our wise men (Solomon) began his book by saying: "To understand an analogy and a metaphor, the words of the wise and their riddles" (Prov. 1:6).

All students of rhetoric know the real concern of a riddle is with its hidden meaning and not with its obvious meaning, as: "Let me now put forth a riddle to you" (Judges 14:12). Since the words of the sages all deal with supernatural matters which are ultimate, they must be expressed in riddles and analogies. How can we complain if they formulate their wisdom in analogies and employ such figures of speech as are easily understood by the masses, especially when we note that the wisest of all men did precisely that, under the guidance of the Holy Spirit? I have in mind Solomon in Proverbs, the Song of Songs, and parts of Ecclesiastes.*

It is often difficult for us to interpret words and to educe their true meaning from the form in which they are contained so that their real inner meaning conforms to reason and corresponds with truth. This is the case even with Holy Scriptures. The sages themselves interpreted Scriptural passages in such a way as to educe their inner meaning from literal sense, correctly considering these passages to be figures of speech, just as we do. Examples are their explanations of the following passages: "he smote the two altar-hearths of Moab; he went down also and slew a lion in the midst of a pit" (II Sam. 23:20); "Oh, that one would give me water to drink of the well of Bethlehem" (*ibid.* 23:15). The entire narrative of which these passages are a part was interpreted metaphorically. Similarly, the whole Book of Job was considered by many of the sages to be properly

*See *Guide*, introduction.

understood only in metaphoric terms. The dead bones of Ezekiel (Ezek. 37) were also considered by one of the rabbis to make sense only in metaphoric terms. Similar treatment was given to other passages of this sort.

Now if you, reader, belong to either of the first two groups, pay no attention to my words nor to anything else in this section. You will not like it. On the contrary, it will irritate you, and you will hate it. How could a person who is accustomed to eating large amounts of harmful food find simple food in small quantities appealing, even though they are good for him? On the contrary, he will actually find them irritating, and he will hate them. Do you not recall the reaction of the people who were accustomed to eating onions, garlic, fish, and the like? They said: "Now our soul is dried away; there is nothing at all; we have nought save this manna to look to" (Num. 11:6).

But if you belong to the third group, when you encounter a word of the sages which seems to conflict with reason, you will pause, consider it, and realize that this utterance must be a riddle or a parable. You will sleep on it, trying anxiously to grasp its logic and its expression, so that you may find its genuine intellectual intention and lay hold of a direct faith, as Scripture says: "To find out words of delight, and that which was written uprightly, even words of truth" (Eccles. 12:10). If you consider my book in this spirit, with the help of God, it may be useful to you.

Now I can begin to discuss the matter with which I am really concerned. Know that just as the blind man cannot image color, as the deaf person cannot experience sounds, and as the eunuch cannot feel sexual desire, so bodies cannot attain spiritual delights. Like fish, who do not know what the element of fire is, because they live upon its opposite, the element of water, so are the delights of the spiritual world unknown in this material world. Spiritual delight does not come within our experience at all. We enjoy only bodily pleasures which come to us through our physical senses, such as the pleasures of eating, drinking, and sexual intercourse. Other levels of delight are not present to our experience. We neither recognize nor grasp them at first thought. They come to us only after great searching.

It could hardly be otherwise, since we live in a material world and are, therefore, able to achieve only inferior and discontinuous delights. Spiritual delights are eternal. They last forever; they never break off. Between these two kinds of delight there is no similarity of any sort. It is, therefore, inappropriate for us who are masters of Torah or theologians to say that angels, stars, and spheres experience no delight. On the contrary, they really experience great delight in that they know by experience the true being of God the Creator. With this knowledge they enjoy delight which is both perpetual and uninterrupted. They have no bodily delight, nor could they, since they have no physical senses, as we do, through which they could get our kind of gratification.

We will be like them after death. Those men who choose to purify themselves will reach this spiritual height. They will neither experience bodily pleasures, nor will they want them. They will resemble a powerful king. He would hardly want to go back to playing ball with children as he did before he became king. Such games attracted him when he was a child and was unable to understand the real difference between ball playing and royal power. Like children we now praise and glorify the delights of the body and do not understand the delights of the soul.

If you consider carefully the nature of these two kinds of delight, you will perceive the inferiority of the first and the superiority of the second, even in this world. Thus, you find that most men will exert extraordinary amounts of intellectual and physical energy laboring at ordinary tasks in order to acquire honor and be exalted by their fellowmen. The pleasure which honor brings is not of the same sort as the pleasure derived from eating and drinking. Similarly, many men pursue vengeance over their enemies more intensely than they pursue any bodily pleasures. Many others deny themselves the keenest of bodily delights because they fear shame and public disgrace or because they seek to acquire a reputation for virtue. If this is the case even in this material world, how much more must it be so in the spiritual world! That world is the world to come.

In the world to come our souls will become wise out of the knowledge of God the Creator, as the higher physical bodies do, or even wiser. This spiritual delight is not divisible into parts, nor can it be described, nor can any analogy explain it. It is as the prophet said when he was awe-stricken at the lofty magnificence of that good: "How great is Your goodness which You have hidden away for them that fear You" (Ps. 31:30). Our sages also wrote: "In the world to come there is no eating, drinking, washing, anointing, or sexual intercourse; but the righteous sit with their crowns on their heads enjoying the radiance of the Divine Presence" (Berakhot 17a). In this passage the expression "with their crowns on their heads" signifies the immortality of the soul being in firm possession of the Idea which is God the Creator. The "crown" is precisely the Idea which great philosophers have explicated at length. The expression, "they delight in the radiance of the Divine Presence" means that souls enjoy blissful delight in their attainment of knowledge of the truly essential nature of God the Creator, a delight which is like that experienced by the holy angels who know His existence first-hand.

The ultimate good, the final end is to achieve this supernal fellowship, to participate in this high glory in which the soul is forever involved with the existence of God the Creator, who is the cause and source of its existence and its goal. This has already been explained by the earlier philosophers.

This is incomparably good, for how could that which is eternal and endless be compared with anything transient and terminable? That is the meaning of the Biblical statement: "That it may be well with you, and that you may prolong your days" (Deut. 22:7)—in the world that is infinitely long, add the rabbis (Kiddushin 39b, Hullin 142a).*

Utterly evil punishment consists in the cutting off of the soul so that it perishes and does not live eternally. This is the penalty of karet to which the Torah refers, as in the phrase: "That soul shall utterly be cut off" (Num. 15:31). Interpreting this phrase, our sages said: "The word hikkaret (utterly cut off) refers to the world to come" (Sanhedrin 64b, 90a). On the other hand, Scripture also says: "The soul of my master shall be bound in the bundle of life with the Lord your God" (I Sam. 25:29).

It follows that if a person has deliberately and regularly chosen physical delights, has despised the truth and loved falsehood, he will be cut off from that high level of being and remain disconnected matter. The prophet has already explained that the world to come cannot be apprehended by the bodily senses, in the verse: "The eye has not seen it, O Lord, except You" (Is. 64:3). The sages taught emphatically that the prophets prophesied only about the days of the Messiah, but that concerning the world to come, "eye has not seen it, O Lord, only You" (Berakhot 34b, Shabbat 63a, Sanhedrin 99a).

Now let me explain the meaning of the promises of good and the threats of evil punishment which are contained in the Torah. What these promises and punishments mean is that God says to you,

*See Guide, III, ch. 28; also Mishneh Torah, Book I, Repentance, ch. VIII.

"If you do these commandments, I will help you in your effort to do them and to achieve perfection in them. I will remove all the obstacles and difficulties which stand in your way." For it is impossible for a man to perform the commandments when he is sick or hungry or thirsty or when he lives in a time of war and siege. God, therefore, says that He will remove all these obstacles to fulfillment, so that men who strive to do the commandments will be healthy and safe until they attain that degree of knowing through which they will merit the life of the world to come. However, he must understand that the ultimate reward of doing the commandments of the Torah is not in any of these things themselves. And if one violates the commandments of the Torah, punishments ensue. All kinds of hindrances will come into being, so that the transgressor will no longer be able to perform the commandments. It is precisely as Scripture states it: "Because you did not serve the Lord your God with joyfulness and with gladness of heart, by reason of the abundance of all things; therefore, you shall serve your enemy whom the Lord shall send against you, in hunger and in thirst and in nakedness, and in want of all things; and he shall put a yoke of iron upon your neck, until he has destroyed you (Deut. 28:47 ff.).

If you consider these things carefully and fully, you will understand that it is as though He were saying to you, "If you do some of these commandments out of love and with genuine effort, I will help you to do all of them, and I will remove the oppressive obstacles that prevent you from doing them. But if you refuse to attempt to perform any of them out of disdain for the commandment, then I will bring upon you the very obstacles that prevent you from doing all of them, so that you cannot achieve perfect existence in the world to come." This is the meaning of the statement of the sages: "The reward of a commandment is the commandment itself, and the reward of a sin is sin" (Ethics of the Fathers 4:2).

The Garden of Eden is a fertile place containing the choicest of the earth's resources, numerous rivers, and fruit-bearing trees. God will disclose it to man some day. He will teach man the way to it, and men will be happy there. It is possible that many exceedingly wonderful plants will be found there, plants which are far pleasanter and sweeter than those which we now know. None of this is impossible or improbable. On the contrary, paradise would be possible even if it were not written of in the Torah. How much more sure then is it since the Torah specifically promises it!

Gehenna is a name for the pain and the punishment which will come upon the wicked. No specific description of this punishment is contained in the Talmud. One teacher says that the sun will come so close to the wicked that it will burn them. He finds proof for this belief in the verse: "For behold, the day comes, it burns as a furnace; and all the proud and all that work wickedness shall be stubble; and the day that comes shall set them ablaze, says the Lord of hosts, that it shall leave them neither root nor branch" (Mal. 3:19). Others say that a strange heat will be produced within their own bodies to incinerate them. They find support for this position in the Scriptural words: "Your own spirit is a fire which will consume you" (Is. 33:11).

The resurrection of the dead is one of the cardinal principles established by Moses our Teacher. A person who does not believe in this principle has no real religion, certainly not Judaism. However, resurrection is only for the righteous. This is the meaning of the statement in *Bereshit Rabbah* (ch. 13) which declares: "The creative power of rain is for both the righteous and the wicked, but the resurrection of the dead is only for the righteous." How, after all, could the wicked come back to life, since they are dead even in their lifetimes? Our sages taught: "The wicked are called dead even while they are still alive; the righteous are alive even when they are dead" (Berakhot 18b). All men must die and their bodies decompose.

The "days of the Messiah" refers to a time in which sovereignty will revert to Israel and the Jewish people will return to the land of Israel. Their king will be a very great one, with his royal palace in Zion. His name and his reputation will extend throughout all the nations in even greater measure than did King Solomon's. All nations will make peace with him, and all countries will serve him out of respect for his great righteousness and the wonders which occur through him. All those who rise against him will be destroyed and delivered into his hands by God. All the verses of the Bible testify to his triumph and our triumph with him. However, except for the fact that sovereignty will revert to Israel, nothing will be essentially different from what it is now. This is what the sages taught: "The only difference between this world and the days of the Messiah is that oppression by other kingdoms will be abolished" (Berakhot 34b; Shabbat 63a, 151b; Pesahim 68a; Sanhedrin 91b, 99a). In the days of the Messiah there will still be rich and poor, strong and weak. However in those days it will be very easy for men to make a living. A minimum of labor will produce great benefits. This is what the sages meant when they said: "In the future, the land of Israel will bring forth ready baked rolls and fine woolen garments" (Shabbat 30b). This is rather like what people say when someone finds something ready for use. They say, "So-and-So has found his bread already baked and his meal already cooked." The Scriptural support for all of this is in the expression, "and aliens shall be your plowmen and your vinedressers" (Is. 61:5). This verse suggests that there will be sowing and reaping even in the Messianic time. The Talmud (Shabbat 30b) records the irritation of one of the sages with a student whose objection to this passsage showed that he did not understand his teaching on it because he understood the verse literally. The sage replied to him incorrectly, in accordance with the student's inadequate understanding of the matter. The reason for the sage's refusal to give a true answer is found in the verse: "Answer not a fool according to his folly" (Prov. 26:4).

The great benefits which will occur in those days include our release from oppression by other kingdoms which prevents us from fulfilling all the commandments—a widespread increase of wisdom, in accordance with the Scriptural promise: "For the earth shall be full of the knowledge of the Lord, as the waters cover the sea" (Is. 11:9)—and the end of the wars, again in accordance with the Scriptural statement: "Nation shall not lift up sword against nation, neither shall they learn war any more" (Micah 4:3). In those days perfection will be widespread, with the result that men will merit the life of the world to come.

But the Messiah will die, and his son and his grandson will reign in his stead. The prophet has already predicted his death in the verse: "He shall not fail nor be crushed till he has set the right in the earth" (Is. 42:2). However, his reign will be a very long one. All human life will be longer, for when worries and troubles are removed men live longer. There is no reason for surprise that the Messiah's reign will extend for thousands of years. As our sages have put it: "When good is gathered together it cannot speedily be dissipated."

We do not long and hope for the days of the Messiah because of an increase of productivity and wealth which may occur then, or that we may ride on horses and drink wine to the accompaniment of song, as some confused people think. The prophets and the saints looked forward to the days of the Messiah and yearned for them because then the righteous will be gathered together in fellowship, and because goodness and wisdom will prevail. They desired it also because of the righteousness and the abundant justice of the Messianic king, because of the salutary influence of his unprecedented wisdom, and because of his nearness to God, as described: "The Lord said to me: 'You are My son: this day have I begotten you'" (Ps. 2:7). They also anticipate the performance of all of the commandments of the Torah of Moses our Teacher, with neither inertia on the one hand nor compulsion on the other, in fulfillment of the Scriptural promise: "And they shall teach no more every man his neighbor and every man his brother, saying: 'Know the Lord': for they shall all know Me, from the least of them to the greatest of them, says the Lord: for I will forgive their iniquity and their sin will I remember no more" (Jer. 31:34). Similarly, it is written: "I will put My Torah in their inward parts, and I will write it in their heart" (Jer. 31:33). Scripture also says: "And I will take away the stony heart of your flesh, and I will give you a heart of flesh" (Ezek. 36:26). There are many other verses with the same promise.*

Thus, men will achieve the world to come. The world to come is the ultimate end toward which all our effort ought to be devoted. Therefore, the sage who firmly grasped the knowledge of the truth and who envisioned the final end, forsaking everything else, taught: "All Jews have a share in the world to come" (Sanhedrin 10:1).

Nevertheless, even though this is the end we seek, he who wishes to serve God out of love should not serve Him to attain the world to come. He should rather believe that wisdom exists, that this wisdom is the Torah; that the Torah was given the prophets by God the Creator; that in the Torah He taught us virtues which are the commandments and vices that are sins. As a decent man, one must cultivate the virtues and avoid the sins. In so doing, he will perfect the specifically human which resides in him and will be genuinely different from the animals. When one becomes fully human, he acquires the nature of the perfect human being; there is no external power to deny his soul eternal life. His soul thus attains the eternal life it has come to know which is the world to come, as we have explained. This is the meaning of the verse: "Be not as the horse or as the mule, which have no understanding; whose mouth must be held in with bit and bridle" (Ps. 32:9). Restraints which prevent animals from acting in accordance with their nature are external ones, like the bit and the bridle. With man, the influences which restrain

*See *Mishneh Torah*, Book XIV, Kings, chs. XI–XII.

him are his control of self. When a man achieves human perfection, it restrains him from doing those things which are called vices and which withhold perfection from him; it urges and impels him toward those things which are called virtues and which bring him to full perfection. This is what all the teaching of the sages have made clear to me about this most important matter.

I hope to write a book collecting all the sages' teachings on this subject from the Talmud and other works. I shall interpret them systematically, showing which must be understood literally and which metaphorically, and which are dreams to be interpreted by a wakeful mind. There I shall explain the many principles of our faith of which I have discussed a few here. You must make your own comparisons. Let no one blame me for the freedom with which I have used certain expressions or made certain statements in this book, though they may irritate some scholars. For I have expatiated on these points precisely in order to teach those with no training in theology, a subject which not every man can understand. . . .*

We must remember in connection with this subject, and indeed with all others, that our religion is based on the following thirteen principles:

The First Fundamental Principle: To believe in the existence of the Creator; that there is an Existent complete in all the senses of the word "existence." He is the cause of all existence. In Him all else subsists and from Him derives. It is inconceivable that He not exist, for should He not exist the existence of all else would be extinguished, and nothing could persist. If we imagine the absence of any other existent thing, however, God's existence would not thereby be extinguished nor diminished. For unity and mastery are only God's, since He is sufficient to Himself. All else, whether angels or celestials and whatever is in them or below them, needs Him to exist. This first fundamental principle is taught in the Biblical verse: "I am the Lord your God" (Ex. 20:2).

The Second Fundamental Principle: We are told to believe that God is one, the cause of all oneness. He is not like a member of a pair, nor a species of a genus, nor a person divided into many discrete

*See Guide, introduction.

elements. Nor is He one in the sense that a simple body is, numerically one but still infinitely divisible. God, rather, is uniquely one. This second fundamental principle is taught in the Biblical verse: "Hear, O Israel, the Lord our God, the Lord is One" (Deut. 6:4).

The Third Fundamental Principle: We are to believe that He is incorporeal, that His unity is physical neither potentially nor actually. None of the attributes of matter can be predicated of Him, neither motion, nor rest, for example. They cannot refer to Him accidentally or essentially. That is why our sages denied Him composition and separation, and said: "On High there is neither sitting nor standing, neither want nor weariness" (Hagigah 15a), *i.e.*, neither composition nor separation, as the Biblical usage of these words attests. The prophet asked: "To whom can you compare God, whom might He resemble?" (Is. 40:18). If He were a body, He would be like other bodies. Whenever Scripture describes Him in corporeal terms like walking, standing, sitting, speaking, and the like, it speaks metaphorically. Thus our sages said: "The Torah speaks in human language" (Berakhot 31b). This third fundamental principle is taught in the Biblical verse: "You have seen no image" (Deut. 4:15). This verse means to say, one cannot conceive of Him as one would a Baal image, since, as we have shown, He has no body at all, actually or potentially.

The Fourth Fundamental Principle: We are to believe that the One is absolutely eternal; no thing existed before Him, as many Scriptural verses prove. This fourth fundamental principle is taught in the Biblical verse: "A dwelling-place is the Eternal God" (Deut. 33:27).

The Fifth Fundamental Principle: Only He, blessed be He, is rightfully worshiped, magnified, and obeyed. One must not pray to anything beneath Him in existence: angels, stars, planets or elements, or anything composed of these. All of them are natural processes without self-determination or free will. Only God is free and puissant. Hence, we must not worship those powers which can serve only as means to bring us nearer to Him. We must think only of Him, leaving to one side all else. The fifth fundamental principle has all Biblical warning against idolatry as its warrant, in other words, the bulk of the Torah.

The Sixth Fundamental Principle is Prophecy. One should know that among men are found certain people so gifted and perfected that they can receive pure intellectual form. Their human intellect clings to the Active Intellect, whither it is gloriously raised. These men are the prophets; this is what prophecy is. A full explanation of this root principle would require much more time. We do not wish to cite proof-texts for every principle or to explain each fully. However, I remind you in passing of the many Scriptural passages which testify to the prophecy of many different prophets.

The Seventh Fundamental Principle is the prophecy of Moses our Teacher. We are to believe that he was the chief of all other prophets before and after him, all of whom were his inferiors. He was the chosen one of all mankind, superior in attaining knowledge of God to any other person who ever lived or ever will live. He surpassed the normal human condition and attained the angelic. There remained no veil he did not rend and penetrate behind, nothing physical to hold him back, no deficiency, great or small, to confuse him. All his powers of sense and fantasy were repressed, and pure reason alone remained. This is what is meant by saying that he spoke to God without angelic mediation.

I should have wished to explicate this mystery from Biblical sources, explaining such verses as "God spoke to Moses mouth to mouth" (Num. 12:8), but I see they would require a great many preparatory comments about the remarkable existence of angels, which derives from God, and about the powers of the soul. And the discussion would have to be widened to include the prophetic descriptions of God and angels, including the Divine Dimension of which even the briefest description would require a hundred pages. I have, therefore, left these matters to my exegetical book, the book on prophecy on which I am working, or to a book I hope some day to write explaining these fundamental issues.

Returning to our seventh fundamental principle: Moses' prophecy must be distinguished from that of all other prophets in four respects:

1. All other prophets were addressed by God through intermediaries, only Moses immediately. This is indicated by the phrase, "mouth to mouth I addressed Him."

2. Prophecy came to all others in sleep (cf. the verses which refer to "a dream of night" [Gen. 20:3]; "a vision of night" [Job 33:15]), or in daytime when a trance fell on the prophet so that his senses and intellect would be as useless as in a dream. This state is called

"vision" or "insight" as in the expression "visions of God." But the Word came to Moses in broad daylight when he stood by the two cherubs, as God had promised, "I will meet you there" (Ex. 25:22). God said: "Moses, my servant, is not like other prophets; to him alone I speak mouth to mouth."

3. Even if another prophet should receive a vision of God through an angel, his powers would fail; he would be overcome with dread, and nearly lose his mind. When, for example, Daniel was addressed by Gabriel in a vision, he said: "I had no strength; my vigor turned against me, I retained no power, but fell swooning on my face to the ground, writhing in a vision" (Dan. 10:8 ff., 10:16). This never happened to Moses. When the Word came to him he would neither shiver nor tremble. "God spoke to Moses face to face, as a man to his friend" (Ex. 33:11). This means that, since a friendly talk produces no anxiety, Moses had no fear. Face to face with God, he had no terror of the revelation, because he clung to Him in a wholly conscious way, as we have implied.

4. The other prophets could not attain a vision whenever they pleased. All depended on God's will. A prophet might wait days or years before prophecy would come to him. He would beg God to reveal Himself in prophecy, but he would have to wait for days or months before the prophecy came. Sometimes God would not reveal Himself at all. There were many sects who prepared themselves by purifying their minds as Elisha did—"and now take me a musician that prophecy might reach me" (II Kings 3:15). But prophecy did not necessarily follow their preparation. Moses our Teacher, on the other hand, could say whenever he wished: "Wait, and I shall hear what the Lord commands you" (Num. 9:8). Scripture says: "Tell Aaron, your brother, not to enter the holy place anytime at all" (Lev. 16:2). Our sages interpret this to mean that Aaron could not come to God whenever he pleased, but Moses might (Midrash to Ahare Mot).

The Eighth Fundamental Principle is that the Torah came from God. We are to believe that the whole Torah was given us through Moses our Teacher entirely from God. When we call the Torah "God's Word" we speak metaphorically. We do not know exactly how it reached us, but only that it came to us through Moses who acted like a secretary taking dictation. He wrote down the events of the time and the commandments, for which reason he is called "Lawgiver." There is no distinction between a verse of Scripture like "The sons of Ham were Cush and Mizraim" (Gen. 10:6), or "His wife's name was Mehetabel and his concubine was Timna" (Gen. 36:39, 12), and one like "I am the Lord your God" (Ex. 20:2), or "Hear, O Israel" (Deut. 6:4). All came from God, and all are the Torah of God, perfect, pure, holy and true. Anyone who says Moses wrote some passages on his own is regarded by our sages as an atheist or the worst kind of heretic, because he tries to distinguish essence from accident in Torah. Such a heretic claims that some historical passages or stories are trivial inventions of Moses and not Divine Revelation. But the sages said that if one accepts as Revelation the whole Torah with the exception of even one verse, which Moses himself and not God composed, he is referred to in the verse, "he has shamed the Word of the Lord" (Num. 15:31), and is heretical.

Every word of Torah is full of wisdom and wonders for one who understands it. It is beyond human understanding. It is broader than the earth and wider than the sea. Each man must follow David, anointed of the God of Jacob, who prayed: "Open my eyes that I may behold wonders out of Your Torah" (Ps. 119:18).

The authoritative commentary on the Torah is also the Word of God. The sukkah we build today, or the lulav, shofar, fringes, phylacteries, etc. we use, replicate exactly those God showed Moses which Moses faithfully described for us. This fundamental principle is taught by the verse: "And Moses said, 'Thus shall you know that the Lord sent me to do all these things, and that they are not products of my own mind'" (Num. 16:28).

The Ninth Fundamental Principle is the authenticity of the Torah, i.e., that this Torah was precisely transcribed from God and no one else. To the Torah, Oral and Written, nothing must be added nor anything taken from it, as is said, "You must neither add nor detract" (Deut. 13:1). We have already sufficiently explained this principle in our introduction to this Commentary on the Mishnah.

The Tenth Fundamental Principle is that God knows all that men do and never turns His eyes away from them, as those who say "The Lord has abandoned this earth" (Ezek. 8:12, 9:9) claim. Rather, as Scripture has it, "Great in counsel, mighty in insight (is God) whose eyes are open to all the ways of men" (Jer. 32:19). Or again, "And the Lord saw that great was the evil of man on earth" (Gen. 6:5), or the verse, "The cry of Sodom and Gomorrah is powerful" (ibid. 18:20). All these citations point to our Tenth Fundamental Principle.

The Eleventh Fundamental Principle is that God rewards those who perform the commandments of the Torah and punishes those who transgress its admonitions. The greatest reward is the world to come; the worst punishment is extinction. We have already made this sufficiently clear. The Scripture which teaches this fundamental principle is "If you will not forgive their sin, extinguish me." To which God replied, "I will expunge from My book only the man who has sinned against Me" (Ex. 32:32 ff.). This proves He knows both the obedient and the sinner, and rewards or punishes each.

The Twelfth Fundamental Principle refers to the Messianic Era. We are to believe as fact that the Messiah will come and not consider him late. If he delays, wait for him (Hab. 2:3); set no time limit for his coming. One must not make conjectures based on Scripture to conclude when Messiah will come. The sages said: "May the Spirit depart from those who calculate the end-time" (Sanhedrin 97b). One must believe that the Messiah will have more station and honor than all the kings who ever lived, as all the prophets from Moses to Malachi prophesied. Whoever doubts this or minimizes it denies the Torah which testifies to it explicitly, in the Balaam story and in the passage that begins, "You are standing ..." (Deut. 29:9). A corollary of this principle is the assertion that the king of Israel must come only from the house of David and the seed of Solomon. Anyone who rejects this family denies God and the words of His prophets.

The Thirteenth Fundamental Principle is the Resurrection of the Dead, which we have already explicated.

When a man believes in all these fundamental principles, and his faith is thus clarified, he is then part of that "Israel" whom we are to love, pity, and treat, as God commanded, with love and fellowship. Even if a Jew should commit every possible sin, out of lust or mastery by his lower nature, he will be punished for his sins but will still have a share in the world to come. He is one of the "sinners in Israel." But if a man gives up any one of these fundamental principles, he has removed himself from the Jewish community. He is an atheist, a heretic, an unbeliever who "cuts among the plantings." We are commanded to hate him and to destroy him. Of him it is said: "Shall I not hate those who hate You, O Lord?" (Ps. 139:21).

I have spent too much time on these matters, leaving the general subject of my book. But I have done so because I saw their usefulness for faith. So I have collected a number of scattered but useful statements from our great books. You must know them well. Repeat them frequently. Meditate on them carefully. If you mind seduces you into thinking that you comprehend them after one reading—or ten readings—God knows you are deceived! Do not read them hurriedly, for I did not just happen to write them down. Only after careful research and introspection, when I came to see which opinions are clearly true and untrue, did I come to know what to accept. I have proved each point systematically. May God fulfill my wish and lead me on the way of goodness.

*I*NASMUCH as the Book of Commandments was a byproduct of the Mishneh Torah—actually an indispensable preparation for it—it is not surprising that the introduction to the former contains the fullest description of the Mishneh Torah and pointedly notes its most distinctive features. In this introduction, Maimonides reveals the decision-making process that affected the scope, style, and structuring of his code. The introduction also stresses his deep-seated independence and consistently critical attitude toward predecessors, especially the eighth-century author of the Halakhot Gedolot. His plea is for objective evaluation of the cogency and persuasiveness of arguments, not blind reliance on whatever has already been printed. Maimonides does not conceal the fact that he finds the whole mood of intellectual conservatism uncongenial. It should be noted that his sharp arraignment of poets who sacrifice substance for style and whose scholarship is generally defective is usually taken as referring to Solomon ibn Gabirol (cf. Guide, I, ch. 59).

The Book of Commandments was written in Arabic and only subsequently translated into Hebrew; hence, it was not widely studied and its impact on rabbinic literature was not so great or extensive as that of the Mishneh Torah.

Besides the introduction, I have included a few paragraphs which illustrate Maimonides' method, brevity of presentation, and skillful definitions (e.g., the striking ethical emphasis in number 317). The last selection broaches the very fundamental question elaborated in the Mishneh Torah and the Guide—of the rationalization of the Law.

INTRODUCTION

After having completed our previous well-known work wherein we included a commentary to the whole Mishnah—our goal in that work having been satisfied with the explanation of the substance of each and every *halakhah* in the Mishnah, since our intention there was not to include an exhaustive discussion of the law of every commandment which would embrace all that is necessary (to know) of the prohibited and the permissible, liable and free, as will be made clear to him who studies that work—I deemed it advisable to compile a compendium which would include all the laws of the Torah and its regulations, nothing missing in it. In this compendium I would try, as I am accustomed to do, to avoid mentioning differences of opinion and rejected teachings, and include in it only the established law, so that this compendium would embrace all the laws of the Torah of Moses our Teacher—whether they have bearing in the time of the exile or not.

It also appeared to me to be advisable to omit the *asmakhtot**
and the proofs brought (for the various laws), by mentioning the bearers of the tradition; thus, I would not say with each and every law, "These are the words of this Rabbi," or "This Rabbi says so-and-so" but instead I would mention in a general way at the beginning of this compendium all the sages of the Mishnah and the Talmud, peace be upon them, and I would say that all the laws of the Torah—that is, the Oral Torah—have been received and handed down from teacher to pupil (through the ages) until Ezra (and thence) until Moses our Teacher. Together with the leader of every

generation that received the tradition, I would mention also the outstanding persons in his generation, who were associated with him in
the imparting of the Oral teaching. All this (I would do) out of a
desire for brevity.

Similarly, I also found it advisable not to compose (this work)
in the language of the Holy Scriptures, since that sacred language is
too limited for us today to write the whole complex of the law in it.
Nor would I compose it in the language of the Talmud (namely,
Aramaic), since only a few individuals among us understand it today,
and even the erudite of the Talmud find many of its words foreign
and remote. Instead, I would compose it in the language of the
Mishnah, so that it should be easily understood by most of the
people. And I would include in it everything of the Torah that has
been established and confirmed, omitting no question which might
arise, or at least I would mention the principle by means of which
that question can easily be resolved without too deep reflection. Such
was my goal to be in this work: brevity with completeness—so that
the reader thereof might encompass all that is found in the Mishnah
and Talmud, *Sifra*, *Sifre*, and *Tosefta*, and more than that, all
decrees and ordinances of the later Geonim, of blessed memory, as
well as all that they have explained and commented upon concerning
the prohibited and permissible, unclean and clean, invalid and valid,
liable and free, pay and not pay, swear and free from swearing. In
short, outside of this work there was to be no need for another book
to learn anything whatsoever that is required in the whole Torah,
whether it be a law of the Scriptures or of the rabbis.

As I directed my attention toward this goal, I began thinking as
to how the division of this work, and the arrangement of its parts,
were to be done. (I wondered:) should I divide it in accordance with
the divisions of the Mishnah and follow in its footsteps, or should I
divide it in some other way, arranging the subjects at the beginning
or at the end of the work as logic will dictate, since this is the proper
and easier way for learning? Then it became clear to me that in place
of the tractates of the Mishnah, it would be best to arrange this work
in groups of *halakhot* (Laws), so that it read: "The Laws of the
Tabernacle, the Laws of the Palm-Branch, the Laws of the Mezuzah,
the Laws of the Fringes"; and that I should divide every group of
halakhot into chapters and paragraphs, even as the Mishnah had
done, so that, for example, in the Laws of the *Tefillin* there be chapters one, two, three, four, and each chapter be (sub)divided into

various laws, so that a knowledge of it by heart should render it easy
for one who wishes to learn something from it by memory.

With a division of this kind, it was clear that it would not be
necessary to divide the laws of any specific topic—whether it concern
a positive or negative commandment—into two general *halakhot*, but
that all necessary divisions could be made within the chapters of one
general section.

At times one general section would contain a number of commandments, either because there be some general topic which
embraces them, or because many commandments relate to one goal.
For example, in speaking of idolatry, I would designate this general
topic the "Laws of Idolatry," and then I would proceed to discuss
under this general topic a number of commandments: (against)
beguiling an individual Israelite (after the idols), leading a community astray, causing (our offspring) to pass (through the fire) in the
worship of Molech, prophesying in the name of an idol, worshiping
it, and other similar commandments specifically applying to idolatry.
Similarly, in the section entitled "The Laws of Things Forbidden to
be Brought on the Altar," I would mention (the commandments
against offering) leaven or honey, blemished offerings, the hire of a
harlot, or the price of a dog, and similar matters, since all these commandments are embraced in one general topic, namely, things forbidden to be brought (on the altar).

Now on account of this plan I deemed it advisable to enumerate
first in the introduction to that work the number of all commandments, positive and negative, so that the scope of the work embrace
all of them, not one commandment being left out without being fully
discussed, whether singly, such as the tabernacle, the palm-branch,
the fringes, or the phylacteries, since each of these topics can be discussed by itself; or in a group of commandments, such as those mentioned above, in which case we would enumerate them, saying,
"These are the Laws of Idolatry, containing this number of positive
commandments, which are as follows, and this number of negative
commandments, which are as follows." All this (I would do) in
order to guard against omitting any topic from discussion, for only by
including them in the enumeration of the commandments (heading
the various *halakhot*) would I insure against such omission.

When this plan became clear to me, and I desired to compose
the work and list briefly all the commandments by enumerating
them in the Introduction, I was overcome with a feeling of distress,

which in fact I have experienced for a number of years, which was as follows. Scholars engaged in enumerating the commandments, or in writing anything whatsoever on this topic, have all come forward with the strangest of theories that I could hardly describe their magnitude. This is due to the fact that they followed the lead of the *Halakhot Gedolot*, turning aside from his enumeration only minutely, as if opinions have become stifled with the work of that man. Even the author of the famous *Book of the Commandments* criticized some small part of the fantasies of the author of the *Halakhot Gedolot*, finding it untenable to count (among the 613 commandments) the visiting of the sick, and the consoling of mourners, as did the author of the *Halakhot Gedolot*—and indeed, that which appeared to him to be remote is truly so; but in other respects (the author of the *Book of the Commandments*) has gone even further and followed (the *Halakhot Gedolot*) in matters which are even stranger, as will be clarified to him who studies our words in this (book).

Now the Lord, exalted be He, is witness, that the more I thought about their fantasies in the enumeration (of the commandments)—counting as they did matters which even on first thought would appear that they should not have been included, and all (authors) following one another without understanding—the more our ill-fortune grew upon me, and I was conscious that His indication of impending evil was being realized upon us: "And the revelation of all those things has become to you like the words of a scroll that is sealed, which if one hand to a scholar with the request, 'Pray, read this,' he will say, 'I cannot, for it is sealed' " (Is. 29:11).

Similarly, whenever I heard the many azharot* which have been composed among us in the land of Spain, "My pangs have come writhing upon me" (Dan. 10:16), because I saw how popular and disseminated these were. True, these authors are not to be criticized; they are poets, and not rabbis, and as far as their art is concerned—namely, well-balanced expressions and beauty of rhyme—they have performed with perfection. Yet in the context of their poems they have followed after the author of the *Halakhot Gedolot* and some other later rabbis.

With these thoughts uppermost in my mind, and knowing moreover how widely accepted is this enumeration (of the command-

*Poetic compositions enumerating the 613 commandments.

ments by the *Halakhot Gedolot*) among the people, I knew that if I were just to list the true and proper enumeration, without (advancing) proofs for it, the first person that will chance to read it will suppose that this is a mistake—his proof being that it is contrary to what some author had written. Such (unfortunately) is the mentality of even the elect of our times, that they do not test the veracity of an opinion upon the merit of its own content but upon its agreement with the words of some preceding authority, without troubling to examine that preceding source itself. And if this is true of the elect, how much more so of the populace.*

Therefore, I thought it advisable to precede the book I mentioned with a treatise, in which I would explain the enumeration of the commandments and how they are to be counted. To that end I would bring proofs from the verses of the Torah and from the words of the sages, of blessed memory, concerning their interpretation, and I would also precede it with a discussion of the principles that are to guide us in the counting of the commandments. When the enumeration (of the commandments) will be firmly established by this treatise, founded upon clear proof beyond a doubt—then the reader will clearly see the mistake of all those who counted (certain commandments) in a way contrary to ours. There will then be no need for me to answer any particular person, nor to explain to him (the source) of his mistake, since the benefit and object for which this treatise was designed will be achieved by those who seek them without (my going) into any (argumentation). Thus will I explain all the commandments, listing commandment after commandment, bringing proof wherever there is a doubt, or where one not adept in the laws of the Torah is liable to have some unfounded opinion; these will I remove, and further explain everything about which there is some doubt.

My intention, however, in this treatise is by no means to delve into the details of the laws of any of the commandments; only to enumerate them (is the object of the work). And if I shall explain some small part of it in the process of mentioning (the commandment), it will be only by way of explaining its name, so that the contents of that positive or negative (commandment) be understood, and the reason why that name has been attached to it. When a knowledge of the enumeration (of the commandments) will be

*See *Guide*, I, ch. 34; *Epistle to Yemen*.

attained in accordance with the proofs in this treatise, then I shall list them briefly at the head of that general work,* as we have mentioned.

THE PRINCIPLES

Now I shall begin to mention the principles—fourteen in number—which are to guide us in the enumeration of the commandments. I shall begin by saying that the sum total of the commandments, wherein we have been commanded by God, as contained in the scroll of the Law, are 613. Of these, 248 corresponding to the number of limbs in the human body, are positive commandments; 365 corresponding to the number of days in a solar year, are negative commandments. This number (613) is mentioned in the text of the Talmud, at the end of tractate Makkot (23b), where it is said: "Six hundred and thirteen commandments were declared to Moses at Sinai: three hundred sixty-five (prohibitions) corresponding to the days in a solar year, and two hundred forty-eight (injunctions) corresponding to the limbs in the human body." By way of derash (the sages) have further said about (the number of) positive commandments corresponding to the number of limbs (in the human body), that it is as if each and every limb says to the person, "Perform a commandment with me," and about (the number of) negative commandments corresponding to the number of days in a solar year, they said, it is as if each and every day says to the person, "Do not do this day a transgression." This point—that (613) constitutes the number of the commandments—has not eluded even one of the (scholars) engaged in the enumeration of the commandments; but in the process of the actual enumeration they have counted matters which are the product of baseless imagination, as will be explained in this work. This was due to their lack of knowledge of these fourteen principles, which I shall now explain.

The First Principle: we are not to include in this enumeration commandments having only rabbinic authority.

*The Mishneh Torah.

The Second Principle: we are not to include in this enumeration (laws) derived from Scripture by any of the thirteen exegetical principles by which the Torah is expounded,* or by (the principle of) Inclusion.†

The Third Principle: we are not to include (in this enumeration) commandments which are not binding for all time.

The Fourth Principle: we are not to include charges which cover the whole body of the commandments of the Torah.

The Fifth Principle: the reason given for a commandment is not to be counted as a separate commandment.

The Sixth Principle: where a commandment contains both a positive and negative injunction, its two parts are to be counted separately, the one among the positive commandments, and the other among the negative.

The Seventh Principle: the detailed laws of a commandment are not to be counted (among the commandments).

The Eighth Principle: a negative statement excluding a particular case from the scope of a commandment is not to be included among the negative commandments.

The Ninth Principle: the enumeration is not to be based on the number of times a particular negative or positive injunction is repeated in Scripture, but instead it is to be based upon the nature of the action prohibited or enjoined.

The Tenth Principle: acts prescribed as preliminary (to the performance of a commandment) are not to be counted.

The Eleventh Principle: the different elements which go together to form one commandment are not to be counted separately.

The Twelfth Principle: the successive stages in the performance of a commandment are not to be counted separately.

The Thirteenth Principle: where a certain commandment has to be performed on more days than one, it is not to be counted once for each day.

*The thirteen exegetical principles are enumerated in the famous *Baraita* of Rabbi Ishmael, included in the morning service in the traditional prayer book. Its original source is the opening of the *Sifra* on the Book of Leviticus.

†Based upon an extra word, particle, or letter in Scripture.

The Fourteenth Principle: how the modes of punishment are to be counted as positive commandments.

I now turn to explain each and every principle, and bring proofs for it, God be willing.

❨ 3 LOVE OF GOD*

By this injunction we are commanded to love God (exalted be He); that is to say, to dwell upon and contemplate His commandments, His injunctions, and His works, so that we may obtain a conception of Him, and in conceiving Him attain absolute joy. This constitutes the Love of God, and is obligatory. As the *Sifre* says: "Since it is said, 'And you shall love the Lord your God' (Deut. 6:5), the question arises, how is one to manifest his love for the Lord? Scripture therefore says: 'And these words which I command you this day, shall be upon your heart' (*ibid.* 6:6); for through this (*i.e.,* the contemplation of God's words) you will learn to discern Him whose word called the universe into existence."

We have thus made it clear to you that through this act of contemplation you will attain a conception of God and reach that stage of joy in which love of Him will follow of necessity.

The sages say that this commandment also includes an obligation to call upon all mankind to serve Him (exalted be He), and to have faith in Him. For just as you praise and extol anybody whom you love, and call upon others also to love him, so, if you love the Lord to the extent of the conception of His true nature to which you have attained, you will undoubtedly call upon the foolish and ignorant to seek knowledge of the truth which you have already acquired.

As the *Sifre* says: " 'And you shall love the Lord your God': this means that you should make Him beloved of man as Abraham your father did, as it is said, 'And the souls they had gotten in Haran' (Gen. 12:5). That is to say, just as Abraham, being a lover of the Lord—as Scripture testifies, 'Abraham My friend' (Is. 41:8;)—by the

*See *Mishneh Torah*, Book I, Repentance, ch. X.

power of his conception of God, and out of his great love for Him, summoned mankind to believe, you too must so love Him as to summon mankind to Him."

❨ 5 WORSHIPING GOD*

By this injunction we are commanded to serve God (exalted be He). This commandment is repeated several times in Scripture, e.g., "And you shall serve the Lord your God" (Ex. 23:25); "And Him shall you serve" (Deut. 13:5); "And Him shall you serve" (*ibid.* 6:13); "And to serve Him" (*ibid.* 11:13).

Although this commandment is of the class of general precepts which are excluded from the 613 commandments under the fourth principle, it nonetheless imposes a specific duty, viz. that of prayer. The *Sifre* says: " 'to serve Him' means prayer." The sages also say: " 'to serve Him' means study of the Law."

In the Mishnah of R. Eliezer, the son of R. Yose ha-Galili, the sages say: "Where do we learn that prayer is obligatory? From the verse, 'You shall fear the Lord your God; and Him shall you serve.' " The sages also say: "Serve Him through His Torah, and serve Him in His Sanctuary," which means that we should aspire to pray either in the Temple or toward it, as Solomon clearly said in I Kings 8:30.

❨ 9 SANCTIFYING GOD'S NAME†

By this injunction we are commanded to sanctify God's name. It is contained in His words, "But I will be hallowed among the children of Israel" (Lev. 22:32). The purport of this commandment is that we are in duty bound to proclaim this true religion to the world,

*See *Mishneh Torah*, Book II, Prayer, ch. I.

†See *Mishneh Torah*, Book I, Basic Principles, ch. V; Idolatry, ch. I; *Guide*, III, ch. 29.

undeterred by fear of injury from any source. Even if a tyrant tries to compel us by force to deny Him, we must not obey, but must positively rather submit to death; and we must not even mislead the tyrant into supposing that we have denied Him while in our hearts we continue to believe in Him (exalted be He).

This is the commandment concerning the Sanctification of the Name which is laid upon every son of Israel: that we must be ready to die at the tyrant's hands for our love of Him (exalted be He), and for our faith in His Unity, even as Hananiah, Mishael, and Azariah did in the time of the wicked Nebuchadnezzar, when he forced people to prostrate themselves before the idol (Dan. 3:1), and all did so, the Israelites included, and there was none there to sanctify the Name of Heaven, all being in terror. This was a sore disgrace to Israel, in that this commandment was disregarded by them all, and there was none to fulfill it, all being afraid.

This commandment applies only in circumstances such as those of that great occasion, when the whole world was in terror, and it was a duty to declare His Unity publicly at that time. The Lord had already promised through Isaiah that Israel would not be completely disgraced on that hard occasion, but young men would appear among them, undeterred by death, and would sacrifice their lives and proclaim the faith, sanctifying the Name publicly, as He commanded us through Moses our Teacher. This promise is in the words, "Jacob shall not now be ashamed, neither shall his face now wax pale; when he sees his children, the work of My hands, in the midst of him, that they sanctify My name" (Is. 29:22–23).

§ 317 CURSING AN ISRAELITE*

By this prohibition we are forbidden to curse any Israelite. It is contained in His words, "You shall not curse the deaf" (Lev. 19:14).

I will now explain the meaning of the term *heresh* (deaf).

When a person is moved by a desire to revenge himself on one who has wronged him by inflicting upon him an injury of the kind which he believes he has suffered, he will not be content until he has requited the wrong in that fashion; and only when he has had his

---

*See *Mishneh Torah*, Book XIV, Sanhedrin, XXVI, 1.

revenge will his feelings be relieved, and his mind cease to dwell on the idea. Sometimes a man's desire for revenge will be satisfied by merely cursing and reviling, because he knows how much hurt and shame this will cause his enemy. But sometimes the matter will be more serious, and he will not be content until he has completely ruined the other, whereupon he will be satisfied by the thought of the pain caused to his enemy by the loss of his property. In yet other cases the matter will be more serious still, and he will not be satisfied until he has thrashed his enemy or inflicted bodily injury upon him. Or it may be even more serious, and his desire for revenge will not be satisfied except by the extreme measure of taking his enemy's life and destroying his very existence. Sometimes, on the other hand, because of the lightness of the offense, the desire for vengeance will not be strong, so that he will find relief in uttering angry imprecations and curses, even though the other would not listen to them if he were present. It is well known that hot-tempered and choleric persons find relief in this way from the (annoyance caused by) trivial offenses, though the offender is not aware of their wrath and does not hear their fulminations.

Now we might suppose that the Torah, in forbidding us to curse an Israelite, (was moved by) the shame and the pain that the curse would cause him when he heard it, but that there is no sin in cursing the deaf, who cannot hear and therefore cannot feel hurt. For this reason He tells us that cursing is forbidden by prohibiting it in the case of the deaf, since the Torah is concerned not only with the one who is cursed, but also with the curser, who is told not to be vindictive and hot-tempered. Thus, we find, the bearers of the tradition deduce the prohibition against cursing an Israelite from the words of Scripture, "You shall not curse the deaf."

❲ 365 A KING AMASSING GREAT PERSONAL WEALTH*

By this prohibition the king is forbidden to amass great wealth for himself. It is contained in His words (exalted be He), "Neither shall he greatly multiply to himself silver and gold" (Deut. 17:17). The

---

*See *Mishneh Torah*, Book VIII, Trespass, ch. VIII.

limit prescribed is that he may not go beyond what is strictly required for the upkeep of his army and his personal attendants. He is permitted, however, to amass wealth for the needs of all Israel.

The Exalted One explains in Scripture the reason for these three commandments, namely, "Only he shall not multiply horses to himself . . . neither shall he multiply wives to himself . . . neither shall he greatly multiply to himself silver and gold" (ibid. 17:16–17); and the knowledge of the reasons for them led to their being disobeyed, as in the notorious case of Solomon, peace be upon him, notwithstanding his preeminence in knowledge and wisdom, and his being "the beloved of the Lord" (II Sam. 12:24).

Our sages learned from this that if men knew the reasons for all the commandments, they would find ways to disobey them. For if a man so perfect (as Solomon) wrongly supposed that his action (in taking many wives) would in no wise lead him into transgression, how much more would the weak-minded multitude (if they knew the reasons for the commandments) be led to disregard them, arguing thus: He forbade this, and ordered that, only for such-and-such reason; so we will carefully avoid the sin to prevent which this commandment was laid down, but will not be particular about the commandment itself; and this would destroy the very basis of religion. For this reason the Exalted One has withheld the reasons; but there is not even one commandment which has not a reason, and a cause, remote or immediate. Most of these causes and reasons, however, are beyond the intelligence and understanding of the multitude; yet of all (the commandments) the prophet testifies: "The precepts of the Lord are right, rejoicing the heart; the commandment of the Lord is pure, enlightening the eyes" (Ps. 19:9).

I beseech the help of the Lord in fulfilling all that He has commanded, and in refraining from all that he has forbidden.

Here ends what we intended to include in this work.

*T*HIS letter, described earlier as eloquent and philosophical, sensitive and empathetic, again reveals Maimonides as a resourceful pedagogue using literary skill, scientific knowledge, philosophical reasoning, and exegetical virtuosity in order to persuade his readers to remain steadfast in their faith. It not only is an example of medieval polemical literature but contains a philosophy of history as well.

The reader should pay special attention to the following:

(1) The phenomenology of persecutions of the Jews, the theory of suffering which is a constant of Jewish reality, and the promise of eternity which sustains this reality.

(2) The reliance upon special interpretation of Scripture, particularly the Book of Daniel.

(3) The summary of Maimonides' fundamental doctrine that all commandments in Judaism have an inner meaning designed to lead man to perfection.

(4) The notion that Christianity and Islam, Judaism's "daughter religions," are only surface imitations of Judaism.

(5) The refutation of the contention, frequently repeated by Muslim apologists, that Scripture has veiled allusions to Islam.

(6) The plea not to calculate the advent of the Messianic era

coupled with the recording of a family tradition which nevertheless suggests a date for this.

(7) The centrality of the problem of prophecy.

The thoughtful reader of this text will be in a position to gauge the stylistic and substantive transformations that occur when a philosopher becomes a polemicist and popularizer.

. . . You write that the rebel leader in Yemen decreed compulsory apostasy for the Jews by forcing the Jewish inhabitants of all the places he had subdued to desert the Jewish religion just as the Berbers had compelled them to do in Maghreb. Verily, this news has broken our backs and has astounded and dumbfounded the whole of our community. And rightly so. For these are evil tidings, "and whosoever hears of them, both his ears tingle" (I Sam. 3:11). Indeed our hearts are weakened, our minds are confused, and the powers of the body wasted because of the dire misfortunes which brought religious persecutions upon us from the two ends of the world, the East and the West, "so that the enemies were in the midst of Israel, some on this side, and some on that side" (Josh. 8:22). The prophet upon learning of such difficult and dreadful times prayed and interceded in our behalf, as we read, "Then said I, O Lord God, cease, I beseech You: how shall Jacob stand? for he is small" (Amos 7:5). Indeed, this is a subject which no religious man dare take lightly, nor any one who believes in Moses put aside. There can be no doubt that these are the Messianic travails concerning which the sages invoked God that they be spared seeing and experiencing them. Similarly the prophets trembled when they envisioned them as we learn from the words of Isaiah, "My heart pants, fearfulness frightens me, the twilight I have longed for has been turned for me into trembling" (Is. 21:4). Note also the divine exclamation in the Torah expressing sympathy for those who will experience them, as we read, "Alas, who shall live when God does this!" (Num. 24:23).

You write that the hearts of some people have turned away, uncertainty befalls them and their beliefs are weakened, while others have not lost faith nor have they become disquieted. Concerning this matter we have a divine premonition through Daniel who predicted that the prolonged stay of Israel in the Diaspora, and the continuous persecutions will cause many to drift away from our faith, to have misgivings, or to go astray, because they witnessed our feebleness, and noted the triumph of our adversaries and their dominion over us, while others would neither oscillate in their belief, nor be shaken in their convictions. This may be gathered from the verse, "Many shall purify themselves, make themselves white, and be refined, but the wicked shall do wickedly, and none of the wicked shall understand; but they that are wise shall understand" (Dan. 12:10). Further on he foretells that even men of understanding and intelligence who would have brooked milder misfortunes and remained firm in their belief in God and in His servant Moses, will yield to distrust and will err, when they are visited by sterner and harsher afflictions, while only a few will remain pure in faith as we read, "And some of them that are wise shall stumble" (Dan. 11:35).

And now, my coreligionists, it is essential for you all to give attention and consideration to that which I am going to point out to you. You should impress it upon the minds of your women and children, so that their faith which may be enfeebled and impaired may be strengthened, and that they be re-established in an unceasing belief. May the Lord deliver us and you from religious doubt!

Remember, that ours is the true and authentic divine religion, revealed to us through Moses, the master of the former as well as the later prophets, by means of which God has distinguished us from the rest of mankind, as Scripture says, "Only the Lord had a delight in your fathers to love them and He chose their seed after them, even you above all peoples" (Deut. 10:15). This did not happen because of our merits, but rather as an act of divine grace, and on account of our forefathers who were cognizant of God and submitted to Him as we read, "The Lord did not set His love upon you, nor choose you, because you were more in number than any people ... but because the Lord loved you, and because He would keep the oath which He swore to your fathers" (Deut. 7:7). God has made us unique by His laws and precepts, and our pre-eminence is manifested in His rules and statutes, as Scripture says, in narrating God's mercies to us, "And what great nation is there, that has statutes and ordinances so righteous as all this law, which I set before you this day?" (Deut. 4:8). Therefore all the nations instigated by envy and impiety rose up against us, and all the kings of the earth motivated by injustice and enmity applied themselves to persecute us. They wanted to thwart

God, but He cannot be thwarted. Ever since the time of Revelation, every despot or slave that has attained to power, be he violent or ignoble, has made it his first aim and his final purpose to destroy our law, and to vitiate our religion, by means of the sword, by violence, or by brute force, such as Amalek, Sisera, Sennacherib, Nebuchadnezzar, Titus, Hadrian, may their bones be ground to dust, and others like them. This is one of the two classes which attempt to foil the divine will.

The second class consists of the most intelligent and educated among the nations, such as the Syrians, Persians, and Greeks. These also endeavor to demolish our law and to vitiate it by means of arguments which they invent, and by means of controversies which they institute. They seek to render the Law ineffectual and to wipe out every trace thereof by means of their polemical writings, just as the despots plan to do it with the sword. But neither the one nor the other shall succeed. We possess the divine assurance given to Isaiah concerning any tyrant that will wish to undermine our Law and to annihilate it by weapons of war, that the Lord will demolish them so that they will have no effect. This is only a metaphorical way of saying that his efforts will be of no avail, and that he will not accomplish his purpose. In like manner whenever a disputant shall attempt to demonstrate the falsity of our Law, the Lord will shatter his arguments and prove them absurd, untenable, and ineffective. This divine promise is contained in the following verse, "No weapon that is formed against you shall prosper; and every tongue that shall rise against you in judgment you shall condemn" (Is. 54:17).

Although the exponents of both methods persuade themselves that this is a structure which can be demolished, and they exert themselves to undermine its firmly established foundations, they only increase their pain and toil. The structure remains as firmly planted as ever, while the God of truth mocks and derides them, because they endeavor, with their feeble intelligence, to achieve a goal that is beyond the powers of mortal man. The inspired writer describes their attempt and God's scorn of them in the following verses: "Let us break their bands asunder, and cast away their words from us. He that sits in heaven laughs, the Lord has them in derision" (Ps. 2:3–4). Both of these parties have harassed and afflicted us incessantly throughout the epoch of our political independence, and partly during the period of our dispersion.

After that there arose a new sect which combined the two methods, namely, conquest and controversy, into one, because it believed that this procedure would be more effective in wiping out every trace of the Jewish nation and religion. It, therefore, resolved to lay claim to prophecy and to found a new faith, contrary to our divine religion, and to contend that it was equally God-given. Thereby it hoped to raise doubts and to create confusion, since one is opposed to the other and both supposedly emanate from a divine source, which would lead to the destruction of both religions. For such is the remarkable plan contrived by a man who is envious and querulous. He will strive to kill his enemy and to save his own life, but when he finds it impossible to attain his objective, he will devise a scheme whereby they both will be slain.

The first one to have adopted this plan was Jesus the Nazarene, may his bones be ground to dust. He was a Jew because his mother was a Jewess although his father was a Gentile. For in accordance with the principles of our law, a child born of a Jewess and a Gentile, or of a Jewess and a slave, is legitimate (Yevamot 45a). Jesus is only figuratively termed an illegitimate child. He impelled people to believe that he was a prophet sent by God to clarify perplexities in the Torah, and that he was the Messiah that was predicted by each and every seer. He interpreted the Torah and its precepts in such a fashion as to lead to their total annulment, to the abolition of all its commandments and to the violation of its prohibitions. The sages, of blessed memory, having become aware of his plans before his reputation spread among our people, meted out fitting punishment to him.

Daniel had already alluded to him when he presaged the downfall of a wicked one and a heretic among the Jews who would endeavor to destroy the Law, claim prophecy for himself, make pretenses to miracles, and allege that he is the Messiah, as it is written, "Also the children of the impudent among your people shall make bold to claim prophecy, but they shall fall" (Dan. 11:14).

Quite some time after, a religion appeared the origin of which is traced to him by the descendants of Esau, albeit it was not the intention of this person to establish a new faith. For he was innocuous to Israel as neither individual nor groups were unsettled in their beliefs because of him, since his inconsistencies were so transparent to every one. Finally he was overpowered and put a stop to by us when he fell into our hands, and his fate is well known.

After him arose the Madman who emulated his precursor since he paved the way for him. But he added the further objective of procuring rule and submission, and he invented his well-known religion (Islam). All of these men purposed to place their teachings on the same level with our divine religion. But only a simpleton who lacks knowledge of both would liken divine institutions to human practices. Our religion differs as much from other religions for which there are alleged resemblances as a living man endowed with the faculty of reason is unlike a statue which is ever so well carved out of marble, wood, bronze or silver. When a person ignorant of divine wisdom or of God's works sees the statue that superficially resembles a man in its contours, form, features, and color, he believes that the structure of the parts of a statue is like the constitution of a man, because he is deficient in understanding concerning the inner organization of both. But the informed person who knows the interior of both, is cognizant of the fact that the internal structure of the statue betrays no skillful workmanship at all, whereas the inward parts of man are truly marvellously made, a testimony to the wisdom of the Creator, such as the prolongation of the nerves in the muscles and their ramifications, the branching out of the sinews and their intersections and the network of their ligaments and their manner of growth, the articulations of the bones and the joints, the pulsating and non-pulsating blood vessels and their ramifications, the setting of the limbs into one another, the uncovered and covered parts, every one of these in proportion in form and proper place.

Likewise a person ignorant of the secret meaning of Scripture and the deeper significance of the Law would be led to believe that our religion has something in common with another if he makes a comparison between the two. For he will note that in the Torah there are prohibitions and commandments, just as in other religions there are permitted and interdicted acts. Both contain a system of religious observances, positive and negative precepts, sanctioned by reward and punishment.

If he could only fathom the inner intent of the law, then he would realize that the essence of the true divine religion lies in the deeper meaning of its positive and negative precepts, every one of which will aid man in his striving after perfection, and remove every impediment to the attainment of excellence. These commands will enable the throng and the élite to acquire moral and intellectual qualities, each according to his ability. Thus the godly community becomes pre-eminent, reaching a twofold perfection. By the first perfection I mean, man's spending his life in this world under the most agreeable and congenial conditions. The second perfection would constitute the achievement of intellectual objectives, each in accordance with his native powers.

The tenets of the other religions which resemble those of Scripture have no deeper meaning, but are superficial imitations, copied from and patterned after it. They modelled their religions upon ours in order to glorify themselves, and indulge the fancy that they are similar to so and so. However, their counterfeiting is an open secret to the learned. Consequently they became objects of derision and ridicule just as one laughs and smiles at an ape when it imitates the actions of men.

This event was predicted in the divinely inspired prophecy of Daniel, according to which, in some future time a person would appear with a religion similar to the true one, with a book of Scriptures and oral communications, who will arrogantly pretend that God had vouchsafed him a revelation, and that he held converse with Him, besides making other extravagant claims. Thus Daniel in his description of the rise of the Arabic kingdom after the fall of the Roman Empire, alluded to the appearance of the Madman and his victories over the Roman, Persian, and Byzantine Empires in the vision concerning a horn which grew, became long and strong. This is clearly indicated in a verse that can be understood by the masses as well as by the select few. Since this interpretation is borne out by the facts of history, no other meaning can be given to the following verse: "I considered the horns, and, behold, there came among them another horn, a little one, before which three of the first horns were plucked up by the roots; and, behold, in this horn were eyes like the eyes of a man, and a mouth speaking great things" (Dan. 7:8).

Now consider how remarkably apt the symbolism is. Daniel says that he saw a small horn that was going up. When it became longer, even marvellously longer, it cast down before it three horns and, behold, in the side of the horn there were two eyes similar to the two eyes of man, and a mouth speaking wanton words. This obviously alludes to the person who will found a new religion similar to the divine law, and make claims to a revelation of a Scripture, and to prophecy. He will, furthermore, endeavor to alter and abolish the Law, as it is said, "And he shall seek to change the seasons and the law" (Dan. 7:25).

Daniel was divinely informed that He would destroy this person notwithstanding his greatness and his long endurance together with the remaining adherents of his predecessors. For the three parties that warred against us will ultimately perish, *i.e.*, the one that sought to overpower us with the sword, the second which strove to conquer us by arguments, as well the third that founded a religion similar to ours.

Though they shall appear to be triumphant for a while, and be in the ascendancy for a longer or shorter period of time, they shall not last nor endure. We have a divine assurance from time immemorial that whenever a decree of apostasy is passed against us, God will ultimately terminate it. When King David inspired by the Holy Spirit and speaking in the name of the community reflected, how many peoples ruled over Israel in the past, and how many trials and tribulations they had undergone from the beginning of their history, and nevertheless were not exterminated, he was moved to exclaim, "Much have they afflicted me from my youth up; but they have not prevailed against me" (Ps. 129:2).

My brethren, you all know that in the time of Nebuchadnezzar the Wicked, the Jews were compelled to worship idols and none was spared save Hananiah, Mishael, and Azariah. Ultimately God destroyed Nebuchadnezzar, and put an end to his laws, and the religion of truth came back to its own.

Similarly during the Second Commonwealth when the wicked Greek rulers gained control of Palestine, they instituted severe persecutions against Israel in order to abolish the Torah. The Jews were compelled to profane the Sabbath, and were forbidden to observe the rite of circumcision. Every Jew was forced to write on his garment the words, "We have no portion in the Lord God of Israel," and also to engrave this sentence on the horns of his ox and then plough with it. This state of affairs lasted about fifty-two years. Finally, God brought to an end simultaneously their empire and their laws.

The sages, of blessed memory, frequently allude to persecutions in the following manner: "once the wicked government passed the following decree of persecution," or, "they decreed so and so." After a while God would make the decree null and void by destroying the power which issued it. It was this observation that led the rabbis, of blessed memory, to affirm that persecutions are of short duration (Ketuvot 3b).

The divine assurance was given to Jacob our father that his descendants would survive the people who degraded and discomfited them as it is written: "And your seed shall be like the dust of the earth" (Gen. 28:14). That is to say, although his offspring will be abased like dust that is trodden under foot, they will ultimately emerge triumphant and victorious, and as the simile implies, just as the dust settles finally upon him who tramples upon it and remains after him, so shall Israel outlive its persecutors.*

The prophet Isaiah has long ago predicted that various peoples will succeed in vanquishing Israel and lording over them for some time. But that ultimately God will come to Israel's assistance and will put a stop to their woes and affliction as is suggested in the following verse: "A grievous vision is declared to me; the treacherous one will deal treacherously, and the spoiler will spoil; Go up O Elam, besiege O Media! but ultimately the sighing thereof I shall make to cease" (Is. 21:2).

We are in possession of the divine assurance that Israel is indestructible and imperishable, and will always continue to be a preeminent community. As it is impossible for God to cease to exist, so is Israel's destruction and disappearance from the world unthinkable, as we read, "For I the Lord change not, and you, O sons of Jacob, will not be consumed" (Mal. 3:6). Similarly He has avowed and assured us that it is unimaginable that He will reject us entirely even if we disobey Him, and disregard His behests, as the prophet Jeremiah avers, "Thus says the Lord: If heaven above can be measured, and the foundations of the earth searched out beneath, then will I also cast off all the seed of Israel for all that they have done, says the Lord" (Jer. 31:36). Indeed this very promise has already been given before through Moses our Teacher who says, "And yet for all that, when they are in the land of their enemies, I will not reject them, neither will I abhor them, to destroy them utterly, and to break My covenant with them; for I am the Lord their God" (Lev. 26:44).

Put your trust in the true promises of Scripture, brethren, and be not dismayed at the series of persecutions or the enemy's ascendancy over us, or the weakness of our people. These trails are designed to test and purify us so that only the saints and the pious ones of the pure and undefiled lineage of Jacob will adhere to our religion and remain within the fold, as it is written, "And among the remnant are those whom the Lord shall call" (Joel 3:5). This verse makes it clear that they are not numerous, being the descendants of those who were present on Mount Sinai, witnessed the divine Revela-

*See *Mishneh Torah*, Book V, Forbidden Intercourse, ch. XIV.

tion, entered into the covenant of God, and undertook to do and obey as is signified in their saying, "We will do and obey" (Ex. 24:7). They obligated not only themselves but also their descendants, as it is written, "To us and to our children forever" (Deut. 29:28). We have been given adequate divine assurance that not only did all the persons who were present at the Sinaitic Revelation believe in the prophecy of Moses and in his Law, but that their descendants likewise would do so, until the end of time, as it is written, "Lo, I come to you in a thick cloud, that the people may hear when I speak with you, and may also believe you forever" (Ex. 10:9).

Consequently it is manifest that he who spurns the religion that was revealed at that theophany is not an offspring of the folk who witnessed it. For our sages, of blessed memory, have insisted that they who entertain scruples concerning the divine message are not scions of the race that were present on Mount Sinai (Nedarim 20a). May God guard us and you from doubt, and banish from our midst confusion and suspicion which lead to it.

Now, my coreligionists in the Diaspora, it behooves you to hearten one another, the elders to guide the youth, and the leaders to direct the masses. Give your assent to the truth that is immutable and unchangeable, and to the following postulates of a religion that shall never fail. God is one in a unique sense of the term, and Moses is His prophet and spokesman, and the greatest and most perfect of the seers. To him was vouchsafed by God what has never been vouchsafed to any prophet before him, nor will it be in the future. The entire Torah was divinely revealed to Moses of whom it was said, "With him do I speak mouth to mouth" (Num. 12:8). It will neither be abrogated nor superseded, neither supplemented nor abridged. Never shall it be supplanted by another divine revelation containing positive and negative duties. Keep well in mind the Revelation on Sinai in accordance with the divine precept to perpetuate the memory of this occasion and not to allow it to fall into oblivion. Furthermore, we were enjoined to impress this event upon the minds of our children, as it is written, "Only take heed to yourself, and keep your soul diligently, lest you forget the things which your eyes saw, and lest they depart from your heart all the days of your life; but make them known to your children and your children's children" (Deut. 4:9).

It is imperative, my fellow Jews, that you make this great spectacle of the Revelation appeal to the imagination of your children. Proclaim at public gatherings its momentousness. For this event is the pivot of our religion, and the proof which demonstrates its veracity. Evaluate this phenomenon at its true importance, for Scripture has pointed out its significance in the verse, "For ask now of the days past, which were before you since the day that God created man upon the earth, and from the one end of heaven to the other, whether there has been any such thing as this great thing is, or has been heard like it?" (Deut. 4:32).

Remember, my coreligionists, that this great, incomparable, and unique historical event is attested by the best of evidence. For never before or since, has a whole nation witnessed a revelation from God or beheld His splendor. The purpose of all this was to confirm us in the faith so that nothing can change it, and to reach a degree of certainty which will sustain us in these trying times of fierce persecution and absolute tyranny, as it is written, "For God is come to test you" (Ex. 20:17). Scripture means that God revealed Himself to you thus in order to give you strength to withstand all future trials. Now do not slip nor err, be steadfast in your religion and persevere in your faith and its duties.

Solomon, of blessed memory, has compared our people to a beautiful woman with a perfect figure, marred by no defect, in the verse, "You are all fair, my love; and there is no spot in you" (Song of Songs 4:7). On the other hand, he depicted the adherents of other religions and faiths, who strive to entice and win us over to their convictions, as courtesans who lure virtuous women for lewd purposes. Similarly they seek devices to trap us into embracing their religions, and subscribing to their doctrines. To these who endeavor to decoy her into avowing the superiority of their creed, our nation deftly replies, "Why do you take hold of me, can you confer upon me something like the felicity of the two companies?" She reasons thus, "If you can furnish us with something like the Revelation on Sinai, in which the camp of Israel faced the camp of the Divine Presence, then we shall espouse your doctrines." This is metaphorically expressed in the verse, "Return, return, O Shulammite; return, return, that we may look upon you. What will you see in the Shulammite? As it were a dance of two companies" (ibid. 7:1). Now "Shulammite" signifies the perfect one; "A dance of the two companies" alludes to the joy of the theophany in Mount Sinai in which both the camp of Israel and the camp of God showed as is intimated in the two following verses: "Moses brought forth the people out of the camp to meet God" (Ex. 19:17), and "The chariots of God are myriads, even thousands upon thousands; the Lord is among them, as in Sinai, in holiness" (Ps. 68:18).

Note well the apt imagery and the deeper significance of the aforementioned verse. The fourfold occurrence of the word "return" is an allusion to the four empires, each of which will endeavor to coerce us to abandon our faith and embrace theirs. Incidentally, it may be mentioned that we are now living under the aegis of the Fourth Empire. A prediction to this effect is found in the Torah, that our enemies will force us to accept their faith, for we read, "And there shall you serve gods, the work of men's hands" (Deut. 4:28). However, it will not be general throughout the world and God will never deprive us of His Law. As He assured us saying: "For it shall not be forgotten from the mouth of his seed" (ibid. 31:21). Indeed, Isaiah, the herald of the national redemption, has already stated that Israel's indestructibility is the result of a divine pact betokened by the perpetuation of the Torah in our midst, and our devotion to its tenets and teachings, as he says, "And as for Me, this is My covenant with them, says the Lord; My spirit that is upon you, and My words which I have put in your mouth, shall not depart out of your mouth, nor out of the mouth of your seed, nor out of the mouth of your seed's seed, says the Lord, from henceforth and for ever" (Is. 59:21).

Our nation speaks with pride of the virulent oppression it has suffered, and the sore tribulations it has endured, to quote the words of the psalmist, "Nay, but for Your sake are we killed all the day" (Ps. 44:23). The rabbis, of blessed memory, remark that the verse "Nay, but for Your sake" alludes to the generation that undergoes persecution (Midrash Song of Songs 1:3). Let those persons exalt who suffered dire misfortunes, were deprived of their riches, forced into exile and lost their belongings. For the bearing of these hardships is a source of glory and a great achievement in the sight of God. Whoever is visited by these calamities is like a burnt offering upon the altar. We may apply in commendation the verse to them, "Consecrate yourselves today to the Lord, that He may also bestow upon you a blessing this day" (Ex. 32:29).

It behooves the victim for the sake of his religion to escape and flee to the desert and wilderness, and not to consider separation from family or loss of wealth. For they are a slight sacrifice and a paltry offering due to God, King of kings, possessor of all things, the Lord your God, whose Name is glorious and awesome. God may be trusted to compensate you well in this world and in the world to come.

We have noted that godly and pious folk who are animated by a desire to get acquainted with the truth and those who are engaged in its pursuit, rush to the divine religion and wend their way from the most distant parts to the homes of scholars. They seek to gain increased insight into the law with the concomitant hope that God will amply reward them. How much more is it one's duty to go into exile, if the question of observing the whole Torah is at stake.

When a man finds it arduous to gain a livelihood in one country he emigrates to another. All the more is it incumbent upon a Jew who is restricted in the practice of his religion to depart for another place. If he finds it impossible to leave that locality for the time being, he must not become careless and indulge with abandon in the desecration of the Sabbath and the dietary laws on the assumption that he is exempt from all religious obligations. It is the eternally inescapable duty of everyone belonging to the stock of Jacob to abide by the Law. Nay, he exposes himself to punishment for the violation of each and every positive or negative precept. Let no man conclude that he may freely disregard the less important ceremonies without liability to penalty because he has committed under duress some major sins. For Jeroboam, son of Nebat, may his bones be ground to dust, was chastised not only for the sin of worshiping the calves and inciting Israel to do the same, but also for his failure to construct a booth on the Feast of Tabernacles. This is one of the fundamental principles of our religion. Understand it aright, teach it, and apply the principle widely.

In your letter you mention that the apostle has spurred on a number of people to believe that several verses in Scripture allude to the Madman, such as "bimeod meod" (Gen. 17:20); "He shined forth from Mount Paran" (Deut. 33:2); "A prophet from the midst of you" (Deut. 18:15); and the promise to Ishmael, "I will make him a great nation" (Gen. 17:20). These arguments have been rehearsed so often that they have become nauseating. It is not enough to declare that they are altogether feeble; nay, to cite as proofs these verses is ridiculous and absurd in the extreme. For these are not matters that can confuse the minds of anyone. Neither the untutored multitude nor the apostates themselves who delude others with them, believe in them or entertain any illusions about them. Their purpose in citing these verses is to win favor in the eyes of the

Gentiles by demonstrating that they believe the statement of the Koran that Mohammed was mentioned in the Torah. But the Muslims themselves put no faith in their arguments, they neither accept nor cite them, because they are manifestly so fallacious. Inasmuch as the Muslims could not find a single proof in the entire Bible nor a reference or possible allusion to their prophet which they could utilize, they were compelled to accuse us saying, "You have altered the text of the Torah, and expunged every trace of the name of Mohammed therefrom." They could find nothing stronger than this ignominious argument the falsity of which is easily demonstrated to one and all by the following facts. First, Scripture was translated into Syriac, Greek, Persian, and Latin hundreds of years before the appearance of Mohammed. Second, there is a uniform tradition as to the text of the Bible both in the East and the West, with the result that no differences in the text exist at all, not even in the vocalization, for they are all correct. Nor do any differences affecting the meaning exist. The motive for their accusation lies, therefore, in the absence of any allusion to Mohammed in the Torah. . . .

In your letter you have adverted to the computations of the date of the Redemption and R. Saadiah's opinion on the subject. First of all, it devolves upon you to know that no human being will ever be able to determine it precisely as Daniel has already intimated, "For the words are shut up and sealed" (Dan. 12:9). Indeed, many hypotheses were advanced by scholars, who fancied that they have discovered the date, as was anticipated in Scripture, "Many will run to and fro, and opinions shall be increased" (ibid.). That is, there shall be numerous views concerning it. Furthermore, we have a divine communication through the medium of the prophets that many persons will calculate the time of the advent of the Messiah but will fail to ascertain its true date. We are cautioned against giving way to doubt and distrust because of these miscalculations. The longer the delay, the more fervently shall you hope, as it is written, "And it declares of the end and does not lie, though it tarry, wait for it, because it will surely come, it will not delay" (Hab. 2:3).

Remember that even the date of the termination of the Egyptian exile was not precisely known and gave rise to differences of opinion, although its duration was fixed in Scripture, where we read, "And they shall serve them and afflict them four hundred years" (Gen. 15:13). Some reckoned the period of four hundred years from the time of Jacob's arrival in Egypt, others dated it from the beginning of Israel's bondage, which happened seventy years later, while still others computed it from the time of the Covenant of the Pieces when this matter was divinely predicted to Abraham. At the expiration of four hundred years after this event, and thirty years before the appearance of Moses, a band of Israelites left Egypt because they believed that exile had ended for them. They were subdued and slain by the Egyptians. The lot of the Israelites who remained was consequently aggravated as we learn from our sages, the teachers of our national traditions. David already alluded to the vanquished Israelites who miscalculated the date of the redemption in the verse, "The children of Ephraim were as archers handling the bow that turned back in the day of battle" (Ps. 78:9).

In truth, the period of four hundred years commences with the birth of Isaac, the seed of Abraham, par excellence, as may be gathered from the verse, "For in Isaac shall seed be called to you" (Gen. 21:12), and the verse, "Your seed shall be a stranger in a land that is not theirs, they shall serve them and afflict them four hundred years" (ibid. 15:13). In exile, they would rule, enslave, and maltreat them, this is the implication of this text. The four hundred years mentioned in this verse refer to the duration of the exile, and not (solely) to the Egyptian bondage. This fact was misunderstood until the great prophet (Moses) came, when it was realized that the four hundred years dates back precisely to the birth of Isaac. Now, if so much uncertainty prevailed in regard to the date of the emancipation from the Egyptian bondage, the term of which was fixed, how much more would it be the case in respect to the date of the final redemption, the prolonged and protracted duration of which appalled and dismayed our inspired seers, so that one of them was moved to exclaim, "Will You be angry with us forever? Will You draw out Your anger to all generations?" (Ps. 85:6). Isaiah, too, alluding to the long drawn out exile, declared: "And they shall be gathered together as prisoners and gathered in the dungeon, and shall be shut up in prison, and after many days shall they be released" (Is. 24:22). Inasmuch as Daniel has proclaimed the matter a deep secret, our sages have interdicted the calculation of the time of the future redemption, or the reckoning of the period of the advent of the Messiah, because the masses might be mystified and bewildered should the Messiah fail to appear as forecast. The rabbis invoked God to frustrate and destroy those who seek to determine precisely the advent of the Messianic era, because they are a stumbling block to the people, and that is why they uttered the imprecation "May the calculators of the final redemption come to grief" (Sanhedrin 97b).

As for R. Saadiah's Messianic calculations, there are extenuating circumstances for them though he knew they were disallowed. For the Jews of his time were perplexed and misguided. The divine religion might well nigh have disappeared had he not encouraged the pusillanimous, and diffused, disseminated, and propagated by word of mouth and pen a knowledge of its underlying principles. He believed, in all earnestness, that by means of the Messianic calculations, he would inspire the masses with hope for the truth. Verily all his deeds were for the sake of heaven. Consequently, in view of the probity of his motives which we have disclosed, one must not decry him for his Messianic computations.

I note that you are inclined to believe in astrology* and in the influence of the past and future conjunctions of the planets upon human affairs. You should dismiss such notions from your thoughts. Cleanse your mind as one cleanses dirty clothes. Accomplished scholars, whether they are religious or not, refuse to believe in the truth of this science. Its postulates can be refuted by real proofs on rational grounds. But this is not the place to enter into a discussion of them. Mark well, however, what Scripture has to say about the astrologers. At the time when Moses rose to leadership the astrologers had unanimously predicted that our nation would never be freed from bondage nor gain its independence, but fortune smiled upon Israel, for the most exquisite of human beings appeared and redeemed them at the very time which was supposedly most inauspicious for them. Furthermore, Egypt was smitten with the plagues at the very time for which the astrologers foretold an epoch of wholesome climate, abundance, and prosperity for its inhabitants. To the failure of their vaticination, Isaiah alludes when he says, "Where are they then your wise men? And let them tell you now, and let them know what the Lord of hosts has purposed concerning Egypt" (Is. 19:12).

Similarly the pundits, astrologers, and prognosticators were all of one mind that the administration of Nebuchadnezzar, the wicked, marked the beginning of an era of enduring prosperity. Indeed, his dynasty was extinguished and destroyed, as was divinely forecast by Isaiah. He derided them for pretending to foreknowledge, and held

---

*See Letter on Astrology. Also: *Mishneh Torah*, Book I, Idolatry, XI, 16.

up to scorn the state which fancied itself in possession of sapient folk versed in futurity, as we read, "Let now the astrologers, the star-gazers, the monthly prognosticators, stand up and save you" (Is. 47:13).

They are likewise wrong in their predictions concerning the era of the Messiah, may he speedily come. For while the Gentiles believe that our nation will never constitute an independent state, nor will they even rise above their present condition, and all the astrologers, diviners, and augurs concur in this opinion, God will prove false their views and beliefs, and will order the advent of the Messiah. Again, it is Isaiah who makes reference to this event in the verse: "That frustrate the tokens of the impostors, and makes the diviners mad; that turns wise men backward, and makes their knowledge foolish; that confirms the word of His servant, and performs the counsel of His messengers; that says of Jerusalem, 'She shall be inhabited'; and of the cities of Judah, 'They shall be built, and I will raise up the waste places thereof'" (Is. 44:25–26). This is the correct view that every Israelite should hold, without paying any attention to the conjunctions of the stars, of greater or smaller magnitude.

I have observed your statement that science is little cultivated, and that learning does not flourish in your country, which you attribute to the influence of the conjunctions in the earthly trigon. Remember that this low state of learning and science is not peculiar to your country, but is widely prevalent in Israel today. Indeed, a divine premonition of such a state of affairs is contained in a verse in Isaiah which reads, "Therefore, behold, I will again do a marvelous work among this people, even a marvelous work, and a wonder, and the wisdom of the wise men shall perish, and the prudence of the prudent men shall be hid" (Is. 29:14).

This condition is not due to the earthly or fiery trigon, as is proven by the fact that Solomon, king of Israel, lived during the earthly trigon, and yet Scripture testifies that "He was wiser than all men" (I Kings 5:11). So did Abraham, of blessed memory, who was designated the Pillar of the World, discovered the First Cause of the entire universe, and demonstrated the central importance of the principle of the Unity of God for all mankind. He, Isaac, and Jacob, all three of them, carry the throne of glory in their hearts, to make use of a rabbinical metaphor, "The patriarchs are the chariots" (Gen. Rabbah 82:7), which in turn was suggested by the verse, "And God rose up over him" (Gen. 35:13). The meaning is that they have attained a true conception of the Deity. Now the three patriarchs lived during the earthly trigon.

This matter will become clear if the following facts are borne in mind. There is, first, the smaller conjunction, that is, the meeting of Saturn with Jupiter, which occurs once in approximately twenty solar years. These conjunctions continue to take place twelve times within the same trigon, covering a period of two hundred and forty years. Then conjunctions take place in the second trigon, which occur every two hundred and forty solar years. The shift to the next trigon is known as the medium conjunction. According to this calculation an interval of nine hundred and sixty years will elapse between the first and second meeting of two planets in the same point of the Zodiac. This is termed the great conjunction, and occurs once in nine hundred and sixty years. This is the time that must elapse between the first and second meeting of Saturn and Jupiter in the same degree of Aries. If you will calculate back, you will understand my statement above that Abraham, Isaac, and Jacob as well as David lived during the earthly trigon. My purpose in going into details was to dispel any suspicion of yours that the trigon exercises any influence upon human affairs.

Furthermore, you write that some people have calculated the forthcoming conjunction and have determined that all the seven planets will meet in one of the constellations of the Zodiac. This forecast is untrue, for no meeting of the seven planets will occur in the next conjunction, nor in the following ones. For such an event will not happen even in ten thousand years, as is well known to those who are familiar with the astronomical law of equation. Verily this is the calculation of an ignorant person, as is evinced by other remarks of his, quoted by you, to the effect that there will be a deluge of air and of dust. It is essential for you to know that these and similar assertions are fabricated and mendacious. Do not consider a statement true because you find it in a book, for the prevaricator is as little restrained with his pen as with his tongue. For the untutored and uninstructed are convinced of the veracity of a statement by the mere fact that it is written; nevertheless its accuracy must be demonstrated in another manner.

Remember that a blind person submits to an individual having power of sight for intelligent direction knowing that he lacks the vision to guide himself safely; and an ailing person, unskilled in the art of medicine, and uninformed as to matters detrimental to or beneficial for his health, defers to a physician for guidance and obeys him implicitly. Just so is it indispensable for the laity to yield unswervingly to the prophets, who were men of true insight, and to confide in them in respect to matters affecting the truth or the error of a given teaching. Next in importance are the sages who have studied day and night the dogmas and doctrines of our faith and have learned to distinguish between the genuine and the spurious.

After this exposition you may trust me that the statements you have previously quoted are inaccurate and this applies equally to similar views which you heard expressed in conversation or met with in books. For the author of such sayings is either ignorant, a mountebank, or seeks to destroy the law and to demolish its bulwarks. Do you perceive the brazenness of these people who assert that there will be a deluge of air, and dust, and fire, in order to deceive and delude others to believe that the Deluge in the time of Noah was merely due to a concentration of water, and was not a divine punishment for the immorality of the time, as is explicitly stated in Scripture that guides us against error and fallacy. Similarly, Sodom and the other cities were not destroyed because of the unbelief and wickedness of their inhabitants in direct contradiction to the Bible which says, "I will go down now, and see whether they have done altogether according to the cry of it which is come to Me" (Gen. 18:21). Thus whatever happens in this world through divine intervention, they say is the inevitable consequence of the planetary conjunctions.

They have affirmed the truth of their propositions in order to undermine the principles of our religion, and to give free reign to their animal instincts and passions as do the beasts and the ostriches. We were divinely admonished against those views in Scripture to the following effect: If you rebel against Me so that I bring disaster upon you as a punishment for your misdeeds, but you ascribe your reverses to chance rather than to your guilt, then shall I increase your afflictions and make them more grievous. This is the intent of the verse in the Chapter of Admonition: "If you will walk with Me bekeri, I, too, shall walk with you in the wrath of keri" (Lev. 26:27–28).* Now "keri" signifies chance, hazard. Scripture means to say: If you regard My chastisement as a fortuitous event, then shall I bring the most severe calamities upon you "sevenfold for your sins" (ibid. 26:28).

---

*See Mishneh Torah, Book III, Fast Days, ch. I.

These foregoing remarks have made it abundantly clear that the advent of the Messiah is in no way subject to the influence of the stars.

Indeed one of our keen minds in the province of Andalusia calculated by means of astrology the date of the final redemption and predicted the coming of the Messiah in a particular year. Every one of our distinguished scholars made little of his declaration, discounted what he did and censured him sharply for it. But grim fate dealt with him more sternly than we could have. For at the very time when the Messiah was supposed to arrive, a rebel leader appeared in Maghreb who issued an order of conversion as you are well aware. The event proved to be a great debacle for the partisans of this prognosticator. Indeed, the hardships experienced by our people in the Diaspora are responsible for these extravagances, for a drowning man catches at a straw.

Therefore, my coreligionists, "be strong and let your heart take courage, all you that wait for the Lord" (Ps. 31:25). Strengthen one another, affirm your faith in the Expected One, may he speedily appear in your midst. "Strengthen the weak hands and make firm the tottering knees" (Is. 35:3). Remember! Isaiah, the herald of Israel's redemption, predicted that the prolongation of the adversities of exile will impel many of our people to believe that God has relinquished and abandoned us (far be it from Him), as we read "But Zion said: 'The Lord has forsaken me, and the Lord has forgotten me'" (ibid. 49:14). But he was given the divine assurance that such is not the case, to quote the following, "Can a woman forget her sucking child, that she should not have compassion on the son of her womb? Yes, these may forget, yet I will not forget you" (ibid. 49:15). In truth, this divine promise had already been divulged by the first prophet, who declared: "For the Lord your God is a merciful God. He will not fail you, neither destroy you, nor forget the covenant of your fathers which He swore to them" (Deut. 4:31). "Then the Lord your God will turn your captivity and have compassion on you, and will return and gather you from all the peoples where the Lord your God has scattered you" (ibid. 30:3).

It is, my coreligionists, one of the fundamental articles of the faith of Israel, that the future redeemer of our people will spring only from the stock of Solomon, son of David. He will gather our nation, assemble our exiles, redeem us from our degradation, propagate the true religion, and exterminate his opponents as is clearly stated in

Scripture, "I see him, but not now; I behold him, but not nigh; there shall step forth a star out of Jacob, and a sceptre shall arise out of Israel. And shall smite through the corners of Moab, and break down all the sons of Seth. And Edom shall be a possession, Seir also, even his enemies, shall be a possession, while Israel does valiantly" (Num. 24:17–18). He will be sent by God at a time of great catastrophe and dire misfortune for Israel as was predicted in the verse, "There will be none remaining, shut up or left at large" (Deut. 32:36). And when he appears, he will fulfill the promises made in his behalf. A later prophet, too, was alluding to the Messianic tribulations when he delared, "But who can endure the day of his coming" (Mal. 3:2). This is the proper understanding of this article of faith. . . .*

Remember, my coreligionists, that on account of the vast number of our sins, God has hurled us in the midst of this people, the Arabs, who have persecuted us severely, and passed baneful and discriminatory legislation against us, as Scripture has forewarned us, "Our enemies themselves shall judge us" (Deut. 32:31). Never did a nation molest, degrade, debase, and hate us as much as they. Therefore when David, of blessed memory, inspired by the holy spirit, envisaged the future tribulations of Israel, he bewailed and lamented their lot only in the Kingdom of Ishmael, and prayed in their behalf, for their deliverance, as is implied in the verse, "Woe is me, that I sojourn with Meshech, that I dwell beside the tents of Kedar" (Ps. 120:5). Note the distinction between Kedar and the children of Ishmael, for the Madman and imbecile is of the lineage of the children of Kedar as they readily admit. Daniel alludes only to our humiliation and degradation "like the dust in threshing" suffered at the hands of the Arabs, may they speedily be vanquished, when he says, "And some of the host and of the stars it cast down to the ground, and trampled upon them" (Dan. 8:10). Although we were dishonored by them beyond human endurance, and had to put up with their fabrications, yet we behaved like him who is depicted by the inspired writer, "But I am as a deaf man, I hear not, and I am as a dumb man that opens not his mouth" (Ps. 38:14). Similarly our sages instructed us to bear the prevarications and preposterousness of Ishmael in silence. They found a cryptic allusion for this attitude in the names of his sons "Mishma, Dumah, and Massa" (Gen. 25:14),

*See *Mishneh Torah*, Book XIV, Kings, chs. XI–XII.

which was interpreted to mean, "Listen, be silent, and endure" (Targum Pseudo-Jonathan, *ad locum*). We have acquiesced, both old and young, to inure ourselves to humiliation, as Isaiah instructed us, "I gave my back to the smiters, and my cheeks to them that plucked off the hair" (Is. 50:6). All this notwithstanding, we do not escape this continued maltreatment which well nigh crushes us. No matter how much we suffer and elect to remain at peace with them, they stir up strife and sedition, as David predicted, "I am all peace, but when I speak, they are for war" (Ps. 120:7). If, therefore, we start trouble and claim power from them absurdly and preposterously we certainly give ourselves up to destruction.

I shall now narrate to you succinctly several episodes subsequent to the rise of the Arabic kingdom, from which you will derive some benefit. One of these refers to the exodus of a multitude of Jews, numbering hundreds of thousands, from the East beyond Ispahan, led by an individual who pretended to be the Messiah. They were accoutered with military equipment, and drawn swords, and slew all those that encountered them. They reached, according to the information I received, the vicinity of Baghdad. This happened in the beginning of the reign of the Umayyads.

The king then said to all the Jews of his kingdom: "Let your scholars go out to meet this multitude and ascertain whether their pretension is true and he is unmistakably your Expected One. If so, we shall conclude peace with you under any conditions you may prefer. But if it is dissimulation, then I shall wage war against them." When the sages met these Jews, the latter declared: "We belong to the children of the district beyond the river." Then they asked them: "Who instigated you to make this uprising?" Whereupon they replied: "This man here, one of the descendants of David, whom we know to be pious and virtuous. This man, whom we knew to be a leper at night, arose the following morning healthy and sound." They believed that leprosy was one of the characteristics of the Messiah, for they found an allusion to the verse: "stricken, smitten of God, and afflicted" (Is. 53:4), that is by leprosy. Whereupon the sages explained to them that this interpretation was incorrect, and that he lacked even one of the characteristics of the Messiah, let alone all of them. Furthermore, they advised them as follows: "O brethren, you are still near your native country and have the possibility of returning there. If you remain in this land you will not only perish, but also undermine the teachings of Moses, by misleading people to believe that the Messiah has appeared and has been vanquished, whereas you have neither a prophet in your midst, nor an omen betokening his coming." Thereupon they were persuaded by these arguments. The Sultan turned over to them so and so many thousand of denars by way of hospitality in order that they should leave his country. But after they had returned home, he had a change of heart with respect to the Jews upon whom he imposed a fine for his expenditures. He ordered them to make a special mark on their garments, the writing of the word "cursed," and to attach one iron bar in the back and one in the front. Ever since then the communities of Khorasan and Ispahan experienced the tribulations of the Diaspora. This episode we have learned from oral reports.

The following incident we have verified and know to be true because it occurred in recent times. About fifty years ago or less, a pious and virtuous man and scholar by the name of Moses Al-Dari came from Dara to the province of Andalusia to study under Rabbi Joseph ha-Levi, of blessed memory, Ibn Migash, of whom you very likely have heard. Later he left for Fez, the center of Maghreb. People flocked to him because of his piety, virtue, and learning. He informed them that the Messiah had come, as was divinely revealed to him in a dream. Yet he did not pretend on the basis of a divine communication, as did the former lunatic, that he was the Messiah. He merely affirmed that the Messiah had appeared. Many people became his adherents and reposed faith in him. My father and master, of blessed memory, endeavored to dissuade and discourage people from following him. However only a few were influenced by my father, while most, nay, nearly all clung to R. Moses, of blessed memory. Finally, he predicted events which came true no matter what was going to occur. He would say: "I was informed yesterday—this and this would happen," and it did happen exactly as he foretold. Once he forecast a vehement rain for the coming Friday and that the falling drops would be blood. This was considered a sign of the approaching advent of the Messiah, as was inferred from the verse, "And I will show wonders in the heavens and in the earth, blood and fire, and pillars of smoke" (Joel 3:3). This episode took place in the month of Marheshvan. A very heavy rain fell that Friday and the fluid that descended was red and viscous as if it were mixed with clay. This miracle convinced all the people that he was undoubtedly a prophet. In itself this occurrence is not inconsistent with the tenets of the Torah, for prophecy will return to Israel before the Messianic advent, as I have previously explained. When the majority of the people put their trust in him, he predicted that the Messiah would come that very year on Passover eve. He advised the people to sell their property and contract debts to the Muslims with the promise to pay back ten *denars* for one, in order to observe the precepts of the Torah in connection with the Passover festival, for they would never see them again, and so they did. When Passover came and nothing transpired, the people were ruined as most of them had disposed of their property for a trifling sum, and were overwhelmed with debt. When the Gentiles in the vicinity and their serfs learned of this hoax they were minded to do away with him, had they located him. As this Muslim country no longer offered him protection he left for Palestine where he died, may his memory be blessed. When he left he made predictions, as I was informed by those who saw him, concerning events both great and little in Maghreb which were later fulfilled.

My father, of blessed memory, told me that about fifteen or twenty years before that episode, there lived respectable folk in Cordova, the center of Andalusia, some of whom were given to the cult of astrology. They were all of one mind that the Messiah would appear that year. They sought a revelation in a dream night after night, and ascertained that the Messiah was a man of that city. They picked a pious and virtuous person by the name of Ibn Aryeh who had been instructing the people. They wrought miracles and made predictions just as Al-Dari did until they won over the hearts of all the people. When the influential and learned men of our community heard of this, they assembled in the synagogue and had Ibn Aryeh brought there and had him flogged in public. Furthermore, they imposed a fine upon him and put him into the ban, because he gave assent by his silence to the professions of his adherents instead of restraining them and pointing out to them that they contradict our religion. They did the same thing to the persons who assembled about him. The Jews escaped the wrath of the Gentiles only with the greatest difficulty.

About forty years preceding the affair of Ibn Aryeh in Andalusia, there appeared a man in Linon, a large center in the heart of France, which numbered more than ten thousand Jewish families. He pretended that he was the Messiah. He was supposed to have performed the following miracle: On moonlit nights he would go out and climb to the top of high trees in the field and glide from tree to tree like a bird. He cited a verse from Daniel to prove that such a miracle was within the power of the Messiah: "And behold, there came with the clouds of heaven one like a son of man ... and there was given him dominion" (Dan. 7:13–14). Many who witnessed the miracle became his votaries. The French discovered this, pillaged and put many of his followers to death, together with the pretender. Some of them maintain, however, that he is still in hiding until this very day.

The prophets have predicted and instructed us, as I have told you, that pretenders and simulators will appear in great numbers at the time when the advent of the true Messiah will draw nigh, but they will not be able to make good their claim. They will perish with many of their partisans.

Solomon, of blessed memory, inspired by the holy spirit, foresaw that the prolonged duration of the exile would incite some of our people to seek to terminate it before the appointed time, and as a consequence they would perish or meet with disaster. Therefore he admonished and adjured them in metaphorical language to desist, as we read, "I adjure you, O daughters of Jerusalem, by the gazelles and by the hinds of the field, that you awaken not, nor stir up love, until it please" (Song of Songs 2:7, 8:4). Now, brethren and friends, abide by the oath, and stir not up love until it please (Ketuvot 111a).

May God, who created the world with the attributes of mercy, grant us the privilege to behold the return of the exiles, to the portion of His inheritance, to contemplate the graciousness of the Lord, and to visit early in His Temple. May He take us out from the Valley of the Shadow of Death wherein He put us. May He remove darkness from our eyes, and gloom from our hearts. May he fulfill in our days as well as yours the prophecy contained in the verse, "The people that walked in darkness have seen a great light" (Is. 9:1). May He darken our opponents in His anger and wrath, may He illuminate our obscurity, as it is written, "For behold, darkness shall cover the earth . . . but upon you the Lord will shine" (Is. 60:2). Greetings to you, my dear friend, master of the sciences, and paragon of learning, and to our erudite colleagues, and to all the rest of the people. Peace, peace, as the light that shines, and much peace until the moon be no more. Amen.

I beg you to send a copy of this missive to every community in the cities and hamlets, in order to strengthen the people in their faith and to put them on their feet. Read it at public gatherings and in private, and you will thus become a public benefactor. Take adequate precautions lest its contents be divulged to the Gentiles by an evil person and mishap overtake us (God spare us therefrom). When I began writing this letter I had some misgivings about it, but they were overruled by my conviction that the public welfare takes precedence over one's personal safety. Moreover, I am sending it to a personage such as you, "and the secret of the Lord may be entrusted to those who fear Him" (Ps. 25:14). Our sages, the successors of the prophets, assured us that persons engaged in a religious mission will meet with no disaster (Pesahim 8b). What more important religious mission is there than this. Peace be to all Israel. Amen.

*I*N THIS answer to inquiries from scholars of southern France, Maimonides exposes foibles and fallacies of astrology, while touching upon such questions as the sources of knowledge, creation of the world, divine providence and free will, and the Messiah. The rationalistic temper of the letter is characteristic of Maimonidean writing in general and accurately reflects many basic Maimonidean attitudes. Inasmuch as this letter was intended for general circulation, with no pretense to esotericism, the references to the Guide and the statements concerning the rationalization of the commandments are highly significant. Noteworthy is the oft-quoted comment that the Second Temple was destroyed and national independence forfeited because the Jews were preoccupied with astrology. On the whole, the letter is a model of compression, precision, and clarity, revealing Maimonides' ability to address himself to different people on different levels.

... Such is the wish of their brother and friend, who prays on their behalf and rejoices in their tranquillity, Moses, son of Rabbi Maimon (may the memory of the righteous be a blessing), the Spaniard. This inquiry testifies to the purity of their soul and the excellence of their understanding and shows that they pursue science and search into the chambers of understanding and hasten to ascend the steps of knowledge in order "to find out desired words and that which was written uprightly" (Eccles. 12:10), and to understand the "word" and the "interpretation" (Eccles. 8:1). May the hand of the Lord be their help and lay open for them everything that is hidden and "make level every rugged place" (Is. 40:4). Amen. I perceive in this inquiry that although its boughs are many, they are all branches of a single tree, which is their common root: namely, all the statements of "the astrologers, the stargazers" (Is. 47:13). It is evident that the compilation we have made of the statutes of the Torah, which we entitled *Mishneh Torah*, has not reached you. If it had, you would have known directly my opinion regarding all those things of which you have inquired; for we have made this entire matter clear in (the section of that work called) Laws Concerning Idolatry and the Ordinances of the Nations. It seems to me that it will come to you before this reply, since it is already widespread on the island of Sicily, as well as in the West and in the East and in the South. In any case, I myself need to make this clear to you.

Know, my masters, that it is not proper for a man to accept as trustworthy anything other than one of these three things. The first is a thing for which there is a clear proof deriving from man's reasoning—such as arithmetic, geometry, and astronomy. The second is a thing that a man perceives through one of the five senses—such as when he knows with certainty that this is red and this is black and the like through the sight of his eye; or as when he tastes that this is bitter and this is sweet; or as when he feels that this is hot and this is cold; or as when he hears that this sound is clear and this sound is indistinct; or as when he smells that this is a pleasing smell and this is a displeasing smell and the like. The third is a thing that a man receives from the prophets or from the righteous. Every reasonable man ought to distinguish in his mind and thought all the things that he accepts as trustworthy, and say: "This I accept as trustworthy because of tradition, and this because of sense-perception, and this on grounds of reason." Anyone who accepts as trustworthy anything that is not of these three species, of him it is said: "The simple believes everything" (Prov. 14:15). Thus you ought to know that fools have composed thousands of books of nothingness and emptiness. Any number of men, great in years but not in wisdom, wasted all their days in studying these books and imagined that these follies are science. They came to think of themselves as wise men because they knew that science. The thing about which most of the world errs, or all of it—save for a few individuals, "the remnant of whom the Lord shall call" (Joel 3:5)—is that thing of which I am apprising you. The great sickness and the "grievous evil" (Eccles. 5:12, 15) consist in this: that all the things that man finds written in books, he presumes to think of as true—and all the more so if the books are old. And since many individuals have busied themselves with those books and have engaged in discussions concerning them, the rash fellow's mind at once leaps to the conclusion that these are words of wisdom, and he says to himself: "Has the pen of the scribes written in vain" (Jer. 8:8), and have they vainly engaged in these things? This is why our kingdom was lost and our Temple was destroyed and why we were brought to this; for our fathers sinned and are no more because they found many books dealing with these themes of the stargazers, these things being the root of idolatry, as we have made clear in Laws Concerning Idolatry. They erred and were drawn after them, imagining them to be glorious science and to be of great utility. They did not busy themselves with the art of war or with the conquest of lands, but imagined that those studies would help them. Therefore the prophets called them "fools and dolts" (Jer. 4:22). And truly fools they were, "for they walked after confused things that do not profit" (I Sam. 12:21 and Jer. 2:8).

Know, my masters, that I myself have investigated much into these matters. The first thing I studied is that science which is called judicial astrology—that is, (the science) by which man may know what will come to pass in the world or in this or that city or kingdom and what will happen to a particular individual all the days of his life. I also have read in all matters concerning all of idolatry, so that it seems to me there does not remain in the world a composition on this subject, having been translated into Arabic from other languages, but that I have read it and have understood its subject matter and have plumbed the depth of its thought. From those books it became clear to me what the reason is for all those commandments that everyone comes to think of as having no reason at all other than the decree of Scripture. I already have a great composition on this subject in the Arabic language (namely, the *Guide of the Perplexed*) with lucid proofs for every single commandment but this is not required of us now. I now return to the subject of your inquiry.

Know, my masters, that every one of those things concerning judicial astrology that (its adherents) maintain—namely, that something will happen one way and not another, and that the constellation under which one is born will draw him on so that he will be of such and such a kind and so that something will happen to him one way and not another—all those assertions are far from being scientific; they are stupidity. There are lucid, faultless proofs refuting all the roots of those assertions. Never did one of those genuinely wise men of the nations busy himself with this matter or write on it; no (nation) wrote such compositions or committed the error of calling it a science, other than the Chasdeans, Chaldeans, Canaanites, and Egyptians, for that was their religion in those days. But the wise men of Greece—and they are the philosophers who wrote on science and busied themselves with all the species of science—mock and scorn and ridicule these four nations that I have mentioned to you, and they rally proofs to refute their entire position—"root and branch" (Mal. 3:19). The wise men of Persia also recognized and understood that all that science which the Chasdeans, Chaldeans, Egyptians, and Canaanites produced is a falsehood and a lie. Do not imagine that those refutations are mere assertions and that we therefore should not put our trust in them; rather there are lucid and correct, faultless proofs to refute that entire position, and the only one who would cling to it would be "a simple one who believes everything"(Prov. 14:15), or one who wishes to deceive others.

And know, my masters, that the science of the stars that is genuine science is knowledge of the form of the spheres, their number, their measure, the course they follow, each one's period of revolution, their declination to the north or to the south, their revolving to the east or to the west, and the orbit of every star and what its course is. On all this and the like, the wise men of Greece, Persia, and India wrote compositions. This is an exceedingly glorious science. By means of it the onset of the eclipses of luminaries may be known and when they will be eclipsed at any given place; by means of it there may be known the cause for the moon's (yareah) appearing just like a bow, then waxing great until it is full, and then gradually waning; by means of it there may be known when the moon (levanah) will or will not be seen; and the reason why one day will be long and another day short; and the reason why two stars will rise as one, but not set together; and the reason why a given day at a given place is thirteen hours long and in another place fifteen or sixteen or twenty hours long, yet being a single day. (In one place the day and the night will be of equal duration; in another place the day will be like a month or two months or three—so that a place may be found where the entire year is a single day, six months daytime and six months nighttime.) How many amazing conditions are made intelligible by this science, all of which is undoubtedly true. It is this calculation of astronomical cycles of which the (Talmudic) sages said that it is wisdom and understanding in the sight of the (Gentile) peoples (Shabbat 75a). But as for these assertions of the stupid astrologers, they are nothing. I am now making clear to you the main points of those matters that are the mystery of the world.

Know, that all the wise men of the Gentile nations—and they are the great philosophers, men of intellect and science—were all in accord that the world has a Governor; He makes a sphere revolve, the sphere not revolving of itself. They have many books advancing a lucid proof for this; on this point there is no controversy among men of science. There is, however, a great controversy among them regarding this entire world, namely, the sphere and what is beneath it.*

(1) Most of them say that it is not subject to generation and corruption, but that as it is now, it was and it will be for ever and ever. Just as the Holy One, blessed be He, who was always the same as He is now, is making it revolve, so was He always making it revolve, and it was always being revolved; the two of them were always together, never was one without the other.

(2) Among them there are those who maintain that this sphere has come into being and that the Deity has created it, but that there is a single thing that exists together with the Creator, "like the clay in the potter's hand" (Jer. 18:6). From that thing which exists together with Him, He makes whatever He pleases. Sometimes He will use some of that clay, as it were, to make heaven and some of it

*See *Guide*, II, chs. 13–16.

to make earth; and sometimes, if He pleases, He takes some of that out of which He has made heaven and makes something else out of it. But to bring forth something out of nothing is impossible.

(3) Among the philosophers there are those who maintain—just as the prophets maintained—that the Holy One, blessed be He, created all created things out of nothing and that there is no other thing with the Creator aside from the creation that He has brought forth.

Now the great controversy is over this point, and this is the very point that Abraham our Father discerned. A thousand books have already been written on this, with proofs that each and every one of them rallies to support its position. It is the root of the Torah that the Deity alone is primordial and that He has created the whole out of nothing; whoever does not acknowledge this is guilty of radical unbelief and is guilty of heresy. I myself have already written a great composition in Arabic (*Guide of the Perplexed*) on these matters. I have explained the lucid proofs of the existence of the Creator and that He is one and that He is not a body or corporeal in any respect. I have shattered all those proofs that the philosophers advance as proving that the world was not created. In addition, I have resolved all the great difficulties that they have raised against us on account of our maintaining that the Deity has created everything that exists out of nothing. . . . All these, then, are the three sects into which the wise men of the world fall, from the earliest antiquity down to now.

(1) Those who maintain that the sphere is not a created thing, but that it eternally has been and will be just as it is.

(2) Those who maintain that the Deity has created it out of that matter which always exists by Him.

(3) Those who maintain—just as all the prophets did—that there is no other thing that is with the Deity, just He Himself, and that when He wished, He brought forth this world out of nothing, in conformity with His will.

All of these three sects are in accord on the following point. Everything that comes into being in this lower world—namely, every "living soul" (Gen. 1:30) and every tree and every species of grass and every one of the species of minerals—the whole has the Deity as its maker, through a power coming from the spheres and the stars. And they are in accord that the power of the Creator flows first upon the spheres and the stars; from the spheres and the stars it flows and spreads through this (lower) world—everything that is, thereby coming into being. Just as we maintain that the Holy One, blessed be He, performs signs and wonders through the angels, so do these philosophers maintain that all these occurrences in the nature of the world come through the spheres and the stars. They maintain that the spheres and the stars possess souls and knowledge. All these things are true. I myself have already made it clear, with proofs, that all these things involve no damage to religion. And not only this, but what is more I have understood from the sayings of the sages in all of the Midrashim that they maintain as the philosophers maintained. There is no controversy whatever between the sages of Israel and the philosophers on these matters, as I have made clear in those chapters (in the *Guide of the Perplexed*).

All three of these sects of the philosophers, which maintain that everything is made by means of the spheres and the stars, also maintain that whatever happens to each and every human being is due to chance; it is not due to any cause coming from above, and neither the constellation under which one is born nor nature will avail against it. There is no difference for them between this individual who was torn to pieces by a lion that happened upon him, or this mouse that was torn to pieces by a cat, or this fly that was torn to pieces by a spider. Neither is there a difference between a roof's falling upon and killing someone, or a rock's breaking loose from a mountain and falling upon a tree or upon another rock and breaking it. All this, they maintain, is simply fortuitous. It is said as well of those human beings who are warring with one another over a great kingdom, that they are like a pack of dogs warring over a carcass. This is not due to any cause coming from the stars. Furthermore, this one being poor and that one rich, this one having children and that one being childless—all the philosophers maintain that this is due to chance. The summary of the matter is that they maintain that what happens to each and every thing—be it man or beast or trees and minerals—is all due to chance. But the being of all the species and the things comprehended in the entire world—in which there is not the activity of a living soul—all of this stems from the power of the spheres whose root, in turn, comes from the Holy One, blessed be He. The controversy lies in this, that the true religionists, and that is the religion of Moses our Teacher, maintain that what happens to individuals is not due to chance, but rather to judgment—as the Torah says: "For all His ways are judgment" (Deut. 32:4). The prophet explained: "Whose eyes are open upon all the ways of the sons of men, to give every one according to his ways, and according to the fruit of his doings" (Jer. 32:19). It is regarding this that the

Torah warned and bore witness and told Israel: "But if you will not hearken to Me" (Lev. 26:14), I shall bring hardship upon you. If you maintain that that hardship is not an affliction brought on by your sins, but rather due to chance and one of those things that happen by chance, why then I Myself shall heap more of that chance upon you—as it is written: "And if you walk with Me in (the way of) chance, I too shall walk with you in the wrath of chance" (Lev. 26:27–28). This is a root of the religion of Moses our Teacher, that everything happening to human beings is a (just) decree and judgment. Hence, the sages maintained: "There is no death without sin and no affliction with transgression" (Shabbat 55a).

And know, my masters, that it is one of the roots of the religion of Moses our Teacher—and one that all the philosophers also acknowledge—that every action of human beings is left to them and that there is nothing to constrain or draw them. Rather, if he so pleases, a man will worship God and become wise and sit in the house of study. And if he so pleases, he will follow the counsel of the wicked and run with thieves and hide with adulterers. There is no influence or constellation under which one is born that will draw him in any manner toward any one of these ways. Hence it was commanded and told to him: "Do this and do not do that." We have made clear many of the things involved in these matters in most of our Arabic compositions, in the *Commentary on the Mishnah* and in the rest of the compositions. Thus we ought to know that what happens to human beings is not—as the philosophers maintain—like what happens to the beast.*

Three disagreements are to be found in these matters. Imagine this situation. Here is Reuben, a tanner, poor, and his children have died in his own lifetime. And here is Simon, a perfumer, rich, and his children stand before him.

(1) The philosopher will maintain that this due to chance. It is possible that Reuben could become a perfumer, grow rich, and have children; and it is possible that Simon could become impoverished, turn into a tanner, and witness his children's death. All this is simply fortuitous. There is no nature in the world and no power emanating from a star that caused this individual to be or not to be thus. This is the position of the philosophers.

(2) The second position is that of those who believe in judicial astrology and whose sayings you have heard and whose follies are

---

*See *Mishneh Torah*, Book I, Repentance, ch. V.

widespread among you. They maintain that it is impossible that a given thing should ever change. Never will Reuben be anything other than a tanner and poor and childless, for it was thus fixed by the power of the sphere at the time of his birth. Similarly, it is impossible for Simon to be anything other than a perfumer and rich and with surviving children, just as it was fixed by the power of the sphere at the time of his birth.

. . . These two ways, or these two positions, are regarded as false-hoods by us. The position of the astrologers is given the lie by reason, for correct reasoning has already refuted, by means of lucid proofs, all those follies that they have maintained. It also is regarded as a falsehood by us because of the religious tradition, for if the matter stood thus, of what utility would the Torah and the commandment and the Talmud be to a particular individual? For in that event, every single individual would lack the power to do anything he set his mind to, since something else draws him on—against his will—to be this and not to be that; of what use then is the command or the Talmud? The roots of the religion of Moses our Teacher, we find, refute the position of these stupid ones—in addition to reason's doing so with all those proofs that the philosophers maintain to refute the position of the Chasdeans and the Chaldeans and their associates. The position of the philosophers who maintain that these things are due to chance is also regarded as a falsehood by us because of the religious tradition.

(3) The true way upon which we rely and in which we walk is this: We say regarding this Reuben and Simon, that there is nothing that draws on the one to become a perfumer and rich, and the other to become a tanner and poor. It is possible that the situation will change and be reversed, as the philosopher maintains. But the philosopher maintains that this is due to chance. We maintain that it is not due to chance, but rather that this situation depends on the will of "Him who spoke, and (the world) came into being" (Ps. 33:9); all of this is a (just) decree and judgment. We do not know the end of the Holy One's wisdom so as to know by what decree and judgment He required that this should be this way and that that should be the other way; "for His ways are not like our ways, neither are His thoughts like our thoughts" (Is. 55:8). We rather are obliged to fix in our minds that if Simon sins, he will be punished with stripes and impoverished and his children will die and the like. And if Reuben repents and mends his ways and searches his deeds and walks in a straight path, he will grow rich and will succeed in all his undertak-

ings and "see (his) seed and prolong (his) days" (*ibid.* 55:10). This is a root of the religion. If a man says, "But look, many have acted in this way and yet have not succeeded," why this is no proof. Either some iniquity of theirs caused this, or they are now afflicted in order to inherit something even better than this.

The summary of the matter is that our mind cannot grasp how the decrees of the Holy One, blessed be He, work upon human beings in this world and in the world to come. What we have said about this from the beginning is that the entire position of the star-gazers is regarded as a falsehood by all men of science. I know that you may search and find sayings of some individual sages in the Talmud and Midrashim whose words appear to maintain that at the moment of a man's birth, the stars will cause such and such to happen to him. Do not regard this as a difficulty, for it is not fitting for a man to abandon the prevailing law and raise once again the counterarguments and replies (that preceded its enactment). Similarly it is not proper to abandon matters of reason that have already been verified by proofs, shake loose of them, and depend on the words of a single one of the sages from whom possibly the matter was hidden. Or there may be an allusion in those words; or they may have been said with a view to the times and the business before him. (You surely know how many of the verses of the holy Law are not to be taken literally. Since it is known through proofs of reason that it is impossible for the thing to be literally so, the translator [Aramaic Targum] rendered it in a form that reason will abide.) A man should never cast his reason behind him, for the eyes are set in front, not in back.*

What has reached you in my name concerning the Messiah does not correspond to the facts; it was not in the East, in Isfahan. It was rather in Yemen that an individual arose (it is now some twenty-two years ago), and proclaimed that he was a messenger come to prepare the way for the King Messiah and told them that the Messiah was in the land of Yemen. Many people—Jews and Arabs—gathered about him, and they would move around in the hills. Our brethren in Yemen wrote me a long letter informing me of his way and judgment, of the innovations he had made for them in the prayers, and of what he was saying. They said that they had already seen certain marvels of his. They questioned me about this. I gathered from all the circumstances that this poor individual is ignorant and

*See *Guide*, introduction; II, ch. 25.

God-fearing, indeed he possesses no wisdom at all, and that everything that they say he did or that came to sight through him is a falsehood and a lie. I trembled for the Jews who were there, and composed some three or four tablets for them on the subject of the Messiah and his signs and the signs of the time during which he shall appear; and I warned them to beware of this individual lest he be ruined and ruin the (Jewish) communities. The summary of the matter is that after a year he was seized, and all who had joined with him fled. The king of the Arabs who had seized him asked him: "What is this that you have done?" He replied: "What I have done, I have indeed done, and according to God's word." Then he said: "What is your authenticating wonder?" He replied: "Chop off my head and I shall revive at once." He said to him: "You (can) have no greater sign than this. Certainly I—and the whole world—shall trust and know that my forefathers have bequeathed a falsehood." At once they killed the poor fellow. May his death be an atonement for him and for all Israel. The Jews in most places were punished by fines, and even now there are some ignoramuses there who maintain that presently he will come to life and rise. Such were the circumstances. If you heard that my letter has come to Fez, it is only because those remarks of mine that I sent to Yemen were copied and arrived in Fez.

I have already told you that all the details of your inquiries on this subject are all branches of a single tree. I myself command you, out of my knowledge: "Hew down the tree and cut off its branches," and so on (Dan. 4:11). Plant in its stead "the tree of the knowledge of good and evil" (Gen. 2:9), and "eat of its goodness and its fruit" (Jer. 2:7), and put forth your hands and take also from the tree of life. The Holy One, blessed be He, will absolve us and will absolve you for plucking off its fruit and for eating our fill of its goodness until we live forever. Amen. Written in great haste on 11 Tishri 1507 (of the Seleucid era) (1194) in the land of Egypt. May salvation be nigh. . . . Do not censure me, my masters, for the brevity of these remarks, for the writing makes it clear that I wrote it to fill a present need. For I was very busy with many Gentile affairs. The Deity knows that if Rabbi Pinhas had not sent a messenger who "urged me till I was ashamed" (II Kings 2:17) and did not leave my presence until I had written it, I would not be replying now since I have no leisure. On this account, judge in my favor. Farewell, my brothers, friends, and masters; may you increase and be exalted forever. Amen.

OCCASIONAL writings often provide special insight into an author's inclinations, convictions, and sensitivities, which are sometimes submerged in more formal works. The following medley from the letters of Maimonides shows him drawing upon his vast reservoirs of knowledge, relating new situations to old categories, and responding vigorously to everchanging stimuli. They reveal his brilliance of mind, delicacy of feeling, and sensitivity of heart, his precision of style and range of interest. The autobiographical references are of great interest. (See the autobiographical section in the letter to Samuel ibn Tibbon which is cited in the introduction to this book.)

Especially noteworthy is the Letter to Obadiah, the humiliated and confused convert whom Maimonides encourages by expounding a lofty, spiritual conception of Judaism in which biological factors are rather insignificant. Converts to Judaism enjoy complete equality and are, in fact, objects of special love. The Letter to Hasdai is a rare testament of spirituality, accentuating some of the more universalist sentiments of Judaism. The Letter to Ibn Gabir shows the author's pedagogical and psychological skill in encouraging a serious student, whose interest in matters which seem forbidding and inaccessible must be sustained. The Letter to the Rabbis of Lunel reflects the melancholy of Maimonides as he surveyed the contemporary scene.

474

LETTER TO OBADIAH THE PROSELYTE

Thus says Moses, the son of Rabbi Maimon, one of the exiles from Jerusalem, who lived in Spain:

I received the question of the master Obadiah, the wise and learned proselyte, may the Lord reward him for his work, may a perfect recompense be bestowed upon him by the Lord of Israel, under whose wings he has sought cover.

You ask me if you, too, are allowed to say in the blessings and prayers you offer alone or in the congregation: "Our God" and "God of our fathers," "You who have sanctified us through Your commandments," "You who have separated us," "You who have chosen us," "You who have inherited us," "You who have brought us out of the land of Egypt," "You who have worked miracles to our fathers," and more of this kind.

Yes, you may say all this in the prescribed order and not change it in the least. In the same way as every Jew by birth says his blessing and prayer, you, too, shall bless and pray alike, whether you are alone or pray in the congregation. The reason for this is, that Abraham our Father taught the people, opened their minds, and revealed to them the true faith and the unity of God; he rejected the idols and abolished their adoration; he brought many children under the wings of the Divine Presence; he gave them counsel and advice, and ordered his sons and the members of his household after him to keep the ways of the Lord forever, as it is written, "For I have known him to the end that he may command his children and his household after him, that they may keep the way of the Lord, to do righteousness and justice" (Gen. 18:19). Ever since then whoever adopts Judaism and confesses the unity of the Divine Name, as it is prescribed in the Torah, is counted among the disciples of Abraham our Father, peace be with him. These men are Abraham's household, and he it is who converted them to righteousness.

In the same way as he converted his contemporaries through his words and teaching, he converts future generations through the testament he left to his children and household after him. Thus Abraham our Father, peace be with him, is the father of his pious posterity who keep his ways, and the father of his disciples and of all proselytes who adopt Judaism.

Therefore you shall pray, "Our God" and "God of our fathers," because Abraham, peace be with him, is your father. And you shall pray, "You who have taken for his own our fathers," for the land has been given to Abraham, as it is said, "Arise, walk through the land in the length of it and in the breadth of it; for I will give to you" (Gen. 13:17). As to the words, "You who have brought us out of the land of Egypt" or "You who have done miracles to our fathers"—these you may change, if you will, and say, "You who have brought Israel out of the land of Egypt" and "You who have done miracles to Israel." If, however, you do not change them, it is no transgression, because since you have come under the wings of the Divine Presence and confessed the Lord, no difference exists between you and us, and all miracles done to us have been done as it were to us and to you. Thus it is said in the Book of Isaiah, "Neither let the son of the stranger, that has joined himself to the Lord, speak, saying, 'The Lord has utterly separated me from His people'" (Is. 56:3). There is no difference whatever between you and us. You shall certainly say the blessing, "Who has chosen us," "Who has given us," "Who have taken us for Your own" and "Who has separated us": for the Creator, may He be extolled, has indeed chosen you and separated you from the nations and given you the Torah. For the Torah has been given to us and to the proselytes, as it is said, "One ordinance shall be both for you of the congregation, and also for the stranger that sojourns with you, an ordinance for ever in your generations; as you are, so shall the stranger be before the Lord" (Num. 15:15). Know that our fathers, when they came out of Egypt, were mostly idolaters; they had mingled with the pagans in Egypt and imitated their way of life, until the Holy One, may He be blessed, sent Moses our Teacher, the master of all prophets, who separated us from the nations and brought us under the wings of the Divine Presence, us and all proselytes, and gave to all of us one Law.

Do not consider your origin as inferior. While we are the descendants of Abraham, Isaac, and Jacob, you derive from Him through whose word the world was created. As is said by Isaiah: "One shall say, I am the Lord's, and another shall call himself by the name of Jacob" (Is. 44:5).

LETTER TO AN INQUIRER

... When your teacher called you a fool for denying that Muslims
are idolaters he sinned grievously, and it is fitting that he ask your
pardon, though he be your master. Then let him fast and weep and
pray; perhaps he will find forgiveness. Was he intoxicated that he
forgot the thirty-three passages in which the Law admonishes concerning "strangers"? For even if he had been in the right and you in
error, it was his duty to be gentle; how much more, when the truth is
with you and he was in error! And when he was discussing whether a
Muslim is an idolater, he should have been cautious not to lose his
temper with a proselyte of righteousness and put him to shame, for
our sages have said, "He who gives way to his anger shall be
esteemed in Your eyes as an idolater." And how great is the duty
which the Law imposes on us with regard to proselytes. We are commanded to honor and fear our parents; we are ordered to hearken to
the prophets. A man may honor and fear and obey without loving.
But in the case of "strangers" we are bidden to love with the whole
force of our heart's affection.* And he called you fool! Astounding! A
man who left father and mother, forsook his birthplace, his country
and its power, and attached himself to this lowly, despised, and
enslaved race; who recognized the truth and righteousness of this
people's Law, and cast the things of this world from his heart—shall
such a one be called fool? God forbid! Not witless but wise has God
called your name, you disciple of our father Abraham, who also left
his father and his kindred and inclined Godward. And He who
blessed Abraham will bless you, and will make you worthy to behold
all the consolations destined for Israel; and in all the good that God
shall do to us He will do good to you, for the Lord has promised good
to Israel. . . .

LETTER TO HASDAI HA-LEVI

... As to your question about the nations, know that the Lord
desires the heart, and that the intention of the heart is the measure

*See *Mishneh Torah*, Book I, Moral Dispositions, II, 3; VI, 4; Book V, Forbidden Intercourse, ch. XIV.

of all things. That is why our sages say, "The pious men among the Gentiles have a share in the world to come" (Sanhedrin 105a), namely, if they have acquired what can be acquired of the knowledge of God, and if they ennoble their souls with worthy qualities. There is no doubt that every man who ennobles his soul with excellent morals and wisdom based on the faith in God, certainly belongs to the men of the world to come. That is why our sages said, "Even a non-Jew who studies the Torah of our teacher Moses resembles a High Priest" (Bava Kamma 38a). What is essential is nothing else than that one tries to elevate his soul toward God through the Torah. Thus said David, "I put the Lord always before me; because He is on my right hand I do not waver" (Ps. 16:8). And Moses is praised for this reason: "This man was very humble" (Num. 12:3), because this is the height of perfection. Our sages said also, "Be exceedingly humble" (Ethics of the Fathers 4:4).... And the philosophers declared that it is very difficult to find a man who is completely perfect in morality and wisdom. He in whom this perfection is found is called a saint, and surely such a man is on the steps which lead to the higher world. . . . Besides, there is no doubt that the patriarchs as well as Noah and Adam, who obviously did not observe the Torah, by no means became denizens of Gehenna. On the contrary: as they achieved what pertains to the ennoblement of man they are raised aloft. All this cannot be secured by fasting, praying, and lamentation if knowledge and true faith are absent, because in such behavior God can be near to the mouth but far from the heart. The basis of all things is (knowledge) that nothing is eternal save God alone. . . .*

LETTER TO JOSEPH IBN GABIR

I gather from the letter of the esteemed Mar Joseph called Ibn Gabir that he regrets being an am ha-aretz (ignoramus), because he knows Arabic only but not Hebrew and that he, therefore, while studying our Commentary on the Mishnah with great zeal, is unable to read

*See Guide, III, ch. 51; Mishneh Torah, Book I, Study, III, 2; Book XIV, Kings, VIII, 10.

our code *Mishneh Torah*. He reports further in that letter that some scholars in Baghdad reject some of my decisions. I have been asked for the benefit of learning to give my opinion in my own handwriting. I am going to fulfill these requests herein.

First of all I must tell you, may the Lord keep and increase your welfare, that you are not justified in regarding yourself as an *am ha-aretz*. You are our beloved pupil; so is everybody who is desirous of studying even one verse or a single *halakhah*. It makes also no difference whether you study in the holy language, or in Arabic or Aramaic; it matters only whether it is done with understanding. This is the important thing whichever language may be used in the commentaries or in the summaries. But of the man who neglects the development of his spirit it is said: "he has despised the word of the Lord" (Num. 15:31); this applies also to a man who fails to continue his studies even if he has become a great scholar, for the advancement of learning is the highest commandment. I say, therefore, in general, that you must not belittle yourself nor give up the intention of improving. There are great scholars who did not begin their studies until an advanced age, and who became scholars of distinction in spite of this.

If you want to study my work you will have to learn Hebrew little by little. It is not so difficult, as the book is written in an easy style, and if you master one part you will soon be able to understand the whole work. I do not intend, however, to produce an Arabic edition, as you suggest; the work would lose its specific color. How could I do this, when I should like to translate my Arabic writings into the holy language! In any case, you are our brother; may the Lord guard you, lead you to perfection and grant you the happiness of both worlds. . . .

The statement you have heard, namely, that I deny in my work the resurrection of the dead, is nothing more than a malicious calumny. He who asserted this is either a wicked man who misrepresents my words, or an ignorant one who does not understand my views on *Olam ha-Ba* (the world to come). In order to make impossible any further mistake or doubt, I have composed in the meantime a special treatise on this subject.

You mention also an objection made against me concerning the sign of the covenant which by some is considered not as a Mosaic law but as a tradition dating from the time of Abraham. My opponents rely in this regard upon a Talmudic sentence according to which the Lord, on the occasion of that commandment, made a thirteen-fold covenant with Abraham. This objection is futile, and the pretended evidence shows that those people do not understand the foundations of our religion in the least. My explanation is right. That commandment as well as, for example, the prohibition of the sinew belongs also to those 613 Sinaitic commandments which, although they existed in earlier times, were transmitted by Moses; they have been in force as religious prescriptions since the time of Moses. Ask those people who cite in evidence against me the "thirteen-fold covenant" made with Abraham, those blind men who pretend to be seers, ask them if Abraham himself had perhaps written that commandment together with all the verses of Scripture referring to this matter in such a way that Moses had nothing more to do than to copy them as we are wont to copy an ancient work of another author, or if the verses concerned belong to the Torah through having been composed by Moses for the first time under inspiration? Whoever does not believe the latter alternative denies that the Torah is of divine origin. The matter is clear, but unknown to people who have never reflected and who, instead of considering the roots of religion, look upon its branches. The Torah in its totality has been given to us by the Lord through Moses; if ancient laws are comprised in it, as for instance the Noahide Laws and the above-mentioned prescriptions, we are not bound by them because they were observed in former times, but because they have become obligatory for us since the general legislation. . . .*

I have been informed—although I do not know whether it is true—that there is in your city somebody who speaks evil against me, and tries to gain honor by misrepresentation of my teaching. I have heard also that you protested against this, and reprimanded the slanderer. Do not act in this way! I forgive everybody who is opposed to me because of his lack of intelligence, even when he, by opposing, seeks his personal advantage. He does no harm to me. . . . While he is pleased, I do not lose anything. . . . You trouble yourself with useless quarrels, as I do not need the help of other men, and leave it to the people to follow their own will.

May the Lord help you to serve Him in all sincerity, may He lead all your doings and words to His name. May your peace and the peace of the elders and disciples be great. May our God bless them.

---

*See *Mishneh Torah*, Book XIV, Mourning, I, 1; *Guide*, II, ch. 39. Also: *Hullin*, 7:7.

LETTER TO THE RABBIS OF LUNEL

... I have already apologized for the delay of my answer. I have dealt with your doubts, and am forwarding to you now the third part of the *Guide of the Perplexed* in the Arabic language. However, with regard to your request that I may translate the text into the holy tongue for you—I myself could wish that I were young enough to be able to fulfill your wish concerning this and the other works which I have composed in the language of Ishmael, and I should be very pleased thus to free their superior from their inferior elements and to give back the stolen goods to the rightful owner. But I must blame the unfavorable times for preventing me from doing so. I have not even time to work out and to improve my commentaries and other works composed in the rabbinic language, which contain various obscurities, in order to arrange new editions—to say nothing of making translations from one language into another.

Yes, my honored friends, I have no leisure even for writing a little chapter, and only for the sake of showing my respect to your congregation do I undertake to write you with my own hand.

But you have in your midst the learned and well instructed R. Samuel ben Judah (Ibn Tibbon), on whom the Lord has bestowed the necessary insight and excellent penmanship for performing the translation you have asked for. I have already written to him about this subject.

To you, my honored friends, may you remain confident and strong, I have now to tell the truth: You, members of the congregation of Lunel, and of the neighboring towns, stand alone in raising the banner of Moses. You apply yourselves to the study of the Talmud, and also cherish wisdom. The study of the Torah in our communities has ceased; most of the bigger congregations are dead to spiritual aims; the remaining communities are facing the end. In the whole of Palestine there are three or four places only, and even these are weak, and in the whole of Syria none but a few in Aleppo occupy themselves with the Torah according to the truth, but even they have it not much at heart. In the Babylonian Diaspora there are only two or three groups in Yemen, and in the rest of Arabia they know little of the Talmud and are merely acquainted with aggadic exposition.

Only lately some well-to-do men came forward and purchased three copies of my code which they distributed through messengers in these countries, one copy for each country. Thus the horizon of these Jews was widened and the religious life in all communities as far as India revived. The Jews of India know nothing of the Torah and of the Laws, save the Sabbath and circumcision. In the towns of Berbery which belong to the realm of Islam, the Jews read the Torah and observe it according to its literal meaning. What was inflicted upon the Jews of Maghreb as punishment for their sins you know. Thus is remains for you alone to be a strong support to our religion.

Therefore be firm and courageous for the sake of our people and our God; make up your minds to remain brave men. Everything depends on you; the decision is in your hands. Do not rely upon my support, because I am an old man with gray hair. And know that for this not my age but my weak body is responsible. . . .

The following abbreviations have been used. *CCAR:* Central Conference of American Rabbis; *HUCA:* Hebrew Union College Annual; *JJS:* Journal of Jewish Studies; *JQR:* Jewish Quarterly Review; *PAAJR:* Proceedings of the American Academy for Jewish Research.

WORKS OF MAIMONIDES

The Commandments (Sefer ha-Mitzvoth), tr. Charles B. Chavel (London: Soncino Press, 1967), 2 vols.

The Commentary to Mishnah Aboth, tr. Arthur David (New York: Bloch, 1968)

Eight Chapters (Shemonah Perakim), ed. Joseph I. Gorfinkle (New York: Columbia University Press, 1912)

Epistle to Yemen (Iggeret Teman), ed. Abraham Halkin, tr. Boaz Cohen (New York: American Academy for Jewish Research, 1952)

The Guide of the Perplexed (Moreh Nevukhim), tr. Shlomo Pines (Chicago: University of Chicago Press, 1963). Older translation by M. Friedlander (1904; now in Dover paperback ed.). Note also abridged edition, with introduction and commentary by Julius Guttmann, tr. from Arabic by Chaim Rabin (London: East and West Library, 1952)

Helek: Sanhedrin, Chapter Ten, tr. by Arnold J. Wolf as "Maimonides on Immortality and the Principles of Judaism," *Judaism,* XV (1966), pp. 95–101, 211–216, 337–342

Letter on Astrology in Ralph Lerner and Muhsin Mahdi, *Medieval Political Philosophy* (Glencoe: Free Press, 1963), pp. 227–237

Memoirs of My People, ed. Leo W. Schwarz (New York: Farrar and Rinehart, 1943), pp. 15–20

A Treasury of Jewish Letters, ed. Franz Kobler (Philadelphia: Jewish Publication Society, 1954), I, pp. 178–222

Treatise on Logic (Millot ha-Higgayon), ed. Israel Efros (New York: American Academy for Jewish Research, 1938)

483

The Code (Mishneh Torah)

Book of Knowledge, Book I; *Book of Adoration*, Book II, tr. Moses Hyamson (1937; reprinted 1962, Jerusalem: Boys Town Publishers)

The Code of Maimonides (New Haven: Yale University Press). The following volumes have appeared: Book III, *Seasons*, tr. Solomon Gandz and Hyman Klein (1961); Book III, Treatise VIII, *Sanctification of New Moon*, tr. Solomon Gandz (1956); Book V, *Holiness*, tr. Louis I. Rabinowitz and Philip Grossman (1965); Book VI, *Asseverations*, tr. B. D. Klein (1965); Book VIII, *Temple Service*, tr. Mendell Lewittes (1957); Book IX, *Offerings*, tr. Herbert Danby (1950); Book X, *Cleanness*, tr. Herbert Danby (1954); Book XI, *Torts*, tr. Hyman Klein (1954); Book XII, *Acquisition*, tr. Isaac Klein (1951); Book XIII, *Civil Laws*, tr. Jacob J. Rabinowitz (1949); Book XIV, *Judges*, tr. Abraham M. Hershman (1949)

Maimonides' Mishneh Torah, ed. Philip Birnbaum (New York: Hebrew Publishing Co., 1967). An admirable selection from all fourteen books.

GENERAL WORKS

Medieval Jewish History and Philosophy

Baer, Yitzhak, *A History of the Jews in Christian Spain* (Philadelphia: Jewish Publication Society, 1961), I, especially pp. 96–110

Baron, Salo W., *A Social and Religious History of the Jews* (New York: Columbia University Press), VI (1958), pp. 97–107 (on the *Mishneh Torah*); VIII (1958), pp. 55–138 (on philosophy)

Cohen, Gerson D., ed., *The Book of Tradition* by Abraham ibn Daud (Philadelphia: Jewish Publication Society, 1967)

Goitein, Shlomo D., *A Mediterranean Society* (Los Angeles: University of California Press, 1967)

Guttmann, Julius, *Philosophies of Judaism* (New York: Holt, Rinehart and Winston, 1964), pp. 47–265, especially 150–183

Husik, Isaac, *A History of Mediaeval Jewish Philosophy* (New York: The Macmillan Co., 1916; reprinted, Philadelphia: Jewish Publication Society, 1944. Also available in Harper Torchbooks, 1966)

Mann, Jacob, *The Jews in Egypt and in Palestine Under the Fatimid Caliphs* (London: Oxford, 1920; reprinted, New York: Ktav, 1970)

Neuman, Abraham A., *The Jews in Spain* (Philadelphia: Jewish Publication Society, 1948), 2 vols.

Wolfson, Harry A., *Philo*, 3rd printing (Cambridge: Harvard University Press, 1962), 2 vols., especially II, ch. XIV, pp. 439–460

————, *Crescas' Critique of Aristotle* (Cambridge: Harvard University Press, 1929)

Biographical

Ashtor-Strauss, E., "Saladin and the Jews," *HUCA*, XXVII (1956), pp. 305–326

Friedlander, Israel, *Past and Present: Selected Essays* (New York: Burning Bush Press, 1961), pp. 113–147

Goitein, Shlomo D., "Maimonides as Chief Justice," *JQR*, XLIX (1959), pp. 191–203

————, "The Title and Office of the Nagid: a Re-Examination," *JQR*, LIII (1962), pp. 93–120

Graetz, Heinrich, *History of the Jews* (Philadelphia: Jewish Publication Society, 1894), III, pp. 446–493, 522–545, 623–634

Lewis, Bernard, "Maimonides, Lionheart, and Saladin," *Eretz-Israel*, VII (1964), pp. 70–75

Marx, Alexander, *Essays in Jewish Biography* (Philadelphia: Jewish Publication Society, 1947), pp. 87–111

Munz, J., *Maimonides* (Boston: Winchell-Thomas Co., 1935)

Yellin, David and Israel Abrahams, *Maimonides* (Philadelphia: Jewish Publication Society, 1903)

Zeitlin, Solomon, *Maimonides, a Biography* (New York: Bloch, 1955)

SPECIAL STUDIES AND MONOGRAPHS

Altmann, Alexander, "Essence and Existence in Maimonides," *Bulletin of the John Rylands Library*, XXXV (1953), pp. 294–315; reprinted in idem., *Studies in Religious Philosophy and Mysticism* (Ithaca: Cornell University Press, 1969)

Atlas, Samuel, "The Contemporary Relevance of the Philosophy of Maimonides," *CCAR Yearbook*, LXIV (1954), pp. 186–213

————, "Moses in the Philosophy of Maimonides, Spinoza, and Solomon Maimon," *HUCA*, XXV (1954), pp. 369–400

Baron, Salo W., ed., *Essays on Maimonides: An Octocentennial Volume* (New York: Columbia University Press, 1941)

————, "The Historical Outlook of Maimonides," *PAAJR*, VI (1934–35), pp. 5–113; reprinted in idem., *History and Jewish Historians* (Philadelphia: Jewish Publication Society, 1964)

Berman, Lawrence, "Maimonides' 'Statement on Political Science,'" *Journal of the American Oriental Society*, LXXXIX (1969), pp. 106–112

Blumberg, Harry, "The Problem of Immortality in Avicenna, Maimonides, and St. Thomas Aquinas," *Wolfson Jubilee Volume*, ed. S. Lieberman (Jerusalem: AAJR, 1965), I, pp. 165–185

Blumenfield, Samuel, "Towards a Study of Maimonides the Educator," *HUCA*, XXIII (1950–51), part II, pp. 555–593

Cohen, Boaz, "The Classification of the Law in the Mishneh Torah," *JQR*, XXV (1935), pp. 519–540

Cohen, Gerson D., *Messianic Postures of Ashkenazim and Sephardim* (New York: Leo Baeck Institute, 1967)

Cronbach, Abraham, "The Maimonidean Code of Benevolence," *HUCA*, XX (1947), pp. 471–540

Davidson, Herbert, "Maimonides' *Shemonah Peraqim* and Alfarabi's *Fusul Al-Madani*," *PAAJR*, XXXI (1963), pp. 33–50

Dienstag, Jacob, "The Prayer Book of Maimonides," *Leo Jung Jubilee Volume*, eds. Menahem Kasher, et al. (New York: Jewish Center, 1962), pp. 53–64

Diesendruck, Zevi, "On the Date of the Composition of the *Moreh Nebukim*," *HUCA*, XII–XIII (1937–38), pp. 461–497

———, "The Philosophy of Maimonides," *CCAR Yearbook*, XLV (1935), pp. 355–368

———, "Samuel and Moses ibn Tibbon on Maimonides' Theory of Providence," *HUCA*, XI (1936), pp. 341–66

Epstein, Isidore, "The Distinctiveness of Maimonides' Halakhah," *Leo Jung Jubilee Volume*, eds. Menahem Kasher, et al. (New York: Jewish Center, 1962), pp. 65–76

———, ed., *Moses Maimonides: Anglo-Jewish Papers* (London: Soncino Press, 1935)

Etziony, Mordecai, "Apropos of Maimonides' Aphorisms," *Bulletin of the History of Medicine*, XXXV (1961), pp. 163–168

Finkel, Joshua, "A Link Between Hasidism and Hellenistic and Patristic Literature," *PAAJR*, XXVI (1957), pp. 1–24; XXVII (1958), pp. 19–41

Fox, Marvin, "Prolegomenon" to Arthur Cohen, *The Teachings of Maimonides* (New York: Ktav, 1968), pp. XV–XLIV

Friedenwald, Henry, *The Jews and Medicine* (Baltimore: Johns Hopkins Press, 1944), pp. 193–216

Gandz, Solomon, "Date of the Composition of Maimonides' Code," *PAAJR*, XVII (1948), pp. 1–7; reprinted in idem., *Studies in Hebrew Astronomy and Mathematics*, ed. S. Sternberg (New York: Ktav, 1970)

Ginzberg, Asher, (Ahad Ha-am), "Supremacy of Reason," *Ten Essays*, tr. L. Simon (London: George Routledge and Sons, 1922), pp. 162–222

Goldman, S., "The Halachic Foundation of Maimonides' Thirteen Principles," *Essays Presented to Israel Brodie*, ed. H. J. Zimmels (London: Soncino Press, 1967), pp. 111–118

Goshen-Gottstein, Moshe H., "The Authenticity of the Aleppo Codex," *Textus*, ed. Chaim Rabin, I (1966), pp. 17–58

Halkin, Abraham, "Yedaiah Bedershi's Apology," *Jewish Medieval and Renaissance Studies*, ed. A. Altmann (Cambridge: Harvard University Press, 1967), pp. 165–184

Heller, Joseph, "Maimonides' Theory of Miracles," *Between East and West*, ed. A. Altmann (London: East and West Library, 1958), pp. 112–127

Hershman, Abraham M., "Textual Problems of Book Fourteen of the Mishne Torah," *JQR*, XL (1950), pp. 401–413

Husik, Isaac, "Maimonides and Spinoza on the Interpretation of the Bible," *Supplement to the Journal of the American Oriental Society*, LV (1935), pp. 22–40

———, "The Philosophy of Maimonides," *Philosophical Essays*, eds. M. C. Nahm and L. Strauss (Oxford: Blackwell, 1952), ch. XI, pp. 173–236

Hyman, Arthur, "Maimonides' Thirteen Principles," *Jewish Medieval and Renaissance Studies*, ed. A. Altmann (Cambridge: Harvard University Press, 1967), pp. 119–145

Kravitz, Leonard S., "Maimonides and Job: An Inquiry as to the Method of the Moreh," *HUCA*, XXXVIII (1967), pp. 149–158

Laks, Joel, "The Enigma of Job: Maimonides and the Moderns," *Journal of Biblical Literature*, LXXXII (1964), pp. 345–364

Lamm, Norman, "The Fifth Amendment and its Equivalent in the Halakah," *Judaism*, V (1956), pp. 53–59

Lerner, Ralph, "Maimonides' Letter on Astrology," *History of Religions*, VIII (1968), pp. 143–158

Levey, Irving, "Maimonides as Codifier," *CCAR Yearbook*, XLV (1935), pp. 368–396

Levy, S., "English Students of Maimonides," *Miscellanies of the Jewish Historical Society of England*, part IV (1942), pp. 61–84

Marx, Alexander, "Texts by and about Maimonides," *JQR*, XXV (1935), pp. 371–428

———, "The Correspondence between the Rabbis of Southern France and Maimonides about Astrology," *HUCA*, III (1926), pp. 311–358

Mihaly, Eugene, "Isaac Abravanel on the Principles of Faith," *HUCA*, XXVI (1955), pp. 481–502

Pines, Shlomo, "The Philosophic Sources of the Guide," *Guide of the Perplexed* (Chicago: University of Chicago Press, 1963), pp. lvii–cxxxiv

————, "Spinoza's Tractatus Theologico-Politicus, Maimonides and Kant," *Scripta Hierosolymitana*, XX (1968), pp. 3–54

Rawidowicz, Simon, "Knowledge of God: A Study in Maimonides' Philosophy of Religion," *Jewish Studies*, Issued in Honor of the Chief Rabbi J. L. Landau (Tel Aviv: 1936), pp. 78–121

————, "On Maimonides' 'Sepher Hamadda,'" *Essays in Honour of the Very Rev. Dr. J. H. Hertz*, eds. I. Epstein, E. Levine and C. Roth (London: Edward Goldston, 1942), pp. 331–339

Rosenthal, Erwin I. J., "Torah and Nomos in Medieval Jewish Philosophy," *Studies in Rationalism, Judaism and Universalism*, ed. Raphael Loewe (London: Routledge and Kegan Paul, 1966), pp. 215–230

Rosner, Fred, "Maimonides the Physician: A Bibliography," *Bulletin of the History of Medicine*, XLIII (1969), pp. 221–235

Roth, Leon, *Spinoza, Descartes and Maimonides* (New York: Russell & Russell, 1963), ch. 3

————, *The Guide for the Perplexed* (London: Hutchinson's Universal Library, 1948)

Sarachek, Joseph, *The Doctrine of the Messiah in Medieval Jewish Literature* (New York: 1932)

————, *Faith and Reason: Conflict over Rationalism of Maimonides* (Williamsport: Bayard Press, 1935)

Schechter, Solomon, "The Dogmas of Judaism," *Studies in Judaism* (Cleveland & Philadelphia: Meridian, and Jewish Publication Society paperback, 1960), pp. 73–105

Scholem, Gershom, *The Messianic Idea in Judaism* (New York: Schocken, 1971), especially pp. 24–32

Silver, Abba Hillel, *A History of Messianic Speculation in Israel* (Boston: Beacon Press, 1959)

Silver, Daniel J., *Maimonidean Criticism and the Maimonidean Controversy* (Leiden: E. J. Brill, 1965)

Sonne, Isaiah, "A Scrutiny of the Charges of Forgery against Maimonides' 'Letter on Resurrection,'" *PAAJR*, XXI (1952), pp. 101–117

Strauss, Leo, "The Literary Character of the Guide for the Perplexed," *Persecution and the Art of Writing* (Chicago: University of Chicago Press, 1952), pp. 38–95

————, "Notes on Maimonides' Book of Knowledge," *Studies in Mysticism and Religion Presented to Gershom Scholem*, eds. E. E. Urbach, et al. (Jerusalem: Magnes Press, 1967), pp. 269–285